LANGUAGE AND CHARACTERISATION

TEXTUAL EXPLORATIONS

General editors:

MICK SHORT Lancaster University
ELENA SEMINO Lancaster University

LANGUAGE AND CHARACTERISATION

PEOPLE IN PLAYS AND OTHER TEXTS

JONATHAN CULPEPER

Longman

An imprint of **Pearson Education**

Harlow, England · London · New York · Reading, Massachusetts · San Francisco
Toronto · Don Mills, Ontario · Sydney · Tokyo · Singapore · Hong Kong · Seoul
Taipei · Cape Town · Madrid · Mexico City · Amsterdam · Munich · Paris · Milan

Pearson Education Limited
Edinburgh Gate
Harlow
Essex CM20 2JE
England

and Associated Companies throughout the world

Visit us on the World Wide Web at:
www.pearsoneduc.com

First published 2001

© Pearson Education Limited 2001

ISBN 0-582-35753-5 PPR

British Library Cataloguing-in-Publication Data
A catalogue record for this book is available from the British
Library

Library of Congress Cataloging-in-Publication Data
Culpeper, Jonathan, 1966–
    Language and characterisation : people in plays and other texts / Jonathan Culpeper.
        p.   cm. — (Textual explorations)
    Based on the author's thesis.
    Includes bibliographical references and index.
    ISBN 0–582–35753–5 (ppr)
    1. Discourse analysis, Literary.   2. Characters and characteristics in literature.   3.
Shakespeare, William, 1564–1616—Characters—Katherine.   I. Title.   II. Series.

P302.5.C85 2001
808'.001'4—dc21   00–069023

Set in 11/13 pt Bembo by Graphicraft Ltd, Hong Kong
Produced by Pearson Education Asia Pte Ltd
Printed in Singapore

To my father
and in memory of my mother

CONTENTS

PART ONE: CHARACTERISATION AND THE MIND

CHAPTER 2: CHARACTER CATEGORIES AND
IMPRESSIONS OF CHARACTER

PREFACE

It seems insufficient just to acknowledge the help and support I have received from a vast array of people. This book started its life as a thesis, but it would never have been started at all without my parents, who made innumerable sacrifices on my behalf. My mother saw less of me than she should have during the final years of her life: I can only comfort myself with the hope that this book would have made her proud. And my father is a constant reminder that there is more to being a real academic than having letters after your name.

Mick Short — my thesis supervisor, colleague, mentor, and friend — is more than a little responsible for steering me through my thesis, and then providing me with sharp editorial comment for the book. Specific chapters of the book have also benefited a great deal from the following individuals (perhaps more than they realise!): Stanley Hussey, Geoffrey Leech, Willie van Peer, Paul Simpson, Katie Wales, and an anonymous reviewer for the journal *Language and Literature*. I must also thank Dawn Archer and Daniel McIntyre for helping me with the index. If the principle of end focus means anything, I reserve my most profound expression of my debt, gratitude and thanks to Elena Semino. Without her, this book would never have been finished. She supported me throughout, psychologically and academically. She pulled me through moments of crisis and listened patiently to my muddled ideas. Moreover, she shouldered more than her share of looking after our daughters, Emily and Natalie, in order to give me time in which to complete the book. Thanks are not enough.

ACKNOWLEDGEMENTS

Three chapters in this book draw material from previous publications. Chapter 3 draws upon Culpeper, J. (1996b) 'Inferring character from text: Attribution theory and foregrounding theory', *Poetics*, 23, 335–61; Chapter 5 draws upon Culpeper, J. (1998) '(Im)politeness in dramatic dialogue', in J. Culpeper, M. Short and P. Verdonk (1998) (eds) *Studying Drama: From Text to Context*, London: Routledge, 83–95; and Chapter 6 draws upon Culpeper, J. (2000) 'An approach to characterisation: The case of Katherina in Shakespeare's *The Taming of the Shrew*', *Language and Literature*, 9, 4, 291–316.

We are grateful to the following for permission to reproduce copyright material:

American Psychological Association for a table from 'A closer examination of causal inference: The roles of consensus, distinctiveness and consistency information' by B.R. Ovis et al. published in *The Journal of Personality and Social Psychology*. Copyright © 1975 by the American Psychological Association; the author's agent Roger Hancock Ltd for a dialogue extract from 'The Big Sleep' episode (1990) of *One Foot in the Grave* produced and directed by Susan Belbin; Elsevier Science for article based on 'Inferring character from text: Attribution theory and foregrounding theory' by J. Culpeper, published in *Poetics*, 23, pp. 335–61; Faber and Faber Ltd for an extract from 'Ernie's incredible illucinations' from *Plays 2* by Alan Ayckbourn; Faber and Faber Ltd/ the author's agent David Higham Associates Ltd for an extract from *The Entertainer* by John Osborne; F. Hoffmann-La Roche Ltd for transcript of a radio advertisement for *Sanatogon Classic 50 Plus*; Rogers, Coleridge & White, on behalf of the author, Arthur Miller for a dialogue extract from *The Crucible* pp. 46–8; Routledge for an extract from '(Im)politeness in dramatic dialogue' by Jonathan Culpeper from *Studying Drama: From Text To Context* edited by Culpeper et al; Sage Publications Ltd for an extract from 'An approach to characterisation: The case of Katherina in Shakespeare's *The Taming of the Shrew*' by J. Culpeper in *Language and Literature*, 9, (4) © Sage Publications Ltd; TV Times for a review of 'Holby City' in *TV Times* 20–26 November 1999; and University Publishing Rights, a division of Universal Studios for extracts from the screenplay of *Scent of a Woman* © 2000 by Universal City Studios Inc. All rights reserved.

CHAPTER 1

MODELLING CHARACTERISATION

1.1 Introduction

In this book, I explore how the words of a text create a particular impression of a character in the reader's head. I focus on three inter-related questions:

1) How does the reader's prior knowledge contribute to characterisation?
2) How does the reader infer characteristics from the text?
3) What are the textual cues in characterisation?

From these questions, it will immediately be apparent that my concern is mainly with the *process* of characterisation, rather than with character — the output of that process. The approach I take is multi-disciplinary: the book draws together theories from linguistics (particularly from pragmatics), cognitive psychology (such as schema theory), social psychology (for example attribution theory), and stylistics (for example fore-grounding theory). I will show through the analysis of textual examples how these theories interrelate and how they can explicate the mechanisms of characterisation. It may help readers to know that I consider this book to be part of the emerging field of 'cognitive stylistics' (see for instance Freeman 1995; Emmott 1997; Semino 1997). Like the works just cited, the general approach of this book will be to hypothesise about comprehension through an examination of the text, although I will also report some limited empirical work (see Emmott 1997: 94–98 for a description of this approach).

The dialogue of plays is the primary focus of this book. Most recent research on characterisation has dwelt on prose fiction. In two fairly recent special journal issues on literary character, *Poetics Today* (1986) and *Style* (1990), only one article addressed the issue of character in drama. A number of books have theorised about character in the novel, but none about character in drama.[1] This is surprising, since it is in drama that characters are particularly salient. Unlike typical prose fiction, in drama there is usually no narrator who intervenes and guides our perception of a character: we are exposed in a direct way to their words and actions, and, of course, on stage we are exposed to their very physical presence.

Although I will discuss the characterisation of a wide variety of characters (ranging from the characters of the children's television series *Teletubbies* through to the characters of medieval Morality plays), I will draw the majority of my examples from Shakespeare's plays.[2] This is for three reasons: (1) Shakespeare's plays offer a rich collection of characters; (2) since Shakespeare is a playwright who uses few stage directions, we rely almost exclusively on dialogue for characterisation; and (3) Shakespeare's characters are well known and frequently the subject of discussion. However, relying solely on examples from Shakespeare would be problematic. Firstly, the audience of 400 years ago will have had rather different background knowledge from that of the present day, and, secondly, Shakespeare does not exploit the full textual range of characterisation (for example, spelling, lexis and grammar are little used in the creation of a particular social dialect). Thus, I also discuss examples from other more recent plays. In addition, I analyse examples from other text-types, both literary (such as prose fiction) and non-literary (such as advertisements). The involvement of a wide range of text-types is important as a way of demonstrating that what I propose constitutes a general theory of characterisation.

At this early point, I need to address some tricky terminological issues. The problem with the word 'character' is that it is ambiguous. Amongst the various usages, it can be used to refer to the qualities — the characteristics — that combine to form a person's personality, or the people that inhabit the fictional worlds of books, plays, films, and so on. In this book, I will use 'characteristics' for the former sense, and 'character' for the latter sense; the only exceptions being if I am reviewing someone else's work or if the context makes my particular sense clear. However, none of these terms really captures the focus of this book. My concern is the process of characterisation — how we form impressions of characters in our minds — not just characters themselves or their personalities. Thus, I will also use the term 'impression' or 'character impression'. In part, I have borrowed the term from research on impression formation in social psychology, where the issue is how we form impressions of people in the real world. A further advantage of the term 'impression' is that it suggests a less stable notion than, say, 'conception'. This enables me to better maintain a distinction between our evolving impression of a character and the background concepts stored in memory that may be used in shaping that impression. However, the term 'character impression' does have a downside. It may be seen to suggest that the text impresses character on the mind, as if on a wax tablet. For example, the drama scholar J.L. Styan uses the term in this way when he talks of the 'playgoer absorbing meaningful impressions' (1969: 68). This is a false analogy: the mind is not a passive recipient of information, but an active manipulator of that information.

This chapter provides not only the backdrop for the up-coming chapters, but also presents a model for characterisation, the various components of which are individually discussed in the following chapters. In the following section, 1.2, I aim to give the reader a more concrete sense of the issues I will address by discussing in broad terms characterisation in an extract from a play. I will return again to this extract and examine it in more detail in Chapters 2 and 3. In section 1.3, I briefly examine some approaches to characterisation developed in literary studies. In section 1.4, I consider how the issue of language and people has been approached in linguistics. In section 1.5, I overview a model of text comprehension, in order to provide some background for how we might comprehend characters. In section 1.6, I propose a model for characterisation. Finally, in section 1.7, I describe two background assumptions about plays, one concerning the discourse structure of plays and the other the relationship between the play text and the performance of the play. This chapter has been written so that different readers may take different paths through it. If, for example, you are not particularly interested in section 1.4 on language and real-life people, then you could skip it or skim it (and the book should still make sense!). Sections 1.3 (literary approaches to characters), 1.4 (linguistic approaches to people) and, to a lesser extent, 1.5 (matters of text comprehension) are optional: they aim to give the reader a sense of how to place the ideas developed in this book.

1.2 Raising the issues

Let us consider a short example from near the beginning of Osborne's *The Entertainer* (1957). Jean has just arrived in order to visit Billy.

    Jean   Hello, Grandad.
    Billy   I wondered who the hell it was.

Jean	I'm sorry.
Billy	I thought it was some of that mad lot carrying on. Well, come in if you're coming, it's draughty standing about in the doorway. I've only just sat down.
Jean	(*coming in*). Did I disturb you, I am sorry.
Billy	I'd just sat down to read the evening paper. It's a bloody farm-yard this place.
Jean	Well, how are you?
Billy	Bloody farm-yard [. . .]

Osborne 1957: 15

Clearly, Jean's opening greeting 'Hello, Grandad' characterises both Billy and Jean: we assume that they occupy the roles of grandfather and granddaughter. However, this interaction is unusual in a number of respects. In my experience, relationships between grandfathers and grand-daughters are not normally so acerbic. The beginnings of interactions are usually characterised by reciprocal phatic talk — both participants greeting each other — but Billy withholds his greeting. Also, Billy, whilst issuing repeated complaints, seems reluctant to accept Jean's apologies. Her polite question 'how are you?' does not receive an answer. Furthermore, Billy uses 'bloody' (x 2) and 'hell' which are striking because they are mildly taboo words.[3] Overall, this kind of conversational behaviour is clearly unusual, and it raises the question 'Why?'. It is difficult not to be curious about why Billy's behaviour is odd. Is being grumpy part of his personality? Is he grumpy because he has been disturbed? Is he grumpy because he has had too much beer (an earlier stage direction informs us that he has had at least some beer)? Or is it a combination of these factors? Jean's behaviour is also odd. Is being patient and apologetic part of her personality? Has experience taught her that this is the best way to handle Billy? Or is she simply in a good mood? Or is it some combination of these factors?

What does all this show us about characterisation? Firstly, note how just one word from Jean — 'Grandad' — enables us to fill out the characteristics of Jean and Billy. This is because 'Grandad' does not merely tell us about the kinship relationship between Billy and Jean (a kind of dictionary definition of 'Grandad'), but it also triggers our prior knowledge about grandfathers and granddaughters. Thus we might infer prototypical values for various characteristics. For example, the prototypical age for grandfathers is, say, fifties plus. (The reason why my next-door neighbour is a non-prototypical grandfather is because he is in his early forties.) This also relates to appearance characteristics:

grandfathers and older people usually have white hair. And there are typical values for behaviour: grandfathers usually exhibit 'respectable' and friendly behaviour in the context of their granddaughters. Secondly, note how characterisation is also triggered via what the characters say and do in interaction. Billy's use of taboo words is not what we might have predicted for a grandfather/granddaughter interaction, and in order to explain why Billy uses these words we may infer something about Billy (such as 'he's grumpy', 'he's been disturbed'). Billy issues complaints, Jean apologises, and these speech acts and the interaction between them may characterise Billy and Jean — Billy the complainer, Jean the apologetic type. Note also that characterisation is triggered by what they fail to do: Jean greets Billy, apologises to him, and asks him how he is, but none of these acts receives the expected response (a greeting, an acceptance of the apology and an answer). Thirdly, note that in explaining these interactional oddities one option is to infer something about the characteristics of Billy and of Jean, but that there are other options too: the explanation may lie in some contextual factor (such as 'Billy was disturbed', 'Billy was drunk'). Clearly, before a characterising inference can be made we need to assess such contextual factors.

The extract I have discussed here is in fact part of a longer passage that will form the basis of analysis and discussion in 2.6 and 3.8.3. In this book, Chapter 2 is particularly concerned with the role of prior knowledge as a source of inferences for fleshing out characters, and as a means of producing clashes with readers' expectations. Chapter 3 looks at how character inferences might be triggered by linguistic choices, and how such inferences have to be balanced against contextual factors. Chapter 4 surveys the range of linguistic items that can be used to trigger some characteristic. Chapter 5 takes a more dynamic look at language, and how characterisation is achieved in interaction. Finally, Chapter 6 pulls all these threads together through a demonstration analysis.

1.3 Characters: Approaches in literary criticism

Given the importance of characters in discussions of literary works — both by the lay person and the professional — one might suppose that the study of characterisation would have attracted much attention. However, as Chatman points out (1978: 107), 'It is remarkable how little has been said about the theory of character in literary history and criticism'.

Similar remarks are made by Culler (1975: 230) and van Peer (1989: 9). Much literary critical energy, such as it is, has been spent debating the ontological status of character; in other words, they have debated the question 'Where do characters exist?'. Broadly speaking, there are two opposite approaches. The first consists of those who 'humanise' characters and argue that they can be usefully discussed, at least to some extent, independently of the text. The second, which partly developed as a reaction to the first approach, consists of those who argue that characters are products of the plot or simply a textual phenomenon. The extremes of these two approaches are polarised to the extent that there is a tendency in the debate to throw the baby out with the bath water. Below, in sections 1.3.1 and 1.3.2, I present these polarised extremes. Then, in 1.3.3, I will argue for a mixed approach.

1.3.1 Humanising approaches

The humanising approach is represented by a diverse array of scholars who tend to make the assumption either that characters are imitations or representations of real people, or — the more extreme view — that they are actually real people. Their argument is that 'we recognise, understand and appreciate fictional characters insofar as their appearances, actions, and speech reflect or refer to those of persons in real life' (Mead 1990: 442).

A.C. Bradley's book *Shakespearean Tragedy* ([1905] 1960) is perhaps the best known example of the 'humanising' camp, partly because it has been singled out for criticism. L.C. Knights's essay 'How many children had Lady Macbeth?' ([1933] 1963) has been in the vanguard of this attack. The title of this essay is an obvious parody of the approach of the 'humanising' camp. Knights criticises Bradley for speculating about the psychological experiences and motivations of Shakespearean characters and for constructing a past and future for them outside the play texts. In fact, these criticisms apply more to Bradley's analytical practice than his stated critical position. For example, in discussing the nature of tragedy, Bradley is at pains to point out that 'action' is of equal importance to character, and that to say Shakespeare's main interest 'lay in *mere* character, or was a psychological interest, would be a great mistake' (1960: 12–3). However, in his discussion of the plays it is not difficult to find examples of psychological speculation. Often they come in the form of rhetorical questions, as, for instance, his comment on some of Hamlet's words: 'Would any other character in Shakespeare have used those words?' (Bradley 1960: 151). Clearly, Shakespeare supplied those words as part of Hamlet's character, and thus contemplating whether another character would have used them is pure speculation. Elsewhere, Bradley, acknowledging that he does indeed engage in 'speculation' (1960: 264), talks about some characters in *King Lear* as if they were real people:

> How can there be such men and women? We ask ourselves. How comes it that humanity can take such absolutely opposite forms? And, in particular, to what omission of elements which should be present in human nature, or, if there is no omission, to what distortion of these elements is it due that such beings as some of these come to exist?

Since Bradley, only a relatively small number of scholars (for example Harvey 1965) have explicitly adopted anything like a humanising approach to character. However, we need to bear in mind that if we move outside the academic study of literature and consider people's everyday literary encounters, a different picture emerges. I suspect that humanising characters is part of most people's appreciation of literature: part of the enjoyment of plays and films is imagining characters as if they were real people. This might explain why the humanising approach in literary criticism has never really taken off, and why it evoked such a bitter backlash from other critics. Developing a humanising approach would require the literary critic to abandon their familiar and exclusive haven, and venture into the realms of psychology in attempting to understand how the 'ordinary' person comprehends. It is much easier, therefore, to dismiss the humanising approach: 'at its best it represents a slacker criticism' (Styan 1969: 164).[4]

1.3.2 De-humanising approaches

The general thrust of the de-humanising approach is to deny that characters are human and to insist that they have a purely textual existence.

L.C. Knights, reacting to the kind of criticism practised by Bradley, argued that Shakespeare's plays should be treated as dramatic poems, and that character is part of the verbal fabric of the play, nothing more. His critical position is made clear (1963: 18):

> The main difference between good and bad critics is that the good critic points to something that is actually contained in the work of art, whereas the bad critic points away from the work in question; he introduces extraneous elements into his appreciation — smudges the canvas with his own paint.

A similar kind of line is taken by some semioticians. Weinsheimer (1979: 195) has championed what might be seen as the extreme of this critical camp:

> As segments of a closed text, characters at most are patterns of recurrence, motifs which are continually recontextualized in other motifs. In semiotic criticism, characters dissolve.

According to this position, characters dissolve into 'textuality' and we should resist attempts to revitalise them by applying psychological theories. Weinsheimer proceeds to analyse Jane Austen's character Emma, during which he makes the following provocative statement: 'Emma Woodhouse is not a woman nor need be described as if *it* were' (1979: 187, *my emphasis*).

Another line within the de-humanising approach has been to argue that characters are primarily functions within the text. A debate that has been running at least from the time of Aristotle concerns the relationship between characters and plot. In his *Poetics*, Aristotle argues that in drama action comes first, and that characters are foremost 'agents' of the action. This position was taken up by the early Formalists and Structuralists. Chatman summarises their argument thus:

> They [. . .] argue that characters are products of plots, that their status is 'functional', that they are, in short, participants or *actants* rather than *personnages*, that it is erroneous to consider them as real beings. Narrative theory, they say, must avoid psychological essences; aspects of character can only be 'functions'. They wish to analyze only what characters do in a story, not what they are — that is, 'are' by some outside psychological or moral measure. Further, they maintain that the 'spheres of action' in which a character moves are 'comparatively small in number, typical and classable'.
>
> (1978: 111; see also Culler 1975: 230)

Scholars such as Propp ([1928] 1968) and Greimas (1966) devised frameworks which attempted to capture the universal actant roles that underlie narratives and plays (I will return to these frameworks in 2.2.2). Here, as far as characterisation is concerned, the focus is on the kind of doer (such as hero, villain) as a function of the kind of deed (such as good deeds, bad deeds), but not on, for example, what might have motivated the doer to do the deed. The difference between this approach and the humanising approach is neatly put by Bennison (1997: 118): 'The question asked by Proppian critics is "what does this action lead to?", rather than "what is it that causes a character to act in this way?"'.

1.3.3 A mixed approach

As far as the de-humanising approaches are concerned, one would have to admit that character is what we interpret from the text. As Knights points out, the critic, 'however far he may ultimately range — begins with the words of which a play is composed' (1963: 4). And the organisation of the text must play a part in our impression of a character. This point is forcefully made by van Peer (1989: 9):

> Both in narrative and dramatic genres (to a much lesser extent in poetry) the issue of character is an important one. [. . .] More important still is that the category of character is, for its very formation, dependent on linguistic forms. Character, it can hardly be denied, is what readers infer from words, sentences, paragraphs and textual composition depicting, describing or suggesting actions, thoughts, utterances or feelings of a protagonist. Thus the linguistic organisation of a text will predetermine to a certain degree the kind of 'picture' one may compose of a protagonist. Therefore the particular *forms* by which this is achieved need to be studied in detail. It appears that at this moment there is hardly a theoretical framework providing for this necessity.

One aim in this book is to shed light on the textual cues and styles that create characters. In Chapter 4, I look at a wide variety of linguistic phenomena and consider whether they act as cues for particular characteristics. In Chapter 5, I take a more dynamic view of text and character, and, using politeness theory as my basis, consider how character is shaped in interaction.

However, Weinsheimer's (1979) comment on Emma Woodhouse demonstrates how one can throw the baby out with the bath water. His use of the neuter third person pronoun borders on the absurd: Emma's female gender is an undeniable part of her character for any reader. Characters remain as words in the text only when those words have no readers or listeners. As Toolan (1988: 92) puts it:

> The fact is, whatever theorists keep telling us, most readers do unshakably continue to apprehend most novel characters

as individuals (whether seen dimly or sharply, whether recognizable, comprehensible, lisible or impenetrable, alien, unfathomable), and as those apprehensions are built up, revised, and articulated, all sorts of extra-textual knowledge, including our knowledge of characters in the real world, is brought to bear.

And a similar view is put forward by Emmott (1997: 58):

In reading narrative texts, we imagine worlds inhabited by individuals who can be assumed to behave, physically and psychologically, in ways which reflect our real-life experiences of being situated in the real world.

It is difficult to deny that what we all do when we watch a play or a film is to attempt to *interpret* characters with the structures and processes which we use to interpret our real-life experiences of people. We also frequently talk about characters in terms applicable to real people. Even writers who express some doubt about the humanising camp admit that you cannot entirely get away from this idea:

But in some sense we *must* feel Lear, Macbeth, Hamlet are human. We pity or admire because we are throughout the performance in contact with humanity in human situations: the figures in the pattern are, after all, human figures in a human pattern.

(Styan 1969: 164)

[. . .] we have a natural urge to talk about, say, Cordelia as a daughter or Edgar as a son. [. . .] We talk about what we are more sure of: human qualities and attributes.

(Styan 1969: 163)

On the other hand, the extreme humanising view, that characters are actually real people, is, of course, naïve. Even on stage, the actor is the real person; the character is, generally, who they are pretending to be.[5]

The first half of this book has the particular aim of showing how the cognitive structures and inferential mechanisms that readers have already developed for real-life people might be used in their comprehension of characters. However, an awareness that character stems from a fictional text means that we might modify our interpretative procedures. For example, we may attribute particular significance to the words or actions of a character, because we know they have been selected for a particular reason by the author; or we may make particular predictions about a character (for example whether they get happily married or killed), because we assume them to belong to a particular fictional role (such as hero, villain). Modifications such as these will be explored mainly in Chapters 2 and 3.

Clearly, then, the aim of this book is to describe both the textual factors and the cognitive factors that jointly lead a reader to have a particular impression of a character. In fact, my position is not too far removed from that of more recent structuralist critics. Margolin (1989), in an article on the 'state of the art' in structuralist approaches to character, notes scholars' dissatisfaction with 'rather reductive, functionally oriented schemes of character' (1989: 10), and adds:

> Plainly speaking, I suspect that the scholars who expressed the dissatisfaction with the current state of affairs feel, like Wallace Martin, that 'our sense that [many] fictional characters are uncannily similar to people is not something to be dismissed or ridiculed, but a crucial feature of narration that requires explanation'
>
> (Martin 1986: 120) (Margolin 1989: 10)

In fact, in an earlier article Margolin (1983) proposed a scale of humanisation for characters, with 'character as actant' at the least human end and 'character as individual or person' at the most human end. Approaches which are mixed, at least to some degree, have become increasingly popular (such as Hochman 1985; Fishelov 1990; Mead 1990; Phelan 1990). An approach that considers both textual and psychological (cognitive) levels of description is entirely consistent with the current goals of stylistic analysis:

> Stylistic analysis (sometimes known as literary linguistics or linguistic criticism) is an approach to the analysis of literary works which involves a detailed and systematic account of their linguistic properties, linked to what we know about the details of the reading process, in order to arrive at a detailed account of how readers understand particular texts in the ways they do (see, for example, Fowler 1986, Herman 1995, Leech 1969, Leech and Short 1981, Semino 1997, Short 1996, Simpson 1993, 1996, Toolan 1988).
>
> (Short and Semino forthcoming)

In section 1.6, drawing upon ideas from text comprehension, I will outline the mixed approach to characterisation which I take in this book.

1.4 People: Approaches in linguistics

My aim in this section is to give readers a sense of how my approach to language and characterisation fits in with research on language and real people. I will also point out which aspects I shall draw upon in upcoming chapters, and I will keep an eye out for 'lessons to be learnt' from this research.

The various approaches to language and real people are all inter-disciplinary (even multi-disciplinary), and, obviously, the particular combination of disciplines for any one approach lends it its particular flavour. Language attitude research, which I shall look at first, has combined language research with social and cognitive psychological research. The methodology here often resembles that of experimental psychology. The focus of this approach has been on how certain aspects of some-one's language performance trigger beliefs and evaluations in the hearer about that person. A research question in this approach might be: 'What kind of attitudes are triggered by, for example, a high-pitched voice?' It is important to note that this approach has tended to restrict itself to perception in first encounters with unfamiliar others.

The second area I shall consider is the discussion of language and people, and in particular the notion of 'identity', in sociolinguistics.[6] Clearly, sociolinguistics combines linguistics with fields such as socio-logy and anthropology. Here, a typical research question might be, for example: 'What linguistic features does a speaker select in order to iden-tify him/herself with or distinguish him/herself from particular groups?' I shall introduce relevant views in sociolinguistics via a discussion of developments in gender studies. My reasons for this are two-fold. Firstly, the notion of identity in sociolinguistics has been approached from a number of different angles (it even overlaps with language attitudes research). Gender has been studied from a variety of perspectives from within sociolinguistics, and thus it is a good way of introducing that diversity. Secondly, gender is a fundamental social category which people use in making sense of others and which is modelled in the discourses around us. Gender is likely, I would argue, to be one important way in which readers comprehend most characters.

The third area I introduce is the 'social constructivist' approach to identity, which stresses the idea that people have multiple identities and that their identities are not fixed. This approach has developed in two rather separate fields: critical discourse analysis and ethnomethodology (or, more specifically, conversation analysis). Critical discourse analysis is a multi-disciplinary field combining, for example, linguistics, sociology and politics. Identity, in this view, is both shaped and constituted by social practices, including discourse. A research question in this approach might be: 'How does X discourse sustain the power relations between Y groups (e.g. women/men, social classes, ethnic majorities/minorities) by 'positioning' them in certain ways or by making some less visible than others?' Ethnomethodology is a field within sociology, and conversation analysis straddles both sociology and linguistics. Here, identity is what interactants understand by it and use it for in the ebb and flow of talk. A research question in this approach might be: 'How is X identity category used in the management of Y interaction?'

Finally, I develop and argue for a pragmatic view of language and people. Pragmatics is notoriously difficult to define, but let us start by saying that it is an area within linguistics that deals with the construction of meaning in context.[7] Some areas of pragmatics overlap with sociology, and some with cognitive psychology. In this section, I begin by arguing that presenting and understanding characteristics is a communicative matter, and point out that other approaches in linguistics have taken an inadequate view of communication. I will note one line of research in pragmatics which proposes that taking account of participant characteristics is a communicative 'rule'. I also suggest how the concept of character can be related to the concept of context.

1.4.1 Language attitude research

Robyn Lakoff points out (1990: 257) that

> Language is an intrinsic component of personality. Linguistic style is an outgrowth of psychological style, and a diagnostic of it as well. We assume that the way people talk tells us the truth about them.

Of course, one does not have to be a linguist to know this. Imagine you are on a first date. Your informational antennae would be fully switched on, trying to discover what the other person is like. One important source of information would be the other's speech style, for here may lie information about a person's socioeconomic background, intellect, sociability, dynamism, and so on. Of course, you have to allow for the fact that the other person may be 'putting on an act' for the purposes of the occasion, but, in spite of this, your language-derived information will be a crucial foundation for your impression of the other person.

Modern 'scientific' research on language attitudes is usually traced back to the work of Wallace Lambert and his colleagues, which began in the late 1950s. Lambert *et al.*'s (1960) famous study, based in Montreal, investigated listeners' reactions to French and English. Using a sophisticated experimental procedure (the Matched Guise Technique) to rule out speaker idiosyncrasies, they discovered that *both* English-speaking and French-speaking respondents reacted more favourably to the English speakers on several traits, including kindness and intelligence. Similar kinds of study have been carried out on various British accents, particularly with regard to some kind of 'standard' versus 'nonstandard' dimension (for example Strongman and Woolsey 1967; Cheyne 1970; Giles 1970). Overall, the general conclusion seems to be that 'standard accents usually connote high status and competence; regional accents may be seen to reflect greater integrity and attractiveness' (Edwards 1982: 25).

Much of the early work on language attitudes considered geographically linked language varieties. Since then, research broadened and identified other varieties which are perceived to have particular associations. These include, for example, gender-linked language, powerful and powerless styles, and language intensity and obscenity (see Bradac 1990: 395–8, for brief summaries of and references for these styles). In addition, many studies have investigated the attitudinal significance of particular linguistic features. These features have included various vocal characteristics (such as pitch, intensity and quality), and also aspects of lexis, syntax and conversation (see, for example, the studies reviewed in Scherer 1979, and Giles and Robinson 1990). This broadening of the field, however, has had a downside. Scherer (1979), writing a comprehensive and often-cited review of American and European research, makes the following bleak observation:

> 'Style is the man himself' (Cuvier, cited after Busemann 1948: 76). Statements like this, asserting a strong link between linguistic style and the individuality or personality of a speaker, are not difficult to find. At a time when quantitative, statistical analyses of linguistic style started to mushroom and 'speech and personality' was still a hot area within psychology, Sanford (1942: 814) wrote: 'If we set up the hypothesis that a study of the individual's verbal behaviour will disclose

a facet of his personality, it appears unlikely that we are weaving a rope entirely of sand.' Today, more than thirty-five years later, we seem to have just quicksand and no rope.

(1979: 168)

The reasons for this unhappy situation, Scherer argues, not only included lack of research, but also confusion and controversy on both sides of the link between style and personality. On the one hand, researchers debated the nature of personality, and, on the other hand, the nature of style. Neither area had an agreed conceptual or descriptive framework.

Twenty years on, whilst these are still real problems, the situation is not all bad. As Bradac (1990: 405) points out, 'the field has matured to the point where there are sets of stable results capable of yielding general-izations'. For example, one of the generalisations Bradac can formulate is: 'Valued linguistic forms are positively associated with message recipi-ents' judgements of a message sender's status or competence' (1990: 406). The research in this field provides a valuable data baseline, which I will refer to in Chapter 4, where I consider the textual cues in characteris-ation. However, importantly, research on language attitudes is still lacking an adequate account of the communicative context, despite some re-searchers' pointing out the deficit (for example Bradac 1990: 399–403). Influenced by experimental design in psychology, the aim, particularly in the earlier studies, has often been to strip away the messiness of context, so that the remaining contextual variables could be held constant across experiments. Even in more recent studies, whilst some have investigated interaction between variables and stressed the importance of context (see, for example, McCann and Higgins 1990, 1992), there is still a tendency to view context as relatively stable and a given, rather than something which might be defined or negotiated by participants. I will present a more dynamic view of context in section 1.4.4 below. Language attitude research also suffers from an over-concentration on perception in first encounters with unfamiliar others. A particular concern in Chapter 2 is to think about how one's impression of a character develops, and Chapter 5 will touch on the linguistic changes that accompany familiarity.

1.4.2 Identity in sociolinguistics: Insights from gender studies

More than a dozen years ago I — a bright-eyed youth from London — arrived in Lancaster, a small city in the north-west of England. Although

I felt like something of an outcast at first, over the years I have come to enjoy living in Lancaster: I like the environment and I like the people. Simultaneously, my negative attitudes towards those southerners who think that anyone north of Watford must be a barbarian have hardened. Sometimes, I am dimly aware that my linguistic usage reflects my feelings. For example, when a local greets me with 'How are you?', I find myself saying 'Not so bad'. To my personal knowledge, this response is common in Lancaster, but much rarer in London. I also find myself cringing, if I hear the southern back 'a' vowel in the second syllable of 'Lancaster'. Clearly, there has been a shift in the speech communities with which I wish to identify.

In sociolinguistics, identity is most frequently understood to be the way in which people identify themselves with social groups, categories or stereotypes (see, for example, the papers in Abrams and Hogg 1990a). For instance, Le Page and Tabouret-Keller (1985: 181), discussing Creole-speaking communities, propose the hypothesis that

> 'the individual creates for himself the patterns of his linguistic behaviour so as to resemble those of the group or groups with which from time to time he wishes to be identified, or so as to be unlike those from whom he wishes to be distinguished'.

This understanding of identity is clearly present in some of the work on language and gender. Researchers in the variationist tradition of William Labov have treated gender as one dimension of variation. Typically focussing on a single phoneme, morpheme or lexical item, the major finding claimed for this research is that women, regardless of their social characteristics, use more standard forms of the language than men, and that women are generally innovators in linguistic change (see for example Trudgill 1983; Labov 1990, 1994). The explanation for this finding put forward by Labov and Trudgill relates to women's social roles: for example, women's lack of opportunity to pursue social status through work in the same way as men and thus their reliance on the 'symbolic status' of language rather than economic status, and their particular responsibility for transmitting speech to children and thus their sensitivity to correctness.[8] Thus, in this view, women use language as a means of identifying themselves with higher status groups. However, as the language and gender field has developed, different perspectives have emerged. Broadly speaking, issues of language and gender have also been approached in terms of speech style and in terms of social construction. I will briefly describe these below.

The speech style strand in gender research is similar to — and is sometimes seen as part of — the language attitudes research, as outlined in section 1.4.1 above. Robyn Lakoff's *Language and Women's Place* ([1973] 1975) has given rise to a vast number of studies aiming to reveal a particular speech style for women.[9] She included the following features in her discussion of what characterises 'women's language': tag questions, hedges, exaggerated politeness, 'empty' adjectives (that convey an emotional reaction as opposed to information), mild expletives and direct quotations (instead of paraphrase). Lakoff explained the assumed difference in male/female speech style in terms of what has been called the 'dominance' view, which sees differences as a reflection of men's dominance and women's subordination.[10] Clearly, there is much overlap between the kind of style Lakoff describes and powerless styles (see O'Barr 1982). However, Lakoff's work has been criticised on a number of counts, not least because the features she claims to be typical of 'women's language' are not empirically derived, but seem to reflect linguistic stereotypes. Kramarae (1974, 1977), for example, explored students' perceptions of stereotypical male speech (for instance dominant, loud, concise, blunt) and female speech (gentle, emotional, verbose, polite), and these are clearly consistent with the 'women's language' hypothesis. Nevertheless, it should be acknowledged that knowing what the linguistic stereotypes are is valuable, since these are the currency of the layperson.

Both the variationist and the speech style approaches outlined above have tended to focus on individual speech features and treat them as relatively static in meaning. The more recent 'social constructionist' approach (such as Hall and Bucholtz 1995; Crawford 1995) takes a more 'holistic' view of language, typically focussing on spoken interactions, their function and their social context, and draws analytical and theoretical input from the fields of critical discourse analysis and ethnomethodology. Whereas both the variationist and the speech style approaches tend to see gender as a relatively static property of the individual and a relatively clear-cut concept (sex as a binary biological category),[11] the constructionist view emphasises gender as a dynamic social construct. Gender is not viewed as an attribute of an individual, but 'a way of making sense of transactions' (Crawford 1995: 12). Language is not merely a reflection of gender, but a way of shaping it. Within this approach, the discussion is typically of identities (or, specifically, 'femininities' and 'masculinities') which are shaped by social forces outside the individual. In the next section (1.4.3), I will briefly describe three approaches to social construction.

1.4.3 Social constructivist approaches

Fairly recently, I became a father. But what does that mean? As I rapidly discovered, not one single thing: it depends on who I am talking to, what I am reading or what television programme I am watching. One television advertisement portrays a father in charge of the baby and getting the dinner: mayhem ensues. Is being a bumbling no-hoper part of being a father? I have had my crisis moments, but then, so has our daughter's mother.

In the critical discourse analysis perspective, father discourse, like all discourses, is not only

> shaped by situations, institutions and social structures, but also shapes them. [. . .] [Discourse] constitutes situations, objects of knowledge, and the social identities of and relationships between people and groups of people.
>
> (Fairclough and Wodak 1997: 258)

Thus, in this view, my identity as a father is a matter of how I am positioned by these father discourses. Some discourses I may resist, as in the case of the above advertisement, but this will be harder in the case of more dominant discourses. To make all this more concrete, I will refer here to Sunderland (2000), who presents an analysis of parenthood discourses in 'parentcraft' texts. Parentcraft texts, for those who don't know, are the voluminous 'advice' literature inflicted upon new parents: they vary from the ancient writings of Benjamin Spock to those of the modern day sage, Miriam Stoppard. Sunderland focusses on how certain grammatical and lexical choices are used to construct particular father discourses. For example, she shows how the lexical item *help* plays a role in constructing what she calls 'part-time father discourse':

> In particular [. . .] what fathers do is represented by the transactive verb *help*. There are instances of *help* in Text 1, 'Helping [her] with baby': the title, line 1: 'You can help with the baby's care by changing nappies . . .', and l.4: 'If your baby is bottle-fed you can help by making up and giving feeds' [. . .] *Help* also appears as a noun in Text 2, 'Dad Chat', in the subtitle 'Your wife still needs lots of support and help with all the chores'; and in Text 6, 'Accepting help', addressed to mothers: 'If you do need to ask for help, go to your partner first' (l.16) [. . .] *Help* applied to the

father can be seen as 'vague language', compared to the other possible verbs such as *bathe, change, wash, cook* [. . .] this vagueness can also be seen as legitimizing the father's *part-time*, essentially supporting and non-responsible role, in that in most of these cases of *help*, no actual, specific tasks are represented for him. These different uses of *help* thus suggest that the father has some role to play in childcare, in that he is expected to act in ways which have an effect on the world around him, but that he will not be the one left holding the baby.

(Sunderland 2000: 257–8)

Sunderland goes on to show how other father discourses are constructed (such as 'Father as baby entertainer', 'Father as mother's bumbling assistant', 'Father as line manager').

Sunderland, for parts of her analysis, found it useful to draw upon van Leeuwen's (1995, 1996) work on the representation of social actors. Van Leeuwen's work is currently very popular in critical discourse analysis, and so it is worth saying a few words about it here. Van Leeuwen's aims are neatly formulated in two questions:

[. . .] what are the ways in which social actors can be represented in English discourse? Which choices does the English language give us for referring to people?

(1996: 32)

In other words, van Leeuwen aims to provide a set of sociological categories for representing people and to show how they are realised linguistically. Van Leeuwen's primary representational distinction concerns inclusion versus exclusion:

Representations include or exclude social actors to suit their interests and purposes in relation to the readers for whom they are intended.

(1996: 38)

Exclusion can take two forms: *suppression*, where 'there is no reference to the social actor(s) anywhere in the text' (1996: 39), or *backgrounding*, where 'the excluded social actors may not be mentioned in relation to a given activity, but they are mentioned elsewhere in the text' (1996: 39)

19

and where 'they are not so much excluded as de-emphasised, pushed into the background' (1996: 39). For example, Sunderland (2000) points out that part of the 'part-time' father discourse is the use of phrases such as 'someone else', as in ' "you may want to express some milk for someone else to give to your baby in a bottle" '. If the father or partner is mentioned in the vicinity, as in fact happened with the quoted example, then we can infer that the father is a likely candidate for being that 'someone else'. Here then, the father is backgrounded. As far as inclusion is concerned, van Leeuwen develops a complex hierarchy of alternatives, such as whether the actor has an active or passive role, whether they are represented as specific individuals or in groups, whether they are named or categorised. Regarding the linguistic choices which form these representations, van Leeuwen draws eclectically on various linguistic systems, including transitivity, reference, the nominal group, and rhetorical figures.

My aims in this book bear some similarity to van Leeuwen's. I am interested in finding out what the categories for character are and in describing how these are realised linguistically. Can I not, then, simply take van Leeuwen's framework and apply it to my data? There are some important reasons why this is not possible. Firstly, van Leeuwen generated his framework from a corpus of written texts, including 'fictional narratives, comic strips, news stories, newspaper editorials, advertisements, textbooks and scholarly essays, all dealing, in some form or other, with the subject of schooling' (1996: 35). What this does not cover is spoken interaction, or even, as in the case of dramatic dialogue, writing posing as spoken interaction. Clearly, the linguistic features used for representing people in dramatic dialogue are rather different. To take a simple example, a fundamental way of excluding people in spoken interaction, real or fictional, is not to give them the conversational floor. There is no mention of this in van Leeuwen's scheme. Doubtless one could extend van Leeuwen's linguistic inventory to cover spoken interaction. Indeed, my aim in Chapter 4 is to investigate the linguistic resources in dramatic dialogue for constructing character. Secondly, van Leeuwen's approach seems to assume a re-presentation: the re-presentation of an anterior event, person or context. In fictional discourse, however, there is no anterior — it is a matter of *presenting* a fiction. Thirdly, the inclusion/ exclusion dimension fits critical discourse analysis, because it can help reveal the ideologies and power relations that underlie the discourse. But is this dimension the best one for the presentation of character? As I pointed out in 1.3.3 above, stylistic analysis focusses on both the text and the reader, and the interaction between them. Van Leeuwen's framework has nothing to say about how readers might actually go about comprehending a text. For example, one dimension I discuss in Chapter 3 is foregrounding. Van Leeuwen also uses the terms foreground and background when discussing his inclusion/exclusion dimension, but here it is a sociological dimension. My understanding of foregrounding, following stylisticians such as van Peer (1986), relates to perceptual salience. And, of course, a concept such as perceptual salience belongs to a cognitive dimension.

There is another social constructivist approach within critical discourse analysis that has a cognitive dimension. This is the approach taken by van Dijk to the communication of ethnic prejudices and racism (e.g. 1987, 1991). Van Dijk's theoretical framework incorporates aspects of his work in the 1970s and early 1980s on discourse comprehension (see, for example, van Dijk and Kintsch 1983). Fairclough and Wodak (1997: 265–6) neatly summarise van Dijk's argument:

> [van Dijk] argues that no direct relationship can or should be constructed between discourse structures and social structures, but that they are always mediated by the interface of personal and social cognition. Cognition, according to van Dijk, is the missing link of many studies in CL [=Critical Linguistics] and CDA [= Critical Discourse Analysis], which fail to show how societal structures influence discourse structures and precisely how societal structures are in turn enacted, instituted, legitimated, confirmed or challenged by text and talk.

I will not say any more about van Dijk's approach here, because I will return to his work in more detail when I consider text comprehension and characterisation in section 1.5.2 below and when I discuss social cognition in the following chapter.

The final approach to constructing identity developed, not within critical discourse analysis, but within ethnomethodology (see, for example, the founding work of Garfinkel 1967), or, more specifically, within conversation analysis (see for instance Sacks 1992, an edited collection of his lectures from 1964 to 1972; see also 4.4.1). This approach lies at the opposite extreme from the language attitudes research (outlined in 1.4.1), both in terms of theory and methodology. In contrast with language attitudes research, ethnomethodology is anti–cognitivist: one looks for patterns in naturally occurring situated conversation, rather than constructing linguistic examples as 'input' for the psychological processes of experimental 'subjects' in laboratory situations. The state-of-the-art in this approach to identity is captured in the set of papers in Antaki and Widdicombe's *Identities in Talk* (1998b). They describe the approach in all their papers thus (1998a: 2):

> Once we are at a scene [where people are interacting], the ethnomethodological argument runs, we shall see a person's identity as his or her display of, or ascription to, membership of some feature-rich category. Analysis starts when one realizes that any individual can, of course, sensibly be described under a multitude of categories. [. . .]
>
> The interest for analysts is to see which of those identifications folk actually use, what features those identifications seem to carry, and to what end they are put. The ethnomethodological spirit is to take it that the identity category, the characteristics it affords, and what consequences follow, are all knowable to the analyst only through the understandings displayed by the interactants themselves.

To make this more tangible, let us briefly consider Sacks's (1992: vol. 1, 597–599) discussion of a short stretch of data from a group therapy session in the 1960s.[12] The participants are Californian teenagers. Louise is the only female. Dan is the therapist.

> Ken: So did Louise call or anything this morning?
>
> Dan: Why, didju expect her t'call?
>
> Ken: No, I was just kinda hoping that she might be able to figure out some way t-to come to the meetings and still be able to work. C'z she did seem like she d-wanted to come back, but uh she didn't think she could.
>
> Dan: D'you miss her?
>
> Ken: Well in some ways yes, it's — it was uh nice having — having the opposite sex in — in the room, you know, havin' a chick in here.
>
> (Sacks 1992, vol. 1: 597)

What Sacks focusses on here is Ken's shift from the specific nomination *Louise* to a generalised gender category *the opposite sex . . . a chick* in explaining his interest in Louise.[13] This, so Sacks argues, enables Ken to block any inference that his interest is personal: gender is identified as the relevant thing about Louise. It is also a means by which Ken can avoid implying anything unfavourable about the other members of the group (for example, saying 'It was nice having someone smart in the room' might imply that the people in the room were not smart). In Sacks's analysis, then, the emphasis is on how identity categories are set to work: how they are used in the performance and management of social interaction, and in the context of that social interaction.

1.4.4 Developing a pragmatic view of language and people

What one understands about people on the basis of language is part of communication. If I met you, you would use language to present — consciously or unconsciously — a certain identity to me, and I would interpret your presented identity on the basis of your language (and other behavioural) choices and the context. However, it is surprising how much of the language research on real life people has taken a wholly inadequate view of communication. Particular approaches have tended to focus on particular aspects of communication, to the exclusion of others. Language attitudes research, particularly in the earlier years, tended to focus on what the *hearer* made of some linguistic feature, to the exclusion of what the producer of that utterance might have meant by it. In fact, in Robinson and Giles's (1990) review of the field, they suggest that the lack of a theory of motivation may be the 'greatest hazard' (1990: 6) to this research paradigm. Interestingly, they suggest that speech act theory (such as Searle 1975b) may provide a starting point. I will return to speech act theory in parts of Chapters 3, 4 and 5. In sociolinguistics, the focus is frequently on the identifying acts of the *speaker*, to the exclusion of what the hearer makes of them. In the social constructivist approaches, the focus is on the *utterance* or text, to the exclusion of both the hearer, as an interpreter, and the speaker, as an individual with goals of their own (see, for example, the critique offered in Abrams and Hogg 1990b).

In my view, the construction of people — or characters — through interaction is an aspect of meaning construction, and, as such, it is a pragmatic matter. Note here the view of pragmatics espoused in Thomas (1995: 22):

> [. . .] meaning is not something which is inherent in the words alone, nor is it produced by the speaker alone, nor by the hearer alone. Making meaning is a dynamic process, involving the negotiation of meaning between speaker and hearer, the context of utterance (physical, social and linguistic) and the meaning potential of an utterance.

Characterisation, as I shall demonstrate in the course of this book, is part of this dynamic process, involving the speaker, the hearer, the context and the utterance. What has been said in the pragmatics literature about people's identities and perceived characteristics, and how might these be involved in communication? The short answer is not much. The main theoretical contributions, such as speech act theory (Austin 1962; Searle 1969), conversational implicature (Grice 1975), and relevance theory (Sperber and Wilson 1986, 1995), although they can — I shall argue — be useful in describing aspects of characterisation, say nearly nothing about the presentation and perception of identities, or even about the fact that some people might be different from others. People only feature insofar as they are the anonymous 'speaker' or 'hearer' of an utterance. Politeness theory (see, for example, Leech 1983; Brown and Levinson 1987) is something of an exception. It is true that politeness theory tends to overlook the hearer's role in communication and does not treat interactants as 'characterful' entities. Brown and Levinson (1987), for example, introduce the notion of the Model Person — a ' "rational face-bearing [agent]" ' (1987: 58), obliterating differences between speakers. However, it has a lot to offer in describing relationships between people. This is because it is a theory that takes on board people's interpersonal goals, how they relate to each other in terms of power and social distance, and the kind of linguistic features they use. The value of politeness theory in the presentation and perception of identities has been noted and built upon by some researchers (such as Holtgraves 1992; Tracy 1990). I will devote Chapter 5 to politeness theory and characterisation.

So far, I have mentioned major theories in mainstream pragmatics. If one casts the net a little wider, one can find models of communication that allow for both the presentation of identities and/or the perception of them. Notable here is the work of Douglas McCann and Tory Higgins, two cognitively-oriented social psychologists, who describe a model of communication which they call the 'Communication Game' (see, for example, Higgins 1981; McCann and Higgins 1992). Their model is a distillation of other people's, including, for example, Goffman (1959), Austin (1962) and Grice (1975). Since I will describe in detail many of the theories they draw upon in later chapters of this book, I will not fully describe their model. But what is of interest to me is one of the assumptions behind their model, that:

> [. . .] effective and efficient communication entails a continuous process of co-orientation and monitoring between

participants along with accurate appraisal of each other's
characteristics and intention [. . .]

(McCann and Higgins 1992: 147)

From this assumption and four others, they generate their communication model as a set of eight context-dependent 'rules' for the speaker
and six for the hearer. Thus, from the assumption quoted above, they
generate a rule for communicators, 'take the audience's or recipient's
characteristics into account', and a rule for recipients, 'take the communicator's characteristics into account' (McCann and Higgins 1992: 147).
McCann and Higgins cite an impressive array of research to support this
rule (cf. McCann and Higgins 1990). To take an obvious example, it is
well known that communicators modify their language when speaking
to children, foreigners and elderly adults (see, McCann and Higgins
1990: 22, for references).

The final idea I want to get across in this section is to suggest a
pragmatic view of what character *is*. I will begin with a couple of
examples. In the evening, if I say 'bath' to my daughter, it is unlikely to
be taken by anybody else who hears it as a rapture about the wonderful
city of that name or even as some kind of order to my daughter to
take a bath, but as an announcement that bath time has arrived. This
is because my daughter is only two years old, and thus clearly neither
appreciative of the pleasures of Georgian architecture nor capable of
going to have a bath on her own. Knowing something about the target
of the message enables us to narrow down the interpretative possibilities
of the utterance. Knowing something about the speaker also enables us
to narrow down the interpretative possibilities of an utterance. Thus, if
your academic work is praised, your estimation of that praise is determined by knowing who gave it. If you discover that an anonymous
referee is in fact a famous authority in the field, any praise that they
might have given becomes veritable praise indeed. What I am working
towards here is a view of character as a sub-set of context, broadly
understood to be the assumptions that interact with an utterance in the
generation of meaning. This view is similar to Zimmerman's (1998)
notion of 'identity-as-context':

[. . .] identity-as-context refers to the way in which the
articulation/alignment of discourse and situated identities
furnishes for the participants a continuously evolving framework within which their actions, vocal or otherwise, assume

a particular meaning, import and interactional consequentiality (Goodwin 1996: 374–6).

(1998: 88)[14]

However, unlike Zimmerman, I will adopt a cognitive view of context, and thus of character. This cognitive view is described in the following section.

So far, my discussion in this section has considered language and real-life people. I would argue that the same basic ideas also apply to dramatic dialogue, though with some important modifications, which I will attend to in various parts of the upcoming chapters. Let us consider the notion of 'character-as-context'. Imagine the kind of speaker who would say, 'I've been to the zoo'. We all know that children like going to the zoo, so our default hypothesis for the 'speaker-context' is likely to be that the speaker is a child. Also, one might have some hypotheses about the likely goal of this speaker: for example, to get the hearer to pay attention. In fact, these are the first spoken words of Edward Albee's play *The Zoo Story* ([1958] (1962)). We have already been told in a stage direction that the speaker is Jerry, a man in his late thirties. So, there is a clash between the speaker-context one might have inferred from the stage direction and the kind of speaker-context one might infer from what he says. Let us now turn to the 'hearer-context'. Jerry is addressing Peter, a complete stranger who is sitting on a park bench reading a book, for the first time. Now, if the speaker were a child, 'I've been to the zoo' would be acceptable as the opening gambit for a conversation, since we would not expect a child to be au fait with the usual phatic routines for opening a conversation with a stranger.[15] But, of course, Jerry is not a child. It is no surprise, then, that Peter does not know he is being addressed in spite of the fact that Jerry repeats 'I've been to the zoo' (1962: 113) three times with increasing volume. The upshot of all this is that the utterance 'I've been to the zoo' is at odds with both its character-contexts. This mismatch may lead us to infer that Jerry is an oddball, with peculiar conversational assumptions or goals. And so, this one utterance sets the tenor for Jerry's character throughout the play.

1.5 Text comprehension and characterisation

It is probably best for me at the onset of this section to state clearly my position with regard to cognition and discourse. My view accords with van Dijk's (1987: 37):

Although grammar deals with meanings and interpretation in abstract terms, it should be emphasized that, empirically, meanings and interpretations of utterances or activities are to be accounted for in cognitive terms. No serious account of discourse meaning, coherence, or other semantic properties is possible without notions such as concepts, knowledge and beliefs, frames scripts, or models, that is in terms of mental representations and cognitive processes of various kinds. The same is true for the analysis of action and interaction: notions such as plans, intentions, goals, strategies, control, and monitoring are essential in both the theoretical and empirical description of speech acts and social action. The same holds at all levels, for the representation of the communicative context, including speakers, communicative goals and the social properties of the participants and the situation.

Note here that van Dijk regards 'speakers, communicative goals and the social properties of the participants' as (a) part of the context, and (b) part of a mental representation — the cognitive re-presentation of some aspect of the world in the mind.[16] In the understanding of language, 'the human mind actively constructs various types of *cognitive representations* (that is, codes, features, meanings, structured sets of elements) that interpret the linguistic input' (Graesser *et al.* 1997). I have already argued that people or characters in communication are part of the context; here, I shall argue that they are also part of what goes on in a comprehender's mind.

My aim in the rest of this section is to sketch out the backdrop that lies behind the chapters in this book, and thereby show how those chapters relate to one another. Firstly I will briefly indicate what information sources are available to the comprehender. Then, drawing upon van Dijk and Kintsch's (1983) work, I will show how these information sources feed into a model of text comprehension. Finally, I will suggest how this model of text comprehension relates to literary comprehension in general and characterisation in particular.

1.5.1 Information sources and cognitive processes: Top-down and bottom-up

In formulating a hypothesis or cognitive representation about anything in the outside world there are, in a very general sense, two potential sources of information: the external 'stimuli' and our 'prior knowledge'.

Psychologists, however, seem loath to say exactly what constitutes a stimulus.[17] For my purposes, stimulus is best understood as the raw text (real-life communicative situations would, of course, have a rich array of linguistic and non-linguistic stimuli). On the other hand, there seems to be more consensus about the term prior knowledge. By prior knowledge, I mean the past knowledge and experience stored in the mind. The prior knowledge I am particularly interested in is held in 'long-term memory', as opposed to 'short-term memory', which has limited capacity (often said to be up to about seven random items or one or two simple sentences).[18] I will have much more to say about the nature of prior knowledge in Chapter 2, where I shall talk in particular about the role of 'schemata' — structured bundles of generic knowledge.

Cognitive processes that are primarily determined by an external stimulus have been referred to as 'bottom-up' or 'data-driven' processes, while cognitive processes that are primarily determined by the application of past knowledge have been referred to as 'top-down' or 'conceptually-driven' processes (see, for example, Eysenck and Keane 1990). Intuitively, one might suppose that both processes are involved in forming a hypothesis. That this is indeed the case has been argued and demonstrated for person perception (see McArthur and Baron 1983, for example) reading comprehension (Rumelhart and Ortony 1977; McClelland 1987) and cognitive activity in general (Neisser 1976; Eysenck and Keane 1990). I shall argue that one's impression of a character is formed in the interaction between the text and the interpreter's background knowledge; in other words, as a result of both bottom-up and top-down processes. The next two Chapters, 2 and 3, concentrate on top-down processes, whilst Chapters 4 and 5 focus more on bottom-up processes. However, it should be remembered that this separation is simply for expository convenience.

1.5.2 Mental representations in text comprehension

This section is concerned with what we do when we comprehend a text. My brief description of text comprehension is largely based on the model described in van Dijk and Kintsch (1983).[19] Their model has stayed the course of time (one might note, for example, its influence on many of the papers in Britton and Graesser 1996), and it is compatible with more recent approaches.[20] Furthermore, van Dijk (e.g. 1987) showed how this model could be used in the study of social interaction, notably the communication of ethnic prejudices and racism. Characterisation clearly needs a model that can cope with social aspects. However, a limitation of van Dijk and Kintsch (1983) is that it overly concentrates on propositions, on how they are derived from the text and represented in the mind. Johnson–Laird (1983), for example, argues for 'mental models' which are made up of visual elements. Thus, a reader would not compute propositions for a sentence like 'Mary is taller than Jane, Jane is taller than Ann', but would build a spatial model; the reader could image three individuals of varying heights, or, minimally, could have some visual representation akin to plotting their heights on a graph. (See Emmott 1997: 43–50, 109–10, for a critical discussion of van Dijk and Kintsch 1983).

In the van Dijk and Kintsch (1983) model, the reader is an active comprehender, allocating varying amounts of scarce mental resources to different levels of representation. Van Dijk and Kintsch (1983) suggest that there are three levels of representation, and the fact that these exist and are distinct is widely agreed upon by other researchers (see references in Zwaan 1996: 243). The levels are surface or verbatim representation, textbase representation, and the situation model.

Surface or verbatim representation
This is a kind of mirror image of the surface structure of the text. The surface representation is often thought to be lost from memory after only a few seconds (see Long 1994: 213 for numerous references, and also Kintsch *et al.* 1990).

Textbase representation
This is defined in terms of the propositional content of the text, and is thought to last longer in memory than the surface structure (see, for instance, Kintsch *et al.* 1990). This definition begs the question of what a proposition is. A clear definition is given in Graesser *et al.* (1997: 294):

> A *proposition* is a theoretical unit that contains a *predicate* (for example, main verb, adjective, connective) and one or more *arguments* (for example, nouns, embedded propositions), with each argument having a functional role (for example, agent, patient, object, location). A proposition refers to a state, an event, or an action and frequently has a truth value with respect to a real or an imaginary world.

For example, the sentence 'The tall man appeared and Tom fled from him' contains the following propositions (the predicates are to the left of parentheses; arguments and their functional roles are in parentheses):

PROPOSITION 1 — appeared (AGENT = man)

PROPOSITION 2 — tall (OBJECT = man)

PROPOSITION 3 — fled (AGENT = Tom, LOCATION = from him)

PROPOSITION 4 — and (PROPOSITION 1, PROPOSITION 3)

The textbase includes both explicit text propositions and a small number of inferences that provide *local coherence* between the propositions. Precisely what and how many coherence inferences are made at this level of representation is a matter of controversy. In the above example, it is likely that a bridging inference would be made that the pronoun *him* refers to the *man*. Temporal relations between propositions may also be inferred; thus, proposition 1 above occurred before proposition 3. In addition, a causal antecedent inference may be made; thus, the tall man caused Tom to flee. Note that the example inferences given here only connect adjacent text elements. However, van Dijk and Kintsch (1983) also propose that the textbase can include a macropropositional textbase, a representation that establishes global coherence over longer stretches of text by the higher-level organisation of textual information. This, for example, may concern the theme of the text or its main point. Global coherence involves world or genre schemata (van Dijk and Kintsch 1983: 196–7). Thus, my knowledge of the normal sequence of events in restaurants would help me organise a narrative scene taking place in a restaurant (see Schank and Abelson 1977); or my knowledge of detective fiction would help me organise the stages in the plot — crime, investigation, resolution, for example. I will discuss both types of knowledge in Chapter 2.

Situation model
This is the 'representation of events, actions, persons, and in general the situation a text is about' (van Dijk and Kintsch 1983: 11–12).[21] This is created through the integration of new information from the above levels of representation and old information from memory. For example, regarding the above sentence 'The tall man appeared and Tom fled from him', we may infer an emotional reaction of Tom to the appearance of the tall man, namely, that he was frightened. This inference would rely on prior knowledge such as 'people are often frightened of tall men' and 'people often run away when they are frightened'. This inference may also lead to a further inference that Tom is a child, since we know that children are often frightened of tall men. Note that if more text followed, other descriptions could be used in the textbase to

refer to the same individuals in the situation model. Being able to create a situation model is, in van Dijk and Kintsch's view, the major goal in understanding the text: 'If we are unable to imagine a situation in which certain individuals have the properties or relations indicated by the text, we fail to understand the text itself' (1983: 337). This view is also reflected in Garnham and Oakhill (1996: 314).

Two further points about van Dijk and Kintsch's (1983) model need to be made. Firstly, van Dijk and Kintsch (1983) emphasise that comprehension takes place in a social context and that this has important cognitive implications. Thus, for example, in understanding a story a comprehender not only constructs a representation of the story, but also matches this with a representation of what the teller of the story intends the comprehender to understand. More specifically:

> [. . .] a person who interprets a story will also construct a representation of the possible speech acts involved, by assigning a specific function or action category to the discourse utterance, and hence to the speaker.
>
> (1983: 7)

But the comprehender also has intentions or goals, and so

> [. . .] the representation of the discourse in memory will depend on the assumptions of the listener about the purposes (goals) and further underlying motivations of the speaker, as well as on the listener's own goals and motivations when listening to a story.
>
> (1983: 7)

In addition, the interaction between the story teller and the comprehender is part of a social situation, and so the comprehender will also bring a representation of the situation (containing the general norms for participants and discourse in that situation) into play. Thus, to use van Dijk and Kintsch's (1983: 8) example, a car crash story would be interpreted differently in the informal context of a chat between friends, from when it is told in the courtroom.

The second point concerns the idea that comprehension is strategic. Clearly, the willy-nilly activation of prior knowledge in the understanding of a text would quickly overload the system. The use of knowledge depends on the goals of the language user, the amount of available knowledge from text and context, [and] the level of processing or the degree of coherence needed for comprehension [...]

(1983: 13)

These factors act as criteria for the 'control system' which

will supervise processing in short-term memory, activate and actualize needed episodic and more general semantic knowledge, provide the higher order information into which lower order information must fit, coordinate the various strategies, decide which information from short-term memory should be moved to episodic memory, activate the relevant situation models in episodic memory, guide effective search of relevant information in long-term memory, and so on.

(1983: 12)

1.5.3 Mental representations in literary texts and characterisation

In this section, I shall revisit aspects of text comprehension mentioned in the previous section and highlight points of interest for reading literary texts in general and for fictional characterisation in particular. In my discussion, I shall draw in particular upon Zwaan (1996).

Let us first return to the various levels of mental representation.

Surface or verbatim representation
Van Dijk and Kintsch (1983: 343) point out that specific stylistic features of the surface representation may be recalled from episodic memory 'long after' the text is comprehended. Zwaan (1996: 243–4) suggests that whether or not the surface representation is lost from memory depends on the pragmatic context. Long (1994), for example, found that subjects had good long-term memory for the surface form of dialogues in literary prose, especially when it provided information about the speaker's attitudes and when such information was present in a formulaic expression. Moreover, Zwaan (1996: 245–6) argues that literary devices such as rhyme and alliteration attract the reader's attention to the surface form of the text, presumably at the expense of other higher-level processes. This, I would suggest, also works for character.

An example is Kaa, the personified snake in Walt Disney's *Jungle Book* (1967). Our attention is drawn to his alliterative sibilants in utterances like 'It's simply terrible. I can't eat, I can't sleep, so I sing myself to sleep, you know, self-hypnosis. Let me show you how it works'. Thus the feature 'sibilant-producing' is incorporated into his character.[22]

Textbase representation

Zwaan (1996) argues that literary texts can also draw attention to the textbase level by not presenting information in a coherent and unambiguous manner. Zwaan's example in fact relates to fictional characterisation:

> A detail may be mentioned in a detective novel that does not seem to bear immediate relevance to information previously stated in the text. For example, the narrator may mention out of the blue that a particular character is left-handed. In nonliterary prose comprehension, this information probably would be quickly deactivated because it would not receive activation from other nodes in the propositional network. In literature, however, seemingly irrelevant information can be relevant at a later stage, for example, when it turns out that the murderer is left-handed. In the case of literary prose therefore, seemingly irrelevant information has to be kept active in memory for a relatively long period.
>
> (1996: 247–8)

Situation model

It is clear from van Dijk and Kintsch (1983) that one's representation of 'persons' is part of the situation model. There is no reason to suppose that the representation of fictional persons — their goals, motives, beliefs, traits and emotions — is any different in this respect. In fact, in the text comprehension literature it is not only assumed that this is the case, but there is also some supporting empirical evidence (such as Gernsbacher *et al.* 1992; Graesser *et al.* 1994). Of course, in the construction of a unique situation model both the kind of new information derived from the text and the kind of old information recalled from memory may be different in the case of fiction. For example, we may draw upon old information about the particular character types that inhabit a certain genre, such as a Western (for example the 'goodies' and the 'baddies').

Zwaan (1996) makes much of the cognitive control system in literary comprehension, as indeed do other researchers (e.g. Meutsch 1986).[23]

Zwaan argues that readers develop, through their exposure to different text types, control systems for different types of discourse. In informational texts, such as scientific and news discourse, the reader focusses on the construction of a situation model; in literary texts, the reader focusses on the surface and textbase levels (1996: 245). He suggests (1996: 248–9) that control systems adapt to deal with the indeterminacies of literary comprehension. For example, we might delay the creation of a situation model. Thus, to extend Zwaan's example given above for the textbase representation, if it turned out that another suspect was also left-handed, we would potentially have two different situation models: one in which our character was the murderer and one in which our character was not. However, rather than try and keep two complex situation models active, we would simply construct a strong textbase representation which could accommodate either interpretation.[24]

Finally, it is worth mentioning here that other researchers (e.g. Graesser *et al.* 1994), whilst agreeing with work like van Dijk and Kintsch (1983) that comprehenders attempt to construct meaning representations that are coherent and that address their goals, also emphasise that comprehenders attempt to explain *why* actions, events and states occur in the text. Understanding why something happens is a kind of higher-level coherence (that is, above the level at which, for example, one works out the reference of a pronoun) that leads to deeper understanding. Understanding the reasons why characters act as they do is a major part of characterisation, and so I will devote the bulk of Chapter 3 to this issue.

1.6 A model for characterisation

My aim in this section is to present a diagram showing how characterisation might work. I want to show how a representation of character (an impression of character) might be constructed in the mind during the process of reading. The cognitive notion of 'representation of character' and the pragmatic notion of 'character-context', referred to in section 1.4.4, are the same thing, but seen from two different points of view: one cognitive, the other pragmatic. Diagrams, unfortunately, are fraught with danger. They are two-dimensional and static. This is quite unlike the human mind, which processes things in parallel (that is, it is multi-dimensional) and is dynamic. There are also limits to the amount of information that can be captured in a diagram (for example, there are more connections between components than I can possibly show). Thus,

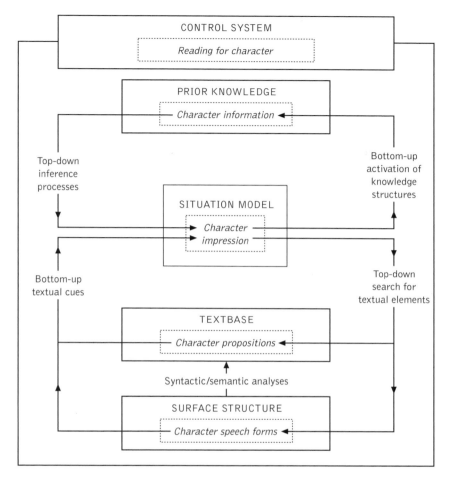

Figure 1.1   Comprehending character

what I present here is both idealised and simplified. Taking inspiration from Meutsch's (1986: 324) diagram for literary reading and incorporating aspects of text comprehension mentioned in previous sections, Figure 1.1 displays how characterisation might work.

Each solid box represents an important and identifiable component in the text comprehension process. Within each of these boxes a dotted box suggests that part of each of these components is at least theoretically specific to characterisation.[25] Note here my ontological view that character potentially exists in all these components. The line arrows show some of the linkages between components. Moreover, they show that comprehension is a combination of both top-down processes (that is,

35

determined by knowledge in memory) and bottom-up processes (determined by textual elements) and that comprehension is cyclic: what you see influences what you know, and what you know influences what you see. I will briefly comment on each component.

Control system
The control system oversees the entire comprehension process. It regulates the level of processing required and the degree of coherence, according to (in particular) the goals of the reader. Part of the literary control system will be 'reading for character', whereby, for example, a greater level of incoherence is tolerated in the textbase and the creation of a specific situation model containing certain characters may be postponed for longer than for other text types.

Prior knowledge
This concerns the knowledge held in long-term memory which can be used in the comprehension process. A subset of this knowledge will contain information that is relevant to the understanding of character. It is worth noting that prior knowledge can vary greatly in type. For example, it can include knowledge of 'facts' (for instance, men are biologically different from women), knowledge about the future ('prospective' knowledge) as well as the past ('retrospective' knowledge — for instance, knowledge of a person's intentions is knowledge about their intended future), knowledge about solutions for problems (such as solutions for 'whodunnit' murder mystery novels), and knowledge about the causes of things (such as what makes people happy).

Situation model
Here, prior knowledge and textual elements combine to create a meaning representation — our sense of what the text is about. Part of the situation model may (depending on the text type) constitute our impression of a character. This part will include an array of character-related inferences, for example, inferences about goals, beliefs, traits, emotions, and social relationships. A character in the situation model may be shaped by prior knowledge about real people, as well as prior knowledge about fictional characters. Textual cues may influence the balance of real people knowledge versus fictional character knowledge. Thus, if we have identified a play as a Morality Play (for example *Everyman*, c. 1500), then we are likely to retrieve and use our knowledge about personified vices and virtues such as the fictional Seven Deadly Sins; whereas if we have identified a play as a 'kitchen sink drama' (for instance Arnold Wesker's

plays), then we are likely to give more weight to our knowledge about real people.

Textbase

Like the situation model this is a meaning representation, but unlike the situation model it only includes the propositional content of the text. Some of these propositions will, of course, relate to character. The literary control system may allow a richer textbase to be constructed than might be the case for other text types. This is one way of coping with incoherent or indeterminate textual information about characters. To put it non-technically, we may keep the various bits of character information in mind for longer when reading for character, rather than attempt to integrate them with our prior knowledge. For some characters, their propositional existence in the textbase may be incorporated in the situation model and play an influential part. For example, allegorical characters, such as those of John Bunyan's *Pilgrim's Progress* (1678), represent abstract qualities and ideas, as the propositional content of their names makes clear — Fellowship, Giant Despair, Sloth, Hypocrisy and Piety. Furthermore, the textbase can include a macropropositional textbase, which uses prior knowledge to organise information at a higher level. For instance, this can include genre knowledge (such as a romance), or world knowledge, such as a restaurant script. Characters can be included in the macropropositional textbase insofar as they are defined by some function within the frame. The notion of character here would accommodate the functional understanding of characters as 'actants' or 'dramatic roles' (to be discussed in 2.2.2 and 2.2.3). Note that this prior knowledge here has an organisational role, whereas in a situation model it is integrated with textual information, in order to produce new information.

Surface structure

This is the surface structure of the text. It will include the particular linguistic choices attributed to characters. The surface structure will undergo syntactic and semantic analyses in order to form the textbase. However, it is not the case that the surface structure will always dissolve into the propositions of the textbase. Formal surface features, if they are deemed relevant, may be incorporated into the situation model. For example, a central part of Sheridan's character Mrs. Malaprop in *The Rivals* (1775) relates to surface features. She tends inadvertently to replace one word with another which is similar in sound but has a different meaning. Thus, she regrets her lack of 'affluence' over her niece. This linguistic trait has become so well-known that our term for it, malapropism, is eponymous. Furthermore, the surface structure is a particular issue for Shakespearian characterisation. Some character speeches are rhetorical showpieces in their own right. In *Romeo and Juliet*, for example, Mercutio's dazzling displays of linguistic dexterity are an important part of his character.

Importantly, the model for characterisation outlined above can accommodate a scale of humanisation for characters (see 1.3.3, and Margolin 1983 in particular). Some characters — such as the protagonists in Arnold Wesker's plays — are relatively humanised individuals. Other characters — such as allegorical characters, actants (typically, the characters in folk tales), Mrs. Malaprop, and Mercutio — are relatively textual.

I will refer back to the above diagram at various points in the coming chapters. Where the various aspects of characterisation are treated separately, it is for reasons of expository clarity. It is important to note that what this diagram lacks, in particular, is a sense of the communicative context. Thus, reading the dialogue of a play will involve us, minimally, in (1) constructing representations (or character-contexts) for all relevant characters, (2) constructing a representation of the situation the characters appear in, and (3) constructing a representation of what the writer of the text intends us to understand by the character discourse. And characterisation involves another mental juggling act: we do not just have to construct all these representations, but also compare them with each other and thereby make inferences.

1.7 Characterisation in plays: Some preliminaries

This book rests upon a number of assumptions about the nature of the dramatic text, in particular its relationship with performance and its discourse structure. I shall briefly address these issues below.

1.7.1 Discourse structure

It is important to remember that dramatic dialogue is constructed by playwrights for audiences to overhear. Thus, the basic issue is not — as often in real life — 'What did a speaker mean me to understand by their utterance in this particular context?', but 'What did a playwright mean me to understand by one character's utterance to another in this particular context?'

At various points in this book I shall refer to or assume a particular discourse structure for drama, which I shall briefly describe here. Short

(1989: 148–9) suggests that the canonical communicative event in ordinary discourse is one in which an addresser conveys a message to an addressee within a particular communicative context. Drama, he argues, also has this same base form, but it is complicated by the fact that it has an additional level of discourse embedded within it. At one level characters convey messages to other characters; at another level the playwright conveys a message to the audience. Short represented this structure in diagrammatic form (see Figure 1.2).

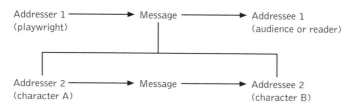

Figure 1.2   The discourse structure of drama (from Short 1989: 149)

The conversation that takes place between characters is designed to be 'overheard', and presumably 'overseen', by the audience: it is part of what the playwright 'tells' the audience. Short points out (1989: 149) that

[. . .] the important thing to notice is the general *embedded* nature of drama, because features which, for example, mark social relations between two people at the character level become messages *about* the characters at the level of discourse which pertains between author and reader/audience.

Clearly, then, the discourse structure of drama will be important in explaining how character is inferred. I shall return to this particular aspect in Chapters 3 and 4. Finally, it should be noted that the number of embedded discourses is not fixed. If the words of a third character are reported or we have a play within a play (as in, for example, Shakespeare's *Hamlet* or *A Midsummer Night's Dream*), then the number of embedded discourses will increase.

1.7.2 Text and performance

Social psychologists (such as Jones 1990) often point to the important influence of appearance in forming impressions of people, and sociolinguists (such as Giles and Powesland 1975) highlight the importance of speech features, such as accent, in evaluating people. It may be that these features are equally important in forming impressions of characters. But if one wishes to study these features in drama, one immediately encounters a problem: Where should we be looking for these features — the text or the performance of the text?

Given that the features mentioned above are only directly observable in performance, one might suppose that we should study performance. Indeed, many have argued that it is only in performance that the words of the text can be fully understood:

> Proper plays can only be understood when performed.

> (Brecht 1964: 15)

> Yet it is only on the stage that drama can be revealed in all its fullness and significance.

> (Stanislavski 1968: 115)

The general assumption here is that the actor must supply those aspects which the text cannot:

> [. . .] even for the clearest, the most precise, and the most forceful writer, words can never be more than symbols that designate a thought, a feeling, or an idea; symbols whose meaning is completed by movement, gesture, and tone, by facial expression, by the eyes, and by the context [. . .]

> (Josephs 1969: 58, translation of Diderot 1875: 363)[26]

The text is assumed to provide the verbal component and the actor the nonverbal component.

Of course, an actor does have a hand in determining the performance of a play. If this were not the case, then there would be much less variation between different performances of a play. However, the above commentators are wrong to diminish the role played by the text in determining a performance. Ionesco was adamant that this role was an essential part of his play texts:

> [. . .] my text is not just dialogue, but also 'stage directions'. These should be respected as much as the text, they are essential [. . .]

> (Ionesco 1964: 216)

The philosopher Searle, discussing the ontological status of fiction in general, went further and argued that

> [. . .] the illocutionary force of the text of a play is like the illocutionary force of a recipe for baking a cake. It is a set of instructions for how to do something, namely, how to perform the play.
>
> (Searle 1975a: 329)

Searle's analogy is perhaps a little misleading. Recipes usually contain a list of explicit 'instructions'; the nearest equivalent in drama is a stage direction. Unlike a recipe, the vast majority of 'instructions' in a play text are implicit — they have to be inferred. A play text provides us with the words that should be spoken, and from these words we can infer how they should be spoken, what should be done (including what gestures, expressions, and so on, should be made), and how one should appear (see Short 1998 for a demonstration of how this works).

My view — which is in tune with Short (1989, 1998) — is that a play text lays down parameters which guide performance. Within these parameters an actor is relatively free to perform the text in different ways in order to achieve different theatrical effects. For instance, an actor would be free to choose the exact accent of the Porter in Shakespeare's *Macbeth*, as long as it was not socially prestigious. The notion that mediates the idea of staying within the performance parameters laid down by the text is that of remaining *faithful* to the text. If Lady Macbeth appeared wearing rags and the porter wearing a crown, then the parameters determining dress would clearly be transgressed. Such dress is not motivated anywhere in the text, and, moreover, is inconsistent with any reasonable interpretation of the text. In other words, though the performance might well be interesting, such dress would not be faithful to the text. A consequence of this argument is that for any character there will be a range of faithful characteristics and a much larger range of unfaithful ones.[27]

The upshot of my argument, then, is that nonverbal features — the features that constitute a performance — are specified, to a degree, within the text. Thus we *can* study the text in order to investigate the role of such features in characterisation. Moreover, it has been argued by Short (1989, 1998) that we *should* study the text rather than a performance. He points out (1989: 140) that variability is a particular problem in studying performance:

Both meanings and value will change not just from one production to another but also from one performance of a particular production to another. There then becomes no play to criticize. Instead we will have to talk about 'X's production of *Hamlet* in theatre Y on the evening of Z', and critical discussion becomes impossible unless the two critics concerned have both seen and are arguing about exactly the same performance.

Furthermore, he notes that teachers and students of literature have traditionally read plays and found it possible to interpret them without the necessity of seeing them performed, and, similarly, that producers of plays must be able to read and interpret plays in order to decide how to produce them.

However, one particular *caveat* needs to be mentioned. Dr Johnson asserted that 'A play read affects the mind like a play acted' (Johnson [1765] 1908: 28). Whilst I think it is the case that a performance is an interpretation of a play, it is also a realisation of that interpretation. There is no guarantee that the way a reader is affected by a text will be the same as the way an audience is affected by the more concrete realisation of that text. For example, it is not clear whether visual and aural cues have the same perceptual salience for a reader as they do for an audience. This is not an area I have space to develop within this book, though I will briefly discuss the notion of 'eye-dialect' — dialect and accent suggested through 'nonstandard' writing — in Chapter 4.

Notes

1 I exclude books that just discuss, say, Shakespeare's characters, without addressing the theoretical basis of character or characterisation.

2 All Shakespearian examples are taken from Kökeritz's ([1954] 1963) facsimile edition of the First Folio, unless stated otherwise. However, for some plays in the First Folio no act or scene divisions are made. Therefore, although the extract is from the First Folio, all act, scene and line references are to Alexander's (1951) popular *The Complete Works of Shakespeare*.

3 In my empirical work (see 3.7.3) these words have been frequently identified as striking, and the reason given by informants for this is that they are taboo (i.e. they break the 'rules' of 'good' or 'clean' language). It is quite possible that they are also striking against the frequency norms of play texts, rather than what might actually be said in informal real-life contexts where taboo words are common. However, this is an empirical question that has as yet not been addressed.

4 It might be argued that Freudian psychoanalysis is humanising in some sense. However, psychoanalytical approaches stand apart from the rest of the humanising camp in that they focus on the unconscious rather than the conscious. I would

also argue that psychoanalysis is unlikely to be the best of starting points for a theory of characterisation. In accord with Knapp (1990), I would claim that it has a very restrictive view of personality (concentrating, for example, on childhood determinacy), it is remote from the 'ordinary' psychological processes readers bring to texts, and it ignores about 100 years of research in mainstream psychology.

5   Of course, it is possible that aspects of the actor's personality may overlap with the character. Also, it is worth bearing in mind that other genres, such as 'docu-dramas', work differently.

6   Concerning what sociolinguistics is, I take the broad view that 'any research which improves our understanding of language and society and the relationship between the two can be called "sociolinguistic" ' (Coates 1989: 63). The traditional view (e.g. Trudgill 1978) is that sociolinguistics is just the Labovian variationist approach.

7   The continental view of pragmatics is much broader. Here disciplines such as linguistics, psychology and sociology are sub-disciplines of pragmatics.

8   However, this finding has not gone unchallenged. Milroy (1980), for example, did not find the expected correlation in her Belfast data. In particular, the *explanations* put forward for this finding have been hotly debated (see Coates and Cameron 1989 for an incisive critique).

9   Much less work has focussed specifically on language and men. See Johnson and Meinhof (1997) for a notable exception.

10   An alternative explanation is the 'difference' view (e.g. Jones 1980), which sees differences as a reflection of the idea that men and women belong to different subcultures (see Cameron 1992: 74–8 for a discussion of some of the issues).

11   In fact, whilst many studies in the variationist or speech style paradigms have claimed just to consider sex, they often touch on issues of gender in their explana-tory discussions or assume that gender will somehow correlate sex.

12   This fragment of data is also discussed, and used as a point of departure for further discussion, by Edwards (1998).

13   Edwards (1998: 18) points out that it is significant that *chick* is a colloquial gender categorisation, and also that it might possibly have sexist implications.

14   Zimmerman is responsible for the notion of 'identity-as-context'; Goodwin (1996: 374–6) discusses the idea of (communicative) action being situated within 'participation frameworks'.

15   All the points I make about children's conversations in this paragraph are sup-ported by research. Dore (1985), for example, citing his own and others' research, points out that infants' expressions often function to gain attention, that up to about school age accountability for talk is fairly relaxed, and that only at about four years old do children begin to adjust their speech to their addressee.

16   Researchers have tended to define mental or cognitive representation to suit their purposes. A more biological definition would view it as a set of activated neurons in the brain; a more cognitive definition would view it as what lies between two processors in the mind. Some readers may wonder whether a 'schema' is a mental representation. The answer is that a schema is a specific type of mental representa-tion, one that is relatively structured and relatively permanent.

17   Hayes offers a rare definition, 'An external environmental event to which an organism responds' (1994: 1040). This, however, raises the question as to what an event is. Generally, psychologists have tended to use the term stimulus inter-changeably with other terms. Within one particular social psychological theory the

terms 'stimulus', 'event', 'entity', 'thing' and 'target' are all used interchangeably (see Chapter 3).

18 The term 'working memory' is sometimes used for short-term memory, because it captures the fact that short-term memory serves both to store information and to process it.

19 Perhaps it should be noted that many of the concepts that constitute their model are by no means exclusive to this model.

20 Zwaan (1996), for example, is able to slide from a description of literary comprehension in terms of van Dijk and Kintsch (1983) to a description in terms of Kintsch's (1988) model, which is partly based on connectionist cognitive theory.

21 It seems likely that van Dijk and Kintsch's (1983) situation model was inspired by Johnson-Laird's (1983) work on 'mental models'.

22 Further processing is, of course, possible. Sibilants are sound symbolic of the hiss of a snake. In other words, we may construct the proposition that the sibilants 'mean' the snake's hiss. This proposition can then be incorporated into our situation model as one property of Kaa's character. However, the interpretation thus outlined has a bottom-up bias. In fact, the mind is simultaneously working in a top-down fashion. Thus, visual cues may have activated the retrieval of knowledge about snakes from long-term memory, which in turn would predispose the comprehender to notice snake-like qualities in the recognisably human voice of Kaa.

23 Zwaan (1996) cites his earlier work (Zwaan 1991, 1993, 1994) as empirical support for the points in this paragraph.

24 For empirical support, Zwaan (1996) cites Mani and Johnson-Laird (1982) who demonstrate, with regard to spatial descriptions, that readers refrain from constructing multiple situation models and instead construct a richer textbase.

25 I say 'theoretically' because having something specific to character implies that it has been identified as such, and this implies a degree of processing. This is a particular issue for the textbase and surface levels of representation, because, by definition, these levels have only incurred minimal processing.

26 '[. . .] dans l'écrivain le plus clair, le plus précis, le plus énergique, les mots ne sont et ne peuvent être que des signes approchés d'une pensée, d'un sentiment, d'une idée; signes dont le mouvement, le geste, le ton, le visage, les yeux, la circonstance donnée, complètent la valeur [. . .]' (Diderot 1875: 363).

27 One might note that the debate over whether we should study the text or performance was certainly alive in Elizabethan times (see Dessen 1977), and that remaining faithful to the text may well have been an issue for Shakespeare, if we are to assume that Hamlet's instructions to the three Players in *Hamlet* (III.ii.1–44) reflect his own opinions.

PART ONE

CHARACTERISATION
AND THE MIND

CHAPTER 2

CHARACTER CATEGORIES AND IMPRESSIONS OF CHARACTER

2.1 Introduction

Jonathan Culler, discussing cultural and psychological stereotypes, notes that:

> When a character in a novel performs an action, the reader can give it meaning by drawing upon this fund of human knowledge which establishes connections between action and motive, behaviour and personality.

> (1975: 142–3)

And he goes on to say that:

> [. . .] most literary effects, particularly in narrative prose, depend on the fact that readers will try to relate what the text tells them to a level of ordinary human concerns, the actions and reactions of characters constructed in accordance with models of integrity and coherence.

> (1975: 144)

This chapter and the next explore that 'fund of human knowledge', and consider how readers use it to give meaning and coherence to the conversational actions of characters in plays. In these chapters, I focus on the role of 'top-down' processes in the construction of character. These chapters, then, examine the role of the prior knowledge box in Figure 1.1.

In this chapter, I draw upon theories from cognitive psychology, particularly social cognition, and argue that these theories can help describe how readers flesh out and make coherent their impressions of characters, and also explain some of the distinctions found in traditional literary character typologies, notably the distinction between flat and round characters. I shall start with a brief overview of literary approaches to character types. Then, I describe two related cognitive theories, prototype theory and schema theory, that attempt to explain aspects of the organisation and role of prior knowledge. Next, I consider how these theories have been used within social cognition to explain the perception of real people, and then turn to how aspects of social cognition might work in the context of fictional characterisation. Finally, bringing the threads of the chapter together, I consider a passage from John Osborne's *The Entertainer* and discuss relevant findings from an exploratory empirical study.

2.2 Literary approaches to categorising character

The problem of categorising different types of character has occupied the attention of both literary critics and psychologists. Here I shall first review three structuralist approaches, one focussing on traits or 'semes', one on 'actant roles' and the other on 'stock figures'. With regard to Figure 1.1 on page 35, all of these schemes emphasise the textbase: they attempt to capture character within specific propositions or consider the character's function within the textual frame (see 1.6). I conclude this section by considering some character typologies — specifically, those relating to the notion of 'flat' and 'round' characters.

2.2.1 Traits and 'semes'

Structuralist literary scholars, such as Barthes ([1970] 1975), have attempted to capture character by specifying a list of features or 'semes' that distinguish one character from another. This approach has been fairly popular in relatively recent publications (e.g. Fowler 1986: 33–38; Pfister 1988: 166–170; Toolan 1988: 99–101). The methodology is analogous to the componential analysis of meaning developed within semantics (see, for example, Leech 1981). Usually, the features considered form binary opposites like male/female, adult/child, good/bad, beautiful/ugly. This type of analysis has proved useful in highlighting the structural similarities and contrasts between characters. Fowler, for example, uses it to analyse the characters of *The Great Gatsby*:

> [. . .] Tom 'overlaps' with Jordan Baker in respect to some
> semes (athleticism, competitiveness, hardness), with Daisy in
> other respects (handsomeness, selfishness, restlessness). The

three of them share some semes with Gatsby (wealth, ostentation, selfishness) but are polarised from him by others (Gatsby's romantic idealism). Gatsby's 'extraordinary gift for hope, a romantic readiness' [. . .] sets him apart from the other major protagonists in the novel. The semes 'idealism, romanticism, purposefulness' excuse his materialism and criminality; the Buchanan set and the Wilsons, dissimilar in most other attributes, are all distinguished from Gatsby by a pointed lack of any seme of spirituality like the idealism which Nick attributes to Gatsby; they are all classified as purposeless, hopeless, spiritually dead.

(1986: 37–8)

I shall consider structural relationships of similarity and contrast between characters further in 4.4.9. However, the semic approach to characterisation in general does not form a major part of this book, because it offers too little guidance on how to identify semes or on how they might cohere, and it is too static to capture the formation of a character impression during the reading or watching of a play. Culler (1975: 237) recognised that something else was needed in the semic approach, and proposed that:

> The process of selecting and organizing semes is governed by an ideology of character, implicit models of psychological coherence which indicate what sorts of things are possible as character traits, how these traits coexist and form wholes, or at least which traits coexist without difficulty and which are necessarily opposed in ways that produce tension and ambiguity.

Unfortunately, Culler does not pursue this avenue. One of the main goals of this chapter is to consider these 'implicit models of psychological coherence' and the role they play in characterisation.

2.2.2 Actant roles

Other structuralist work on models of character has focussed in particular on developing the ideas of Propp ([1928] 1968). Propp, on the basis of his analyses of Russian folk tales, proposed that the number of character roles is limited to seven: villain, donor, helper, sought for person (and her father), dispatcher, hero and false hero. However, perhaps the most popular classification of character roles or 'actants' was that devised by Greimas (1966), whose work was partly inspired by Propp (1968) and also by the dramatic theorist Étienne Souriau (1950) (see Elam 1980 for an explanation and application of Souriau's work). Greimas (1966) suggested that there are six roles, consisting of three interrelated pairs: sender/receiver, subject/object and helper/opponent. This framework is supposed to be analogous to a functional grammar of language. Thus, for example, sender would correspond to the grammatical subject; receiver to the grammatical object, and so on. The concern here is not with the individual, but with capturing the universal actant roles or functions that underlie narratives and plays.

Such a framework seems to work for relatively simple stories. For instance, the characters of the film *Aladdin* (1992, Walt Disney Productions) fall neatly into Greimas's roles. Aladdin (the subject) falls in love with and wishes to marry the princess (the object). In spite of the help of his pet monkey (helper), he is unable to compete with the wicked rival (opponent) for the princess. However, with the magical support of the genie of the lamp (sender or giver), he is able to defeat his rival and win the princess (thus becoming the receiver).[1] For more sophisticated stories, however, Greimas's model is inadequate, or even reductive:

> The *actantiel* model minimizes not only idiosyncracy but also complexity of character, that is the indeterminacy arising from a multiplicity of traits in a behaviour.
>
> (Chatman 1972: 64)

Furthermore, Greimas offers little advice about how to apply the roles, and this leads to significant difficulties in the analysis of complex stories (see Culler 1975: 234, for a demonstration of this point).

The failure of such frameworks to deal with anything other than simplistic characterisation is not surprising, given the fact that they are largely developed from classical, traditional or oral stories, which tend to rely more on the development of plot than of character.[2] Also, to be fair, one must acknowledge that these frameworks are trying to capture generalisations. A satisfying theory of characterisation would need to do this, as well as capture more specific detail.

2.2.3 Dramatic roles

Like the structuralists working on actant roles, Northrop Frye (1957: 171–2) emphasises the primacy of function in characterisation:

In drama, characterisation depends on function; what a character is follows from what he has to do in the play. Dramatic function in its turn depends on the structure of the play; the character has certain things to do because the play has such and such a shape. The structure of the play in its turn depends on the category of the play; if it is a comedy, its structure will require a comic resolution and a prevailing comic mood.

Frye has a more sophisticated scheme than other structuralists, and one which makes a link between character role and genre. Table 2.1 attempts to capture Frye's scheme for comedy. The first column presents the four general role types proposed by Frye (the classical Greek terms from whence these categories are drawn are given in brackets); the second column gives some of Frye's examples of stock figures within these types; and the third column gives examples of the stock figures (some are from Frye, others I have supplied).

Frye (1957: 172) argues that the four general character types form pairs with different functions: 'The contest of *eiron* [self-deprecator] and

Table 2.1   Character roles and comedy

General type	Stock figures	Examples of stock figures
Impostors (*alazons*)	Heavy father (*senex iratus*)	Squire Western in *Tom Jones*
	Miles gloriosus	The dictator in Charlie Chaplin's *Great Dictator*
	Shrew	Katherina in *The Taming of the Shrew*
Self-deprecators (*eirons*)	Hero	Julia in *The Two Gentlemen of Verona*; Columbo of the American TV detective series[3]
	Tricky slave (*dolosus servus*)	Puck in *A Midsummer Night's Dream*; Jeeves in *Jeeves and Wooster*
Buffoons (*bomolochi*)	Parasite	Mosca in *Volpone*
	Entertainer	Mistress Quickly in Shakespeare's *Merry Wives of Windsor*
Churls (*agroikos*)	Killjoy	Malvolio in *Twelfth Night*
	Plain dealer	Sybil in the BBC TV series *Fawlty Towers*

alazon [impostor] forms the basis of the comic action, and the buffoon and the churl polarize the comic mood'.

Frye's scheme, though not without problems, is rather more sensitive than those for actant roles. Also, as my choice of examples demonstrates, Frye's stock figures seem to have endured for many centuries. Importantly, Frye is not proposing a scheme that contains roles which fit characters exactly, but roles which, as Culler (1975) puts it, 'guide the perception and creation of characters' (1975: 236). This is in tune with the aims of this book. Clearly, the scheme for the perception of characters to be proposed in this chapter needs to be able to accommodate the kind of phenomena discussed by Frye. I will return to this particular issue in 2.5.1.

2.2.4 Character typologies: The 'flat'/'round' distinction

In this section, I shall first focus on the flat/round distinction itself, and then look briefly at how subsequent typologies have taken account of it.

2.2.4.1 Forster's flat/round distinction

Forster's discussion of flat and round characters has been influential since its first appearance in 1927. He defines flat characters as 'humours', 'types', or 'caricatures'. 'In their purest form, they are constructed round a single idea or quality; when there is more than one factor in them, we get the beginning of the curve towards the round' (1987: 73). Round characters are defined by implication: those who are not flat are round. According to Forster:

> The test of a round character is whether it is capable of surprising in a convincing way. If it never surprises, it is flat. If it does not convince, it is flat pretending to be round.
>
> (1987: 81)

These definitions are notoriously problematic (partly because Forster's work took the form of a series of lectures about the novel and thus was not as tightly written as it could have been). An important issue is whether Forster's categories are discrete. Firstly, he defines round characters by implication: those that are not flat are round. Then he suggests that we can have 'a curve towards the round' (1987: 73). This seems contradictory. If the categories are discrete, then we have a weak analytical framework since we would end up with a vast collection of round characters and a relatively small group of truly 'one factor' flat characters. If they are not discrete, flat characters may be identified at one end of the scale, but how are we to determine the degree of roundness thereafter? Is it the multiplication of facets? Forster does not say. He offers a test for roundness that is vague and impressionistic. What is it to be 'surprised in a convincing way'? A further problem lies in the fact that in his discussion Forster vacillates between the textual construction of character ('they are *constructed* round a single idea or quality', my emphasis) and the reader's perception of character (being surprised), or leaves it unclear which he intends.

Forster focusses on an important and intuitively attractive distinction, which, as we shall see, is preserved in other character typologies. Where his work fails it is in not offering clear theoretical guidelines to enable one to make that distinction. One of the aims of this chapter is to offer a less confused description of that distinction.

2.2.4.2 The flat and round distinction in post-Forster typologies

Harvey's book-length study of novelistic characters, *Character and the Novel* (1965), appeared some 40 years after Forster's work, but preserves Forster's basic distinction. Harvey's 'protagonist' and 'background' types correspond roughly to flat and round characters. He suggests three factors that define protagonists (although it is not clear whether these factors are intended to be necessary and sufficient). Firstly, protagonists are 'those characters whose motivation and history are most fully established' (1965: 56). This factor seems particularly flawed, since it seems to rule out major characters, such as Hamlet, because of their enigmatic nature. Secondly, protagonists 'conflict and change as the story progresses' (1965: 56). Harvey, however, neglects to say at what level this change and conflict takes place, or whether it is internal or external to the character. Thirdly, protagonists 'engage our responses more fully and steadily, in a way more complex though not necessarily more vivid than other characters' (1965: 56). How our responses are engaged and what this complexity consists of remain unanswered questions. Background characters are defined in terms of their function within the text, be it their relation to the plot or to other characters:

> Singly they may be merely useful cogs in the mechanism of the plot, collectively they may establish themselves as a chorus to the main action — one thinks, for example, of

> Hardy's rustics — or may exist simply to establish the density
> of society in which the protagonists move if they are to have
> any depth of realization.
>
> (1965: 56)

Harvey labels his two other types of character 'ficelle' and 'card'. The ficelle seems to have the roundness of a protagonist, it is 'more fully delineated and individuated than any background character' (1965: 58), but exists like background characters for functional reasons within the text. Harvey's examples include Banquo embodying what Macbeth might have been, and Gloucester standing as a kind of analogue to Lear's experience. The card is a 'character who is a "character"', 'such a person is "larger than life" or is distinguished by some fiction-like idiosyncrasy' (1965: 58). This character type appears to be in some sense a distortion of 'real life'. Such characters, Harvey says, are relatively changeless, unaffected by external conflict and unaware of internal conflict. A card would seem to suggest a fairly flat character type, rather like one of Jonson's 'humour' characters. This should not be confused with saying that cards are a type of background character. Harvey allows for the possibility that cards can be the main characters within a work, suggesting Don Quixote as an example.

Harvey fails to spell out the implications of each of his criteria for each character type. Rather like Forster, he flits from aspects of reader perception to aspects of the text. Broadly speaking, the protagonist and the card seem to be defined in psychological terms, the ficelle in a combination of psychological and textual terms, and the background character in textual terms. The strength of Harvey's work, however, is in offering insights into the dimensions various character types may be associated with. This is also the focus of Hochman's book *Character in Literature* (1985), one of the more significant attempts to get to grips with characterisation since Harvey's work. Hochman's classification is much more elaborate than the preceding typologies, involving eight categories and their opposites:

Stylization	——	Naturalism
Coherence	——	Incoherence
Wholeness	——	Fragmentariness
Literalness	——	Symbolism
Complexity	——	Simplicity

Transparency	——	Opacity
Dynamism	——	Staticism
Closure	——	Openness

Hochman spends some fifty pages fleshing out these categories. For reasons of space, I shall not provide detailed comment on them here. In any case, there is a certain amount of overlap with the typologies outlined so far. We have met complexity/simplicity and dynamism/staticism (i.e. change) in connection with flat and round characters. The stylization as opposed to naturalism category seems to capture Harvey's cards. Hochman's symbolism category can be applied to characters that perform a thematic function within the text. They 'can be spoken of as . . . signifying something else' (1985: 118). This is a dimension that may exist within Harvey's textually oriented background and ficelle characters.

The wholeness/fragmentariness categories relate to one's overall impression. According to Hochman 'we *feel* that we have been given a whole' (1985: 104), we have a '*sense* of the wholeness of a person' (1985: 105), 'central figures . . . *impress* us as possessing wholes' (1985: 105) [my italics in all quotations]. Clearly, there must be some psychological factors underlying these categories, though Hochman does not say what they are. A character's coherence is not an aspect that has been raised in the other typologies. For Hochman, incoherence relates to uncharacteristic behaviour. His examples include Gertrude's uncharacteristically lyrical account of Ophelia's drowning and Polonius's uncharacteristically wise advice to Laertes. Here again, there are presumably psychological factors involved in deciding what counts as characteristic or uncharacteristic. Transparency/opacity is to do with the degree to which the author allows access into a character's inner life (that is, motives and psychological states). The degree of closure/openness relates to the extent to which questions raised by the presentation of a character are left open and the extent to which the conflicts a character is subjected to are resolved.

It is worth noting that the degree to which we gain knowledge of a character's inner life has been seen as an important distinction in characterisation. For Ewen (1980),[4] it is one of the three axes upon which he bases his character classification (the others were complexity and development, aspects which have been touched on above). It should be remembered that these critics are primarily considering prose fiction. Whether this aspect is as important in drama is an issue which needs to be addressed. Certainly there are specific devices in drama, such as soliloquy, that are often used to present a character's inner life. I shall pursue this further in 4.3.2.

Fishelov (1990) makes two important general criticisms of Hochman's typology. Firstly, although it can make fine distinctions, it is unwieldy as a basic typology. Potentially, combining Hochman's categories leads to the possibility of sixty-four different types of character. Secondly, Hochman claims 'some exhaustiveness' (1985: 89) in his typology, but why stop with just the categories he has? Why not add interesting/dull, or any other categories? Nevertheless, Hochman's typology is impressive in its scope, and touches on aspects of character that have not been mentioned in the other typologies. To be fair to Hochman one should draw attention (Fishelov does not) to the fact that although he often refers to his categories as categories, he intended each of his categories, with its opposite, to represent 'the extreme end of a scale on which we can place characters in literature' (1985: 89). Viewed as dimensions along which characters may vary, they form a more sensitive analytical framework. However, an important problem remains: Hochman offers no real criteria by which to work out which dimensions are relevant to a particular character or where that character lies on that dimension.

2.2.4.3 Assessment

A fundamental problem underlying the character typologies that I have examined is that they make no attempt to discriminate between psychological and textual aspects of character. Of course, in a sense it is artificial to separate these aspects. As I made clear in 1.5 and 1.6, when we read a play-text our conception of a particular character arises as a result of a complex interaction between the contents of our heads and the incoming textual information. However, in suggesting a defining feature or dimension of character, one cannot assume that what applies at a textual level necessarily applies at a psychological or cognitive level. For this reason I focus separately on the cognitive and textual aspects of character below, whilst bearing in mind that they are part of an interactive process.

A common thread through the literary-critical typologies is that they make a distinction between flat and round characters, or at least distinguish some sense of flatness and roundness in characters. I suggest that this distinction is best conceived of as a scale. This allows for more subtle gradations of character. Factors associated with roundness include complexity, change, conflict, and inner life. Flatness is associated with the opposites of these factors: simplicity, stasis, immunity from conflict, and external life (that is, we are not given direct access to a character's thoughts). In addition, flatness is often associated with characters who exist mainly to contribute to a particular aspect of the text such as the plot, or another character's characterisation. Obviously, these factors are inadequately specified. What, for example, does complexity/simplicity consist of? To understand these factors one needs first to understand how characterisation works. What are the building blocks and processes used in forming an impression of a character? What textual features contribute to the construction of a character? In the following sections I shall examine the cognitive building blocks and processes involved in forming impressions of real-life people, and then consider how this might be applied to drama.

2.3 The organisation and role of prior knowledge

Consider this story:

> A father was driving his son home when he had a crash. The father was killed and the son rushed by ambulance to hospital. At the hospital, the surgeon refused to operate, citing the rule that surgeons cannot operate on their own children.

What is odd about this story? Most people who hear or read it are flummoxed. I have been told that if the father is dead he cannot be in the hospital refusing to operate. Sophisticated solutions are often suggested: perhaps the son had two fathers, a natural father and a father through adoption. The fact that the surgeon could be the boy's mother tends to be overlooked. This is because when our knowledge about surgeons is activated we are likely to generate a strong expectation that a surgeon is male.[5] This example demonstrates the fact that our prior knowledge about particular kinds of people affects the way we interpret new information. Such knowledge, and the expectations we may generate from it, can lead us astray, but it does enable us to deal efficiently with the complexity of the world and provides us with the secure feeling of being able to predict and control what confronts us (Fiske and Taylor 1984: 139 et passim; see also Fowler 1986: 16–17).

My aim in this section is to move towards an understanding of how we remember information and experiences, and how we later use that knowledge to help us understand new experiences. Much research, especially since the 1970s, has tried to shed light on the mental organisation and content of our knowledge. Research has mainly been conducted by cognitive psychologists, although their ideas have also been used and developed in many other fields, notably artificial intelligence. In linguistics, these ideas have been used in a number of areas, but particularly to help explain semantic categories (see for example Labov 1973; Lakoff 1977; Coleman and Kay 1981). The bulk of the early research concentrates on nonhuman phenomena, such as colours or animals. I shall consider research that focusses on people separately in section 2.4, which covers 'social cognition'. Here, I shall first outline some ideas about the organisation of memory, and then the organisation of knowledge in memory.

2.3.1 Memory stores

Much discussion of cognition treats the brain as some kind of information processor, and thus it is not surprising that many terms from computing have been employed for cognition (such as 'input', 'processor', 'network'), just as some terms for aspects of cognition have made their way into computing (such as 'memory'). The analogy works — to an extent — for different kinds of memory. Computers can write information to the hard disk for long-term storage, but they also have RAM (Random Access Memory), which has much reduced capacity and thus only stores information that is needed for the task in hand. The hard disk might also be said to be a passive mode of storage, since it does not need electricity to maintain it, whereas RAM can only hold information when it is made active by electricity. Similarly, in models of cognition, there are said to be different types of memory store for information: 'long-term memory', as opposed to 'short-term memory' with its limited capacity (about seven random items or one or two simple sentences). Long-term memory is relatively passive and permanent, whereas short-term memory is relatively active with currently needed memories. In fact, the active role of short-term memory has been stressed by some researchers who have argued that short-term memory is better conceived of as 'working memory' (see, for example, Baddeley 1986). Short-term working memory provides a working space for the interaction between new information received from the environment (the text, in our case) and old information retrieved from long-term memory. Putting this in less technical terms, short-term working memory might be thought of as what is in our mind's eye: it is what we are conscious of at a particular moment in time, and what we are conscious of constantly changes as our attention shifts from one thing to another.

The fact that so much work in cognition is part of the 'information processing paradigm' has its limitations. Some people have pointed out that the notion of memory stores may not accurately reflect the organisation of memory; information may be stored as networks of connections. In the model referred to as connectionism or parallel distributed processing (see for instance McClelland *et al.* 1986), information is not held in stores but distributed throughout the brain. Other people have pointed out that the information processing paradigm ignores the social nature of thinking, and instead treats people as individuals operating in the abstract. I will return briefly to the latter criticism when I consider the nature of social cognition in section 2.4.1.

2.3.2 Semantic memory and episodic memory

With regard to long-term memory, many researchers have found it useful to adopt Tulving's (1972) distinction between 'episodic memory' and 'semantic memory'. An important point to note is that this distinction is not a matter of different memory stores but of different knowledge types. The general idea is that information which has been analysed and interpreted in short-term working memory is provisionally held as an 'episode' in episodic memory. An episode is a personal experience, associated with a particular time and place. For example, my reading of van Dijk and Kintsch (1983) was a personal experience, as was my experience of being in a car crash. Semantic memory, on the other hand, contains more general, abstract knowledge. My knowledge about the *language* used in van Dijk and Kintsch (1983) — the meanings of words, grammatical rules, discourse types, and so on — or my knowledge about driving to work (an activity that happens most mornings) is stored in semantic memory. Episodic memory is assumed to feed semantic memory: an accumulation of related experiences leads to generalisation and abstraction. The upshot of all this is that current or recent experiences (such as my current attempt at writing this section) are stored as episodes in memory; some experiences may remain as personal episodes in memory (for example my memory of my car crash); whilst others blur into semantic memory (for instance I cannot remember the individual episodes that I originally experienced each time I drove to work). Note that in Figure 1.1 the situation model is created as an episode.

The distinction between episodic and semantic memory is a useful way of capturing different types of knowledge in memory. This is not to say that it is an unproblematic distinction. The cut-off point between episodic and semantic memory is not clear — it is probably a continuum — and it is also not clear how exactly episodic memory feeds semantic.

In the rest of this chapter I will focus on the knowledge of semantic memory, because it is this knowledge which has been the particular focus of interest for researchers investigating how prior knowledge helps us to retrieve textual cues and make inferences.[6] It is also this knowledge which authors can assume — at least to some extent — to be shared amongst their readership. Indeed, it is the shared nature of semantic memory that led van Dijk (1987, 1990 for example) to suggest that it be called 'social memory' (see section 2.4.2).

2.3.3 Knowledge structures

In this section I shall consider the organisation of knowledge in long-term semantic memory. Understanding how knowledge is organised will help us understand how it is used in text comprehension. A problem to be tackled immediately is the use in different studies of a bewildering array of interrelated theoretical terms for the cognitive building blocks or knowledge structures of long-term semantic memory. These include 'prototype', 'stereotype', 'schema', 'frame', 'script', 'scenario', 'model', 'memory organisation packet' and 'semantic network'. However, it is safe to say that schema (plural = schemata) tends to be used as a blanket term, whilst some of the other terms tend to be used to refer to particular types of schemata. Scripts (Schank and Abelson 1977), for example, contain knowledge about frequently encountered sequences of actions (for example a restaurant script, a birthday party script).

There is considerable overlap between the two theories I will introduce in this section, namely, prototype theory and schema theory. However, I would argue that there are important differences in emphasis which justify the separate treatment of these theories. Firstly, prototype theory tends to consider single categories or simple hierarchies of categories, whilst schema theory tends to consider clusters of categories organised in complex structures. Secondly, prototype theory tends to deal with the processes involved in applying category or concept labels to the phenomena we encounter (matters of categorisation), whilst schema theory tends to deal with the effects the application of a category or concept label has on processes of perception, memory, and inference.

2.3.3.1 Prototype theory

Categorisation is a pervasive activity. Rosch *et al.* claim that it is 'one of the most basic functions of all organisms' (1976: 382). It is not confined to the concrete, but includes abstract phenomena such as emotions and meanings. Usually categorisation is fairly automatic and trouble-free — I have no problem in telling you that I am sitting on a chair and that a table is in front of me — but sometimes it is more problematic. I feel more awkward about telling you that I am using a 'computer' in creating this text. I am using a portable 'computer' with very limited capabilities. It can only cope with basic word processing, and has been referred to by uncharitable friends as a 'glorified typewriter'. So, the crux of the problem is, am I using an unsophisticated computer or sophisticated typewriter? This problem raises an issue which is central to the study of categorisation: how does one decide whether a particular example fits a particular category? And here lies the specific relevance to characterisation: how do we know that a character belongs to a particular category? For example, the issue of how certain characters fit the category of 'king' is an important part of a number of Shakespeare's plays, including *King Lear*, *Macbeth*, *Richard II* and *Henry IV*. As a corollary to tackling this categorisation issue, one needs to consider what categories consist of and how they are formed.

Prototype theories were developed with the aim of remedying some of the deficiencies of the classical view of categories. The classical view suggests that categories can be defined in terms of a set of necessary and sufficient features (see, for example, Frege 1952; Collins and Quillian 1969). However, it has been criticised, not least because it has difficulty accommodating borderline cases of categories, such as my 'computer' (see Eysenck and Keane 1990: 251–63 for a useful description and critique of the classical view of categorisation). Within prototype theory, Rosch's work on object categories has been particularly influential (Rosch 1973, 1975, 1977, 1978; Rosch and Mervis 1975; Rosch *et al.* 1976). I do not have space to consider each prototype theory in detail. Instead, I shall list the main principles that underpin most prototype theories.

Prototypes and categories
A category consists of a typical or ideal exemplar called a prototype and a range of peripheral or less good examples. For instance, in British culture a robin is a more prototypical example of a bird than an ostrich. People derive the prototype through their experience. An unresolved debate has developed about whether prototype categories exist in the mind as some kind of generalised average abstracted from available examples (birds typically have wings, feathers, can fly, etc.), or as collections of individual examples, or a combination of both (see Smyth *et al.* 1994: 72–88 for a discussion).

Category membership

The degree to which a newly experienced example is considered to be a member of a category depends on the similarity or goodness of fit between its features and those of the category's prototype or central member. Similarity is assessed according to *family resemblance*, a notion adopted from Wittgenstein (1958). There is no fixed set of necessary and sufficient features defining a category, but rather any of a number of features may be involved in a judgement as to whether an example resembles the category prototype. For example, an observer assessing the category of my family on the basis of appearance may have noted that I have the same broad nose and large head as my mother and sister, the same eyes as my father, and that my sister has the same physique and eyes as my mother, and so on. Category members can be ranged on a continuum of prototypicality according to their similarity to the prototype.

Category fuzziness

Given the prototype structure of a category, it follows that there are no fixed, well-defined boundaries between categories. The distinctiveness of categories is achieved by 'conceiving of each category in terms of its *clear cases* rather than its boundaries' (Rosch 1978: 36). Category members can slide into other categories (as is the case with my 'computer/ typewriter').

Category hierarchies

Categories are organised hierarchically according to inclusiveness. For example, a chair can be included within the category 'furniture' and therefore it is subordinate to it. Rosch and her colleagues (1976) argue that hierarchies have three levels which are useful for different purposes. There is a superordinate level (such as furniture), a basic level (table, chair), and a subordinate level (coffee table, kitchen table, rocking chair, armchair). The optimal level for cognitive activity is viewed as the basic level, since it is here that categories are both rich in attributes and well differentiated from one another.

The prototype view is clearly an improvement on the classical view of categories. My computer example can be better accounted for. My 'computer' is low in typicality, far from the prototype, and in the fuzzy area of the computer category. The female surgeon of the story at the beginning of 2.3 is a less prototypical instance of the 'surgeon' category compared with a male surgeon. Hal in Shakespeare's *Henry IV Part I* and the greater part of *Henry IV Part II* is far from a prototypical 'heir apparent'. There are, however, problems with the prototype view (see

Eysenck and Keane 1990: 269–70 for a critique). Lakoff titled his book (1987), *Women, Fire, and Dangerous Things*, after the contents of a category he found in one culture. It is difficult to argue that similarity is the cohesive mechanism underlying the category here. Clearly more research needs to be done on category cohesion. Another aspect of categorisation that needs more attention in prototype research is the effect of function and context. Labov (1973) has pointed out that a container is more likely to be called a cup when subjects had coffee drinking in mind as opposed to flower arranging. If my 'computer' was seen in a shop amidst a range of typewriters, it is much more likely to be seen as a 'glorified typewriter', a non-prototypical typewriter (in fact, I bought it from a computer shop, and thus I consider it a computer). Barsalou's work has highlighted the role of context (for example 1982, 1989). Barsalou argues that categories are unstable. Different subsets of knowledge within a category are activated in different situations. For example, if you read the word 'football' in isolation, the feature 'floats' is likely to remain inactive in memory. If you read 'football' in a context such as 'Tom used a football as a life preserver when the boat sank', 'floats' is likely to be active. The categorisation of people and characters, as we shall see in later sections, is particularly sensitive to context and function. Of course, one cannot assume that the context is a stable given. It, too, has to be interpreted. Schema theory has more to say about the interpretation of context than prototype theory.

2.3.3.2 Schema theory

Bartlett [1932] (1995) is often acknowledged as a founder of modern schema theory, but, as with prototype theory, it was not until the mid-1970s that research took off (for example Minsky 1975; Neisser 1976; Rumelhart and Ortony 1977; Schank and Abelson 1977; Thorndyke 1977; Rumelhart and Norman 1981; Rumelhart 1984). Again, for reasons of space, rather than review this literature I shall outline the general principles behind schema theory and its role in cognition. (For good reviews of schema theory see Thorndyke and Yekovich 1980; Brewer and Nakamura 1984; Eysenck and Keane 1990: 275–86).

The nature of schemata
'A *schema* is a structured cluster of concepts; usually, it involves generic knowledge and may be used to represent events, sequences of events, precepts, situations, relations, and even objects' (Eysenck and Keane 1990: 275). Schemata are higher-order cognitive structures, and consist

of particular configurations of variables or slots that may accept a range of concepts or sub-schemata. The concepts that fill or instantiate slots are called values. Our knowledge about the typical values of slots constrains what may instantiate a slot. Slots can be left unfilled or have an assumed or default value. The classic example in the literature is the schema for a restaurant. A restaurant schema contains role slots (for instance waiters, customers), slots for props (tables, the menu), and slots for actions (entering, ordering, eating). Note that a schema such as this provides a contextual framework for people. A person's restaurant experience may lead to a restaurant schema being instantiated (that is, a certain configuration of slots being filled by a certain configuration of values). The particular values of that instantiation relate to the particular situation (the particular waiters and customers at the restaurant). Only certain concepts would instantiate slots. Somebody frisking customers at the door would not instantiate the waiter slot. Default values might include such things as the main chef being of the same nationality as the cuisine.

Schema formation

Broadly speaking, schemata are assumed to be abstracted or induced from experience, the episodes of episodic memory. For example, my supermarket schema is presumably acquired through noting the similarities between the various supermarkets I have experienced — they tend to have baskets, trolleys, an entrance, an exit, goods displayed in aisles, a row of tills; you select your goods, then you pay, what you pay corresponds to the total value of the goods, and so on. Rumelhart and Norman (1981) and Rumelhart (1984) have attempted to specify what the processes of schema formation are. They suggest three processes. 'Accretion' occurs when our schemata are assumed to be adequate for the interpretation of an experience. A new instantiation of an existing schema is recorded. 'Tuning' occurs when the concepts in a schema undergo elaboration and refinement to make them more in tune with experience. 'Restructuring' involves the creation of new schemata either by analogy (copying an old schema with a few modifications) or induction (the general process mentioned earlier).

Schemata and information processing

Our schematic knowledge shapes how we view, remember, and make inferences about new information. In other words, schemata may form the basis of top-down or conceptually-driven cognitive processes. Neisser (1976: 22) argues that 'schemata are anticipations, they are the medium by which the past affects the future'. Rumelhart suggests (1984: 170) that in a sense 'conceptually-driven processing is *expectation-driven* processing'. The idea that schemata give rise to expectations that guide our processing is fundamental, but a cautionary note is needed. Schemata are not synonymous with expectations: only schemata that are currently active form expectations. Such expectations help us interpret and predict the complexities of the world. Schema theory researchers have made the point that what you see is in part determined by what you *expect* to see (Neisser 1976: 20–1; Rumelhart 1984: 179–80). Schema-based expectations guide perception, memory and inference toward schema-relevant information, and often toward schema-consistent information (see, for example, Taylor *et al.* 1978). Disconfirming or incongruent information requires more effort to process than congruent information; if that effort is made, that information may be well remembered (Fiske and Taylor 1984: 165).

Schemata and text comprehension
Schemata guide our comprehension. They offer a guiding theme, a scaffolding for input data. Read this passage:

> The procedure is actually quite simple. First, you arrange things into different groups. Of course, one pile may be sufficient depending on how much there is to do. If you have to go somewhere else due to lack of facilities that is the next step; otherwise, you are pretty well set. It is important not to overdo things. That is, it is better to do too few things at once than too many. In the short run this may not seem important but complications can easily arise. A mistake can be expensive as well. At first, the whole procedure will seem complicated. Soon, however, it will become just another facet of life [. . .]

(Bransford and Johnson 1972: 722)

This passage is difficult to comprehend and difficult to remember. Comprehension involves finding a configuration of schemata that offers an adequate account of the textual information in the passage. This passage lacks sufficient cues as to what schemata are relevant. Bransford and Johnson discovered that when the passage had the title *Washing Clothes* subjects could use their washing clothes schema to make sense of the passage, and were better able to remember it. This is also a convenient moment to briefly illustrate the van Dijk and Kintsch (1983) text comprehension scheme outlined in section 1.5.2. The point is that if you lack the relevant prior knowledge schema, you will not get much beyond the surface representation and the propositional textbase representation. The lack of a cohesive structure for these representations makes them difficult to hold in memory. The washing clothes schema not only allows us to organise the propositions (that is, to create a macrotextbase), but crucially it allows us to infer what the text is about, that is, to create a situation model — how to wash clothes.

Schemata and text inferencing

Schemata enable us to construct an interpretation, a representation or situation model in memory, that contains more than the information we receive from the text. We can supply, or infer, extra bits of information from our schematic knowledge. In fact, empirical evidence has shown that comprehenders have difficulty in distinguishing what might have been supplied by schematic knowledge and what might have been explicitly stated in the text (see, for instance, Graesser *et al.* 1997). One way in which schematic knowledge enables additional inferencing is by supplying default values for schematic slots. For example, most people when they heard my car crash story inferred that the surgeon was male. The default value for the surgeon gender slot is male. In fact, comprehension typically requires much inferential work, generating information not explicitly available in the text or speech and thereby generating a coherent interpretation. Let us briefly note some of the likely inferences in the first two sentences of the surgeon story.

> A father was driving his son home when he had a crash. The father was killed and the son rushed by ambulance to hospital.

In the first sentence there is no mention of a car. However, I am sure that the majority of readers would have inferred via schematic knowledge that he was driving a car, rather than, say, a horse and carriage, and that it was the car that crashed. Driving a vehicle yourself is an activity associated with cars (carriages are usually driven by professional carriage drivers), and crashes — unfortunately — are strongly associated with cars. The second sentence is grammatically ambiguous because of the ellipsis of the auxiliary '[was] rushed', resulting in two possible interpretations: either 1) the father was killed and the son (we assume) was seriously injured, resulting in an ambulance being called and then the ambulance taking the son to hospital, or 2) the father was killed and then the son rushed by ambulance to the hospital. The first interpretation fits better our schematic knowledge about accidents and ambulances, even though, on the face of it, it relies on a much bigger raft of schematic assumptions being made or default values being filled in (for example, if the father was killed, it is likely that the son was injured; ambulances have to be called to the scene of an accident, they don't appear out of nowhere; ambulances are driven by approved personnel, you can't just get into an ambulance and drive it).[7] Note here that:

> [. . .] the bulk of processing in a schema-based system is directed towards finding those schemata which best account for the totality of the incoming information. On having found a set of schemata which appears to give a sufficient account of the information, the person is said to have 'comprehended' the situation.
>
> (Rumelhart and Ortony 1977: 111–12)

Schema activation

Schemata may be thought of as being in an inactive state in the mind until they are cued and thus made active (instantiated as part of the interpretative process). What determines which schemata get activated? Generally, one might suppose that only relevant schemata are activated, in other words, those that fit the incoming information. But these can be many. What is to stop virtually every word in a text activating a schema? Schema theory does not address this issue. A plausible solution is suggested by Semino:

> It is often pointed out that schema theory tends to be rather vague as to the mechanisms and conditions that lead to schema activation (e.g. Thorndyke and Yekovich 1980). In this respect, Relevance theory (Sperber and Wilson 1986, 1995) offers a useful contribution. Sperber and Wilson claim that in comprehension we always aim to balance the effort involved in searching and activating background knowledge with the resulting cognitive effects. In schema-theory terms, this is equivalent to saying that we activate a schema when its contribution to interpretation counter-balances the effort expended in activating it.
>
> (Semino 1997: 170)[8]

Precisely which category is activated when you perceive someone depends on a number of factors. Researchers in social cognition (such as Fiske and Taylor 1991: 145–6; Zebrowitz 1990: 50) have argued that schemata which have been recently activated and/or frequently activated are more accessible, and thus more likely to spring to mind. Fiske and Taylor (1984: 176) also suggest that observational purpose (for example whether someone is empathising, trying to predict behaviour, trying to recreate someone's perspective) and the situational context may influence which schemata are activated (for instance seeing somebody on a running track is much more likely to activate an athlete category than seeing that person at a desk). (All the factors mentioned in this paragraph are also discussed in Fiske and Neuberg (1990: 9–12), where one can find numerous supporting references.) Within text comprehension, it is emphasised that the activation of prior knowledge is strategic, addressing the reader's goals (see van Dijk and Kintsch 1983: 13; Graesser *et al.* 1994: 377–8). This, of course, ties in with Fiske and Taylor's (1984: 176) suggestion that observational purpose is a factor.

Schemata and the individual
It is worth noting here that differences in comprehension, or indeed remembering, may be due to differences in the schemata held by individuals. This is not to say that people — particularly those sharing a similar culture — will not have significant similarities between their schemata (Emmott 1997: 71; see also section 2.4.2 below), but inevitably people have different experiences which may lead (in conditions where, for example, the different experiences are repeated) to the formation of different schemata. This is most obvious when one considers people from different cultures. Bartlett's [1932] (1995) own experiment on the North American Indian folk tale *The War of the Ghosts* revealed that British informants tended to reconstruct the story in terms of their own cultural schemata. For example, canoes, which were presumably rather less familiar to Bartlett's informants of the early twentieth century, became boats (Bartlett 1995: 128). Work within cross-cultural pragmatics (such as Scollon and Scollon 1995), addresses the fact that communicative misunderstanding or breakdown may occur because people lack the relevant schemata. Cross-cultural differences in schemata are especially important to keep in mind when one examines historical literary texts, such as Shakespeare.

Linguistic triggers for schemata
This is a fairly unexplored area in schema theory research. The most detailed comments are probably those made in Schank and Abelson (1977), where the authors (p. 48) coined the term 'headers' to refer to textual items which activate scripts (their term for a particular type of schema). They proposed four categories of headers, which vary as to

how closely associated they are with a particular script and thus how likely they are to activate it (1977: 48–50). These are listed below in order of increasing strength (the examples, the first two of which are drawn from Schank and Abelson (1977: 49–50), refer to the script or schema for a restaurant).

- Precondition headers: the text contains a reference to a precondition for the application of the script, for example *John was hungry*.
- Instrumental headers: the text contains a reference to actions that can be interpreted as the means towards the realisation of a script, such as *John took the subway to the restaurant*.
- Locale headers: the text contains a reference to the setting associated with a particular script, such as *John took the table near the door of the Chinese restaurant*.
- Internal conceptualisation headers: the text contains a reference to any conceptualisation or role from the script, for example *John signalled to the waiter*.

Schank and Abelson suggest that at least two headers are needed in a text before 'to be certain a script has been invoked' (1977: 50). However, there is no hard experimental evidence for this idea. Rather this suggestion reflects the needs of the artificial intelligence paradigm (in which Schank and Abelson were working) where computers need clear-cut rules. I suspect it would not only depend on the strength of the header, but also the header's context. For example, if John starts out on a trip our restaurant script could be cued, if John's previous trips had always ended in a restaurant.

2.3.3.3 Assessment

Schema theory is plausible and has currency amongst today's researchers. Rumelhart *et al.* (1986), for example, show how valuable parts of schema theory are preserved within the more recently developed cognitive model known as parallel distributed processing. Furthermore, as Thorndyke and Yekovich point out (1980: 39), schema theory is 'clearly outstanding as a descriptive theory'. However, there are serious weaknesses that one needs to be aware of. For example, whilst researchers have shown that there are particular interactions between cognition and affect (for example, people recall memories better when they are in a similar affective state to when they first had the memory), the interaction between schema theory and affect has been neglected (see Semino

1997: 149–52 for a review of the issues). But the most common criticism levelled at schema theory is that it lacks predictive power (see for
example Thorndyke and Yekovich 1980: 41–3; Eysenck and Keane
1990: 283–5). Schema theory, it is said, is so unconstrained that it can
account for virtually any *post hoc* result, and a consequence of this is that
the theory is not testable. This is particularly true for the claimed contents of particular schemata. The weak schema-theoretic analysis has a
rash of different schemata cropping up to account for different phenomena. This is a valueless enterprise. The challenge is to offer a parsimonious
account explaining how comprehension might be achieved. Regarding
testability, all is not completely bleak. 'Open questionnaires' and 'think
aloud protocols' may give one a hint of what is going on in readers'
heads. Also, testing subjects' reading times over an extract of text may
give some indication of whether the subject is experiencing schema-
consistent information or not, since schema-inconsistent information
demands more cognitive work and will thus slow the reading process
down. For example, if a character in a text initially fits a particular
schema but then acts 'out of schema' (for instance an ambulance driver
who then at the scene of an accident asks someone how to drive the
ambulance), the point of inconsistency should slow the reader down.
This then would be the source of a falsifiable hypothesis.

2.4 Social cognition

As a way of introducing social cognition, I begin this section with a
discussion of the different perspectives on social cognition in the literature. From here, I move to an examination of social categories, which
I then link to the notion of social schemata and cognitive stereotypes.
Finally, I introduce a model of impression formation, showing how prior
knowledge need not always dominate one's impression of someone.

2.4.1 Perspectives on social cognition

Condor and Antaki (1997: 343) neatly define social cognition and indicate how it has been approached:

> 'Social cognition' as an intellectual domain — the study of
> people's knowledge of the social world in which they live,
> speak and act — can lean in one of two directions. The
> tendency that has most currency among cognitively oriented

psychologists is towards studying the psychological mechanisms by which individuals mentally represent social objects — themselves and other people. On the other hand, social cognition can orient to the social *nature* of perceivers and the social world they construct. Here the concern is with how people function as members of particular cultures or groups, and with studying the way in which the social world emerges in the course of social interaction.

The first approach — the more traditional approach — is really an extension of the information processing paradigm (see section 2.3.1) to cover social phenomena (see, for example, Wyer and Srull 1984 or Fiske and Taylor 1984, 1991). The research here is typically geared towards people's cognitive biases, and, methodologically, has revolved around questionnaires and laboratory experiments. A vast amount of research has considered how people categorise others, how these categories (often referred to as schemata) contain generalised or stereotypic information, and how this information is used in social inferencing. Thus, as was the case with my surgeon example, categorising someone by gender can result in the inference of stereotypic beliefs about that person (Taylor *et al.* 1978). Within the second approach there are several identifiable research strands, but all of them seek to distance themselves from what they see as the 'individualism' of the first strand. The strand which is at the furthest remove from the first approach is that constituted by the 'discursive psychologists' (such as Potter and Wetherell 1987; Edwards and Potter 1992). As one might gather from their name, the discursive psychologists accord theoretical priority to discourse. Note that many discursive psychologists are ethnomethodologists and have furthered the constructionist approach to identity in talk, which was introduced in section 1.4.3. In discursive psychology, cognition is 'part and parcel of *action*, and *joint action* at that' (Condor and Antaki 1997: 334). Cognition and all its trappings, they argue, is not the abstract goings-on in one's head, but has its 'reality' in the way cognitive concepts are invoked and exploited in discourse. Thus, for example, category labels can become situated descriptions that can be exploited in discourse (see section 1.4.3 for an example from Sacks 1992).

I am sympathetic to the discursive psychologists' view that we should 'attend to the words used as exactly as possible to see what might be going on' (Condor and Antaki 1997: 337). After all, this is clearly a view shared by stylisticians (see 1.3.3). However, as I pointed out in section 1.4.4, meaning is not just encoded in the utterance or text, but is also constructed by the hearer as an interpreter, and the speaker as an individual with goals of their own (for a critique of discursive psychology, see Abrams and Hogg 1990b). Furthermore, the idea that cognition is in no sense individual, but exists in jointly constructed discourse, does not square very well with the particular experiences stylisticians are especially interested in. Reading a book is a rather individualistic activity. The discourse is not jointly constructed: only the author does this. The activity for the reader is to *interpret* the discourse. Thus, apart from attending to the words, the stylistician must also attend to the interpretative activities of the reader. It is the *meaning* of the text which is jointly constructed. Finally, it is worth noting that methodologies of traditional social cognition research, of which the discursive psychologists are so critical, are actually quite relevant to research in cognitive stylistics, since very many of these laboratory-based experiments involved subjects reading short passages (usually constructed) containing fictional characters. However, we must be careful not to over-estimate the validity of experiments based on textual fragments compared with the experience of reading whole texts (see Emmott 1997: Chapter 3).

2.4.2 Cognition, social dimensions and discourse

There is, in fact, a less radical strand in the non-traditionalist approach mentioned above, particularly as represented by work in continental Europe. What researchers in this strand have in common is that they assume individuals are part of a common culture. Rather than attempt to review all research in this strand, I shall focus specifically on the influential work of van Dijk (for example 1987, 1988, 1990). Van Dijk is in the fairly unique position of having contributed to the research in all three areas under discussion here, namely, cognition, social dimensions and discourse. He agrees that information about people and groups of people is processed much like other objects of cognition, but stresses that social cognition is more than this, and, in particular, that social cognition is socially embedded (1988: 130). This is not to say, however, that social dimensions stand apart from cognition or that they have a direct link with discourse. Instead, van Dijk argues, social cognitions act as a link between social dimensions and discourse (1988: 133). People not only share knowledge of social organisation, but also reproduce that knowledge in their daily interactions. Thus, in simple terms, an employee might suppose in their head that a certain power relationship pertains between them and their employer, and so will use particular forms (such as deference) in their discourse and thereby reproduce the power relationship, and, in turn, this reproduction serves to strengthen knowledge of the power relationship.

Clearly, the nature of these social cognitions is of great importance. As I briefly mentioned in section 2.3.2, van Dijk prefers to call semantic memory 'social memory', because much of the information in semantic memory is at least partially shared with other people (though note the points in section 2.3.3.2 on schematic differences).[9] This is distinct from the personal, autobiographic memories of episodic memory. A key aspect in van Dijk's discussion of social cognition is the notion of attitudes. Attitudes are considered to be 'evaluative beliefs', which may be associated with emotive aspects (such as like or dislike) (1987: 188–9). For example, one has evaluative beliefs about particular ethnic minorities, such as 'Blacks make good musicians' (a positive evaluation) or 'Blacks are lazy' (a negative evaluation). Attitudes contain 'general, context-free information', are organised in 'schematic clusters', and are located in social memory (1987: 189–93). Such attitude schemata are distinct from the personal opinions represented in episodic memory. Thus, it is possible to express an opinion which is at odds with one's attitudes. For example, one might have a belief such as 'Blacks are lazy', but for reasons of self-presentation (not to be seen as a racist) express a contrary opinion. Importantly, as I will explain in 2.4.5.1, attitude schemata provide a link to the notion of ideology.

Van Dijk suggests (1987: 192–3) that categories which organise our knowledge about people may also organise our attitudes, and these categories might include:

> [. . .] 'appearance', 'gender', 'age', 'occupation', 'role', or 'class', as well as the (inter)actions associated with these categories, which also underlie our prototypical beliefs about other people.

I shall return to categories of knowledge about people in 2.4.4. It is also worth noting that van Dijk mentions '(inter)actions associated with these categories'. The idea that particular aspects of language are associated with representations of our beliefs about other people is an important idea to which I shall return in Chapters 3 and, more particularly, 4.

2.4.3 From non-social to social categories

An issue of particular concern in social cognition is whether the cognitive structures and processes that are developed in reference to objects or things apply in the same way to people. Note here that the term 'social' is used to mean 'relating to people'.

Cantor and Mischel argue (1979: 8) that '[w]hile people certainly differ from objects as stimuli, the categorisation rules and conceptual structures used in person and object perception may not be fundamentally different'. They claim that Rosch's prototype approach (for instance 1973) to object categorisation (see 2.3.3.1) can usefully be applied to people (Cantor and Mischel 1977, 1979). Person categories can also be formed according to prototypicality, they are fuzzy, and they can be organised into a three-level hierarchy. One example is as follows: superordinate (committed person); basic (religious devotee, social activist); subordinate (Buddhist monk, nun, save the whale campaigner, antiwar protestor) (Cantor and Mischel 1979: 16). Rumelhart suggests (1984: 185) that social knowledge exists like other knowledge in the form of schemata, and that perceptions of people are determined in ways similar to our perception of objects. Brewer (1988: 4) proposes that the 'majority of the time, perception of social objects does not differ from nonsocial perception in either structure or process'. (See also the papers in Wyer and Srull 1984, and indeed many other papers dealing with social cognition.)

In spite of these claims one needs to bear in mind that there tend to be important general (but not absolute) differences between social categories and non-social categories relating to inanimate objects, such as cups and chairs. For example:[10]

- Social categories are highly variable in structure and often overlapping
- Social categories are usually made up of abstract attributes (e.g. intentions, traits) which cannot be observed, but have to be inferred
- Social categories are highly sensitive to context.

These aspects provide additional complexities for the researcher in social cognition. For instance, with reference to the final bullet-point above, Cantor and Mischel (1979: 36–42) discovered that person prototypicality judgements depended on the *interaction* between behaviours and situations. A person who exhibited the same kind of behaviour, say extroversion, consistently across situations, and particularly in situations where such behaviour is not normal (at a library, for instance), would be considered a more prototypical extrovert.

It is worth noting that research on social categories and schemata did not come about just as a side-step from research on object categories. The schema theory approach is anticipated in the research on impression formation — the way in which components relating to a person are combined to form an integrated impression (see 2.4.7). Asch's (1946) work was of particular importance. He argued that traits form a 'gestalt' which is not simply an average of the traits. He argued that the *meaning* of each trait is affected by the other traits present in that context, and that it is not easy to predict the final impression from individual traits. For example, in Asch's experiments a cold, intelligent person was seen as calculating, whereas a warm, intelligent person was seen as wise. However, much research in impression formation and social schemata has been unduly influenced by earlier trait psychologies. As Zebrowitz put it (1990: 86):

> The vast majority of research on impression formation has focused on trait perceptions. Yet we frequently form impressions of more contextual qualities, such as roles and relationships.

Thus, other categories, as we shall see in the following section, besides trait categories are used in our understanding of other people.

2.4.4 Social categories: Three main groups

In this section, my aim is to propose three broad groupings for the social categories which people use in their perception of others.

People frequently perceive others as members of social groups rather than as individuals. These groups are assumed to provide the basis for cognitive categories. Such categories are viewed as having prototype-like structures (see 2.3.3). On the basis of existing work on social cognition (such as Cantor and Mischel 1979; Fiske and Taylor 1984, 1991; van Dijk 1987, 1988; Wyer and Srull 1984), I suggest that social categories include three broad groupings, defined by the kind of information that constitutes them:

Personal categories: These include knowledge about people's preferences and interests (e.g. likes Chinese food), habits (e.g. late for appointments), traits (e.g. extrovert) and goals (e.g. to seduce somebody). These might be seen as quite idiosyncratic features, but note that they can be the basis of groups (e.g. people who are shy, people who are disorganized). Preferences, habits and traits tend to be cross-situational tendencies, whereas goals tend to be powerful predictors of a person's behaviour in a particular setting (Fiske and Taylor 1984: 150).

Social role categories: These include knowledge about people's social functions. They include kinship roles (e.g. parents, grandparents), occupational roles (e.g. doctor, shop assistant), and relational roles (e.g. friends, partners, lovers, colleagues). A particular characteristic of many roles is that they are fluid: one can rapidly move from one role to another, combine multiple roles, or even create them. Holyoak and Gordon (1984: 50) argue for the psychological primacy of role categories (i.e. knowledge of a person's social role places one in a particularly strong position to make inferences about other aspects of the person).

Group membership categories: These include knowledge about social groups: sex, race, class, age, nationality, religion, and so on. Some theorists (e.g. Brewer 1988, Fiske and Neuberg 1990) have argued that a small number of categories, notably, sex, race and age, are used relatively automatically and universally in perception, and so they have termed these categories 'primitive' categories. Certainly such categories are linked to salient appearance cues (it is difficult not to notice somebody's sex, race and age).

Of course, I am not saying that this is the only way of grouping social categories or that there are hard and fast distinctions between the groups. Some schemes (such as van Dijk 1987) would add 'appearance' as another group. It is worth noting that these groupings seem to form a three-level hierarchy of the type suggested by Rosch *et al.* (1976) (see section 2.3.3.1), consisting of group membership as superordinate level, social role as basic level, and person as subordinate level (see Brewer *et al.* 1981, Andersen *et al.* 1990, and Fiske and Taylor 1991: 143–4, for some empirical support for this hierarchy).[11] This supports the Holyoak and Gordon (1984: 50) argument for the psychological primacy of role schemata, since the base level is the optimal cognitive level, where categories are both rich in attributes and well differentiated from one another (see also Fiske and Taylor 1991: 143). Of course, anecdotal evidence would also support this. Discovering someone's occupation ('What do you do?') is a frequent and primary way of finding out about someone.

2.4.5 Social schemata

This section focusses on the important notion of social schemata, high-level cognitive structures that contain links between social categories, such as those outlined in the previous section. In section 2.4.5.1, I introduce social schemata and associate them with cognitive stereotypes;

in section 2.4.5.2, I point out that social schemata are not the only basis for social processing; social episodes may also play a role.

2.4.5.1 Social schemata and cognitive stereotypes

There is some evidence to suggest that people could just activate a particular category and no more, in conditions when they are experiencing high cognitive loads (Gilbert and Hixon 1991). But, generally, when a category is activated, so too is the network of which it is a part. It is this network that I shall describe as a social schema, a concept that I will later associate with the notion of cognitive stereotype. For example, one might categorise someone as male or female, a matter of biological sex, but one would also activate the sex-linked associations that constitute one's gender schema, a social cognitive construct, and one would use that schema to process further information.

> Gender-schematic processing in particular thus involves spontaneously sorting attributes and behaviors into masculine and feminine categories or 'equivalence classes,' regardless of their differences on a variety of dimensions unrelated to gender, for example, spontaneously placing items like 'tender' and 'nightingale' into a feminine category and items like 'assertive' and 'eagle' into a masculine category.
>
> (Bem 1983: 604)

It is particularly important to note that social schemata include links across the three category groupings outlined in 2.4.4. Thus, in the quotation from Sandra Bem above, a female gender schema might include a link to a trait such as 'tender', and a male gender schema might include a link to a trait such as 'assertive' (see also Ashmore 1981 on 'sex stereotypes'). Note that some of these links form evaluative beliefs (that is, may be considered positive or negative features). Such evaluations constitute what van Dijk (1987, 1988) refers to as 'attitude schemata' (see section 2.4.2), and provide a link to the notion of ideology. Different groups would have had different attitudes, or different attitude schemata, associated with the schema for a particular group. These attitudes would influence the way the schema was employed in the interpretation and production of social discourse, which in turn would influence the development of the schema. Here, I am making a distinction between two types of knowledge within a schema: (a) basic category knowledge about a social group (i.e. the prototypical features that constitute a social group), and (b) attitudes towards a category (i.e. evaluative beliefs — positive or negative — about a social group). For example, I may have some knowledge of — or, in other words, a schema for — the social group comprising 'white supremacists'. Part of this schema will consist of knowledge of the basic social category, including features such as white and male. It will also include my attitude towards this social category, which is oppositional: I hold negative beliefs about white supremacists (narrow-minded, bigoted, etc.). Moreover, I share this attitude with others, and it is this shared attitude which constitutes an 'anti-racist' ideology (see van Dijk (e.g. 1988, 1990), for a similar conceptualisation of ideology).

Van Dijk also suggests that these evaluative beliefs may be associated with emotive aspects, such as like and dislike (1987: 188–9). How emotive and affective aspects are dealt with in a cognitive model and whether they belong there at all is controversial (see Semino 1997: 149–52, for an overview of the issues). Ortony *et al.* (1988) associate emotions with certain cognitions, and this association is a result of the way in which a perceiver cognitively constructed the situation that gave rise to the emotion. There is some empirical evidence that emotions are represented in schema-like structures. Conway and Bekerian (1987), for example, found evidence of priming effects: people recognised a word faster if the word had an emotional association with the situation they had just read about. With regard to characterisation, my model needs to cope with emotive aspects, since sometimes authors construct characters in order to create particular emotional effects, as we shall see in 2.5.5. Thus, like Semino (1997), my discussion of schemata will also include their likely emotive associations.

Social schemata relate to research on stereotypes within social cognition. Andersen *et al.* (1990: 192) define stereotypes as 'highly organised social categories that have the properties of schemata'. Taylor *et al.* (1978: 792) argue that stereotyping has its basis in normal cognitive processes such as categorisation: it is a way of structuring and managing potentially overwhelming input data. They suggest that '[s]tereotypes can be thought of as attributes that are tagged to category labels (e.g., race, sex) and imputed to individuals as a function of their being placed in that category'. This is how I have been describing the relationship between categories and social schemata above. A stereotype is a set of beliefs which is 'stored in memory as a cognitive structure and can then influence subsequent perceptions of, and behaviors toward, that group and its members' (Hamilton and Sherman 1994: 15). It can be viewed as an abstract group schema having central tendency beliefs or attributes characterising a group 'as a whole' or 'on average' (Hamilton and Sherman 1994: 31). A newly-encountered person is categorized according to their similarity to the central beliefs (Cantor and Mischel 1979). It is worth noting that the schema-like structure of stereotypes can explain their durability. As noted in section 2.3.3.2, schemata guide perception toward schema-relevant information, and often toward schema-consistent information, since disconfirming or incongruent information requires more effort to process than congruent information — though if that effort is made, the information may be well remembered (see, for example, Taylor *et al.*, 1978; Fiske and Taylor 1984: 149; Hamilton and Sherman 1994: 33–7).[12] Clearly, if schemata bias perception toward schema-consistent information, then that factor operates as a self-perpetuating bias for the stereotype. In this book, I shall refer to stereotypes as social schemata, because this makes clear my view that stereotypes have a particular cognitive structure — they are not simply a loose collection of beliefs.[13]

2.4.5.2 Social schemata and social episodes

It does not take much reflection for one to realise that we do not perceive others wholly on the basis of some set of generalised social schemata. In all the van Dijk publications cited in this book, he stresses the importance of having both semantic and episodic memory in accounting for comprehension. I suggested in section 2.3.2 that the distinction between semantic and episodic memory is scalar. At one end of the scale, we have the social schemata of semantic memory. These contain abstract generalisations about groups of people. The central beliefs of these schemata constitute the stereotype for that group. At the other end of the scale, we have particular experiences of individuals or groups of people stored as episodes. To exemplify, before I met my Italian wife, my stereotypical knowledge of Italians was presumably largely represented as a semantic schema (containing such information as 'Italians are passionate', 'Italians eat pasta', 'Italians have dark hair') and Italians were assumed to be a rather homogeneous group. Over the last few years I have interacted with many different Italians: I have met Italians who do not seem particularly passionate, I have had dinner with Italians who have eaten many other dishes apart from pasta, and I have seen quite a number of fair-headed Italians. Whilst I almost certainly still have a generalised schema for Italians, I cannot apply it with the same confidence, since I have learnt that there is great variation. The idea of specific episodic or exemplar information about individuals or groups of people helps to explain how we cope when we only have very weak schematic knowledge: we simply use the episodic memories as a basis for categorisation (see Smith and Zarate 1990). Furthermore, a single recent or dramatic encounter, stored as an episodic memory, can have a great impact on processing. In one study, Lewicki (1985) showed how subjects judged a short-haired individual to be unfriendly, having recently encountered an unfriendly short-haired individual. It is worth noting that the role of representations or episodic memories of specific individuals in the comprehension of newly-encountered people has tended to be overlooked in popular models of impression formation, including the model I shall introduce in section 2.4.7 (see Smith 1988: 171–4).

2.4.6 Social categories and social schemata in two advertisements

Firstly, consider a short example from a newspaper, the personal advertisement below:

> LONDON MAN, 32, SMART, non smoker. Accountant but Left interests and outlook. Looking to meet attractive, optimistic woman.

> (*New Statesman* 26/8/1994, quoted in Cunico 2000: 49)

Concentrating on the advertiser's self-description (the first two sentences), the descriptors can be analysed with the social category groupings outlined in section 2.4.4. The descriptors can be coded thus:

> LONDON [group membership — area of residence] MAN [group membership — gender], 32 [group membership — age], SMART [appearance feature] non smoker [?]. Accountant [social role — occupation] but Left [group membership — political] interests and outlook.

In the first sentence, the advertiser's strategy seems to be to define himself through a series of group memberships. The status of 'non-smoker' is difficult to determine. The converse, 'smoker', is clearly a person feature, since smoking can be seen as a habit or preference. 'Non-smoker', however, does not involve a proactive choice in the way that 'smoker' does: one can be a non-smoker by doing nothing, but not a smoker. Thus, being a non-smoker is not much of a discriminating feature: it is not very informative about a person. The kind of inferencing lying behind this discussion is fully explained in Chapter 3. 'SMART' is, on the face of it, an appearance feature, but it has a very strong schematic link to a person feature: a person who is smart can be assumed to be a person who likes being smart. The second sentence is of particular interest. Here 'accountant' activates a social role, which in turn activates the schematic network of which it is a part. The problem for the advertiser is that 'accountant' is schematically linked to politically right-wing group membership, which in turn is linked to particular person interests. So the writer has to block this possible schematic inference. This he does through the formal device 'but', a conjunction that carries the conventional implicature (see Grice 1975) that an expectation generated in the preceding text does not apply.

My second example is more extensive. Consider this radio advertisement:[14]

[*Loud disco music is playing throughout. Female A sings to the music. Only her clearly audible words are transcribed.*]

Female A: there I was looking for your love couldn't get enough ooh-ooh .. yeah-eah stop

[*Two loud knocks. Voice B shouting.*]

Female B: turn that racket down .. now . do you hear me. now I said =

Female A: = right now .

Female B: what did you say . how dare you speak to me like that . honestly Mum I don't know what's got into you lately

Voice-over: Sanatogen Classic 50 Plus . with ginkgo–biloba and ginseng vitamins specially formulated for the over 50s . with iron to help maintain vitality in both mind and body . Sanatogen Classic 50 Plus . have you got it in you

(Classic FM, May 1998)

I undertook a small-scale empirical test of this advertisement on the members of the Stylistics Research Group at Lancaster University. All nine participants, having heard the taped advertisement, agreed that the two participants were female, giving the pitch of their voices as evidence (see 4.4.7, for research correlating pitch and gender). However, six of the nine listeners were initially fooled into thinking that Female A was a teenage daughter and Female B her mother, *before* the word 'Mum' is used in Female B's second utterance. They also assumed Female A to be located in a bedroom. The most frequently cited reasons for their interpretation were: (1) loud disco music is favoured by teenagers, (2) the loud knocks suggested that the participants were on either side of a door, (3) Female B uses the typical power talk of a parent (see 5.5.1, for research correlating pragmatic features and power).

Table 2.2 represents the social schematic elements that might be involved in an impression of Voice A and Voice B before the word 'Mum' is uttered.

Table 2.2   Social schematic elements in the Sanatogen advertisement

		Voice A	Voice B
Person	*Goal*	To play loud music	To reduce the music volume
	Preference	Likes disco music	Dislikes disco music
	Trait	Rebellious	Authoritarian
Social role	*Kinship*	Offspring	Parent
Group membership	*Gender*	Female	Female

None of the information displayed in Table 2.2 is explicit in the advertisement; it is derived through inferences based on knowledge of social behaviour, including knowledge of vocal stereotypes, politeness norms and behavioural preferences. Moreover, schematic knowledge enables us to infer how one bit of information coheres with another. Text comprehension involves finding a configuration of schemata that offers an adequate account of the information in the text (for example Bransford and Johnson 1972). In the advertisement, 'daughter' and 'mother' schemata, each consisting of a certain configuration of slots for person, social role and group membership features, with prototypical values, offer an adequate account of the information we receive (until we hear the owner of Voice A being addressed as 'Mum'). Where information about the value of a particular slot is lacking, we can infer the default value. This is how the advertisement works: it tricks the listener into assuming default values, 'offspring' and 'parent', for the social role slot, because explicit textual evidence is lacking. I will briefly return to this advertisement in the following section.

2.4.7 Impression formation

Table 2.2 gives no indication of how the impressions of Voice A and Voice B in the Sanatogen advertisement developed. It is to this general issue that I now turn. The idea that people simplify the complexities of the world by interpreting the specific in terms of the general has been described as the 'most fundamental idea suggested by schema research' (Fiske and Taylor 1984: 141). However, people are not totally constrained by top-down processes. There are times when the emphasis may be on bottom-up processes, which lead to a rather different kind of impression. The aim of this section is to consider the different types of impression and, in particular, the processing decisions that lie behind them.

In person perception, two basic alternatives, which may be viewed as the opposite ends of a scale, can be distinguished: (1) sometimes a category may indeed suffice, and (2) sometimes we may form an impression more on the basis of information about a particular individual than any category. Note that the existence of these two alternatives was raised in section 2.4.5.2. The first alternative involves a greater emphasis on top-down processing and results in a 'category-based' impression. For example, in the advertisement the initial impressions of Female A and Female B are almost entirely category-based. The second alternative involves a greater emphasis on bottom-up processing and results in a 'person-based' or 'attribute-based' impression: the impression is made up of the individual attributes of the target person. How these attributes and features might be inferred is dealt with in Chapter 3. Category-based and person-based impressions have very different characteristics: categorisation entails simplification and, as a consequence, a category-based impression loses much of the richness, complexity and personalisation of detail that a person-based impression has. To fully appreciate the differences between category-based and person-based impressions, one needs to consider the different kinds of processing that lie behind these impression types. However, before considering category-based and person-based processing, let us briefly note that this bipolar scale is fully compatible with the model of text comprehension introduced in 1.5 and 1.6. In this model, category-based processing means greater emphasis on the prior knowledge categories relevant to character in forming an impression of character; person-based processing means greater emphasis on the textbase in forming an impression of character.

Two important studies, Brewer (1988) and Fiske and Neuberg (1990), have attempted to incorporate category-based and person-based impressions within a processing model. There are a number of problems with Brewer's model (see particularly Fiske 1988 and Fiske and Neuberg 1990: 57–9 for critiques), and so I shall concentrate on Fiske and Neuberg (1990) here. Fiske and Neuberg (1990) propose a continuum model of impression formation, with category-based processes dominating one end of the continuum and person-based processes dominating the other. Category-based processes are posited to take priority over person-based processes. Progression towards person-based processes depends on:

1. *Motivational factors.* If the individual is 'minimally interesting or personally relevant enough' (1990: 4), attention is given to other information thereby enabling progression down the continuum. As we move down this processing continuum, more and more cognitive effort is required, and thus we need to be motivated to expend that effort.
2. *The configuration of information received.* If information is not easily categorised, then alternative processes along the continuum may be used.

Fiske and Neuberg (1990) identify four stages on the continuum from category-based to person-based:

1. Upon encountering somebody, the first stage of perception consists of an *initial categorisation*.
2. If the information fits the initial categorisation, then *confirmatory categorisation* occurs.
3. If the information does not fit the initial categorisation, but it is categorisable (by accessing, for example, a new category or sub-category), then *recategorisation* occurs (e.g. from teacher to secondary school teacher to secondary school Maths teacher).
4. If the information does not fit any particular category, then *piecemeal integration* occurs; in other words, the person's attributes are averaged or added up in order to form an impression.

Finally, it should be noted that although progression down the continuum is essentially one-way, it is possible to loop back up to the beginning of the three processes (2, 3 and 4 above), if we decide that further assessment is required.

How might all this work in relation to Female A in the above advertisement? A possible interpretative line is as follows. The loud disco music cues an initial categorisation of 'young person'. Subsequent information (for example, the inference that this event takes place in a home, that Female A is the recipient of 'power' talk, and that Female A ignores Female B's wishes or even may be rudely mimicking her in singing 'right now') is not directly relevant to this specific category, and so might lead to a recategorisation, the activation of a sub-schema such as 'rebellious teenage daughter'. Further information, the fact that Voice A is addressed as 'Mum', fails to fit the 'rebellious teenage daughter' sub-schema. At this point, we may shift towards piecemeal integration, if we are unable to find any particular schema to fit the configuration of information we now have. In this case, the individual attributes we do have (for instance female, mother, likes disco music, is rebellious) are used to form an impression. Thus, the listener abandons the category-based assumption that Voice A is the daughter, and instead constructs the person-based notion that a mother can act like and have the preferences of a much younger, carefree person. And this is the point of the advertisement: Sanatogen Classic 50 Plus is claimed to rejuvenate the older person.

With particular relevance to this book, it should be noted that Fiske and Neuberg's consideration of 'motivation' is far from comprehensive. Fiske and Neuberg (1990: 36–47) concentrate on external motivation, which they illustrate with the following example: if a perceiver whose job it is to evaluate job applicants knows that the boss is concerned with impression accuracy, then that perceiver would be motivated to adopt relatively individuating processes. This kind of motivation is largely irrelevant to normal encounters with literary texts (an exception would be revising a text for an examination). It is beyond the scope of this book to discuss the complex area of motivation. Whilst commenting that no model has fully specified this area, Sherman (1988: 161) points out that the processing mode is probably the result of a complex interaction between

(a) the perceiver's momentary and long-term personal goals,
(b) the processing goals of the perceiver,
(c) the structure, amount and content of incoming information, and
(d) current and anticipated task demands.

It is worth noting that self-involvement may play a part. Brewer (1988), in her impression formation model, made much of this as a reason why one might expend further cognitive effort. She suggests that self-involvement is when 'the perceiver feels closely related to or interdependent with the target person, or feels ego-involved in the judgement task' (1988: 9). In the Sanatogen advertisement, a listener might identify with an individual and feel sympathy for them, or, conversely, might be repelled by them. This self-involvement would result in greater attention being paid to the particular individual(s), and hence more cognitive effort being spent in forming an impression of them.

2.5 Social cognition and fictional characterisation

My overall aim in this section is to relate my discussion of social cognition to the literary approaches to character which I introduced at the beginning of this chapter. In the first section, I consider the extent to which some ideas from social cognition can help explain the building blocks and the processes involved in characterisation. In the second section, I suggest two cases where categories for real people are distorted in fictional contexts. In the third section, I revisit the flat/round character distinction and suggest how ideas from impression formation can provide an explanatory basis for it. Finally, in the fourth section, I consider how category shifts can be used for dramatic effect. Some of the arguments made in this section are supported and illustrated by an empirical study discussed in section 2.6.

2.5.1 Categories in characterisation

A problem that has beset literary scholars is what makes aspects of character, such as traits, cohere. Those working with semic analysis (see 2.2.1) could list individual traits, but there was no sense of what made groups of traits cohere, or made other traits seem inconsistent. Similarly, Hochman (1985) (see 2.2.4.2) argued that an important aspect of characterisation was the '*sense* of the wholeness of a person' (1985: 105), but does not offer a means of understanding 'wholeness'. Culler (1975: 237) took a step in the right direction by suggesting that 'implicit models of psychological coherence' were involved. I would argue that first impressions of characters are guided by the implicit models offered by social schemata. Such schemata, once activated, offer a scaffolding for incoming character information. Moreover, they allow us to make further knowledge-based inferences and thereby flesh out our impressions of character. This, incidentally, enables us to account for the complexity and indeterminacy of character, something which the actantial model of character conspicuously fails to do (see 2.2.2). I would argue that knowledge of real life people is a primary source of knowledge used in understanding characters. Moreover, I would argue that the social categories I have described for real people — personal, social role and group membership — offer a useful means of analysing characters. However, it needs to be stressed that knowledge about real-life people is not the only knowledge used in understanding characters.

Work on actant roles and stock figures (see 2.2.2 and 2.2.3) reminds us that we also need to take on board knowledge about fictional character types. Thus, we need to consider yet another group of categories, which we might label 'dramatic role'. The notion of 'dramatic role', as espoused in the work of Propp (1968), Greimas (1966) and Frye (1957), does not concern the individuality of a character, but the universal roles that underlie narratives and plays. This concern with the generic is, of course, also at the heart of schema theory. Indeed, some scholars (Mandler and Johnson 1977; Rumelhart 1975; Thorndyke 1977) have attempted to describe the global structures of stories in terms of schema theory, and state (for instance Rumelhart 1975: 235) that they are building on Propp's (1968) work. Dramatic role knowledge, however, is not isolated from the kind of information that is used in the perception of real people. For example, if a character in a Western does a series of good deeds, you might infer that that character is the 'hero', and, knowing this dramatic role, you may infer such things as 'this character is unlikely to be killed'. Moreover, because of the schematic associations between dramatic roles and other types of 'real-life' social categories, we may generate additional inferences. For example, the hero is likely to be male and not aged (group membership information), a lover (social role information), as well as good and brave (personal information). This particular example reminds us, as indeed Frye's (1957) work did, that dramatic roles are closely tied to genre. Our knowledge about different genres — comedies, tragedies, romances, Westerns, detective stories, and so on — includes a set of associated dramatic roles. Thus, recognising the genre one encounters can lead to the activation of a set of dramatic roles, which in turn may guide one's perception of the characters. This, in fact, was the point made in 1.5.2 and 1.6, where I introduced van Dijk and Kintsch's (1983) notion that the textbase (the basic propositional content of a text) can include a macropropositional textbase, a representation that establishes global coherence over longer stretches of text by, amongst other things, genre schemata.

How much do readers draw on real-life knowledge of people and how much on dramatic role knowledge in their perceptions of fictional characters? As I have already proposed in section 1.6, this probably depends on the kind of genre one is dealing with. Ultimately, the question is an empirical one. Livingstone (1998) conducted a comprehensive and convincing study of people's perceptions of TV soap characters (specifically from *Coronation Street*, *EastEnders* and *Dallas*). She revealed ways in which knowledge of structural aspects of the genre took precedence over real-life social knowledge. For example:

> Viewers are clearly aware that the characters occupy different moral stances and find the moral narratives or messages central to the programme an appropriate way of conceiving of the characters more generally [. . .] One might suggest that viewers focus on what the characters do with their positive attributes (thereby linking representation of character to that of narrative): the 'baddies' use them for exploitation and deceit; the 'goodies' use them for righting wrongs and helping others. A focus on morality implies judgement of the characters' actions and also an appreciation of the narrative implications of assigning characters to a moral category.
>
> (Livingstone 1998: 142–3)

2.5.2 Prototypicality distortions in fictional contexts

A literary character type not yet accounted for is Harvey's (1965) notion of a card, the character who is ' "larger than life" or is distinguished by some fiction-like idiosyncrasy' (1966: 58). I would argue that cards are perceived as such because they are an exaggerated prototype of some social category. Note that I am not saying that they are simply the prototype of a social category. A prototypical instance of a social category would be someone who was in some sense average or normal, and this is clearly not what is meant by the card. The point is that the character is prototypical in some exaggerated way. Just as a visual caricature of a person exaggerates parts of their appearance (Prince Charles's ears, Mrs Thatcher's handbag), so a writer can exaggerate particular characteristics of a character. How is a high degree of exaggeration achieved? As I noted in section 2.4.3, person prototypicality judgements depend on the *interaction* between behaviours and situations (Cantor and Mischel 1979: 36–42). Characters are perceived as exaggerated prototypes, if (1) they fail to exhibit contextually sensitive behaviour, and/or (2) they simply appear in situations where they are not expected. For example, Bottom in *A Midsummer Night's Dream* and Sly in *The Taming of the Shrew* consistently exhibit the prototypical characteristics of simple country folk, and do so even when positioned as a Queen's lover or a lord. Note that some allegorical characters can be seen as cards. The Seven Deadly Sins, for example, are an exaggerated prototype of their respective personality trait. Such prototypicality distortions are, of course, more typical of fictional worlds than the real world. In fictional worlds, these prototypicality distortions can become established as fictional stock figures in their own right (see the examples given in Table 2.1).

Comedy is rich in prototypicality distortions. Let us consider an extract from Alan Ayckbourn's comedy play *Ernie's Incredible Illucinations* ([1969] 1998: 8–12). Ayckbourn targeted this play largely at children. It turned out to be extremely successful, being produced, Ayckbourn suggests, more than any of his other plays. Prior to this extract, Ernie has been taken to the doctor by his mother and father, because he is suffering from 'illucinations'. Ernie's parents derive this word from 'illusions' and 'hallucinations'; according to Ernie's mother, they are 'more than illusions'. It turns out that Ernie's daydreams have an effect on the current reality. To demonstrate this to the doctor, Ernie describes what happened 'one wet Saturday afternoon', and those events begin to happen in the doctor's surgery. In the first and last turns below, Ernie narrates the story. The 'exciting discussion' referred to in the first turn is an ironic reference to a football match.

> **Ernie** Meanwhile — while this exciting discussion was in progress, I was reading this book about the French wartime resistance workers and of the dangers they faced, often arrested in their homes. I started wondering what would happen if a squad of soldiers turned up at our front door, having been tipped off about the secret radio transmitter hidden in our cistern — when suddenly . . .
>
> *The tramp of feet, and a squad of Soldiers comes marching on and up to their front door.*
>
> **Officer** Halte! *(He bangs on the door.)*
>
> *Pause.*
>
> **Dad** That the door?
>
> **Mum** What?

Dad The door.

Mum Was it?

Officer Open zis door. Open the door! *(He knocks again.)*

Mum Oh, that'll be the milkman wanting his money. He always comes round about now. Albert, have you got ten bob . . .?

Dad (*fumbling in his pockets*) Ah . . .

Officer (*shouting*) Open zis door immediately. Or I shall order my men to break it down! *(He bangs on the door again.)*

Mum Just a minute. Coming.

Dad Should have one somewhere . . .

Officer We know you're in there, English spy! Come out with your hands up . . .

Mum What's he shouting about? Oh, I'd better ask him for three pints next week, if Auntie May's coming . . .

Officer Zis is your last chance . . . *(He knocks again.)*

Mum Oh, shut up . . .

[During the next 35 turns the officer and his men force an entry into the house. Ernie tries to explain that it is not the milkman but enemy soldiers after him and the radio transmitter. Ernie's Mum and Dad misunderstand this, and assume that they are the television licensing authority men, visiting because they have not paid their television licence.]

Officer You will come with me.

Dad What, in this? I'm not going out in this rain.

Officer Outside or I shoot.

Dad Here . . .

Mum Albert . . .

Ernie Hold it! Drop those guns!

Officer Ah, so . . . *(He raises his gun.)*

Ernie Da-da-da-da-da-da-da-da-da-da-da.

The Soldiers collapse and are strewn all over the hall. Mum screams.
Then there is a silence.

Mum Oh. Ernie. What have you done?

Ernie Sorry, Mum.

Dad Oh, lad . . .

Mum Are they — dead?

Dad Yes.

Mum screams again.

Steady, steady. This needs thinking about.

Mum What about the neighbours?

Dad Could create a bit of gossip, this could.

Mum What about the carpet? Look at it.

Dad Hasn't done that much good.

Mum What'll we do with them?

Dad Needs a bit of thinking about.

Ernie steps forward. As he speaks and during the next section, Dad
and Mum carry off the bodies.

Ernie Well, Mum and Dad decided that the best thing to do
was to pretend it hadn't happened. That was usually the way
they coped with all emergencies . . .

Ayckbourn (1998: 8–12)

Ernie's daydreams allow an impossible blend of situations: the World
War II German soldiers searching for a radio transmitter and the present-
day domestic scene with typical English weather and typical Saturday
afternoon football talk. The effect on the readers' perceptions of the
characters is to make them seem exaggerated prototypes. The officer
is characterised through a linguistic stereotype or schema (linguistic
schemata will be discussed at length in Chapter 4). The lexical item *Halte*
and the unconventional spelling *zis* for 'this', signal the group membership — German nationality — of the speaker. The direct ('bald on
record') commands and threats (*Open zis door immediately. Or I shall order*

my men to break it down!), as well as the shouting and banging on the door, suggest the power of the speaker. The reaction of Ernie's Mum and Dad is to assume, first of all, that it is that quintessentially English phenomenon — the milkman. Despite the power talk of the Officer, Ernie's Mum is concerned about ordering enough milk for Auntie May's visit (Auntie May is also a name which conjures up slightly old-fashioned respectability), and even commands the Officer to *shut up*. Similarly, once the Officer and his men have forced their way into the house, Ernie's Dad is oblivious to their power to give commands, refusing to go with them because of the rain. After Ernie has killed the soldiers, leaving bodies all over the hall, Ernie's parents' concerns are limited to the gossip this might cause and the state of the carpet. Finally, Ernie reveals that his parents did what they always do in emergencies — pretend they had not happened. The contrast between Ernie's parents' staid parochial English outlook and the dynamic coercive power of the Officer and his men, as well as the inability of either set of characters to engage in the world of the other, has the effect of exaggerating the prototypicality of the characters, thereby creating dramatic interest and humour.

2.5.3 Possibility distortions in fictional contexts

Another case involving a different kind of distortion is where part of a real-life social schema can be instantiated, but other parts of the schema strongly conflict with the available evidence. Here I am not talking simply about the lack of schematic fit that might lead to more personalised processing, but something rather more dramatic — a conflict that involves impossibility. The following fable by Aesop provides a good illustration:

> A LESSON FOR FOOLS
> A crow sat in a tree holding in his beak a piece of meat that he had stolen. A fox which saw him determined to get the meat. It stood under the tree and began to tell the crow what a beautiful big bird he was. He ought to be king of all birds, the fox said; if only he had a voice as well. The crow was so anxious to prove that he *had* a voice, that he dropped the meat and croaked for all he was worth. Up ran the fox, snapped up the meat, and said to him: 'If you added brains to all your other qualifications, you would make an ideal king.'

Semino (1997: 147) comments that although this is a physically impossible world, containing as it does speaking animals, it conveys a moral that applies to the reader's world. Moreover, she comments (1997: 148) on the real-world relevance of the story, which 'applies generally to situations that involve similar goals (a person A wants an object X), similar conditions (another person B has possession of X), similar plans (A flatters B) and similar features (A is cunning, B is naïve)'. Much of Semino's description involves characterisation. Specifically, the goals and traits of the two participants are inferred from their interaction. In other words, particular personal categories are invoked. Thus, in forming an impression of these participants we apply our real-world social schematic knowledge, but part or parts of the impression — the speaking characters are animals — will clash with what we know to be possible in the real world. It is this combination that I term a 'possibility distortion'.

Let us consider one more example of possibility distortions, the characters in the children's BBC television series *Teletubbies*. In terms of appearance, the Teletubbies have all the key features of humans (legs, bodies, arms, heads, eyes, noses, mouths, ears, etc.), the proportions of very young children (relatively large eyes, heads and bellies), and even the faint trace of a nappy is visible. They speak in the manner of very young children, especially in terms of intonation. Thus, the group membership 'young children' is triggered. They also behave in ways that trigger personal categories such as jealousy. However, some elements clash with what we know to be possible in the real world. They have TV screens in their bellies, aerials coming out of their heads, and short fur on their bodies: human bodies cannot have such things. Finally, rather like prototypicality distortions, possibility distortions can be established as fictional character types. Science fiction must be the genre that is richest in possibility distortions, and it is this genre that established the Martian. In fact, knowledge of the Martian is relevant to an impression of the Teletubbies, who even live in something resembling a space ship.

2.5.4 The flat/round distinction revisited

Impression formation can provide a basis for understanding E.M. Forster's distinction between 'flat' and 'round' characters. This distinction broadly corresponds with the distinction between category-based and person-based impressions. Although Forster's definitions for flat and round characters are rather slippery, it is clear from them and from subsequent work on Forster's distinctions (notably Harvey 1965, and Hochman 1985) that three dimensions are involved: 1) whether the character is simple or complex, 2) whether the character is static or undergoes change, and 3) whether the character 'surprises' the reader or not. The problem is understanding exactly what is meant by these dimensions. However, we can begin to solve these problems, if we relate the dimensions to Fiske and Neuberg's model. The substance of the simple/complex dimension becomes clearer: the attributes and features of a flat character are organised according to a preformed category or schema to form a category-based impression; the attributes and features of a round character combine to form a person-based impression. The staticism/change dimension can be explained: a categorised character implies no change, while the piecemeal integration of a personalised character implies change. And the 'surprise' dimension also follows: the confirmatory categorisation of a character means being satisfied that a current schema adequately accounts for the information you have about that character, whereas piecemeal integration means that a character will not fit an existing schema and is thus 'surprising'.

Consider this review of an episode of the hospital soap opera *Holby City*:

> Even by its own standards, *Holby City* has a spectacularly high cliché count in the series' comeback episode this week. A Sexy (though emotionally flawed) Specialist and Snooty, Super-Cool Consultant board a plane full of passengers from Stereotype City — Irritating Child, Laddish Lager Louts, Daffy New Age Counsellor and Fear-of-Flying Man — just in time to perform a miraculous Caesarean on (wouldn't you know it) Woman-Who-Didn't-Know-She-Was-Pregnant-With-History-of-Miscarriages (married to Potential Heart Attack Man for added value). Back at base, Stroppy Sister, Confused Pregnant Nurse and New Bit of Fluff (male) continue the drama-by-numbers game. Next week we get to meet Boorish Builders, Dowdy Wife/Blowsy Mistress and Chirpy Working Class Waitress at Gentlemen's Club. Oh please! We've met them all before, in every sub-standard series that uses Rolf Harris-sized brushstrokes to sketch in what passes for characterisation. *Holby City*'s in chronic need of emergency life support otherwise it'll haemorrhage viewers because we'll all burst a blood vessel shouting our irritation at the screen.[15]

(*TV Times* 20–26/11/99)

Clearly, according to the reviewer, *Holby City* is made up of flat characters, characters which are based on well-known schemata. Such characters are simple (*Rolf Harris-sized brushstrokes*) and familiar (*We've met them all before*). They do not change or surprise the viewer. The 'distortion' characters discussed in the previous sections are also flat characters: they are simple and do not change. However, they do 'surprise', since they have some unusual distortion, brought about through interaction with an unexpected context, or through the inclusion of an impossible element. This is not the case in *Holby City*.

This discussion can be related to Cook's (1994) work on schema theory and 'literariness'. In essence, Cook (1994) argues for the idea that literary texts are typically associated with 'schema disruption' (a clash between information in the text and the reader's schemata), and lead to 'schema refreshment' (a change in the reader's schemata); and, conversely, non-literary texts are associated with 'schema reinforcement' (the strengthening of the reader's schemata) (see also my discussion of adverts in Further Directions and Exercises on pages 157–8). Weber (1992), taking a similar view but from a critical linguistic perspective, goes further in ascribing greater value to schema refreshment (or 'positive manipulation' in his terms) compared with schema reinforcement (or 'negative manipulation'). Semino (1997: 154), however, points out that 'in practice texts that are regarded as literary range on a continuum from schema reinforcement at one end to schema refreshment at the other end'. Countering Weber's argument, Semino (1997: 157) suggests that some readers 'may prefer texts that confirm their view of the world', and, more importantly, points out that Weber's view is too restricted in that it seems to assume that

> the reader's existing schemata are always narrow-minded, intolerant and stereotyped, and that literary texts always work towards the establishment of non-classist, non-racist and non-sexist views.

With regard to characterisation, one can describe flat characters as typically schema reinforcing and round characters as typically schema refreshing. Whether one can say, however, that round characters have a stronger association with literariness is more controversial. It may be true that round characters are prototypically a feature of literary texts (not least of all because literary texts often afford sufficient space for character development), though exceptions can easily be found, and the role of flat characters in literary texts should not be undervalued. Note that the Sanatogen advertisement discussed above (2.4.6 and 2.4.7) has a round character at its centre. Conversely, note that Oscar Wilde's *The Importance of Being Earnest* has very little by way of roundness for any character, yet there is a vast scholarly literature on the play, and it is also one of the most popular plays ever written. As *The Importance of Being Earnest* illustrates, flat characters can be used for distortion effects and structural contrasts, as well as to keep the focus on the action. Since what flat characters do is more predictable than what round characters do, the focus of interest is more on the interaction with events and contexts. The issue for Jack in *The Importance of Being Earnest* is not how his character will change to resolve the clash between his desire to marry Gwendolen and her desire to marry somebody named Ernest, but on what he does in coping with the clash (for instance, lying about his name). This, of course, is how much of the humour is created. At the end of the play, the plot brings about a resolution of the clash: the final event is the discovery that he is in fact called Ernest.

The argument above may also help explain the success of soap operas. The reviewer of *Holby City* clearly takes a negative view of flat characterisation (cf. *sub-standard*). However, many soaps (such as *Neighbours*) make almost exclusive use of flat characters. Yet these soaps are phenomenally successful: viewers come back day after day for more. It may be the case that some viewers positively value the schema-reinforcing nature of flat characters. Furthermore, as Livingstone (1988: 142–3) comments above (see 2.5.1), the focus for viewers may be on what characters *do* with their attributes. Thus, the issue in *Holby City* is how the 'Super-Cool Consultant' will enact the super-cool consultant, how the 'Irritating Child' will enact the irritating child, and so on, in the context of the plane.

2.5.5 Category shifts in characterisation

One might hypothesise that the unmarked path for character development consists of the following steps: 1) make an initial categorisation, 2) recategorise by accessing a sub-category, and 3) move to piecemeal processing. This would occur in the context of a continual flow of new information about a particular character and motivational factors encouraging one to attend to it. There is, however, a notable deviation from this path. Recategorisation may also take place by abandoning one category totally and activating another. Such recategorisations involve significant cognitive reorganisation, particularly in cases where a superordinate-level group membership categorisation must be rejected (for the different levels in social categories see section 2.4.4). Not surprisingly, these recategorisations are frequently exploited in fiction.

A good example lies at the heart of Neil Jordan's film *The Crying Game* (1992). One of the protagonists, Dil, has prototypically female appearance characteristics (physique, clothes, hair, make-up) and thus a female group membership category is rapidly activated. This activation is strengthened through schematically associated social role and person categories. Dil has jobs (a hairdresser and a singer in a club) typically undertaken by women, and displays typically female preferences (such as male partners). Understandably, when the audience reaches the bedroom scene where a camera pans down her naked body, the sight of a penis produces a dramatic schematic clash. Recategorisation, from female to male, is the most likely change for one's character impression, though, apparently, some viewers persisted in believing that Dil was a woman, explaining away the penis with the belief that a body double was used or that it was a special effect (Giles 1997: 57, 75). Dil in *The Crying Game* is also an interesting example of how the activation of a schema can trigger an emotional response. The seductive 'woman' in the film may elicit feelings of attraction, which are eventually disrupted. This partly explains why some viewers were so reluctant to accept that Dil was a man. As Marjorie Garber puts it: 'Their problem was the same as Fergus's: they had come to desire that which, once they "knew" what it was, they "knew" they didn't desire. Or did they?' (Garber 1996: 231, cited in Giles 1997: 57).

Recategorisation is the staple of murder mystery novels, where, if the novel is successful, the denouement involves the recategorisation of a character we did not think was the murderer as the murderer. Recategorisation is also used for humorous effect. Let's consider an extract from the BBC comedy series *One Foot in the Grave*, which revolves around Victor Meldrew, a grumpy (though inadvertently humorous) man dealing with the trials and tribulations of being retired.

[Context: At the beginning of this episode (*The Big Sleep*), the window cleaner claims that she is going to report Victor to the police for indecent exposure whilst she was cleaning the bathroom window. Later, Victor has just come in from the garden to be told by his wife that there are two men in the living room waiting to speak to him. Victor goes to speak to them. Transcription conventions are as follows: V = Victor; S1 = the dark suited man who first speaks; S2 = the other dark suited man; [= point at which overlap begins; other transcription conventions are given in note 14].

S1   Victor Meldrew

V   Yes

S1   Wondered if we might have a little word with you sir

V   Oh God

S2   On the subject of obscene behaviour

V   Look . it's all very simple really =

S1   = Rather a lot of it going on these days wouldn't you say . acts of unbridled filth perpetrated by perverts and sexual deviants who should know better at their age

V   Look . I . . . I just got out of the bath and I was just rubbing . [I was rubbing

S1   [How do you think God feels about all this

V   What

S1   How do you think the Lord feels about so much sin and wickedness in his holy kingdom on earth

S2   If we look at Proverbs 6 verse 12 I think we can find the answer . . . a naughty person a wicked man walketh [with a

V   [You're Jehovah's Witnesses . you're bloody Jehovah's Witnesses I thought you were policemen

S1   Oh . we are policemen but on our days off we work for God

V   Get out =

S1   = Let me just read you something sir . In the beginning [there was

V   [Get out of my house

S1   Sir . we all of us need a moment of soul searching reflection in these iniquitous times =

V   = I know my rights . you can't search my soul without a warrant now go on get out of it . bloody cheek

One foot in the Grave: *The Big Sleep* (1990)

Given that the audience has fairly recently heard that Victor was reported to the police for indecency, a police-related schema is readily activated. As I noted in 2.3.3.2, research suggests that schemata that have been recently activated are more likely to spring to mind. The 'activity type' here appears to be a police interview. According to Levinson ([1979] 1992), activity types — interviews, lectures, chats, quiz shows, courtroom trials, and so on — are made up of particular 'kinds of allowable contributions' (1992: 69), involving particular participants in particular settings. And this has the important consequence that 'to each and every clearly demarcated activity there is a corresponding set of *inferential schemata*' (1992: 72). The opening turns, checking the identity of the interviewee and requesting permission to commence the interview (with lip service to politeness), are strongly associated with the police interview activity type. It is not surprising then that Victor infers, as probably does the audience, that the men are police detectives, since they are part of the corresponding schema. And, indeed, the two men, S1 and S2, look like prototypical police detectives (dark-suited, male and in advanced middle-age). The recategorisation of the police detectives as Jehovah's witnesses is brought about by a switch in activity types. S1's question *How do you think God feels about all this* clashes with the police interview activity type, and this is clear from Victor's response — *What*. Whilst asking questions is perfectly consistent with the police interview activity type, the religious topic is not. After the question *How do you think the Lord feels about so much sin and wickedness in his holy kingdom on earth* and the quotations from the Bible, Victor realises that the activity type is actually one of religious proselytising, and, consequently, that these are Jehovah's Witnesses, a religious group that is well known for making door-to-door visits. The dramatic recategorisation is a trigger for humour.

2.6 Investigating readers' descriptions of character

In this section, I introduce and then discuss an exploratory study designed to investigate aspects of characterisation.

2.6.1 Aims and methodology

To date, only one empirical study — Potter (1992) — has attempted to correlate readers' perceptions of characters with particular linguistic features of the text. In my view, the major problem with this study is that Potter did not use free response questionnaires, because 'free response to any collection of verbal symbols is not likely to produce common responses' (1992: 18). In other words, she claims that free responses, because they can be so varied, are difficult to analyse quantitatively, and so it is difficult to discover statistical correlations between particular linguistic features and particular responses. Thus, Potter chose a set of traits that would constitute informant rating scales, and her choice of traits was based on 'the hypothesis that they would correlate' (1992: 20) with particular linguistic features. This approach raises a number of issues, for example: Why use these particular traits and not others? Why use traits at all and not other aspects of character?

I conducted a study which did not bias readers' perceptions by presenting them with particular categories (such as particular traits), but attempted to discover what the very categories of their perceptions might be. The questions I wished to pursue included:

1. What kinds of descriptors do readers use to express their perceptions of characters? How do these descriptors relate to one another? Do they reveal anything about the cognitive mechanisms that might be at work?
2. What linguistic features are important in determining readers' perceptions of characters?

I shall address the first question in this chapter and the second in the next. Needless to say, to provide 'answers' to these questions would require an extensive research programme. Here I can but hint at some aspects that need to be considered.

The methodology I adopted was the questionnaire. One needs to bear in mind that the questionnaire has a number of weaknesses as a research tool. There is always the danger that a particular question or task may bias responses (a specific example of this is discussed in the following section). A further weakness is the fact that introspective reports work best when obtained during the performance of a task rather than retrospectively, and when subjects are asked to describe what they are thinking about rather than supply an interpretation (Eysenck and Keane 1990: 38). The written questionnaire is liable to retrospective re-interpretation. On the other hand, the questionnaire is widely used as a research tool in the social sciences, and can yield valuable data. The key point to remember is that the questionnaire is a means of revealing *potential inferences* that might be drawn from the text, but not the *actual inferences* that were drawn. With regard to my study, it makes sense at this initial stage to first consider potential inferences and from these to generate hypotheses about the actual inferences that might occur, hypotheses which can be tested at a later date with an appropriate methodology (such as verbal protocols, reading speeds). In addition to the questionnaire, I also recorded two discussion groups, comprising undergraduates who had completed the questionnaire.[16] The aim of these group discussions was to try to reveal why respondents had put what they did in the questionnaires.

My questionnaire asked readers to look at two characters in an extract taken from near the beginning of John Osborne's play *The Entertainer* (1957). Part of this extract will already be familiar to you, since I briefly discussed it in 1.2. I chose a modern play for my questionnaire in order to avoid the cultural and linguistic complications that might have occurred if I had chosen an older text. The passage I selected is the first dialogue in the play.

> *He settles down. Across from up L. comes a young girl. Billy pours himself out some more beer. The girl knocks on the door. He listens.*

Billy Who is it?

> *The girl knocks again.*

Who is it? Can't get any peace in this damned house.   5

Girl Is that you, Grandad?

Billy What?

Girl It's Jean.

Billy (*rising*). Who is it?

Jean It's me — Jean.   10

Billy (*goes to door and stands behind*). Can't even read the paper in peace. Who?

Jean It's your granddaughter.

> *Jean tries to push the door open but the rug prevents it.*   15

Billy Just a minute! Just a minute! Hold your horses! (*He bends down*).

Jean Sorry.

Billy   Hold your horses!

He releases the rug and opens the door, revealing Jean Rice. 20
She is about twenty-two, with slightly protruding teeth and
bad eyesight. Her mouth is large, generous.

Jean   Hello, Grandad.

Billy   I wondered who the hell it was.

Jean   I'm sorry. 25

Billy   I thought it was some of that mad lot carrying on.

Well, come in if you're coming, it's draughty standing about in the doorway. I've only just sat down.

Jean   *(coming in)*. Did I disturb you, I am sorry.

Billy   I'd just sat down to read the evening paper. It's a 30
bloody farm-yard this place.

Jean   Well, how are you?

Billy   Bloody farm-yard. They want locking up. And you
know what now, don't you? You know who she's
got upstairs, in Mick's old room, don't you? Some 35
black fellow. It's true. I tell you, you've come to a
mad-house this time.

Jean   You're looking very well. How do you feel?

Billy   I'm all right. You expect a few aches and pains when
you get to my age. Phoebe's at the pictures, I think. 40
She didn't tell me you were coming.

Jean   I didn't tell her.

Billy   No, well she didn't say anything. So I wasn't
expecting a knock on the door.

Jean   I only decided to come up this morning. 45

Billy   I'd only just sat down to read the evening paper.

Jean   I'm sorry. I disturbed you.

She has picked up her cue neatly. The fact that his evening
has been disturbed is established. His air of distracted irrita-
tion relaxes and he smiles a little. He is pleased to see her 50
anyway.

Billy   Well, give your Grandad a kiss, come on.

She does so.

Jean   It's good to see you.

Billy   Well, it's nice to see you, my darling. Bit of a sur-   55
prise. Go on, take your things off.

*Jean undoes her coat, and throws a packet of cigarettes on
the table.*

(Osborne 1957: 14–16)[17]

I conducted my investigation at a workshop held during the Poetics and Linguistics Association conference at Lancaster University in August 1991. All respondents were academics or research students in the area of stylistics. Respondents took an average of 30 minutes to complete the questionnaires.[18] In order to reduce linguistic and cultural differences among the respondents, I limited my attention to British native speakers of English. It turned out that ten (in fact, the majority) of my respondents were male. In order to gain ten female respondents, I administered the questionnaire to second- and third-year undergraduates (who had some background in stylistics). Thus, I had 20 respondents, half male, half female. I asked these respondents to rate their knowledge of the play on a five-point scale, from 1 indicating 'Not at all' to 5 indicating 'Very well'. The average score was 1.3. No respondent circled higher than 2. This suited my purposes, since detailed background knowledge of the play might have distorted responses to the text. Individual respondents will henceforth be referred to as 'Respondent 1', 'Respondent 2', and so on. I have not attempted any detailed statistical verification or manipulation of the questionnaire data for a number of reasons, but above all because the number of respondents was quite small.

2.6.2 Discussion

The first task of the questionnaire was designed to elicit character description:

(1) a.   Describe **X** in terms of adjectives or short phrases (EXAMPLE: Mrs. Thatcher = Ex-Prime Minister, domineering, a tyrant, strong, inflexible, a mother, hated by many, etc.)

Though relatively open-ended, it constrains responses in asking for them to be short. This, I hoped, would facilitate analysis of the data. All the data obtained in this task for the characters Billy and Jean is presented in Tables 2.3 and 2.4. I have attempted to identify some provisional groups in the data, according to the social categories outlined in section 2.4.4.[19]

Firstly, note that all of the descriptors elicited are descriptors that could apply equally to 'real' people, none are fictional character-specific (there is no mention of 'stock figures', for example). This would support the validity of my approach to characterisation which rests on the

Table 2.3   Descriptors for the character Billy

Group	Descriptors	Total
Personal	Grumpy (x 8), irritable (x 8), set in his ways (x 7), egocentric (x 5), impatient (x 4), rude (x 4), likes privacy (x 4), loving (x 4), warm (x 3), prejudiced (x 3), affectionate (x 3), caring (x 3), racist (x 3), bigot (x 2), complaining (x 2), inflexible (x 2), lonely (x 2), bad-tempered (x 2), abrupt (x 2), domineering (x 2), traditionalist (x 2), prone to swearing mildly (x 2), intolerant (x 2), dislikes surprises (x 2), irascible, cantankerous, kind-hearted, extrovert, likes routine, short-tempered, likes creature comforts, lover of peace and quiet, wary of neighbours, offensive, moody, narrow-minded, distracted, aggressive, gruff, ignorant, nosey, a gossip, drinker	100
Social roles	Grandfather (x 8), married, not the stereotypical grandfather	10
Group membership	old (x 11), man (x 5)	16
Appearance features	Possibly stooping	1
Health	deaf (x 8), senile (x 2), weak, ill, forgetful, physically quite fit	14
Emotional state	feels oppressed, frustrated, miserable, unsatisfied	4
Other comments	kind-hearted underneath, kind/appreciative underneath, apparently projects annoyance at interruption but neatly welcomes visitors, uses emotions as a front, possibly not as hot-tempered as he seems, but also affectionate	6
Grand total		151

Table 2.4   Descriptors for the character Jean

Group	Descriptors	Total
Personal	polite (x 10), patient (x 8), apologetic (x 5), caring (x 5), shy (x 4), understanding (x 4), kind (x 4), timid (x 3), friendly (x 3), deferential (x 3), concerned (x 3), persistent (x 3), affectionate (x 2), tactful (x 2), quiet (x 2), cheerful (x 2), warm (x 2), smoker (x 2), loving (x 2), pleasant (x 2), tolerant (x 2), lacking in self-confidence, self-effacing, perceptive, thoughtful, generous, flexible, subdued, affable, possibly secretive, sensitive, sympathetic, compassionate, level-headed, solicitous, considerate, calm, spontaneous, prissy, bookish, nervous, impulsive, passive, disruptive, strong personality, forceful, intelligent, possibly an anti-smoker	100
Social roles	granddaughter (x 11), visitor	12
Group membership	young (x 8), female (x 3)	11
Appearance features	plain, peculiar face, not attractive, large generous mouth (x 2), protruding teeth	6
Health	bad eyesight (x 2)	2
Emotional state	cheerful (x 2)	2
Grand total		133

assumption that people, at least in part, apply to characters in drama concepts developed in their real-life experiences with people. It is clear that most descriptors belong to the personal features group. That this is so may in part be due to the nature of the study. Firstly, respondents may have thought I was trying to elicit personal features, especially personality traits, rather than any other character aspect. Personality traits are strongly associated with psychology experiments. Secondly, the fact that the task asked for 'adjectives or short phrases' may have biased respondents towards supplying traits. Personality traits usually have adjectival labels, and in fact it has been suggested that this is a defining feature (Andersen *et al.* 1990: 193), whereas social roles usually have nominal labels. However, it is still the case that descriptors other than personal features were supplied. In fact, for Billy the most frequent lexical item was 'old' (x 11), a group membership feature, and for Jean it was 'granddaughter' (x 11), a social role. Furthermore, it is clear from the tables that some descriptors fall into other groups apart from the three social categories I introduced in 2.4.4. As I already noted in 2.4.4, some researchers would include 'appearance features' as a further social category. I have not done so because all studies relating to appearance as a category are based on *visual* physical properties (as I made clear in section 1.7.2, one cannot assume that the perception of visual properties is the same as the understanding of a description of visual properties in a text), and, unlike the other categories, appearance plays a key role as a stimulus feature cueing other categories. I will have more to say about appearance features in general in 4.4.8. A further social category in Billy's and Jean's descriptors relates to 'health', and I shall comment further on this category below. Finally, some descriptors relate to 'emotional state'. This is a reminder that emotion, just because it is typically viewed as an unstable property, should not be overlooked as a characterising feature within a particular context.

Contrary to Potter's (1992) claims, responses had much in common, in spite of the fact that the task was relatively open-ended. Of the personal descriptors for Billy, 83% can be placed into five approximate groups on the basis of semantic similarity:[20]

Table 2.5   Personal descriptors for the character Billy

Group	Personal descriptors	Total
Disagreeability	Grumpy (x 8), irritable (x 8), impatient (x 4), rude (x 4), complaining (x 2), bad-tempered (x 2), abrupt (x 2), domineering (x 2), intolerant (x 2), irascible, cantankerous, short-tempered, offensive, aggressive, gruff, nosey	41
Agreeability	Loving (x 4), warm (x 3), affectionate (x 3), caring (x 3), kind-hearted	14
Inflexibility	set in his ways (x 7), inflexible (x 2), traditionalist (x 2), likes routine	12
Negative attitudes	Prejudiced (x 3), racist (x 3), bigot (x 2), narrow-minded	9
Selfishness	Egocentric (x 5)	5
Grand total		81

Similarly, 89% of personal descriptors for Jean can be placed into four approximate groups.

Table 2.6   Personal descriptors for the character Jean

Group	Personal descriptors	Total
Agreeability	Polite (x 10), patient (x 8), apologetic (x 5), caring (x 5), understanding (x 4), kind (x 4), friendly (x 3), deferential (x 3), concerned (x 3), affectionate (x 2), tactful (x 2), warm (x 2), loving (x 2), pleasant (x 2), tolerant (x 2), generous, affable, sensitive, sympathetic, compassionate, solicitous, considerate, thoughtful	65
Introversion	shy (x 4), timid (x 3), quiet (x 2), lacking in self-confidence, self-effacing, subdued, nervous, passive	14
Psychological strength	Persistent (x 3), strong personality, forceful	5
Flexibility	Flexible, spontaneous, impulsive	3
Grand total		87

This overlap in descriptors would be consistent with the idea that there are no significant differences in the schemata which respondents activated in the reading of the text. This is not to say, of course, that differences could not be revealed with further experimentation. In fact, there is some slight evidence already that respondents activated different schemata according to whether they were male or female. All the negative evaluative comments on Jean's appearance — 'plain, peculiar face, not attractive' — were supplied by male respondents. This difference was also picked up in the discussion groups, where an individual, commenting on discussions with others in the group, said that there was 'a clear divide between what the males thought and what the females thought' about Billy and Jean.[21] This raises the possibility that male and female respondents were activating different gender schemata.

How do the various descriptors given relate to each other? Some clues were revealed in the second part of the first task:

(1) b.   Number your adjectives/phrases above in order of importance. Those of equal weight may carry the same number. (EXAMPLE: Ex-Prime Minister <2>, domineering <5>, a tyrant <1>, strong <6>, inflexible <4>, a mother <7>, hated by many <3>)

Respondents had difficulty in performing this task. For example, Respondent 1 commented, 'It's difficult to put traits in a fixed order', and Respondent 2 noted, 'Numbering task very difficult: I keep changing my mind', whilst four other respondents used bracketing techniques to identify groups of descriptors of equal weight. Similarly, the discussion groups described the numbering task as 'not easy', and said that they 'couldn't differentiate' between the descriptors. What all this would seem to suggest is that there is no fixed hierarchical order of descriptors, but rather loose, flexible groupings. This, of course, is consistent with the idea that our impressions of characters are partly determined by social schemata.

An interesting aspect of the responses was the way in which some of the descriptors clearly resulted from inferences generated from the informants' prior knowledge. To illustrate this I shall focus on the data displayed in the table containing all the descriptors for Billy (Table 2.3). Under group membership descriptors, 11 respondents described Billy as 'old'. Where does this information come from? Four of the five respondents explicitly indicated that the information was extracted from Jean's word 'Grandad' (line 6). From this, respondents could infer Billy's age from the social role schema for grandfathers: grandfathers are highly likely to be old. As I noted in section 2.4.4, social roles provide, perhaps, an optimal knowledge base from which to infer other features. From our experience of the world we learn that certain types of people tend to fill certain social roles. Similarly, note that appearance features or health features may be readily inferred from social roles or, more particularly, group membership. Whilst Jean's appearance features are triggered by a stage direction (lines 20–2), Billy's appearance feature 'possibly stooping' has to be inferred. Presumably, the inference relies on an association between old people and stooping. In fact, for any characteristic it would seem likely that we can generate expectations about other characteristics in other groups or, indeed, in the same group.

A striking feature of Billy's descriptors is that some inconsistencies arise. This can be seen most clearly in the table displaying Billy's personal features (Table 2.5). The descriptors of the disagreeability group are consistent with those of the inflexibility, negative attitudes and selfishness groups: they are all negative in some way. These descriptors amount to the social schema for a grumpy old man. It is interesting to note that a recent film was actually called *Grumpy Old Men* (1994, directed by Donald Petrie), and revolves around two members of the set of prototypically grumpy old men. However, the descriptors of the agreeability group, representing 17% of the total number of traits, are positive. Of the 20 respondents, 16 indicated that they had inferred the positive traits of Group B from the final part of the passage (lines 50–56). The problem seems to have been how to accommodate this inconsistency within the overall conception of Billy's character. It is clear from the questionnaires that the inconsistency triggered much interpretative work. The table displaying all Billy's descriptors (Table 2.3) includes a group labelled 'Other comments'. Six respondents departed from the adjectives and short phrases which the task asked for and provided more extensive comment in an attempt to explain the inconsistency. Typically, respondents used a metaphor to suggest that beneath a negative 'surface' Billy's true nature was positive.[22] In impression formation terms, Billy is 'recategorised' as a sub-type of grumpy old men: those who are disagreeable in some circumstances, but agreeable in others. The idea of inconsistency acting as a trigger for further interpretative work will be pursued in Chapter 3.

One might note that no such extensive comment was elicited for Jean's character.[23] Compared with Billy, she is a flatter character. In the table displaying her personal descriptors (Table 2.6), 65% of the descriptors used belong to a single group, agreeability, and those of the other groups — introversion, psychological strength and flexibility — are not inconsistent with it. Jean is the opposite of parts of Billy's character: in particular, they contrast on the dominant agreeability/disagreeability group and the flexibility/inflexibility group. One might suppose that this contrastive relationship would affect the way the two characters are perceived, for example, by polarising our perceptions or by encouraging us to assume opposite characteristics for one character because they were clearly present in the other. Thus, one might hypothesise that the elicitation of 65 agreeability descriptors for Jean as opposed to 41 disagreeability descriptors for Billy (in spite of the fact that Billy speaks almost four times as many words as Jean, 207 compared with 58), partly comes about as a reaction to the disagreeability of Billy. Comments in the discussion groups are consistent with this. Several people said that the descriptor 'understanding' was inferred 'from the context' or 'from the whole situation'. This kind of relationship between characters will be further considered in Chapter 4.

To sum up, the main points suggested by this pilot study include:

- Knowledge developed for real-life people is used in the perception of characters.
- Although personal concepts seem dominant in characterisation, other more contextually oriented concepts, such as social roles and group

membership (and even appearance, health and emotional state), are used in the perception of characters.

- Whilst there is substantial agreement in the way different people (but people who also share the same culture) view characters, some impression differences may be due to different schemata (for example different gender schemata).
- Descriptors form loose groups rather than rigid hierarchies. This is consistent with a schema-based approach to knowledge.
- Knowledge-based inferences allow us to enrich our impressions of characters. Social roles — rich in attributes but not overwhelming — seem to be a key inferential source.
- Impressions of character are dynamic and may change over time. Interpretative work may take place at points where one's impression is inconsistent with the textual input.
- The perception of a particular character is coloured by the context that character is perceived in. This context includes impressions of other characters.

2.7 Conclusion

Clearly, within the scope of this chapter I have not been able to demonstrate the full potential of the theories from social cognition which I have introduced. Nevertheless, I hope to have shown that they can make a useful contribution in explaining an array of characterisation aspects, some of which have been poorly dealt with by literary critics for centuries. Some caveats, however, need particular mention. One complex and controversial area, and one whose importance is only recently being recognised, is the relationship between affect (for example emotions, moods, evaluations) and cognition. This chapter has not done justice to this area (for a good review of some of the issues see Fiske and Taylor 1991: 409–61). Furthermore, we must remember that character impression formation arising from dialogue is a complex and dynamic business. Consider that the reader will typically construct an impression of each participant. In addition, an impression of a participant may include that participant's impressions of other participants. Our impression of Othello, for example, includes Othello's impression of Desdemona. Of course, to closely monitor all these impressions against a flow of character information generated from the text requires massive cognitive resources. Thus the reader distributes attention unevenly.

But what determines what captures the cognitive eye? Indeed, how do we decide that something in the text has anything to do with character at all? These are some of the questions I will address in the next chapter.

Notes

1   Culler points out (1975: 233–4) the oddity of Greimas's receiver, which has no equivalent in Propp's scheme and thus no empirical support. Note how in the *Aladdin* analysis the hero is both subject and receiver.

2   In fact, the actant model has not always proved adequate for oral genres, such as the ballad. Leith (1989: 53) notes that ballad is action- rather than character-oriented, but in spite of this discovers that the actant notion of character is strained.

3   It is true that the detective TV series *Columbo* is not of the comedy genre. However, Frye acknowledges that particular character types from one genre can appear in another. My reason for including this example is that Columbo, the bumbling detective, seems a good example of what Frye describes as the self-deprecating hero, and, indeed, is a quietly comic character.

4   This publication is in Hebrew. Ewen's scheme is summarised in Rimmon-Kenan (1983: 41–2).

5   In fact, Britain's first female Professor of Surgery, Averil Mansfield, was appointed in October 1993.

6   It should not be assumed that episodic memory has no role to play here. For example, one's first experience of travelling by aeroplane would presumably be stored as an episodic memory. But one's second experience of travelling by aeroplane would almost certainly be guided by inferences based on the first experience (e.g. inferences about and the order of certain procedures, such as check-in, going through passport control, boarding the aeroplane, and so on).

7   Of course, I would not deny that the grammatical parallelism in 'The father was killed and the son rushed' (SUBJECT + AUXILIARY + VERB + AND + SUBJECT + [AUXILIARY] + VERB) predisposes the reader towards the first interpretation.

8   Semino (1997: 193) points out that it is clear from Sperber and Wilson's comments (e.g. 1986, 1995: 138) that Relevance theory is compatible with schema theory.

9   Other researchers have used the term 'social memory' for memory about social affairs.

10   The first two bullet-points are suggested in Lingle *et al.* 1984.

11   The hierarchical nature of social categories is highly controversial, particularly regarding the status of 'traits', which I have placed under the person grouping. However, much research strongly supports the idea of social roles constituting some kind of basic level.

12   This, needless to say, is something of a simplified summary. See Fiske and Taylor's (1991: 126–31) overview of some of the complexities.

13   The nature of that cognitive structure and how it affects perception are currently areas of hot debate in social cognition. An excellent overview of the issues involved can be found in Hamilton and Sherman (1994: 15–42).

14   The transcription conventions are as follows: pauses are shown as full stops (each full stop represents approximately half a second); an equals sign shows one utterance immediately following on from another; capital letters show loud speech.

15   Rolf Harris is a television personality who used to introduce children's cartoons by first drawing a cartoon character from the up-coming cartoon. These drawings were large (human size) and created rapidly with a broad paint brush or roller.

16   In case I should bias these discussion groups towards saying things I wanted to hear, the group sessions were conducted by John Heywood, to whom I owe my thanks.

17   I made one small cut in the text. The sentence 'She is what most people would call plain, but already humour and tenderness have begun to stake their small claims around her nose and eyes' precedes the final sentence 'Her mouth is large, generous' in line 22. This sentence was cut because it explicitly and directly provides character description to the reader. It would interfere with my interest, namely, the descriptors the reader supplies and how the reader decides that they are appropriate on the basis of character behaviour. Its removal did not appear to affect my informants' ability to interpret the text holistically as they read it.

18   I mixed the questionnaires so that half of the respondents commented on Billy before Jean and half on Jean before Billy, in order to reduce the effect of a possible bias.

19   In cases where there was little doubt that two terms were synonymous, I counted the less frequent synonym as an instance of the more frequent. Thus, 'self-centred' was counted as an instance of 'egocentric'.

20   This approach is supported by the group discussions where it was reported that, although different individuals had used different words, the words 'mean the same thing'.

21   In the discussion group, apart from commenting on the differing perceptions of Jean's appearance, they also suggested that the female respondents had more readily noticed the 'loving' aspect of Billy's character. However, this particular difference was not reflected in the questionnaire data.

22   In an earlier pilot of this test, 4 of my 7 respondents used 'heart' as a metaphor to suggest that Billy had a positive character underneath a negative surface (e.g. 'kind-hearted', 'heart of gold').

23   This is in spite of the fact that one might see some tension between the introversion group and the psychological strength group.

CHAPTER 3

INFERRING CHARACTER FROM TEXTS

3.1 Introduction

Like the previous chapter, this chapter also explores what Culler referred to as the 'fund of human knowledge' and its application in characterisation. Thus the focus remains on the role of 'top-down' processes in the construction of character — the role of the prior knowledge box in Figure 1.1. Chapter 2 focussed on what happened to character information. This chapter focusses on a prior stage: how and when we decide that we have character information. It considers how the reader 'establishes connections between actions and motive, behaviour and personality' (Culler 1975: 142–3). Recent studies (for instance Herman 1995; Short 1996; Culpeper *et al.* 1998) investigating the language of drama recognise that information about characters can be inferred from conversational behaviour, but none of these studies are clear about why they consider some conversational behaviours significant for characterisation but others not. It is this deficit that I hope to address here by considering theories developed for our understanding of real people.

I shall attempt to answer the following questions: What makes us decide to attend to some behaviours, be they linguistic or non-linguistic, but not others in forming an impression of a character? What makes some behaviours more informative about a character than others? An important notion that underlies the first question is salience, and an important notion that underlies the second question is contextual ambiguity. Contextual ambiguity was an issue that informants in my empirical investigation (see section 2.6) considered. Some informants speculated that Billy may have had 'good cause to be angry'; in other words, they considered the possibility that some contextual reason caused him to be angry, rather than some property of his character. In attempting to answer these two questions, I shall again draw upon theories that have been developed within social cognition. Specifically, I shall discuss theories of 'attribution', which are designed to explain how aspects of personality are inferred in real life situations. These theories, however, though well established, tend to be rather underspecified, and sometimes rely more on intuitive appeal and anecdotal evidence than systematic empirical support. Moreover, the two most important attribution theories (Jones and Davis 1965; Kelley 1967) seem to be incompatible. One of my aims will be to strengthen the theoretical position of this work and to show how the two attribution theories can be reconciled, by drawing an analogy with foregrounding theory, a theory developed within literary stylistics to address issues of literary interpretation. I will also argue that attribution theory connects with various areas of language research. Finally, I turn to inferencing in fictional texts and play texts in particular, returning to the exploratory study I discussed in 2.6. I shall start, however, by noting what is probably the only work done in this area by somebody working within literary studies.

3.2 Approaching character inferencing from within literary studies

The only serious attempt within literary studies to think through some of the issues with which this chapter is concerned is in the work of Margolin (1983, 1986, 1989, 1990). However, Margolin's work tends to consist of statements about theoretical fundamentals: it lacks any kind of detailed analytical demonstration or empirical support. As a consequence, I will summarise Margolin's main claims in list form, rather than offer any kind of detailed description of his work. Later sections of this chapter will pick up and expand upon some of these claims.

Margolin (especially 1983: 11–13) makes the following claims about canonical character inferences:

1. Mental/psychological properties cannot be directly observed, but are inferred from other properties of the narrative agent (his term for an uncharacterised character). Thus, such mental/psychological properties are ontologically dependent. For example, an act of a doer must be kind before one can call the doer kind.

2. The same inference rules applied to the same data will lead to several possible conclusions of equal probability. Thus, '[f]rom "x spoke in shrill voice" we may equally infer "x was nervous", "x was impatient", "x was fed up", etc.' (Margolin 1983: 11).

3. The application of inference 'rules' to acts and settings is context dependent. Thus, '[t]he same behavior in small child and adult,

king and peasant, health and sickness will lead in each case to different conclusions' (Margolin 1983: 12).

4. All character inferences are probabilistic. Thus, an inference can
be cancelled if it conflicts with a stronger inference subsequently
recovered.

5. The conclusions resulting from character inferences can include:
(a) the degree to which a narrative agent possesses a certain property
(for example 'somewhat suspicious', 'extremely suspicious'), and
(b) contextual information associated with the property (for instance
whether the property only occurs at specific times in specific situations, or whether the property occurs more generally).

3.3 Attribution theories

We all try to understand why people act as they do, what causes lie
behind behaviour, so that our world may be more predictable and
hence more controllable (Heider 1944). However, our task is complicated by the fact that one cannot see or hear what inclines people to act
as they do. We have no direct access to another person's mind. Of
course, in fictional texts an author can give us such direct access into a
character's mind through such devices as thought presentation or soliloquy. But in general, and even in fictional texts, the causes of a person's
actions have to be *inferred* from observable behaviours, including conversational behaviour (see Margolin's first claim in 3.2). For example, if
a colleague snaps at you in the morning, you may explain it to yourself
by inferring that this is because he or she has just been soaked in a
thunderstorm. Alternatively, if your colleague regularly snaps at you and
other people, you may infer that this is because your colleague is characteristically or dispositionally short tempered.[1] The process by which
we attempt to extract such causal information from behavioural acts is
known in social psychology as *attribution*.

A number of complex theories attempting to explain the process of
attribution have been developed. The two classic theories are Jones's
correspondent inference theory (Jones and Davis 1965; Jones and
McGillis 1976; and Jones 1990) and Kelley's covariation theory (Kelley
1967, 1972, 1973). It should be acknowledged that both Jones and
Kelley were building on many of the ideas which had first appeared in
the writings of Heider (1944, 1958). I will first outline Jones's theory
and then offer a critique.

3.3.1 Correspondent inference theory

The task Jones and his colleagues set themselves is to identify the factors that render behaviour informative about an underlying disposition. They are concerned to identify the circumstances that lead to an inference that there is a degree of correspondence between a person's behaviour and their disposition. They call this a *correspondent inference*. In the above example, a non-correspondent inference is made in deciding that a colleague's snappy behaviour was due to the fact that he or she had been soaked in a thunderstorm, but a correspondent inference is made in deciding that it was due to a short-tempered disposition. In a nutshell, when you make a correspondent inference you are able to transfer your description of a person's behaviour to your description of that person's disposition. So aggressive behaviour results from an aggressive disposition, generous behaviour results from a generous disposition, and so on. Note that this view of disposition inferencing underlies Margolin's first claim in 3.2. Jones also stresses that correspondence is a scalar concept. Some inferences are more correspondent than others; in other words, behaviour varies in the degree to which it is informative about a disposition. This point is also reflected in Margolin's fourth claim in 3.2. I shall briefly outline below the factors that, according to Jones, decrease or increase correspondence.

Jones makes much, at least in his early papers, of the importance of intentionality. He argues that the reason for a behaviour should only be attributed to the disposition of the person involved if the consequences or effects of that behaviour are thought to have been intended by that person. For example, I recently poured some tomato ketchup into my coffee instead of onto my plate. Jones's interpretation of this example would follow these lines:

> It was obviously an accident, I had not intended to do it, and therefore observers would not be able to make a correspondent inference such as 'he has strange tastes'.

There is an issue here about how intention is inferred. I shall briefly return to this in my critique.

A crucial factor in making a correspondent inference is whether the actor of the observed behaviour is free from external constraint. Jones writes that 'freely chosen behaviors should be more informative than behaviors that are required or constrained by the situation' (Jones 1990: 44). For example, films depicting the apparent bravery of British First

World War troops as they leap out of the trenches and charge the enemy obscure the NCOs positioned behind ready to shoot anybody who tries to remain in the trench. A correspondent inference to the effect that they were all acting out of bravery is discounted by the presence of another cause. A less extreme example might be that of a child whose exuberant thanks to a friend's parents upon departure from a birthday party follows closely on a parental prod. Dispositional causes will not, or at least logically should not, be inferred when one is under external pressure to produce a particular behaviour. The importance of the notion that contextual reasons for a behaviour exert a negative effect in attributing cause is not overlooked in Kelley's theory. He supplied the convenient label of the *discounting principle* for this notion (Kelley 1972). The important effect of context is also reflected in Margolin's third claim in 3.2.

A second key factor lies in causal ambiguity: the fewer reasons there are for doing something, the more likely we are to be sure of why a person did it, and thus the more able we are to make a correspondent inference. Note that what lies behind this is Margolin's second claim in 3.2 that the same data and the same inference rules will lead to multiple conclusions (or reasons). What Margolin is not so clear about is that the number of conclusions varies. Jones devised a fairly complicated calculus to enable us to work out what these reasons are and how many they are. Freedom of choice amongst behavioural alternatives implies that there are options chosen and options foregone. The chosen and rejected alternatives may have single effects (that is, consequences), but more often have multiple effects. For example, in choosing a university to study at, the choice is complicated by the fact that each alternative has multiple effects. These can range from the type of course available to the setting of the university (city or countryside), the cost of living or what the social life is like. Some of the effects may be the same for both chosen and rejected alternatives; they are *common effects*. These effects are not informative about a behavioural choice, since they provide no discriminating reason for the choice. So, a choice among Manchester, Bristol, or London universities would not be informative about whether I had a penchant for a large city environment, since all the alternative universities would be in a city. On the other hand, *noncommon effects*, arising from both chosen and foregone alternatives, are informative as they provide discriminating reasons for a particular choice. If in addition to the above universities Lancaster had been an alternative and I had chosen Lancaster, it would be reasonable to infer that I liked a country environment.

A third key factor is that behaviours that are unusual tend to be more informative about a person. In Jones and Davis (1965) this factor was couched in terms of *social desirability*. A perceiver, they argue, draws conclusions about whether the effects of an action are desirable or undesirable to the actor on the basis of cultural assumptions. They write that:

> [. . .] universally desired effects are *not* informative concerning the unique characteristics of the actor. To learn that a man makes the conventional choice is to learn only that he is like most other men.
>
> (1965: 227)

I noted earlier the discounting effect of external factors that constrain or require particular behaviours. An observation, for example, that somebody gave thanks for a gift is not likely to be very informative about that person, since most people would follow the social norm of giving thanks for a gift. What would happen if an action produced only undesirable effects? What would a perceiver make of a person who withheld thanks for a gift? Jones and Davis suggest (1965: 229) two options:

> He may decide that the actor is truly a deviant type, that he desires those goals which are shunned by others; or he may decide that the actor was unaware of the effects of his action.

Whilst these are plausible inferences, I think it needs to be stressed that much more contextual information would be needed to enable one to make either of them. One is unlikely to decide, for example, that somebody is 'truly a deviant type' on the basis of one act. If one knew that that person had acted in a 'deviant' way on other occasions, the inference is much more probable. Note that from a linguistic point of view the social desirability of utterances is very much the business of politeness theory, an area I will specifically focus on in Chapter 5.

An important observation can be made about a behaviour that gives rise to both desirable and undesirable effects. In such a case, assuming no evidence to the contrary, an observer will decide that an 'actor has acted in spite of, rather than because of, any negative effects in the choice area' (Jones and Davis 1965: 227). The important point here is that 'more significance is attached to the desirable effects the more numerous and distasteful the undesirable effects "incurred"' (1965: 229). So, if I bought a book in spite of its very high price, you might reasonably infer that I particularly wanted it. Kelley also highlights the notion that contextual reasons for not doing something can lend weight to the reasons why we go ahead and do it. He labels it the *augmenting principle* (Kelley 1972). As we have already noted, the important effect of context is reflected in Margolin's third claim in 3.2.

3.3.2 Critique of correspondent inference theory

One might agree with Jones that awareness that a person is acting unintentionally can sometimes prevent us from making a correspondent inference. The notion of intentionality, however, is much more complex and problematic than Jones admits. There is no simple correspondence between our intentions and the consequences or effects of our behaviour. I may intend to be helpful, but end up having the effect of hindrance. How do we know what somebody intends? As I have said earlier, we have no access to a person's mind. Jones offers little help here. It is also the case that correspondent inferences are made even in the absence of the assignment of intention to a behavioural effect. Can we say that somebody whose behaviour is hesitant, retiring or nervous intends to exhibit such behaviour? No, but we are still able to make a correspondent inference to the effect that that person has a hesitant, retiring, or nervous disposition. Other factors — factors which I will examine later — enable us to make correspondent inferences without resorting directly to intentionality. This is not to say that we should dismiss the notion of intentionality. It is normally the case that part of an interpreter's construction of what is meant by an act will be what the doer of the act might have intended by it. The focus, then, can reasonably be on what the interpreter understands the doer's intentions to be, rather than on what the doer's intentions actually are. The fact that Jones devoted a decreasing amount of space to the notion of intentionality in his publications over the years may be implicit evidence that he found the notion more problematic and less important than he had originally thought.

Jones does not acknowledge that the cognitive demands of non-common effects analysis seem overwhelming. In order to be in a position where one might make a correspondent inference, one must (a) identify the diverse effects of the various behavioural alternatives (this in itself is an extremely complicated and difficult task), (b) decide which effects are common and which are noncommon, and (c) examine the combination of noncommon effects chosen and foregone. Obviously, we cannot be involved in this sort of processing very often in everyday life. I shall argue later that knowledge about the situation and the people involved, and the use of mental short-cuts, make these cognitive acrobatics largely unnecessary. It is important, however, not to lose sight of the fact that noncommon effects analysis represents a calculus that attempts to understand what reasons are involved and how many there are when we observe a particular behaviour. It is a way of calculating the relative causal ambiguity of an act. Noncommon effects are informative as to why somebody made a particular choice, and the fewer the number of noncommon effects, the lower the ambiguity. The ambiguity of an act affects our ability to make a correspondent inference. As Jones puts it, 'The more reasons there were for adopting a particular course of action, the less confident an observer can be that any of these were especially important or determinative' (1990: 47–8).

The notion of social desirability is weak because it is inadequately specified and not sufficient to capture the ways in which behaviour might be perceived as unusual. Jones and McGillis (1976) in particular, but also Jones (1990), go some way towards providing a remedy. They describe behaviour as unusual to the extent that it does not fit the perceiver's expectancies. An expectancy is defined as 'a probabilistic forecast of behaviour' (Jones 1990: 79), which may be generated from our schematic knowledge. Expectancies fall into three groups: 'normative', 'category-based' or 'target-based'. Normative expectancies are expectancies that are strongly linked to the situation in which one observes the behaviour. These include the social norms that guide behaviour. For example, if I were to go to a dinner hosted by the Vice-Chancellor of the University I would have various expectations about the appropriate dress, the appropriate things to say and do, the appropriate time to leave, and so on. Category-based expectancies are expectancies that we have about the general groupings in our society. These groupings include such aspects as gender, age, class, nationality, and occupation. Obviously people can be members of more than one group. We have various expectations about these groupings. For example, I would usually expect an Italian to speak more than an English person, a child to be more impatient than an adult, and a nurse to be more compassionate than an army sergeant-major. Target-based expectancies are expectancies that one has about a particular person. For example, I may expect a colleague to respond swiftly to a note I had sent, having previously observed that colleague's efficiency in replying to past notes or efficiency in other activities.

It is worth noting here that the distinction between category-based and target-based expectancies is entirely compatible with the approach to impression formation that I proposed in 2.4.7. When our social schemata are activated, they give rise to category-based expectancies. Person-based impressions, on the other hand, may give rise to target-based expectancies. For example, when I first met my wife, I formed an impression of her largely on the basis of schemata in my head. The fact that she was Italian, for instance, would have led to the activation of my schema for Italians. Thus, the expectancies I had about her were largely category-based. As I got to know her better, I acquired more information about her and was motivated to pay attention to that information — my impression became more person-based. Over time, this impression has enabled me to make specific predictions about her as an individual (for instance the kind of people she likes). In other words, I am able to generate target-based expectancies. Two further points about category-based and target-based expectancies should be noted. Firstly, just as category-based and person-based impressions are not distinct but form opposite positions on a scale, so it is with category-based and target based expectancies. Secondly, category-based expectancies take temporal priority over target-based expectancies. This is consistent with models of impression formation which argue that category-based processes take precedence over person-based processes.

Taking account of some of my criticisms of the factors said to affect the correspondence of an inference, I shall attempt to summarize Jones's theory. One can say that a particular behaviour is correspondent to the extent that it is:

1. Free from external pressures.
2. Low in ambiguity, i.e. yields noncommon effects which are few in number.
3. Unusual, i.e. departs from the perceiver's expectations (normative, category-based, or target-based).

The main problem with correspondent inference theory, however, has still not been dealt with. The theory deals in an idealised way with single behaviours that seem to take place in a vacuum. The complexities of context are ignored. Jones highlights part of the problem (1990: 53):

> The original form of correspondent inference theory was definitely a first-impression theory, dealing especially with the meaning of single acts or decisions by an unfamiliar target person.

Correspondent inference theory does not take account of the fact that an act is perceived, more often than not, as part of a sequence of behaviours.

In contrast, Kelley's theory of attribution deals explicitly with sequences of behaviour that occur over time. Jones and McGillis's main aim in their 1976 paper was to tighten up and extend correspondent inference theory so that it could subsume some of the principles of Kelley's model. These modifications, however, have not been well integrated into the social psychology research literature (Zebrowitz 1990: 174, note 1). Furthermore, Jones and McGillis admit that although the models have much in common, they are divergent in important respects (1976: 412). In particular, correspondent inference theory 'does not explicitly incorporate the impact of information regarding the target person's past behaviour' (1976: 412). I intend, therefore, to complement correspondent inference theory with Kelley's covariation theory, rather than to adopt the uncertain modifications to correspondent inference theory, and attempt to stretch the theory yet further in order to cover neglected aspects of attribution. First, I shall briefly digress and consider similarities between correspondent inference theory and, from within pragmatics, speech act theory, whilst focussing on the analysis of play texts.

3.3.3 Correspondent inference theory, speech act theory and play texts

The focus within classic attribution theory has been on behavioural acts. Within linguistic pragmatics, there has also been a focus on acts, specifically, 'speech acts'. The philosophers Austin (1962) and Searle (1969, 1979) developed the notion that an utterance can be thought of as an attempt on the part of the speaker to 'do' something. A conversational contribution or series of contributions may constitute a particular speech act, such as a statement, a command, a promise, or a curse. The 'illocutionary force' of a speech act can be thought of as the speaker's intention in performing the act in a particular context (see Austin 1962: 98–164, and Leech 1983: 14–15). For a speech act to achieve success certain 'felicity conditions' (Austin 1962: 12–45) need to be in place. For example, the words 'I baptise you [. . .]' for performing an act of baptism cannot be said by anyone in order to successfully baptise an individual, but must be said by a priest. The 'perlocutionary act' refers to the achievement of certain effects (Austin 1962: 99–120), for example, the baptism of an individual (the removal of original sin, becoming a member of the church). As we saw above, acts, intentions and effects lie at the heart of correspondent inference theory. In addition, there is an important similarity between the felicity conditions of speech act theory and the discounting principle of attribution theory (that is, dispositional causes logically should not be inferred when one is under external pressure to produce a particular behaviour): they both refer to a set of contextual factors that, if they are not appropriate, can affect how one understands an act. However, the discounting principle is more limited in scope than felicity conditions, in that researchers have only applied it to situational factors, and not to the form of the act or the thoughts and intentions of the doer.

A number of stylisticians have applied speech act theory to play texts, in order to explain how playwrights have exploited particular speech acts for dramatic effect. I will briefly discuss two of these studies, Hurst (1987) and Lowe (1998), pointing out connections with attribution theory. Hurst (1987) analyses the characters of Ivy Compton-Burnett's *A Family and a Fortune* in terms of their speech acts. In her conclusion she remarks (1987: 356): 'We can see how certain personalities gravitate toward certain speech acts [. . .]'. The idea that 'certain personalities' correlate with certain 'acts' is the basic premise behind attribution theories. Hurst (1987: 345) comments that '[e]arly conversations seem designed so that the reader can pick up the identifying patterns of each individual'. Although she does not provide frequencies, Hurst's (1987) approach is to quantify types of speech act, and then draw conclusions for character. For example, she comments on Aubrey (1987: 346–7):

> Aubrey's most common forms of speech are summary statements. Here [pp. 8–9], although Justine first responds to Clement's outburst, Aubrey quickly enters the fray with the summary, ' "Justine understands Clement." ' The summation does more than get in the last word, for the representative borders on an absolute declaration. Often in the novel, characters who are in subordinate positions, like younger brothers or dependent aunts, express their insecurity by overcompensating in their language and making broad, bold statements.

Hurst (1987) is sensitive to the fact that speech acts are context-bound, and, as a consequence, can reveal character relationships. Focussing on the relationship between Dudley and Edgar, Hurst notes Dudley's preference for 'directives' (such as questions, commands, requests), and draws the conclusions that 'Dudley likes to tell people to tell him to do something, and this constitutes devious manipulation', whereas 'Edgar allows himself to be led along' (1987: 348). Clearly, the directives reflect an asymmetric power relationship. Hurst also focusses on the unexpected (1987: 356):

> When a character performs an unusual speech act or when a response does not fit the expected conventions, that character's speech is thereby emphasized and foregrounded.

Of course, unusual behaviours are also focal points in correspondent inference theory (see 3.3.1 and 3.3.2), since it is argued that unusual behaviours tend to be more informative about a person. In 3.4 and 3.5, I will consider more closely the relationship between attribution theories and foregrounding theory, a theory developed within literary stylistics.

Lowe (1998) conducts a detailed analysis of the speech act of confession in Arthur Miller's play *The Crucible* ([1953] 1986). Based on the Salem witchcraft trials of the seventeenth century (with obvious resonances for the McCarthyism of the 1950s), the play revolves around the issue of whether certain characters are witches or not. Accused of witchcraft, a character could either confess to the charge (in which case they lose their reputations and property, and are imprisoned for life), or deny the charge (in which case they are hanged). Given this context, one can immediately see that any 'confession' will theoretically be subject to a discounting effect: characters do not 'confess' because they are guilty but to save their own lives. Lowe (1998) focusses specifically on the 'confession' of Tituba, a black slave. The key turns are given below (and numbered for ease of reference):

(1) HALE: [. . .]When did you compact with the Devil?

(2) TITUBA: I don't compact with no Devil!

(3) PARRIS: You will confess yourself or I will take you out and whip you to your death, Tituba!

(4) PUTNAM: This woman must be hanged! She must be taken and hanged!

(5) TITUBA: [*terrified, falls to her knees*]: No, no, don't hang Tituba! I tell him I don't desire to work for him, sir.

(6) PARRIS: The Devil?

(7) HALE: Then you saw him! [TITUBA *weeps*] Now Tituba, I know that when we bind ourselves to Hell it is very hard to break with it. We are going to help you tear yourself free —

(8) TITUBA: [*frightened by the coming process*]: Mister Reverend, I do believe somebody else be witchin' these children.

(9) HALE: Who?

(10) TITUBA: I don't know, sir, but the Devil got him numerous witches.

(11) HALE: Does he! [*It is a clue.*] Tituba, look into my eyes. Come, look into me.

[*Here follow 12 turns during which Hale tries to persuade Tituba to open up*]

(12) HALE: When the Devil comes to you does he ever come — with another person?
[*She stares up into his face.*]
Perhaps another person in the village? Someone you know.

(13) PARRIS: Who came with him?

(14) PUTNAM: Sarah Good? Did you ever see Sarah Good with him? Or Osburn?

(15) PARRIS: Was it man or woman came with him?

(16) TITUBA: Man or woman. Was — was woman.

(17) PARRIS: What woman? A woman, you said. What woman?

(18) TITUBA: It was black dark, and I —

(19) PARRIS: You could see him, why could you not see her?

(20) TITUBA: Well, they was always talking; they was always runnin' round and carryin' on —

(21) PARRIS: You mean out of Salem? Salem witches?

(22) TITUBA: I believe so, yes, sir.

[*Now HALE takes her hand. She is surprised.*]

(23) HALE: Tituba. You must have no fear to tell us who they are, do you understand? We will protect you. The Devil can never overcome a minister. You know that, do you not?

(24) TITUBA: [*kisses HALE's hand*]: Aye, sir, oh, I do.

(25) HALE: You have confessed yourself to witchcraft, and that speaks a wish to come to Heaven's side. And we will bless you, Tituba.

(Act one, pp. 46–8)

At various points Austin (1962) stresses that appropriate circumstances must be in place for speech acts to be felicitous, and, more specifically, he mentions 'duress' (1962: 21, 39) as a factor that can cause infelicitous speech acts. As is clear from the threats in turns (3) and (4), Tituba is under duress, and thus her 'confession' is infelicitous. In the terms of the discounting principle, given a contextual factor that can cause the 'confession', one cannot logically infer that the 'confession' reflects something about the speaker, namely, her guilt. Moreover, as Lowe (1998: 135) points out, Tituba's 'confession' is 'unhappy' with respect to other felicity conditions for speech acts. Tituba does not use a form of words associated with 'confessions' (such as 'I confess', 'I admit'), and there is no evidence that Tituba has appropriate thoughts (for example that she believes herself to be guilty).

Lowe (1998: 138) attributes the wilful '(mis)interpretation' of Tituba's conversational acts to the Salem belief system and Tituba's relative lack of status. More generally, Lowe (1998: 130) comments:

> This potential for misunderstanding is often exploited in literary works, and can become a source of entertainment and enjoyment, or sadness, as in this play, when the reader is placed in the privileged position of being able to judge what a speaker means, and to witness the reaction of those who listen.

Indeed, it is not difficult to think of plays where the readers' or audience's appreciation of '(mis)interpretation' or '(mis)attribution' by particular characters is the major source of dramatic interest. Shakespeare's *Othello* is a prime example of this, since the play focusses on Othello's (mis)-attribution of Cassio's and Desdemona's verbal and non-verbal acts (for instance Cassio's supposed gift of a handkerchief to Desdemona, Cassio's supposed confession of adultery). The audience can see that Othello fails to acknowledge the presence of contextual factors which can account for the acts in other ways: he fails to apply the discounting principle. And the reason for this failure? Iago comments: 'his unbookish jealousy must construe / Poor Cassio's smiles, gestures, and light behaviours, / Quite in the wrong.' (IV.i.101–3).

3.3.4 Covariation theory

Jones and Kelley approach attribution theory from opposite ends: Jones is concerned with the validity of inferences regarding the person, and attempts to rule out environmental or situation-based sources of interference; Kelley is concerned with the validity of inferences regarding the environment and attempts to rule out person-based sources of interference (Kelley 1967: 209). Kelley's model is valuable in lending a different and, as I shall argue, complementary perspective to the problem of inferring person or character information. It provides a basis for ruling out contextual causes of behaviour, as well as for reducing the correspondence of unintentional behaviour, an aspect that was inadequately handled in Jones's model.

The main thrust of Kelley's model is not, as was the case with Jones, to find out the precise cause of a particular behaviour, but to decide whether the cause is located in the person or in the environment. This distinction between internal and external causal *loci* was borrowed from Heider (1958). In addition, Kelley distinguishes two types of environmental cause: the entity or event to which a response is made, and the particular circumstances in which a behaviour occurs. We thus end up with three possible attributions: a *person* attribution, a *stimulus* attribution, or a *circumstance* attribution.[2] For example, if you see me laughing, you may decide that it is because I am characteristically a jovial person (a person attribution), or because the film I am watching is very funny (a stimulus attribution), or because I have just consumed a bottle of wine (a circumstance attribution).

Kelley (1967: 194) suggests that the covariation of cause and effect enables us to decide where to make our attribution:

> The effect is attributed to that condition which is present when the effect is present and which is absent when the effect is absent.

This variation can be assessed according to three major dimensions. In the above example, a stimulus attribution (the cause of my laughter lay in the film) would be the case if:

a) I had responded in a *distinctive* way to the film (i.e. I did not laugh at every film I saw),

b) I had responded in a *consistent* way to the film (i.e. I laughed at other times and in other situations), and

c) I had responded in agreement or *consensus* with other persons' responses.

In other words, a perceiver would be in a good position to make a stimulus attribution (to infer that the cause of the laughter lay in the film), if he or she had high *distinctiveness*, high *consistency*, and high *consensus* information. Distinctiveness, consistency, and consensus are briefly defined below:

Distinctiveness: The extent to which the target person reacts in a distinctive way to different stimuli.

Consistency: The extent to which the target person reacts to the same stimulus in the same way at other times and in other situations.

Consensus: The extent to which others react in a similar way to this stimulus.

(adapted from Kelley 1967: 194 and 197)

Different information patterns would lead to different attributions. These are summarised in Table 3.1.

Table 3.1 Information patterns for 3 causal attributions (Orvis *et al.* 1975: 607)

	Information Pattern		
Attribution	Distinctiveness	Consistency	Consensus
Stimulus	High	High	High
Person	Low	High	Low
Circumstance	High	Low	Low

Obviously, the information pattern for a person attribution — low distinctiveness, high consistency, and low consensus — is of particular relevance to this book. In the above example, low distinctiveness would apply if I tended to laugh at all sorts of films. High consistency would apply if I had laughed at that particular film every time I had seen it over the years, and when I had seen it at home on video as well as at the cinema. Low consensus would apply if the other people watching the film with me had not laughed. If observers saw this pattern of information, they would be likely to conclude that I was given to laughter.

3.3.5 Integrating two attribution theories

Adding the notions that we have gained from Kelley's model to correspondent inference theory we can say that a particular behaviour is correspondent to the extent that it is:

1. Free from external pressures.
2. Low in ambiguity, i.e. yields noncommon effects which are few in number.

3. Unusual, i.e. departs from the perceiver's expectations (normative, category-based, or target-based).
4. Part of the following behavioural pattern: low distinctiveness, high consistency, and low consensus.

The integration of the two models works up to a point, but scrutiny of this summary will reveal apparent overlap and contradiction between conditions 3 and 4. Consensus can be happily subsumed within normative and category-based expectations. Distinctiveness and consistency relate to a particular individual's past behaviour and thus *appear* to be subsumed within target-based expectations. This is in accord with Jones and McGillis's integrated framework (1976: 413). Problems arise when we consider that 3 involves behaviour that departs from expectations. This is compatible with low consensus, but not low distinctiveness and high consistency. Low distinctiveness and high consistency imply that a behaviour is perceived to some degree as equivalent to previous behaviours, and thus *conforming* with target-based expectancies, not departing from them. These difficulties will be examined more closely in the sections on foregrounding theory and attribution theories below. I shall argue that in a number of respects foregrounding theory is analogous to attribution theory, and that by investigating this analogy one can gain a better understanding of the relationship between Jones's and Kelley's models. To begin with, I shall briefly summarise foregrounding theory.

3.4 Foregrounding theory

The theory of foregrounding has been a keystone in stylistics and literary theory for the last 30 years. Though rooted in Russian Formalism and the work of the Prague School, its main development came about in the 1960s and 70s, notably through Jakobson (1960) and Leech (1969, 1970, 1985). Foregrounding has been seen as a notion that can help explain the nature of 'literariness', and also guide the interpretation of literary texts.

In visual art the term 'foreground' denotes the elements that achieve salience by standing out in relief against a background. In Formalist literary theory, it is argued that in texts foregrounded elements achieve salience through deviation from a linguistic norm (Mukařovský 1970). Foregrounding involves intentional divergence from what usually happens. The characteristics of such foregrounded elements includes 'unexpectedness, unusualness, and uniqueness' (Mukařovský 1970: 53–4).

For example, in *Antony and Cleopatra* when Antony says, 'Let Rome in Tiber melt' (I.i.33), deviation occurs at a semantic level, since, quite obviously, a city cannot melt. Our attention is captured and we can work to construct an interpretation. In Antony's wish the defeat of Rome is presented as a physical process of liquefaction and dissolving. This is consistent with other foregrounded features in the play that work to enforce this vision of the decay of Rome, of Antony, and, ultimately, of life. Towards the end of the play, Cleopatra's reaction to Antony's death contains a similar semantic deviation: 'The crown o'th'earth doth melt' (IV.xv.63). The firm substance of Antony's life, the symbol of earthly power, now dissolves. These foregrounded features also correlate with lexical foregrounding achieved through neologism. Shakespeare coined his own vocabulary for dissolution: *discandy* (IV.xii.22; III.xiii.165), and *dislimns* (IV.xiv.10). These foregrounded features are interpreted as part of a meaningful pattern. Leech (1985: 50) referred to this type of patterning as 'cohesion' of foregrounding.

Leech drew attention to the two sides of foregrounding: just as you can have deviation through irregularity, so you can also have deviation through regularity. The parallelism of the same kinds of elements where you would normally expect different ones is a type of deviation. Jakobson has argued (1960: 358) that this patterning of equivalences in the syntagmatic chain is the essence of poetic language.[3] Returning to the above example, one can perceive a high degree of regularity in the metrical pattern:

x　　/　　x　/　x　/

Let Rome in Tiber melt

The strict alternation between stressed and unstressed syllables picks this utterance out. It is foregrounded not only against the natural rhythms of spoken English, but also against the immediately preceding lines which contain no such regularity of patterning. This regularity signals the serious nature of what Antony has to say. It foregrounds his first statement of treason.

Antony's line is not only part of a cohesive pattern of foregrounded features, it also exhibits 'congruence' of foregrounding, that is to say, deviations occurring concurrently at different linguistic levels (Leech, 1985: 50). I have already touched on deviations at the levels of semantics and phonology. There is also some degree of syntactic foregrounding. Syntactic rules are violated in that no definite article precedes *Tiber*.

Furthermore, the ordering of this particular clause, with this kind of adverbial falling between subject and predicator, is odd.[4] My guess is that the syntactic construction here was motivated by a desire to form a regular metrical pattern. Whatever the case, the important point here is that foregrounding occurs on a number of levels.

Van Peer (1986) further developed the notion of congruence of foregrounding. In his terminology, Antony's line is a *nexus* of foregrounding. Van Peer (1986) argued that such nodal points will be more foregrounded, other things being equal, than if deviation had occurred at only one linguistic level. An intuitive sense of this can be gained if one attempts to reduce the degree of foregrounding in Antony's line. 'Let Rome melt in the Tiber' is far less striking, and would surely have received less attention than Shakespeare's version.

Leech (1985) distinguishes three types of deviation according to what type of norm is involved. Primary deviation, or external deviation as it is sometimes called (Levin 1965), involves departure from the norms of language as a whole. The semantic deviation resulting from the fact that Rome cannot melt is an example. Secondary deviation involves departure from the norms of literary composition (for example the norms of author or genre). *Antony and Cleopatra*, for example, contains almost exactly double the normal number of scenes in Shakespeare's tragedies.[5] *Antony and Cleopatra* has 45 scenes compared with an average (mean) of 22 for the other tragedies. Furthermore, the variance of this average is relatively narrow, yielding a standard deviation of only 5.15. This secondary deviation is largely the result of the fact that it is the only Shakespearean play in which substantial parts take place in two different continents. By flitting rapidly backwards and forwards from West to East, our attention is constantly drawn to the contrasts between the two worlds: the solid, harsh, cold barrenness of Rome, and the fluid, lush, warm fertility of the East.

Tertiary deviation, or internal deviation as it is sometimes called (Levin 1965), involves departure from the norms created within a text. A good example from *Othello* appears in Leech (1969: 120):

> O, that the slave had forty thousand lives!
> One is too poor, too weak for my revenge.
> Now do I see 'tis true. Look here, Iago;
> All my fond love thus do I blow to heaven:
> 'Tis gone.
> Arise, black vengeance, from thy hollow cell!
> Yield up, O love, thy crown and hearted throne

> To tyrannous hate! Swell, bosom, with thy fraught,
> For 'tis of aspics' tongues!

(III.iii.446–54)

Leech (1969: 119) uses this example to illustrate the effect of 'defeated expectancy', which arises from the 'disturbance of the pattern which the reader or listener has been conditioned to expect'. Here the reader encounters a textually-established norm with regard to the particular verse form, the iambic pentameter. A deviation from this pattern occurs with the two-syllable line "'Tis gone', which is therefore strongly foregrounded. Our attention is drawn to the fact that Othello is making an emotional transition from love to hate. With regard to *Let Rome in Tiber melt*, I have already noted how its highly regular metrical pattern contrasts with the immediately preceding lines. This, of course, is a matter of deviation from an internally established norm.

To summarise so far, foregrounding can be said to result from the occurrence of unexpected regularity (the establishment of patterns) or unexpected irregularity (the breaking of norms). The latter case may involve, as I have shown, different types of norms, such as linguistic norms, generic norms and text-internal norms or patterns. In a recent development of foregrounding theory, it has been pointed out that a further type of deviation results from the breaking of the expectations that readers form on the basis of their general knowledge of the world, or their world schemata (G. Cook 1990, 1994). G. Cook uses the term 'discourse deviation' to refer to the disruption of readers' existing schematic knowledge in their interaction with the language of texts, and particularly literary texts.

One of the main reasons for the success of the notion of foregrounding lies in its relevance to the study of the process of textual interpretation. Leech, and Leech and Short, point out that more interpretative effort is focussed on foregrounded elements, in an attempt to rationalise their abnormality, than on backgrounded elements (Leech 1969: 68, 1981: 7, 1985: 47; Leech and Short 1981: 29). Leech writes:

> In addition to the normal processes of interpretation which apply to texts, whether literary or not, foregrounding invites an act of IMAGINATIVE INTERPRETATION by the reader. When an abnormality comes to our attention, we try to make sense of it. We use our imaginations, consciously or unconsciously, in order to work out why this abnormality exists.

(1985: 47)

Furthermore, van Peer (1986) has provided empirical evidence to sub-stantiate the claim that foregrounded elements are not only psychologically more striking but are also regarded as more important in relation to the overall interpretation of the text.

3.5 Foregrounding theory and attribution theory: Are they analogous?

As I pointed out earlier, the main problem with adding Kelley's model to Jones's is the apparent contradiction between certain aspects of each. How can one explain increased correspondence if, as Jones would have it, behaviour is unusual, departing from a perceiver's expectations, and yet also if, as Kelley would have it, behaviour is seen to some degree as equivalent to previous behaviours, and thus conforming with expectations? The answer, I think, is that they are different sides of the same coin. Jones concentrates on unexpected irregularity and Kelley on unexpected regularity. Both aspects, as we saw with foregrounding theory, result in behaviour that in some sense deviates from a norm and is thus more interpretable, more informative and, in some circumstances, more correspondent.

Jones's argument that correspondence increased when behaviour de-parted from the perceiver's expectations seems analogous to the idea that the salience of foregrounded elements is achieved through departure from a linguistic norm or expectation. Leech's distinction between primary, secondary and tertiary deviation is reflected in Jones's scheme. Primary deviation involves departure from the norms of language as a whole. Departure from normative expectancies involves departure from what the average person would do in a particular situation. Just as the norms of grammar can be broken, so can the norms of social behaviour. Secondary deviation involves departure from the norms of literary group-ing such as author or genre. Departure from category-based expectations involves departure from expectations associated with general groupings in society. Tertiary deviation involves departure from the particular norms created within a text. Departure from target-based expectations involves departure from expectations that one has about a particular person.

Kelley's model considers the similarity of behaviour across different contexts (that is, in response to different stimuli, times, and situations). It is tempting to draw an analogy here with foregrounding through regularity. Parallelism consists of a pattern of equivalent elements that draw attention and attract interpretative effort. Much the same applies to Kelley's consistency condition. With high consistency the target person reacts to the same stimulus in the same way at other times and in other situations. For example, if somebody exhibits agreeable behaviour when confronted with an imposition, this in itself is not diagnostic of that person's personality. But if that person consistently over time exhibits agreeable behaviour when confronted with an imposition whatever the situation, then we have a noticeable and informative pattern from which we may reasonably infer that this person has an agreeable personality.

Leech's notion of cohesion of foregrounding (1985: 50) seems to be analogous to Kelley's distinctiveness condition (the extent to which a target person reacts in a similar way to different stimuli). Both involve the idea of a cohesive interpretative pattern. For example, if I exhibited nervous behaviour such as an unusually high number of non-fluency features (such as pauses, needless repetition, syntactic anomalies), I may be perceived as deviating from normative expectations. But this would not be strongly diagnostic of my personality (that is, yield a correspondent inference), since my behaviour can easily be attributed to circumstance (for example, my mind was engaged on something else). Consistency information to the effect that I regularly produced such nervous behaviour at other times and in other places would strengthen correspondence. In addition, if my hand had been seen shaking, the perceiver would have a cohesive interpretative pattern lending weight to an attribution of nervousness. In other words, the interpretation or attitude inferred from each different behaviour would be similar: we would have low distinctiveness information increasing the correspondence of an attribution of nervousness.

On the whole, attribution theorists have concentrated on non-linguistic behaviour, whereas foregrounding theorists have concentrated on linguistic behaviour. There seems no reason why there should be a division. Wearing no clothes at a funeral would be foregrounded (deviating from normative expectations), as would telling a joke in the same context. The notion of congruence of foregrounding (Leech, 1985: 50) might be extended to non-linguistic behaviour. Wearing no clothes, laughing and telling jokes in an inappropriate situation would produce, in van Peer's (1986) terms, a nexus of foregrounding.

Although the analogy between attribution theory and foregrounding theory can be pushed quite far, there is some difference in that attribution theory is also explicitly designed to take on board aspects of the context in which behaviour occurs. Unexpected behaviour will not necessarily result in a person attribution. For example, if some behaviour is constrained by context, our person attribution will experience a discounting effect, since behaviour can always be perceived as a result of the stimulus or circumstances involved and therefore not diagnostic of the person who produced that behaviour. In other words, foregrounding theory does not contain explicit mechanisms with which to distinguish different types of causal *loci*.

3.6 Attribution theory in practice

So far my discussion of attribution theory has not paid much attention to whether in everyday life people really make attributions at the times and in the ways suggested by the theory. In the next section, I shall examine some of the empirical evidence to see how, if at all, it supports the theory. In the following section, I shall consider the influence of context in making attributions. It should be emphasised that the attribution theories I have examined were developed as theoretical models, or rational baselines, against which one could evaluate real-life occurrences of attribution. There was no expectation on the part of the theorists that there would be a perfect match between theory and empirical data.

3.6.1 When and how does attribution occur?

In section 3.5 I argued that Jones's and Kelley's theories involve deviation from behavioural norms, and are in some respects analogous to foregrounding theory. If this is the case, then attribution should occur when we are confronted with the unexpected. Both Weiner (1985) and Hastie (1984) not only conduct experiments but also collate a considerable amount of empirical evidence to suggest that unexpected or socially negative events (such as failure as opposed to success) tend to elicit a great amount of attributional activity. Hamilton (1988) goes further than Hastie or Weiner in concluding that attribution *only* occurs when inconsistency interrupts routine processing and forces the perceiver to ask the question 'Why?' This evidence is in accord with van Peer's (1986) empirical work on foregrounding theory, which demonstrates that foregrounded elements attract more interpretative effort. However, although the correlation between the unexpected and attribution is clear, what is not so clear is whether attributions do *not* occur if events are expected or if information is consistent. In other words, is attribution part of normal information processing or limited to those points when we require a more conscious, effortful attributional search? Jones argues that part of the problem is how you want to define attribution: should it exclude the easier and more automatic cases of attribution and just be confined to 'deliberate, effortful attempts to answer the question "Why?"' (1990: 75)?

It seems unrealistic to suggest that attribution regularly occurs according to inference based on the assessment and manipulation of all or most of the variables suggested in either Jones's or Kelley's models. An unreasonable amount of cognitive effort would be required. A possible explanation for the occurrence of attribution, I think, and one that accounts for most of the empirical evidence, is that there is a scale. At one end of the scale the kind of careful analysis described in Jones's and Kelley's models takes place; at the other end of the scale we get by with inferences based on limited information and on our past experience. The idea of different inferential paths being taken in attribution is consistent with the view that people take the path of least resistance, in other words, they try to do the least possible amount of mental work that they can get away with in most situations. In Fiske and Taylor's (1984) terms, people are 'cognitive misers'. Kelley's later paper (1973) takes account of this. He suggests that *causal schemas* allow people to make an attribution on the basis of a single observation with no covariation information at all. People develop schemata about the causes of particular effects. For example, success is usually considered the result of ability and effort — internal causes, whereas laughing is considered the result of external causes such as a comedian or a funny film (Baron and Byrne, 1991: 60). Thus we expect a person attribution for success and a stimulus attribution for laughter. A study undertaken by Orvis *et al.* (1975) showed how people used causal schemas to make up for the fact that they only have partial covariation information. If you look at the information patterns given in Table 3.1, you will see that, for example, low distinctiveness information is peculiar to a person attribution. People who only have low distinctiveness information would infer the other information variables consistent with a person attribution, that is to say, low consensus and high consistency. The notion of causal schemata will be of some importance when I consider links with language in 3.7.3 and in Chapter 4.

3.6.2 Attribution and perceiver biases

Both Jones and Kelley argue that the presence of a reason for doing something in the context in which it is done would have a discounting effect on any correspondent inference made on the basis of that behaviour (the discounting principle); on the other hand, the presence of a reason for not doing something in the context in which it is done would have an augmenting effect on any correspondent inference made on the basis of that behaviour (the augmenting principle). Empirical work, however, has suggested that the role played by the context is more complicated than this. It seems that there is a tendency to underestimate contextual factors, so that there are times when the discounting effect is not as strong as the theory suggests it should be.

In a famous experiment, Jones and Harris (1967) asked subjects to evaluate students' attitudes towards Castro after reading essays supposedly written either under conditions of free choice where the student could choose a pro- or anti-Castro slant, or under the constraint of having to write an essay with a particular slant. The results generally supported the theory, in that stronger attitudes were attributed to the students who wrote under conditions of free choice. This was particularly the case for those students who had apparently chosen to write pro-Castro essays. This further supports the theory since at the time a pro-Castro position was neither common nor considered desirable. In other words, a pro-Castro essay departed from normative expectations. However, contrary to the theory, Jones and Harris discovered a very strong tendency for subjects to infer that the students who wrote the pro-Castro essays were really sympathetic to Castro, *even* when they knew that those students had not been free to choose the slant of the essay. This result seems to fly in the face of the rationale behind the discounting principle. If we know that somebody has not freely chosen a topic to debate, that should reduce the correspondence of any inference we try to make about that person on the basis of the topic being debated.

We tend to make correspondent inferences about a person's dispositions on the basis of behaviour in spite of situational constraints. Ross termed this the *fundamental attribution error*: 'the tendency to underestimate the impact of situational factors and to overestimate the role of dispositional factors in controlling behaviour' (Ross 1977: 183). Whether this tendency can be felicitously described as fundamental or whether it is an error has been questioned (for example by Augoustinos and Walker 1995: 71), but the label has stuck. Jones (1990) prefers the term 'correspondent bias', a term that places this tendency amongst the other biases that affect the rational processes of attribution. A good deal of research has substantiated this tendency; as Jones rather enthusiastically puts it, 'Correspondent bias is the most robust and ubiquitous finding in the domain of interpersonal perception' (Jones 1990: 164).

A number of factors contribute to the fundamental attribution error. Heider noted (1958: 54) that behaviour tends to be more salient than other situational factors:

> [. . .] it tends to engulf the field rather than be confined to its proper position as a local stimulus whose interpretation requires the additional data of the surrounding field — the situation in social perception.

This, in a sense, is reflected in the age-old adage that we believe what we see. The salience of behaviour often leads to its acting as an attributional anchorage point from which we can make adjustments according to the situation. The problem is that we often make insufficient adjustment (Tversky and Kahneman 1974; Gilbert and Jones 1986). Another factor contributing to the fundamental attribution error is to do with the fact that act and actor are more automatically seen as a causal unit and that taking account of situational factors seems to require a more complex kind of processing (Gilbert 1989). In addition, there are practical and social reasons for the existence of the fundamental attribution error. Jones (1990: 154) points out that we are socialised towards accepting what other people do at face value. In spite of the fundamental attribution error, most social interactions are not hampered by 'inaccuracies' in attribution. In fact, it may reflect an inferential process that is efficient, freeing cognitive effort, and on the whole accurate (Gilbert 1989).

Apart from the fundamental attribution error, there are other perceiver biases. In particular, the 'actor–observer' bias deserves a mention here. Heider (1958: 157) notes that perceivers tend to make different kinds of attributions according to whether they subsume the role of 'actor' or 'observer'. Jones and Nisbett (1972) label this the 'actor–observer effect' and describe it thus:

> There is a pervasive tendency for actors to attribute their actions to situational requirements, whereas observers tend to attribute the same actions to stable personal dispositions.

> (1972: 80)

In fact, the actor–observer bias contains the fundamental attribution error, since the second half of the actor–observer bias (i.e. observers tend to attribute the actions of others to dispositions) is a statement of the fundamental attribution error. Although a number of studies appear to support the actor–observer bias (for example Nisbett *et al.* 1973; Ross 1977), this work has been challenged (e.g. Augoustinos and Walker 1995: 72–7). However, an interesting group of studies (e.g. Storms 1973; Taylor and Fiske 1975) attempt to explain the actor–observer bias in terms of differences of perspective. Just as Heider's (1958) point above about the salience of behaviour can help explain the fundamental attribution error, perceptual salience can also explain the actor–observer bias. The argument is neatly put by Augoustinos and Walker (see also Fiske and Taylor 1991: 73).

> Observers see the actor acting, but don't see a situation. The actor is salient; the situation is not. Actors, though, don't see themselves acting. They see the situation around them, and are aware of responding to invisible situational forces. Thus, when actors and observers are asked to explain the same event, they give different accounts because different facets of the same event are salient to them.
>
> (Augoustinos and Walker 1995: 82)

I shall return to both the biases mentioned in this section, and in particular to the link with perspective, in section 3.8.2.

3.7 Attribution theory and language

In spite of the fact that the vast majority of attribution experiments have involved subjects reacting to linguistic data, very little research has actually considered the role of language in attributional processes (notable exceptions being Kanouse 1972 and Hewstone 1983). In this section, I will argue that attribution theory connects with a number of areas of linguistic research, notably conversation analysis, pragmatic inferencing and language attitude research.

3.7.1 Conversational action

Antaki, a discursive psychologist (see 2.4.1), has re-assessed some aspects of attribution theory. Antaki (1994) argues for a move away from focussing, as Jones does, on single acts and cognitive matters such as intention to focussing on the dynamics of action itself, and specifically draws on conversation analysis (see section 1.4.3 for a description of

139

conversation analysis). This parallels developments in pragmatics: a movement away from focussing, as for instance Searle (1969) does, on single speech acts and matters of intention to focussing on the dynamics of interaction (see, for example, Thomas 1995). Consider the conversation below:

1) A: You know that film about the Titanic that's on at the moment?

2) B: Yeah

3) A: Do you want to go to see it with me tonight?

4) B: Well . yes . . . but unfortunately I already have made [an arrangement

5) A: [oh that's okay

The first utterance, although said with rising intonation to signal its questioning force, does not function like a simple question. Rather, it seems to be an opening gambit leading up to A's utterance in turn 3, 'Do you want to go to see it with me tonight?' The speech act status of this utterance in turn 3 seems indeterminate: is it an offer, a request, a question? Clearly, speech acts can be performed by utterances working in conjunction with other utterances, and some utterances may be deliberately indeterminate with regard to their speech act force. This kind of strategic building up and strategic indeterminacy is quite typical in contexts where the speaker risks face-damaging refusal.

Furthermore, the conversation analysts would focus in particular on B's utterance in turn 4. Conversation contains regular patterns. Regularities between pairs of utterances ('adjacency pairs') that tend to co-occur (such as question – answer, greeting – greeting, offer – acceptance) result in 'expectations so powerful that they can actually determine meaning' (Antaki 1994: 69). Conversation analysts use the term 'preferred' for structurally unmarked second parts (see Levinson 1983: 332ff on 'preference organization'). B's utterance provides a context for A's utterance in turn 3 and helps determine its meaning. 'Yes' in turn 4 seems to take A's utterance as a question, since it functions as an answer (that is, 'yes, I want to go to see it with you tonight'). However, 'but' expresses the conventional implicature that what follows is going to contradict an expectation that is associated with what proceeds (if A wants to go, they will accept the offer and go). The remainder of B's utterance takes A's utterance as an offer, since it functions as a refusal. Note that the refusal is the unexpected or 'dispreferred' second part to an offer. In fact, the writing was on the wall with the first hedge 'well' and the pauses, since these frequently accompany dispreferred second parts.

Focussing on expectations is, of course, a familiar theme in attribution theory. But Antaki (1994) would argue for much more than this. Note that it is when a conversational expectation is not met that an *explanation* is provided. This explanation proposes a cause for the disruption. Thus, rather than guessing about the inner workings of a subject's mind, the conversation-analytic approach to attribution would suggest that we study the linguistic realisation of attribution-related phenomena. As Antaki (1994: 69) puts it: 'The flag that conversation analysis flies is that the organisation of conversations — what comes after what — is the most direct evidence possible about people's social reasoning.'

I will return to the issue of speech acts and conversation analysis in drama in the following chapters.

3.7.2 Inferencing in a communicative context

I argued in section 1.4.4 that research on language and personality or identity has been dogged by an inadequate view of communicative context. The typical attribution experiment presents subjects with some language (often a vignette) and elicits their reactions to it. Subjects are allowed little or no sense of the producer of the language, and the language is usually stripped of social context. In a richer communicative context a number of factors come into play that are lacking from most attribution experiments. There is empirical evidence that when people overhear language produced in context they: (1) consider the implications for both the target of the language and the speaker of it (in the case of a favourable description, one would take on board the implications for the person being described and the person who produced the description), and (2) consider the social implications of the language in the context in which it is produced (for example an unfavourable description would seem to break a norm of politeness) (see Wyer and Carlston 1994: 67–72, and the references therein). In this section, I shall begin to look more closely at the communicative norms pertaining between speaker and hearer. Chapter 5 is devoted to a consideration of politeness.

There are clear similarities between attribution theory, foregrounding theory and one of the leading theories in pragmatics, Grice's Conversational Implicature (1975). Conversational Implicature is a theoretical notion about the way in which language is used to convey meaning beyond what is actually said. The idea is that in conversation there is a tacit agreement — the Cooperative Principle — to cooperate in the exchange of information (Grice 1975: 45). The constituent maxims of the Cooperative Principle are:

1. Maxim of Quantity: Make your contribution as informative as is required for the current purpose of the exchange; Do not make your contribution more informative than is required.
2. Maxim of Quality: Do not say what you believe to be false; Do not say that for which you lack evidence.
3. Maxim of Relation: Be relevant.
4. Maxim of Manner: Avoid obscurity of expression; Avoid ambiguity; Be brief; Be orderly.

These maxims can be seen as conversational expectations (see, for example, Antaki 1994: 36). There are various ways in which these conversational expectations can be disrupted. By *flouting* them in a blatant manner, a speaker signals that the hearer should work out his or her intended meaning at some level deeper than the surface sense of the utterance. The meaning thus generated is an *implicature*. Let us consider an example:

[In a BBC comedy series, Victor has been buried up to his neck in the back garden by an irate builder. His wife, Margaret, comes out]

> M: What are you doing?
> V: I'm wallpapering the spare bedroom, what the hell do you think I'm doing?
>
> (*One Foot in the Grave*, BBC 12/11/96)

My interpretation of this example might run thus: (1) I recognise that what Victor has said breaks the maxim of Quality, (2) I assume that Victor is being cooperative at a deeper level, (3) I draw the implicature that Victor thinks that Margaret has asked a ridiculous question. This clearly fits foregrounding theory: the hearer's interpretative effort is triggered by deviation from a conversational expectation. Regarding attribution theory, conversational expectations can be seen as part of normative expectations. A flout breaks those expectations, and the hearer attempts to extract causal information — his belief about Margaret's question — in accounting for why conversational expectations are broken.

Maxims can also be obviously but unintentionally broken. Thomas (1995) calls this an *infringement* of a maxim, and attributes the idea to Grice (1981). For example, a public speaker may infringe the Maxim of Quantity in repeating the same point *ad nauseam*, simply because of nerves. Of course, one can still draw an inference (the speaker is nervous), but it is not an inference *intended* by the speaker. Note that this ties in with my discussion in 3.3.2, where I commented that correspondent inferences do not depend upon a particular intention on the part of the actor. A further way in which one might orientate towards the maxims is to break them intentionally but surreptitiously, often with the intention of misleading the hearer. Grice (1975) labelled this a *violation* of a maxim. Lies are obvious examples of violations of the maxim of Quality — we can deliberately misrepresent the truth. Violations by definition do not attract attention in breaking some norm. For their success, they rely on what one might think of as the linguistic equivalent of the fundamental attribution error. In other words, they rely on hearers taking the words of speakers at face value.

I will return to the Cooperative Principle and drama in Chapter 4.

3.7.3 Language attitude research

I introduced language attitude research in 1.4.1. In this approach the focus has been on how certain aspects of someone's language performance trigger beliefs and evaluations in the hearer about that person. Many studies have pursued the idea that certain social or personality aspects are associated with particular linguistic features (see, for example, Giles and Powesland 1975 and Scherer 1979 for reviews). The link with attribution theory is through Kelley's (1973) notion of the causal schema, which was introduced in 3.6.1. Causal schemas contain knowledge about the causes of particular effects. With regard to language, this can be seen as knowledge about links between language and particular attributions. Furthermore, Kelley suggested that causal schemas allow people to make an attribution on the basis of a single observation with no covariation information. This fits the scenario — first impressions of unfamiliar others — pursued in the bulk of language attitude research.

It is worth noting here that the inferential process does not necessarily proceed directly from language to some individual personality feature, but may go via a social category. Some language features are associated directly with personality features. For example, non-fluency features are associated with anxiety (Scherer 1979). Others are associated with a social category, which in turn may be associated with personality features.

The clearest example relates to accent. The particular linguistic features comprising an accent may be associated with particular social categories (such as socio-economic status, place of abode), and these social categories may be associated with particular personality features. Thus, with regard to British accents, 'standard accents usually connote high status and competence; regional accents may be seen to reflect greater integrity and attractiveness' (Edwards 1982: 25). Of course, the inferential link between social categories (in the above case, group membership categories) and personal categories received much discussion in the previous chapter.

The schematic links between linguistic features and either personal characteristics or social categories will be discussed at greater length in Chapter 4.

3.8 Inferring characteristics in plays

In developing and discussing attribution theories, social psychologists have coined elaborate — but often stilted and improbable — anecdotes, vignettes and short stories in order to illustrate their claims, and latterly to test them.[6] The fact that they use these fictional pieces in their work provides some justification for applying their theories to literary texts. In fact, one might view literary texts as providing a vast quantity of 'authentic' data (in the sense of not being contrived for the purpose in hand) for testing and exemplifying attribution theories. Play texts would seem to be particularly ideal, since characterisation here relies mostly on what we can infer from conversational action. Discussing characterisation in drama, Downes (1988: 226) states:

> Characterization essentially involves the manifestation of inner states, desires, motives, intentions, beliefs, through action, including speech acts. We can ask 'why' a speaker said what he did and propose an intentional description as an answer.

Inferring 'why' is very much the business of attribution theory. However, literary texts do have some particular characteristics which need to be borne in mind. In the next section, I consider some of the assumptions which lie behind inferencing in literary texts; and, in the following section, I note some reader manipulations that can be related to attribution theory; and, finally, I return to my investigation of a passage from *The*

Entertainer, in order to examine how readers might extract character information from a play text.

3.8.1 The inferential context

A cautionary note needs to be sounded with regard to any attempt to extend theories developed for real-life people to fictional characterisation. One cannot assume that the characteristics of real people are inferred in exactly the same way as those of literary characters. In particular, two important differences need to be borne in mind. First, character behaviours are complete (see Margolin 1983: 9). A psychologist may study the behavioural patterns of a patient and conclude that it is safe for that patient to be released from an institution, but there is no guarantee that that patient will not turn around and do something completely unexpected. Similarly, in the course of our daily psychological assessment of people we see in the street, colleagues, friends, partners and so on, we can never be absolutely sure that we have a complete set of behaviours diagnostic of personality (although usually we have enough information to make predictions about a person's behaviour that are strong enough for our purposes). Even if the real-world observer, lay or professional, considered the personality of a dead person, and thus a potentially finite set of behaviours, in practical terms it would be impossible to record or observe that person's complete set of behaviours. This is not the case with a literary character, since by reading the whole text we have access to that character's whole life — complete and finite.

A second difference is that character behaviours have greater relevance and significance (see Margolin 1983: 9). An assumption underlying the process of extracting personality information from the behaviours of people we meet is that people act in ways consistent with their personalities. Thus behaviours ought to be diagnostic of personality. However, this assumption is weak. We cannot assume that any particular behaviour will have strong personality significance. The same assumption also underlies the perception of character behaviour, but the particular discourse framework of most literary texts has the effect of lending additional weight to that assumption. As a result of the fact that character interaction may be described as a discourse level embedded within that of the author and reader (see section 1.7.1), we are in a position to make a much stronger assumption that behaviour will be interpretatively significant. Any character behaviour is part of an act of communication between the playwright and the audience/reader, and as such we can assume that character behaviour has additional significance or relevance. This can be explained with reference to relevance theory (Sperber and Wilson 1986). In relevance theory terms, any character behaviour is part of an ostensive act of communication between the author and the reader, and as such 'communicates the presumption of its own optimal relevance' (1986: 158). In other words, we can assume that character behaviour has additional significance or relevance, so that our processing efforts will receive sufficient cognitive rewards.

Let me illustrate with an example. Yesterday, in the process of reversing the car I was driving, I almost ran over my wife who had been standing in my blind spot. Anybody observing the fiasco probably would not conclude much more than that I had not been paying enough attention at that particular moment. What if the same event had occurred in a film? In this case, one may assume that it has greater interpretative significance. Perhaps the driver is clumsy by nature, perhaps the driver's clumsiness will lead to a serious accident, perhaps he is a murderer trying to bump off his wife, and so on. The conversation and actions that take place between characters are designed to be 'overheard' and 'overseen' by the audience: they are part of what the playwright 'tells' the audience. As I have already noted in section 1.7.1, Short (1989: 149) points out that

> the important thing to notice is the general *embedded* nature of drama, because features which, for example, mark social relations between two people at the character level become messages *about* the characters at the level of discourse which pertains between author and reader/audience.

3.8.2 Reader manipulations

Gerrig and Allbritton (1990) use the fundamental attribution error to explain an intriguing literary phenomenon. Why doesn't a predictable plot, such as that of the James Bond books, destroy the reader's interest in the outcomes of events? We know from our knowledge of the plot that the hero will be all right, so why do we entertain doubts and fears that he might not be? They suggest that the fundamental attribution error aids the author in creating

> [. . .] the illusion that even the most formulaic outcomes are brought about — afresh — by the internal properties of characters [. . .] readers are so solidly predisposed to find

the causes of events in the characters rather than in the circumstances that reflection upon the 'formula' plays no role in their immediate experience of the novel: when events can be explained satisfactorily with recourse to dispositions, we have no reason to look elsewhere.

(Gerrig and Allbritton 1990: 382–3)

Of course, this is something of a simplification. One can never know for sure that the hero will be all right until the end of the novel, and often there is some other, less formulaic, plot element at work (Will he fall in love? Will he marry the girl?). The reader may be more involved in the short-term suspense of 'how is he going to get out of this one?', and less concerned with the long-term suspense of 'will he succeed in the end?' Nevertheless, the fundamental attribution error may be a contributory factor in maintaining reader interest. Clearly, further investigative work is needed here.

Another bias which should be mentioned here is the actor–observer bias. As I noted in section 3.6.2, actors tend to attribute their actions to the situation, whereas observers tend to explain others' actions by attributing them to their dispositions. Graumann (1992 for example) is one of the few scholars who have investigated and found evidence for a possible link with linguistic viewpoint. With regard to prose fiction, Pollard-Gott (1993: 506), although offering no supporting empirical evidence, proposed a link with fictional point of view:

> By manipulating point of view and available information, a novel can affect the salience of the various characters and the features of their situations. Increasing the salience of a character's environment or situation will lead the reader-observer to adopt the character's stance to a greater degree and appreciate the myriad mitigating circumstances that seem to govern the character's behaviour.

Put simply, by looking through a character's eyes (including their mind's eye) a reader gets to view the fictional world as if they were that character. Thus, the reader becomes more of an actor in that world than an observer of it.

What are the mechanisms for point of view manipulations in fictional texts? Broadly speaking, there are three areas to consider. We might be brought closer to a character (or character-narrator), if we have:

1) first-person narration, as opposed to third-person;
2) internal narration (i.e. the expression of a character's thoughts and feelings), as opposed to external (cf. Fowler 1986);
3) more direct speech and thought presentation, as opposed to less (cf. Leech and Short 1981).

Let me briefly illustrate with a couple of examples from Andrew Morton's biography of Princess Diana, *Diana: Her New Life* (1995):

> She [Diana] recalls the 'strange look' the Queen Mother fixed upon her during lunch — 'It's not hatred, it's sort of interest and pity,' she reflects as she complains about the mealtimes with the royal family at Sandringham. 'I was very bad at lunch and I nearly started blubbing. I just felt really sad and empty and thought "bloody hell, after all I've done for this fucking family" [. . .]'
>
> (Morton 1995: 44)

> The man [Charles], who from birth had lived on the auto-pilot of duty and an almost other-worldly obligation to the nation, now had to confront the wretched state of his marriage and his impossible relationship with his wife, which had troubled him long before the difficult summer of 1992.
>
> (Morton 1995: 48)

In the first example, we look through Diana's eyes at the Queen Mother; we are brought relatively close to Diana's words through the use of direct speech; and we gain access to Diana's mind's eye via direct report of thought. Through these techniques, the reader is given the viewpoint of an actor, and, as a consequence, is likely to attribute Diana's emotional troubles to the context — the members of the royal family. In the second example, Charles is described almost entirely through external narration, the only clear exception being the narrator's report of an emotional state ('had troubled'). Here then, the reader is given the viewpoint of an observer, and, as a consequence, is likely to attribute Charles's emotional troubles to his character — his excessive sense of duty to the nation.

Of course, point of view manipulations alone are not enough to ensure that a reader adopts the viewpoint of an actor or an observer. It would presumably also depend on whether the reader identified with the character concerned. With regard to the remit of this book, it should be noted that the specific point of view mechanisms discussed above are typical of prose fiction. They do not play an important role in play texts because, generally, drama lacks a narrator. This is not to say that point of view is not an issue in drama, but here it typically involves one character's thoughts and feelings about another character or some other aspect of the fictional world. Whether this kind of point of view manipulates the reader's perceptions in the same way as point of view in prose is an issue that needs to be researched.

3.8.3 Investigating readers' inferences

In the light of the discussion in this chapter, I will now consider the operation of attribution theory and foregrounding theory in the interpretation of an extract taken from John Osborne's play *The Entertainer* (1957). Thus, I return to the study I introduced in 1.2 and 2.6. Specifically, I will examine the second task of the questionnaire designed to investigate the role of the text in the characterisation of Billy and Jean:

> (2) Why did you decide to describe **Billy/Jean** as you did in question 1? Mark on your text on the preceding page aspects that relate to your impression and add relevant comments on the text itself and/or in the space alongside the text.

In the process of doing this, I also aim to provide a demonstration analysis for the discussion in this chapter.

The segments of text I wish to focus my analysis on are listed below. These are segments which half or more of my twenty informants marked as relating to their impression of Billy. (The number of markings are indicated in brackets, as are the text line numbers. The segments are presented in the order in which they occur).

1. Can't get any peace in this damned house (x 15) (line 5)

2. Can't even read the paper in peace (x 15) (lines 11–12)

3. I wondered who the hell it was. (x 10) (line 24)

4. I'd just sat down to read the evening paper (x 10) (line 30)

5. bloody farm-yard (x 14) (line 31)

6. Bloody farm-yard (x 11) (line 33)

7. Some black fellow (x 12) (lines 35–6)

8. I'd only just sat down to read the evening paper (x 12) (line 46)

9. give your Grandad a kiss (x 14) (line 52)

10. it's nice to see you, my darling (x 13) (line 55)

Segments 1 and 2 and segments 4 and 8 form close lexical and syntactic parallelisms, and are thus foregrounded. Moreover, all four of these segments have the force of the speech act of complaining (as, in fact, does segment 3). Billy's behaviour is highly foregrounded: it is unexpectedly regular. It yields high consistency information.

What character inference does this unexpected behaviour trigger? Wierzbicka (1987: 241–3) suggests that the meaning of the speech act verb of complaining is as follows:

I say: something bad is happening (to me)
I feel something bad because of that
I say this because I want to cause someone to know about it
and to do something because of that that would cause me to
feel better.

Wierzbicka goes on to suggest that '*Complaining* is often regarded as an action which is not particularly dignified, because it involves something akin to feeling sorry for oneself' (1987: 241). It seems reasonable to suppose that Billy's pattern of complaint triggered the inference of negative characteristics, such as 'grumpy' and 'irritable', the two most frequent personal descriptors (see 2.6.2).

Segments 3, 5, and 6 have a regular pattern: they all contain mildly taboo words. It is quite possible that such words are striking against the frequency norms of written play texts, rather than what might actually be said in informal real-life contexts, where mild taboo words are common. However, this is an empirical question that has as yet not been addressed. Whatever the case, my informants frequently identified them as striking, and four informants added a note that they were taboo. Taboo words add a note of disharmony, they break the expectations of 'good' or 'clean' language. These words would contribute to an explanation of descriptors such as 'grumpy' and 'irritable', and, more particularly, 'prone to swearing mildly' (x 2), 'offensive', 'aggressive', and 'gruff'. It is also worth bearing in mind that taboo words are possible indicators of emotional state (and this is an idea that I shall return to in 4.4.3.3).

Thus, the emotional state descriptors 'feels oppressed', 'frustrated', 'miserable', 'unsatisfied' might have been triggered, at least in part, by Billy's taboo words.

Segment 7, *Some black fellow*, was identified as striking. For people who have a non-racist ideology, the expression of a racist attitude conflicts with their attitude schemata (see 2.4.2 and 2.4.5). In this sense, Billy deviates from normative expectations. Of course, it is also possible that some readers underlined this segment because they like to be *seen* as having a non-racist ideology. What character inference does this unexpected behaviour trigger? Eight informants indicated that this segment related to one or more of the negative characteristics 'prejudiced', 'bigot', or 'racist'. The point to note here is that we are beginning to acquire low distinctiveness information for Billy. Billy exhibits intolerance across various stimuli. He reacts in similar ways to the arrival of Jean and the presence of a black man upstairs.

So far we have a high consistency and low distinctiveness information pattern for Billy. This is consistent with the information pattern for a person attribution (see Table 3.1). Thus it is possible to make a reasonably strong correspondent inference that Billy is dispositionally intolerant.

Segments 9 and 10, the only parts of the dialogue to trigger positive characteristics of Billy, represent a deviation from the pattern of negative behaviours Billy has engaged in, and thus they are foregrounded. Here, there is deviation from category-based expectancies, because our impression of Billy has, until here, largely been based on schematic knowledge about grumpy old men, and to a lesser extent target-based expectancies, because it is a deviation from the specific detail of the pattern set up by Billy's behaviour. The positive aspects of segments 9 and 10 clash with expectations generated from this knowledge. A number of informants perceived the clash and undertook much interpretative work in order to try to incorporate the positive elements of Billy into their overall impression (for example by suggesting that he had a positive personality underneath a negative surface).

Turning to the character Jean, the most salient feature of her discourse is her apologies. In my informant questionnaire Jean's apologies attracted more comment than any other linguistic feature:

Informant 4:   apology even though no real fault

Informant 6:   apology — part of persistence

Informant 8:   keeps being apologetic

Informant 9:   multiple apologies

Informant 10:   apology–apology–apology–apology   persistence of Jean's apologies suggestive of apologetic trait

Informant 13:   apologises even though she doesn't appear to have done anything wrong

Informant 19:   repeatedly apologises to Billy

Just as the speech act of complaint played an important role in Billy's characterisation, so the apology is important for Jean. Wierzbicka suggests that 'the person who *apologizes* acknowledges that he has caused something to happen that is bad for the addressee' (1987: 215). Jean's visit has indeed caused disturbance for Billy, but this is more an unfortunate effect rather than a sought-for result. This reasoning probably underlies informant 4's comment above that the disturbance is not really Jean's fault. The augmenting principle — the notion that reasons for not doing something can enhance reasons why we go ahead and do something — is relevant here. Jean apologises even though it is not clear that she should.

As with Billy's complaints, informants pointed to the fact that Jean apologises with unusual regularity. Her apologies form a foregrounded pattern — they yield consistency information. Informants 6, 8, and 10 also note Jean's persistence. This is particularly salient because of Billy's reaction to her apologies and generally polite behaviour:

Informant 4:   ignores apologies

Informant 10:   Jean's repetition of polite questions is also evidence of her patience in the face of Billy's failure to answer

Informant 11:   considerate, polite, deferential — the latter because he is impolite

Again the augmenting principle is relevant here. Jean apologises and is polite in spite of Billy's behaviour, and this has the effect of making her seem all the more apologetic and polite.

Although no informant explicitly comments on it, it is interesting to note that Billy's complaints and Jean's apologies are related in terms of conversational organisation: they form an adjacency triple. Edmondson (1981: 280), discussing the speech act or illocution of the apology, writes that

[. . .] the most predictable function of this illocution in discourse is that it counts as an attempt on the part of the speaker to cause the hearer to withdraw a preceding COMPLAIN: it is an attempt to restore social harmony. In the case that the APOLOGY is accepted (I propose the term *Satisfy* as the relevant interactional move), then the COMPLAIN is no longer a valid focus for talk — the exchange initiated by the COMPLAIN is 'closed' by the illocution by means of which the APOLOGY is accepted or Satisfied. This illocution will thus be what I shall call a FORGIVE.

Billy does not accept Jean's apologies, but instead issues further complaints. The result is a recurring pattern of complaint (lines 5 and 11–12), apology (line 18), complaint (line 24), apology (line 25), complaint (line 28), apology (line 29), complaint (lines 30 and 46), apology (line 47). Billy's constant non-acceptance of Jean's apologies has the effect of making the complaint, the apology, and the interaction between them highly salient in this passage. This salience can be explained by reference to the augmenting principle: Billy complains in spite of Jean's apologies. This recurring sequence is brought to a close when Billy says *give your Grandad a kiss* (line 52). This functions as an acceptance of her apology: she is forgiven.

In sum, this discussion shows that attribution theory can act as an explanatory framework for readers' character inferences. Moreover, it is interesting to note that many of those inferences — specifically, correspondent inferences — involved conversational acts. Thus, for example, the label 'apology' was frequently applied to Jean's conversation, and the label 'apologetic' to her character; and the absence of expected conversational acts led to attributional work. Also, politeness issues — Billy's offensive use of language, Jean's defensive use of language — clearly lay at the heart of this passage. Of course, all this is not to deny that other issues may arise in other texts, but I would suggest that my work here provides some useful pointers for future research.

3.9 Conclusion

The basic notion I have pursued is that at some points behaviour arises as a result of a person's (or character's) dispositional make-up: points where in theory we can make a correspondent inference. By drawing an analogy with foregrounding theory, I have argued that the two classic attribution theories could be reconciled within a framework of deviation from expectations. Jones highlights the importance of behavioural irregularity, behaviour that deviates from category, target, or normative expectations; Kelley highlights the importance of behavioural regularity, behaviour that is in some sense parallel (that is, yields high consistency information). I also noted how in Kelley's theory low distinctiveness seems analogous to the idea of congruence of foregrounding. Furthermore, there is empirical evidence that Jones's and Kelley's models can be integrated, since attribution seems to occur mostly when we encounter the unexpected. It is at these points that we are likely to spend more cognitive effort in making an attribution search, whilst at other points we can short-circuit the attribution process in using causal schemas. With respect to context, Kelley's theory is stronger as it focussed on sequences of behaviour and their relationship with the context. Both Jones and Kelley highlight the discounting and augmenting effects of context, but even here a more sophisticated account is needed. Empirical evidence has shown that people do not always follow the logic of the theory. In particular, we have a tendency to overlook contextual factors, a phenomenon that has been termed the fundamental attribution error.

I argued that some of the basic ideas in attribution theory connect with areas of language research, notably with speech acts, conversation analysis, Grice's conversational implicature, and language attitude research. I will pursue all of these areas further in the next chapter, where I focus on the textual side of characterisation. I argued that attribution theory can provide insights into how characterisation works in literary texts, though I stressed that literary texts have particular discoursal and linguistic features that must be borne in mind. Finally, I investigated my questionnaire data, in order to gain some insight into how readers might have gone about extracting character information from a play text. Here, I demonstrated the power of attribution theory as a descriptive and explanatory framework. Of course, further empirical work is needed to fully assess these arguments, and to investigate other characters, other texts, and other text types.

Notes

1   Throughout this book I shall use the term *disposition* in the way it is used in social psychology, where it is a general term covering a person's relatively stable characteristics (for example, traits, abilities, values).

2   It is clear that Kelley's model has three attribution *loci*. What is not so clear is the exact labels for these. Kelley consistently uses 'person' (Kelley 1967, 1973), although other commentators have used the term 'actor' (Zebrowitz 1990; Orvis *et al.* 1975). Kelley uses 'stimulus', but also 'entity' and 'thing' (Kelley 1967, 1973), and other commentators have used the terms 'event' (Baron and Byrne 1991), or 'target' (Zebrowitz 1990; Orvis *et al.* 1975). Kelley (1967, 1973) uses the term 'circumstance', as indeed do most other commentators. What this term covers is not spelt out. Kelley seems to use 'circumstance' primarily to cover contextual factors that are transient and/or affect the way we interact with the stimulus. Other commentators seem to use it to cover any contextual factor.

3   Of course, the idea that this patterning is a distinctive feature of 'poetic' language has been challenged (for example, see Werth 1976).

4   Needless to say, these were also syntactically odd compared with the norms of Early Modern English.

5   I take as 'tragedies' those plays that are listed as such in the First Folio (1623). In addition, I have included *Troilus and Cressida*, partly because the Folio's editors had originally intended it to be amongst the tragedies (see Alexander 1985: xxv).

6   See Jones and Davis (1965: 230–2) for a good example of this.

FURTHER DIRECTIONS AND EXERCISES

1. Jokes

Characterisation is a crucial part of most jokes. A large set of jokes involve prototypicality distortions (see 2.5.2). Consider the following example:

> You know, there was one time when I would have cut my throat if it wasn't for my mother-in-law.
>
> How was that?
>
> She was using my razor.

This is one of the many 'mother-in-law' jokes. On the face of it, a mother-in-law is a social role, specifically, a kinship role. These jokes typically involve an exaggeration of a schematic link between the social role category and a personal category, that of being domineering. In this particular joke, the mother-in-law has assumed the characteristic 'domineering' to the extent that her gender is challenged: she engages in a male activity. Similarly, there are many jokes that involve prototypicality distortions of schematic links relating to particular group memberships (such as the Irish and stupidity, the Scots and meanness). Of course, all these examples clearly illustrate the connection between social schemata and ideologies. As I noted in section 2.4.5.1, social schematic links such as these represent evaluative beliefs and constitute what van Dijk (1987, 1988) refers to as 'attitude schemata'. The underlying similarities in attitude shared by a social group towards a set of social cognitions collectively constitute an ideology. The social schemata exploited in the jokes mentioned here are part of sexist or racist ideologies, which is why they are offensive to readers not sharing those ideologies.

Another common strategy used in jokes is dramatic recategorisation (see 2.5.5). Consider the following joke:

'Is the doctor at home?' the patient asked in his bronchial whisper. 'No,' the doctor's young and pretty wife whispered in reply. 'Come right in.'[1]

In the first sentence, the social role labels 'doctor' and 'patient' trigger particular categories for the participants. The category 'patient' is also reinforced by the participant's behaviour: 'bronchial whisper'. More-over, the reader probably constructs an event representation such that the patient is seeking help from the doctor for a chest problem. In the second sentence, the information that the doctor's wife is 'young' and 'pretty', and the fact that she 'whispered' too, whilst not inconsistent with the categories we have activated, does not fit them. On the other hand, given the discourse structure of the joke (which would be the same as the canonical form for drama), the reader can assume that these details will have some relevance at some point. The third sentence, 'Come right in', is inconsistent with the model we have constructed so far: if the patient is seeking help from the doctor but he is not at home, there is no point in telling the patient to come in. The solution is to construct a different event, that of an illicit affair, and to recategorise the participants as lovers.

Make a collection of jokes (or find a published collection), and address the following questions: (1) what social categories are involved? (2) what schematic links are exploited? (3) what ideologies are involved? (4) can the joke's humorous potential be explained in terms of a schematic effect, such as prototypicality distortion or recategorisation?

2. Adverts

Characterisation is often exploited in adverts. Indeed, some TV adverts are like mini-plays, and some have fictional characters that appear across a series of adverts in the manner of a TV soap (an example is the Nescafé Gold Blend series). Some would argue, however, that a 'non-literary' discourse type such as advertising tends to relate to schemata in a different way from 'literary' discourse types. As I pointed out in 2.5.4, Cook (1994: 195) argues that 'literature' is 'often primarily schema-refreshing', that is to say, it challenges readers' schemata and results in the destruction of old schemata, the creation of new ones, or new connections between schemata (1994: 191ff.). Adverts, according to Cook, tend to preserve or reinforce world schemata, including those concerning people (see Cook 1994: 193, and also his analyses of adverts on pages 109–18 and 161–7). In my view, Cook's notion of schema refreshment does not square with much of the evidence attested in cognitive psychology. It is unlikely that schemata change in the light of reading a schema-challenging text. Schemata are probabilistic structures: a schema-challenging text can always be seen as an exception. What of the issue that adverts tend to preserve or reinforce schemata? My analysis of the Sanatogen advert suggested that we ended up with a piecemeal impression of Voice A, or, in other words, an impression that was not category-based (see 2.4.7). However, Cook (1994) is careful only to claim a tendency for the literary/non-literary distinction, so the Sanatogen advert could simply be an exception.

Collect some adverts (you could, for example, record all the TV adverts for one particular evening). Discard those that contain no or minimal characterisation (such as a picture of the product and a voice-over). Describe your impressions of the characters. What social schemata are activated (see 2.4.4)? Thinking in terms of the impression formation (see 2.4.7), do your impressions experience (1) confirmatory categorisation, (2) recategorisation (and if so, through accessing a sub-category or switching entirely to another category), or (3) piecemeal processing? Clearly, if piecemeal processing predominates, then you have some tangential support for Cook's hypothesis. Also, note interesting prototypicality and possibility distortions.

3. Personal adverts

Personal adverts are a prime source of self-characterisation data. My analysis of a personal advert in section 2.4.6 demonstrated how my framework can be used to (a) analyse the social categories people place themselves in, and (b) explain certain inferences. Given the space restrictions imposed on these adverts, it is not surprising that the self-presentations are so heavily category-based: the reader can use shared category knowledge to fill in the detail. We also need to keep in mind the pragmatic context of the advert. Compare these two adverts (both from *The Independent: The Weekend Review* 31/7/99):

> Lively, attractive, outgoing, intelligent, 26, 5′4″, slim, blonde, seeks attractive, intelligent male, 24–35, 5′7″+, slim/medium build, N/S, with GSOH, who enjoys life.[2]

> Not-so-old grey mare, wishes to team up with thorough-bred stallion and kick over the traces before being put out to grass for well-earned retirement. Newmarket.

The pragmatic problem confronting the advertiser is how to make the highest possible claims for yourself without attracting negative attributions of boasting or immodesty. A general politeness norm is to be modest (see Leech 1983). Politeness is, of course, contextually sensitive. One might assume that the personal advert is a context where the modesty norm is suspended, since it is recognised that the purpose of the genre is to sell yourself. However, the fundamental attribution error would suggest that such contextual factors tend to be overlooked. Immodesty might be an issue for the first advert above, where the self-presentation consists of a string of positive attributes (even here her age and height are in areas which are generally positively evaluated). The second advert takes a rather different approach. The advertiser uses a possibility distortion to characterise herself: she becomes a communicating horse, and uses this as the basis for a complex extended metaphor. Note that even the advertiser's address, Newmarket, is part of her strategy, since Newmarket is home to one of the most famous racecourses in Britain. This advertiser *demonstrates* the lively intelligence claimed by the first advertiser. The reader can make an attribution on the basis of her linguistic behaviour. I will discuss the explicit/implicit presentation distinction exemplified in these two adverts further in Chapter 4.

Collect some personal adverts. One idea might be to compare personal adverts designed for readerships of different ages. Consider: (1) the kind of social categories used (see 2.4.4), (2) what aspects might be filled in by category-based inferencing (see 2.4.5.1 and 2.4.6), and (3) how the advertiser relates to the pragmatic context of the advert.

4. Newspapers

The representation of people in newspapers has received much attention (for example Fowler 1991: ch. 6). As with other text-types such as adverts, restrictions of space mean that economies are often sought via a category label. But the choice of category label is, of course, crucial, since (a) people can infer the social schematic links that are tied to the label, and (b) it requires cognitive effort to move away from a category-based impression, and people often fail to make sufficient adjustment (Tversky and Kahneman 1974; Gilbert and Jones 1986). As a consequence, the power of writers and editors 'in facilitating and maintaining discrimination against "members" of "groups" is tremendous' (Fowler 1991: 94). For example, Fowler's (1991: ch. 6) analysis of a number of newspapers suggests that men are typically identified by categories associated with power, whereas women are identified according to domestic roles or sexual categories (that is, appearance features). Undoubtedly, this is generally true, though it is worth bearing in mind that (a) different newspapers exhibit somewhat different patterns, and (b) the topic of the news report can affect the category labels chosen. For example, a feature of *The Mirror* is to use domestic role labels in cases where the subject of the story has died, whether that subject is male or female. Often these are used in the title, for example, DAD KILLS WIFE THEN DIES ON RAIL LINE (*The Mirror* 10/8/99). The category labels position the killing within the family unit and also allow the inference that a child (or children) has lost its parents. All this fits the tabloid's goal of dramatising the story.

Of course, newspapers can exploit many other techniques for representing people, including point of view. As I mentioned in section 3.8.2, point of view might be linked to the actor–observer bias: an internal point of view is more likely to result in contextual explanations for behaviour, whereas an external point of view is more likely to result in dispositional explanations for behaviour. Writers and editors may bias their readers simply by — for example — using direct speech to represent some participants, and narration or indirect forms of speech for other participants.

Collect some newspaper data. You could consider setting up a comparison between different types of newspaper. Consider the social category labels used to present individuals (you may wish just to focus on people as they are presented in titles and the first sentences of reports). Are particular types of label used for particular groups? What schematic inferences do these labels allow? What are the implications of the labels in terms of ideology? What factors seem to influence the writers'/editors' use of particular labels? Also, consider the presentation of people in the body of newspaper reports. Can you identify point of view techniques (in particular, the use of speech report) that may bias the readers?

Notes

1   This example is discussed by Raskin (1985: 32). My thanks to Moeko Okada for bringing it to my attention.
2   'N/S' = non-smoker; 'GSOH' = good sense of humour.

PART TWO

CHARACTERISATION AND THE TEXT

CHAPTER 4

TEXTUAL CUES IN CHARACTERISATION

4.1 Introduction

In this chapter and the next, I turn my attention to bottom-up or data-driven aspects of characterisation — the textual cues that give rise to information about character. In other words, I focus on the surface structure and textbase boxes in Figure 1.1. Two literary researchers, Rimmon-Kenan (1983: 59–70) and Pfister (1988: 124–6, 183–95), produce 'checklists' of textual features or techniques that they consider important in characterisation. Although both lists are a valuable starting point, neither supplies much by way of specific detail, or justifies why particular features were chosen and others not. This latter criticism is crucial, because, theoretically, any textual cue can yield character information in a particular context. If a valuable 'checklist' is to be produced, we need some principled way of selecting and justifying what goes in it. In this chapter, I aim not only to construct a more comprehensive and more detailed checklist, but also to (1) relate textual features, where possible, to research on language attitudes (see 1.4.1 and 3.7.3), and (2) show, through mini-analyses, the relevance of particular features for characterisation in plays. Additionally, I aim to shed some light on Shakespeare's characterisation techniques.

The link with language attitudes research builds in particular on an idea raised in the last chapter (3.7.3), where I suggested that people avoid much cognitive work in deciding which attributes are associated with a particular linguistic cue by relying on their schematic knowledge — specifically, their knowledge of causal schemas. For example, conversational interruptions are strongly associated with power and aggression (Robinson and Reis 1989). In describing these schematic associations between communicative behaviour and character, I shall draw upon research which has tried to correlate certain cues with certain characteristics. However, we need to bear in mind that this research concentrates almost exclusively on (1) perceptions in first encounters, and (2) the role of real-life speech. Research into the relationship between written language, including that of fictional texts, and character is virtually non-existent. However, it is improbable that when we interpret fictional texts we switch off the interpretative apparatus we employ for real-life discourses. Simpson (1998: 41) forcefully makes this point:

> [. . .] drama dialogue can only be accessed through its relationship to the social context outside the play-text [. . .] the norms, values and modes of conduct which regulate how 'real' people organize their linguistic behaviour form the basis for interpreting the speech and action of the fictional characters in the world of a play.

One further cautionary note: it cannot be assumed that the schemata suggested by contemporary research necessarily apply in all cultures and all periods — an important point to bear in mind, given that many of my examples will be drawn from Shakespeare's plays.

The organisation of this chapter is inspired by distinctions made in Pfister (1988: 124–6). After some preliminaries, I consider *explicit* characterisation cues, where we find characters explicitly presenting themselves or others — that is, making character statements about themselves or others. Then in the bulk of the chapter I discuss *implicit* characterisation cues, where we have to infer (via causal schemas, for example) character information from linguistic behaviour. Finally, I look at *authorial* cues, where character information comes relatively directly from the author, as in the case of stage directions, for instance. Of course, this kind of direct authorial (or narratorial) character information would be even more common in narrative description in novels, particularly in third-person narration.

4.2 Preliminaries

Two areas need some brief examination before we embark on this discussion. We need to consider (1) the relationship between form and function in the context of impression formation, and (2) the concept of 'idiolect' and how it is realised in different media.

4.2.1 Form, function and context

Studies in language and gender provide some valuable insights, and indeed caveats, for the study of language and character. As I noted in section 1.4.2, Robyn Lakoff's (1975) hypothesis that particular linguistic features (such as tag questions, hedges) characterise 'women's language' was criticised for lacking an empirical basis. This gave rise to many quantitative studies designed to establish whether there were 'real' differences between men's and women's language (see, for example, Crosby and Nyquist 1977; Dubois and Crouch 1975; Shimanoff 1977; Steckler and Cooper 1980). However, these studies have been beset with methodological problems, including the difficulty (impossibility?) of isolating the variable of 'sex' (understood as a biologically determined category) from other contextual variables such as status, and the difficulty in selecting samples of men and women who are comparable in terms of social background. Furthermore, some empirical studies have tended to focus on matters of form, and pay insufficient attention to function. For example, a number of researchers have undertaken empirical studies on hedges, such as 'I think', 'sort of', and 'well' (for example Crosby and Nyquist 1977; McMillan *et al.* 1977; O'Barr and Atkins 1980). Later work has pointed out that in this research there has been an over-reliance on form, and insufficient attention has been given to function and context (see for instance Cameron *et al.* 1989; Holmes 1995). In particular, whether one labels a certain form as having a downtoning function or a boosting function is very much dependent on the context. Holmes's (1995: 92–5) discussion of *I think* makes this especially clear. Most researchers, including Lakoff (1975: 54), have treated *I think* as a clear-cut example of a word which always has a downtoning function. Holmes argues that it can also have a boosting function, as in the following examples:

> *Male committee convenor in radio interview*
>
> Personally I think you can't sustain that position for long
>
> *Female member of a lobby group in radio interview*
>
> I think Mrs McDonald would agree with me (*where interviewer has suggested she wouldn't*)

> (Holmes 1995: 95)

Here 'I think' boosts a disagreeing proposition: it explicitly puts the weight of the high status participants behind what they say.

This discussion raises a number of issues that are also pertinent to the study of language and characterisation. Firstly, we must be wary about assuming that people's linguistic stereotypes or causal schemas, such as

Lakoff's 'women's language' hypothesis, have empirical validity. This is not to say, of course, that they are any less important in forming an impression of a person or, indeed, character. Secondly, identifying which characteristic correlates with a particular linguistic feature is problematic, since some characteristics may be conflated or confused with other characteristics (such as sex and status). Thirdly, the discussion of function and context illustrates that we have to move beyond the simplistic 'X linguistic feature = Y personality feature' equation which has bedevilled more traditional language attitudes research. What a particular form *means* in one context may differ from what it means in another.

Some of these issues account for why in Chapter 5 I consider characterisation in relation to politeness theory, a theory which attempts to relate linguistic features, function and context.

4.2.2 Idiolect, dialect and different media

'Idiolect' is usually taken to be a person's total, individual linguistic thumbprint. For example, when my father telephones me, he never identifies himself. However, within a few words of speech, I can invariably identify him on the basis of his vocal characteristics. 'Dialect' is usually taken to be the linguistic thumbprint of a particular group of people (or speech community). Traditionally, the dialects that have received most attention are regional (the dialect spoken by the people of a particular geographical area) and social (the dialect spoken by the people of a particular social group). The term dialect refers to a variety of language characterised in terms of pronunciation, grammar and lexis; the term 'accent' can be understood to refer to a sub-set of dialect in that it refers to a variety of language characterised in terms of pronunciation only. The dialects one speaks are also part of one's idiolect. For example, part of my father's idiolect are the dialects of a middle-class man living in the south of England. I pointed out in section 2.4.4 that people frequently perceive others as members of social groups rather than as individuals. Dialects, then, are going to be of some importance in this chapter.[1]

In this chapter, I will discuss the dialectal and idiolectal features of characters in play texts, in other words, in writing posing as speech. This means that any dialectal or idiolectal features are restricted to the visual features of writing. This raises a number of issues. Consider the limitations of writing. I recognise my father on the basis of vocal characteristics such as pitch and voice quality, but these characteristics could not be rendered — certainly not precisely — in writing. (If I read 'Hello, is it a good moment to speak?' out of the blue, I would be clueless about the identity of the speaker.) Clearly, writers must rely on other linguistic means for characterisation in texts. Another issue is that of accent. English spelling is not up to the job of presenting different accents accurately. Consider this advertising slogan: 'Yuvgoat taethinko' yerinsides aswell.' When I have shown this to Malaysian students, they have neither known how to pronounce it, or what accent it is supposed to represent. The clue, in fact, is in the accompanying picture of high-land spring water: the spelling reflects the accent of a Scottish speaker. This is all part of the natural, rustic image sought by the brand. Students from the United Kingdom, however, are usually able to guess the accent of the speaker before they see the picture. Clearly, they have know-ledge about spelling conventions for regional accents. It is possible that some speakers may recognise *tae* as the written Scottish dialectal form of the preposition 'to'. In addition, the perceived degree of deviation from spelling norms suggests that this is a highly marked regional accent. Knowledge of accents in the British Isles could produce an inference that the accent concerned was that of a Scottish speaker, since, broadly speaking, the further one is from London, the more marked the accent.

This discussion alerts us to some of the issues that permeate this chapter. We need to remember that writers are limited by the medium they are communicating in. They may utilise conventionalised ways of presenting the dialectal features of speech in writing, and they may stop short of systematic accuracy, relying on the readers' knowledge of accents and dialects to 'fill in the gaps'. Above all, we need to remember that the norms of writing are at issue. As Hughes (1996: 96) points out: 'if a writer chooses to be "realistic", the reader automatically takes this to be a cue that the speaker is abnormal in some way'. Some of the specific issues raised in this section will be pursued further in 4.4.5, concerning dialects.

4.3 Explicit cues: Self-presentation and other-presentation

Self-presentation occurs when a character or person provides explicit information about him or herself, and other-presentation occurs when a character or person provides explicit information about someone else. Perhaps the best example of a text-type involving self-presentation is a personal advertisement (see 2.4.6 and Further Directions and Exercises fol-lowing Part One, pages 158–9), and a good example of other-presentation is a job reference. However, the validity of presentation may be affected by strategic considerations. For example, if a person is at a job interview or in the presence of somebody they are attracted to, they are more likely to emphasise their most positive facets and obscure their negative ones. We rarely gain undistorted information about other people through self-presentation, since self-presentation is inevitably oriented towards others (except for such private forms of communication as writing a diary). As a result, in deciding what a character or person is like, the discounting principle (see 3.3.1) often comes into operation: we must discount aspects of self-presentation that are likely to be motivated by strategic reasons. In plays, however, particularly Shakespearean plays, a soliloquy or aside offers the possibility of self-presentation which is relatively free from strategic inter-character effects. For other-presentation we must similarly pay attention to discounting effects. For example, someone might (unprofessionally!) write a bad reference for someone because of a personal vendetta. If one knew about the vendetta, it should logically discount the characterisation given in the reference.

I shall begin by considering the self-presentation of Shakespearean characters when other characters are present, and then move on to self-presentation when other characters are absent. Finally, I turn to other-presentation.

4.3.1 Self-presentation in the presence of other characters

Doran (1976), discussing Shakespeare's language, touches on the self-presentation of Cleopatra and notes her progression 'from the deviant roles of *whore* and *man* to acceptance of her womanhood and humanity', and to her 'final assertion of dignity through her inherited title of *queen* and her achieved title of wife to Antony' (Doran 1976: 162). These are among the quotations she uses to justify her claims:

> Broad-fronted Caesar,
> When thou wast here above the ground, I was
> A morsel for a monarch;

(I.v.29–31)

> A charge we bear i' th' war
> And, as the president of my kingdom, will
> Appear there for a man.

(III.vii.16–17)

No more but e'en a woman, and commanded
By such poor passion as the maid that milks
And does the meanest chares.

(IV.xv.73–5)

Show me, my women, like a queen. Go fetch
My best attires. I am again for Cydnus,
To meet Mark Antony.

(V.ii.226–8)

Clearly, Cleopatra does provide us with explicit information about herself, and this information also seems to suggest changes that are occurring to her as the play progresses. However, Doran does not point out that all of these speeches take place in the presence of other characters and that this has an important effect on the nature of her self-presentation. The effect is strongest in the first two speeches above. The first speech is spoken in the presence of her attendants, Charmian, Iras and Mardian, with whom she is fairly intimate. Thus, she is very relaxed and enjoying a talk about love. There is more than a hint of boasting as she lists her lovers, and her self-description *A morsel for a monarch* is part of a boast about her sexual attractiveness. Her second speech is to Enobarbus. It is a response to his charge that she weakens Antony's resolve in preparing for the battle at Actium, and his assertion that rumour in Rome has it that the war is managed by the eunuch Photinus and Cleopatra's maids. It is thus not surprising that she casts herself as *the president of my kingdom* and *a man* — both social schemata reinforce her counter-claim to be powerful. The self-presentation in these speeches is thus distorted to some degree by strategic considerations.

4.3.2 Self-presentation in the absence of other characters

The validity of self-presentation within dramatic devices such as the soliloquy and aside is particularly strong. This is partly because of the absence of other characters from the communicative act, and partly because of the nature of the communicative act itself. A key point to note about the communication of information within a soliloquy or aside is that we can make a strong assumption that characters say what they believe. In other words, Grice's maxim of quality (1975) is strongly assumed to apply. This lies behind Hussey's comment that 'By convention [. . .] what the character says in a soliloquy is to be taken as sincere, at least within the limits of his own self-knowledge' (Hussey 1982: 182). This is not to say, however, that a character's self-conception is *necessarily* correct. As Hussey (1982) points out, it is limited by that character's self-awareness, and, presumably, how efficient they are in self-observation. Thus, there can be no strong assumptions about the application of Grice's (1975) other maxims — relation, quantity and manner — in the communication of information within a soliloquy or aside.

Of course, a soliloquy or aside may serve a number of purposes besides self-presentation: other characters may be presented, as may the plot. But self-presentation seems to be a key function, particularly in Shakespeare's early plays (those pre-dating *Richard III*). Warwick in *Henry VI*, Pts *1, 2* and *3*, for example, supplies us with detailed information about his feelings and plans:

> I came from *Edward* as Ambassador,
> But I returne his sworne and mortall Foe:
> Matter of Marriage was the charge he gaue me,
> But dreadfull Warre shall answer his demand.
> Had he none else to make a stale but me?
> Then none but I, shall turn his Jest to Sorrow.
> I was the Cheefe that rais'd him to the Crowne,
> And Ile be Cheefe to bring him downe againe:
> Not that I pitty *Henries* misery,
> But seeke Revenge on *Edwards* mockery.
>
> (*Henry VI, Pt. 3*, III.iii.256–65)

In the later plays Shakespeare went beyond straightforward self-presentation, and developed the soliloquy into a powerful device for thought presentation. It may be remembered that in section 2.2.4.2, I noted that scholars had argued that gaining knowledge of a character's inner life is an important factor in characterisation, and one likely to lead to a 'rounder' impression of character. Shakespeare used the soliloquy to exploit different aspects of a character, in particular the private self and the public self. Richard III indicates his double self when at the end of his first soliloquy he says 'Dive, thoughts, down to my soul' (I.i.41) and in a later soliloquy

> And thus I cloath my naked Villanie
> With odde old ends, stolne forth of holy Writ,
> And seeme a Saint, when most I play the deuill.
>
> (I.iii.336–8)

The self he presents for public consumption is the diametric opposite of the self which he reveals privately to the audience. Also, Shakespeare used the soliloquy to articulate mental and emotional conflicts within a character. Consider, for example, the conflicts voiced by Julia in *The Two Gentlemen of Verona*, who, as a woman in male disguise, is asked by the man she loves to woo her rival for him. These conflicts take place between the private self and the public self, arise from conflicting elements within one of those selves, or result from a clash between an aspect of the self and an action or event within the play. Such conflicts voiced in soliloquy imply self-awareness: conflict would not be an issue, if the character had no self-awareness. The importance of these conflicts is that they stimulate character and plot development in their resolution.

4.3.3 Other-presentation

It would be quite wrong to think that characterisation that stems from *another* character about a particular character is necessarily less important than the cues gleaned directly from the character in question. In fact, it is quite possible to form an impression of a character entirely on the basis of other-presentation. Nell, for example, in *A Comedy of Errors* (III.ii.71–153) is only spoken about and never seen or heard, yet the information we gain is remarkably detailed. We know her name, her job — 'Kitchin wench' — and thus her low social status. We are told about her salubrious physical appearance (the quality of her skin — 'al grease', her complexion — 'swart', her shape — 'sphericall'). We also learn about her disagreeable personality (she is 'a very beastly creature', like a 'beare').

As with self-presentation, an important issue that needs to be addressed here is the validity of other-presentation. Our inferential efforts are complicated: *theoretically*, before we can assess the value of the characterising statement for the target character, we must first discount aspects motivated by the characteriser or the situation. For example, in *King Lear*, Lear's descriptors for Kent (I.i.160–6) — 'Vassall', 'Miscreant', 'recreant' — tell us very little about Kent, since Lear is in a rage. If anything, they suggest that Lear lacks control over his temper. However, in practice there are reasons to think that we do not do as much discounting as in theory we should. In 3.6.2 I argued that we are predisposed to take what someone says at face value. In social psychology, the tendency to underestimate the impact of contextual factors when inferring characteristics has been referred to as the *fundamental attribution error*

(Ross 1977). This is clearly an important factor here: we are predisposed to accept at face value what characters say about other characters.

An important factor influencing whether a cue is discounted is the characteriser's credibility. Characters such as Iago, Falstaff and Richard III, who have their scant regard for the truth established early in their respective plays, are more likely to have their characterisations of others discounted. One way we can be more certain about the validity of a particular characterisation is if a number of different characters have characterised the target in the same way. This, I would argue, can be explained in terms of attribution theory, specifically covariation theory (see 3.3.4). Other-presentation can be viewed as a stimulus attribution, because the issue here is the validity of the stimulus — the target character. The key information pattern for a stimulus attribution is high consensus. Thus, if various characters behave in a similar way towards the target character (high consensus), then their behaviour reflects something about the target character. This pattern will be illustrated in Chapter 6, where I discuss the role of other characters' characterisations of Katherina, the protagonist in *The Taming of the Shrew*.

4.4 Implicit cues

In the following sections, I shall consider both the verbal and non-verbal cues that are important in conveying *implicit* information about a character, that is character information which has to be derived by inference. For example, the fact that somebody speaks fast tells us nothing explicitly about the speaker. However, on the basis of our assumptions about fast speakers we may infer, assuming appropriate contextual factors, an attribute of the speaker such as extroversion. I have constructed a checklist of implicit cues. I shall consider conversational, lexical, grammatical, paralinguistic, non-verbal and contextual features, as well as accent and dialect.

4.4.1 Conversational structure

The kinds of conversational features I wish to outline briefly here have been discussed in studies of naturally occurring conversation, and form the backbone of the field of conversation analysis (see for example Sacks *et al.* 1974; Levinson 1983). This framework has been usefully applied to drama, and succeeded in shedding light on character (Herman 1991;

Bennison 1993). I shall introduce some of the central notions of this framework, and pay particular attention to the following aspects: frequency of turns, length of turns, total volume of talk, turn allocation, interruptions, and topic control. I shall examine these aspects to see what light they can shed on character, and then, in the following section, show their relevance to characterisation by analysing an extract from *Richard III*. In this analysis, I will also make some reference to notions introduced in the sections of the previous chapter dealing with conversational action and inferencing (3.7.1 and 3.7.2).

The way in which people interact with one another can reveal, among other things, the relative distribution of power between them. Discourse partners do not always have the same amount of influence over the progress, structure and contents of the interaction, but can often be divided into more or less powerful participants. In some cases the distribution of power is determined by the social and institutional roles played by different people. In a lecture, for example, the balance of power leans heavily on the side of lecturers, and this is reflected in the unequal amount of speech allocated to lecturers and students, the lecturer's control over the content of the communication, and so on. However, even in casual conversations between friends there may be latent patterns of dominance whereby some people are more confident and influential, and this has an effect on how they interact with other people. In these cases, inequality of power is due to factors other than social and institutional roles, such as personality, attractiveness, and so on.

In describing conversation, we need to take into account the way in which talk is distributed between participants. More specifically, we can look at the number of conversational contributions or turns for each participant, the length of each turn, and the total volume of talk for each participant. The way in which speakers alternate (that is, the transitions between turns) can also be revealing. Speakers may either self-select — spontaneously grab the conversational floor — or they may have a turn allocated to them by another speaker, who may ask them a question or somehow signal that now it is their turn to speak. Speakers may also butt in without waiting for the other speaker to finish their turn, in which case we have an interruption. Sometimes speakers overlap, particularly at the end of one turn and the beginning of another. Another important aspect of conversation is the way in which topics are introduced, maintained and changed. Again, topic management is related to power distribution, as well as to attitudes, degrees of involvement in the interaction, and so on.

As we noted in section 3.7.1, in conversation, particular turns often form conventional sequences. Questions, for example, set up an expectation that a following turn or turns will function as an answer. Similar canonical 'adjacency pairs' include greeting–greeting, and comment–comment. Of course, whether something actually counts as a second part of a sequence is not determined by positioning alone. Whether something is, say, an answer to a question, would require inferential work, in particular an assessment of its relevance. In dialogue, observing who tends to initiate such sequences and who responds can, for example, suggest who may be dominant, a motivator, compliant, or obstructive. Notice also that the presence of a 'dispreferred' response (such as the refusal of an offer as opposed to its acceptance) or the absence of any response is foregrounded, and invites interpretation. If you say 'hello' to someone and they don't say anything back, you might benevolently conclude that they haven't heard you or that they are absent-minded, or, less benevolently, that they are rude.

Is there empirical support for the discussion thus far? Ng (1990: 276) states that a correlation between influence and participation in conversations, and more particularly between influence and the number of successful turns, is a consistent finding. And it is not difficult to find specific studies that support the idea that people associate the features mentioned above with power. For example, Ng (1990: 276) reports Brooke's (1988) study which found that group members perceived those who changed the topic the most as most influential; Robinson and Reis (1989) found that interruptions led to attributions of assertiveness and reduced sociability. This supports the idea that hearers have a causal schema linking power as the cause of such conversational features. However, we need to remember that all this is very dependent on context. Consider research in the area of language and gender. This is pertinent to the discussion here because one of the leading explanations for possible linguistic differences between men and women is the relative powerlessness of women. Researchers appear to disagree about whether men or women contribute most to interaction (see the references given in Thorne et al. 1983: 279–81). Holmes argues convincingly (1992: 132) that the discrepancies arise because of the differing contexts and purposes of talk. For public and formal contexts, Holmes cites (1992: 132–5) numerous studies which demonstrate that in general men have longer turns, and argues that contributing talk in these contexts is status-enhancing. More specifically, Holmes reminds us (1995: 33–4) that in a situation like an interview it is the interviewee, the relatively powerless participant, who contributes most talk, and a cooperative interviewee 'is one who contributes plenty of talk'. Clearly, we need to look closely at how the discourse is working in context.

There are, of course, many other conversational features that may correlate with the social dimension of power. Some of these will be considered in detail at other points in this book (see in particular 5.5.1). Furthermore, one must bear in mind that power is just one of a number of variables that may influence the usage of these features. I shall pay attention to some other variables when I turn to politeness theory in Chapter 5. Drawing upon the aspects I have covered so far, I shall now demonstrate their value to characterisation in an analysis of *Richard III* (IV.ii.86–122).

4.4.1.1 Conversational structure and Richard III

At the end of Act III, scene i, Richard requests Buckingham's help in plotting the death of Hastings, in return for which Buckingham is promised the Earldom of Hereford and the possessions of the late king when Richard ascends to the throne. Buckingham agrees, saying that he will claim the promised things, to which Richard asks him to 'look to have it yielded with all kindness' (III.i.198). In the following act, Buckingham, having fulfilled his part of the bargain, seeks to make his claim. The situation in which the conversation takes place is both public (other nobles, such as Stanley, and attendants being present) and formal (Richard enters, according to the stage direction, in *pomp* having just been crowned king). Richmond, whom Richard talks about, is leading a revolt against Richard. The turns of the passage given below are numbered for ease of reference.[2]

(1)	**Buckingham**	My lord, I have considered in my mind The late request that you did sound me in.
(2)	**Richard**	Well, let that rest. Dorset is fled to Richmond.
(3)	**Buckingham**	I hear the news, my lord.
(4)	**Richard**	Stanley, he is your wife's son. Well, look unto it.
(5)	**Buckingham**	My lord, I claim the gift, my due by promise, For which your honour and your faith is pawn'd:

	Th'earldom of Hereford, and the moveables
	Which you have promised I shall possess.
(6) **Richard**	Stanley, look to your wife; if she convey
	Letters to Richmond, you shall answer it.
(7) **Buckingham**	What says your Highness to my just demand?
(8) **Richard**	I do remember me, Henry the Sixth
	Did prophesy that Richmond should be King,
	When Richmond was a little peevish boy.
	A king . . . perhaps . . . perhaps —
(9) **Buckingham**	My lord!
(10) **Richard**	How chance the prophet could not, at that time,
	Have told me — I being by — that I should kill him?
(11) **Buckingham**	My lord, your promise for the earldom —
(12) **Richard**	Richmond! When last I was at Exeter,
	The Mayor in courtesy show'd me the castle,
	And call'd it Rougemont, at which name I started,
	Because a bard of Ireland told me once
	I should not live long after I saw 'Richmond'.
(13) **Buckingham**	My lord —
(14) **Richard**	Ay — what's o'clock?
(15) **Buckingham**	I am thus bold to put your Grace in mind
	Of what you promis'd me.
(16) **Richard**	Well, but what's o'clock?
(17) **Buckingham**	Upon the stroke of ten.
(18) **Richard**	Well, let it strike.
(19) **Buckingham**	Why let it strike?
(20) **Richard**	Because that like a jack thou keep'st the stroke

		Betwixt thy begging and my meditation.
		I am not in the giving vein today.
(21)	**Buckingham**	May it please you to resolve me in my suit?
(22)	**Richard**	Thou troublest me; I am not in the vein.

Richard III (IV.ii.86–122)[3]

In terms of *total volume* of speech Richard clearly dominates the conversation, speaking 50.9% more words than Buckingham. It is not the case, however, that he consistently hogs the conversational floor. In the first third (turns 1–7), Buckingham actually speaks 29 words more than Richard. It is in this third that Buckingham is making his claim for the promised title and wealth. Richard's reaction is to swamp Buckingham with unilateral talk about another topic, the rebel Richmond, and thus for the second third (turns 8–13) Richard speaks 75 words more than Buckingham. In the final third (turns 14–22), Richard changes tactics and engages Buckingham in a topic of his own choosing. This results in a distribution of words that is much more balanced — Richard speaks only 9 more words than Buckingham.

The fact that Richard systematically denies Buckingham speaking rights is evident in the *allocation of turns*. In turn 1 Buckingham self-selects and engages Richard in dialogue. But in turn 4 Richard switches his address from Buckingham to Stanley. The result is that Buckingham must again self-select in turn 5. This pattern repeats itself: Richard again engages Stanley, so that Buckingham must self-select in turn 7. Over his next three turns (8, 10, 12) Richard reminisces about Richmond, with the result that Buckingham is again forced to self-select in turns 9, 11, 13. A point to note here is that self-selection is not straightforwardly an indicator of power. In this context, Buckingham must self-select if he is to speak at all. Buckingham's self-selection in turn 9 cuts into Richard's turn (it is clear that Richard had not finished his final sentence in turn 8), and thus is an interruption. Richard appears to interrupt Buckingham in turn 12, though we must remember that the dash at the end of turn 11, like all the punctuation here, is an interpretation supplied by a particular editor. Both characters are employing relatively aggressive tactics. In turn 14 Richard again appears to interrupt Buckingham, but also changes tactics and allocates the next turn to him. From this point onwards the conversation takes a more normal course, at least from the point of view of turn allocation.

The *topic* that Buckingham wishes to pursue throughout is his claim for the title and wealth. He introduces this indirectly in his first turn. In his response, Richard explicitly commands Buckingham to drop this topic, *Well, let that rest*, introduces a different topic of his own, *Dorset is fled to Richmond*, and succeeds in eliciting a relevant responding comment from Buckingham in turn 3. Buckingham reintroduces the topic of his claim in turn 5, but Richard 'skips' Buckingham's contribution and continues to pursue his own topic. In turn 7, Buckingham attempts to elicit a relevant response from Richard by formulating a question, but Richard provides no answer, and instead continues with his own topic. This pattern of 'skip-connecting', with Richard ignoring Buckingham's contributions and steadfastly pursuing the topic of Richmond, continues until turn 14. Here Richard does acknowledge that Buckingham is attempting to talk (*Ay*), but also changes tactics and formulates a question to steer Buckingham away from talking about his claim. It is worth noting that the topic of Richard's question, the time, is disarmingly fatuous. Buckingham, nevertheless, is unperturbed. He fails to supply an answer, and continues with the topic of his claim. Richard does acknowledge that Buckingham's topic has been broached (*Well*), as he did in turn 2, but again he asks the time, and succeeds in eliciting a 'preferred' answer from Buckingham.

Richard's next strategy (turn 18) is more sophisticated. It is difficult to make sense of his utterance, *Well, let it strike*. A clock strikes independently of human intervention, so letting the clock strike or not is not an option Buckingham has. Not surprisingly, Buckingham is perplexed and asks Richard to explain. Richard has succeeded not only in getting Buckingham to respond to his topic, but also to further it by asking a question about it. The topic is, however, something of a blind alley. Richard really has no 'answer' to Buckingham's question, but instead rebukes his conversational behaviour, comparing him to a jack striking the bell of a clock. This is doubly offensive since the word 'jack' is also a name for a knave. The offence is further magnified by the public nature of the conversation. The implication of his impoliteness is that Buckingham should desist from this line of conversation. However, Buckingham is undaunted and reintroduces the topic of his claim in the form of a yes/no question, thus attempting to focus Richard's response. Richard fails to provide a 'preferred' answer. Richard employs evasive strategies until turn 20 where, significantly, he characterises Buckingham's conversational action as *begging*. The assumptions behind this are that Richard is in a much more powerful position and that he owes nothing to Buckingham. It is highly condescending to Buckingham. In the next turn Buckingham tries once more, making an indirect request in the form of a question. Richard's response that he is not *in the vein* (in the mood) neither grants Buckingham's request nor refuses it.

The *terms of address* used by the two characters are in stark contrast. All of Buckingham's choices are deferential: *My lord* (6 times), *your Highness*, and *your Grace*. Buckingham acknowledges Richard's higher social status and in doing so produces a counterbalance to the imposition of his request. In other words, Buckingham's terms of address partly function as a politeness strategy (see Chapter 5). Richard, on the other hand, avoids using forms of address until his final two turns. He is not seeking to engage Buckingham in conversation. When he does address Buckingham, he uses the 'thou' form of the second person pronoun. This may indicate that his temper has snapped in the face of Buckingham's persistence, and also that he condescends to Buckingham (note that *thou* lies next to *jack* and *begging*). Richard makes it plain that Buckingham is in no position to request anything of him. Terms of address and pronouns will be discussed further in section 4.4.3.4.

What does all this tell us about Richard's character? Richard employs conversational strategies to deny the just claim of his most loyal supporter. We can infer — via the schematic associations of his conversational features as well as their meaning in context — his power, his lack of scruples, and sheer nastiness. But Richard is no simple tyrannical king. In considering his character, one also needs to think about why it is that Richard does not simply hand over the title and monies — the title is of little value to him and there is no evidence that he is short of cash. If he does not intend to hand them over, why does he not simply say so? It is true that a consistent characteristic of Richard is that he never gives anybody anything, he only takes,[4] but there are other factors involved. At this point in the play Richard's fortunes are beginning to deteriorate, with the rebels massing around Richmond. Buckingham, some fifty lines earlier in the scene, had been less than supportive of Richard's latest plot involving the murder of Prince Edward (*Give me some little breath, some pause, dear lord, / before I speak positively in this*, lines 24–5). If Richard simply hands over what Buckingham wants, then there is less to stop Buckingham from going to join the rebels. Similarly, if he flatly refuses to grant Buckingham's claim, then he also risks losing Buckingham to the rebels. As a result of this, Richard employs a series of conversational strategies in order to avoid the issue altogether, or indicate indirectly, through impoliteness to Buckingham, that he should not pursue his claim. Nowhere does he explicitly deny Buckingham's claim. His final strategy in turns 20 and 22 is to violate the maxim of relation (Grice 1975) in claiming that he is not *in the giving vein*. If he is not in the mood to give things, then clearly Buckingham will not have his claim met at that particular moment. Importantly, Richard leaves it open for Buckingham to infer that he may get what he wants in the future, when Richard is in the mood. We might infer that Richard is a very clever and sophisticated Machiavel.

What does all this tell us about Buckingham's character? Buckingham exhibits remarkable tenacity in pursuit of his claim, not to mention bravery in the face of Richard's impoliteness, bearing in mind that Richard's frequent reaction to those who cross him is to contrive their deaths. Conversationally, he faces Richard out: it is Richard who leaves immediately after turn 22, not Buckingham. He exerts power through conversation, in spite of the fact that he is socially the less powerful participant. According to the augmenting principle (3.3.1), if one does something in spite of reasons for not doing it, the effect can be to strengthen an attribution. Hence, we may infer that Buckingham is especially robust in character. Nevertheless, the fact that he has angered Richard and that Richard has contempt for him does not escape him. He immediately leaves to gather forces against Richard.

4.4.2 Conversational implicature

I have already introduced Grice's Cooperative Principle (Grice 1975), the idea that in conversation there is a tacit agreement to cooperate in the exchange of information, and its constituent maxims of quantity, quality, relation, and manner. I suggested in section 3.7.2 that it provides a framework of conversational expectations, which, when broken, may trigger interpretative activity. As far as drama is concerned, it provides a useful framework for explaining how implicit meanings are generated from character speech, and it is an effective way of capturing differences in conversational behaviour. Its usefulness has been demonstrated in a number of papers (such as Cooper 1981; Short 1989; Bennison 1993). Before I illustrate the value of the Gricean framework in the study of characterisation, I first need to describe the operation of implicature in the discourse situation of drama.

An important point to note about implicatures and drama is that sometimes they can be worked out by the characters on stage as well as the audience, but at other times they can only be worked out by the audience. The most obvious situation where there is this kind of double perspective has been referred to as dramatic irony. Dramatic irony comes about as a result of the peculiar discourse structure of drama (see 1.7.1).

At one level we have the playwright conveying some sort of message to the audience; within that message we have an embedded level of discourse where character A conveys a message to character B. Character A can flout maxims and generate implicatures for character B, implicatures which the audience can usually also work out. However, character A can also generate implicatures which only the audience can work out, and dramatic irony results. For example, Richard, in *Richard III*, keeps the audience well informed through soliloquies. We have much more background knowledge about Richard than the characters on stage have, so we can draw implicatures that the other characters cannot. For example, when Richard says that he will *lie* (I.i.115) for his brother Clarence, the characters on stage might reasonably interpret this as meaning that he will *position* himself, in the place of his brother who has been condemned to death. Richard thus appears magnanimous. But for the audience, *lie* is ambiguous. We can also interpret it to mean that it is his untruths that will condemn his brother to death. By flouting the Maxim of Manner, Shakespeare has conveyed an implicature to us about Richard via his own character.

Let us see how the Gricean maxims might capture the conversational behaviour of a character. In *Henry IV, Pt. II*, Falstaff has supposedly promised to marry Mistress Quickly, who, in the following passage, attempts to get Falstaff to honour his word.

> Marry (if thou wer't an honest man) thyself, & the mony too. Thou didst sweare to mee vpon a parcell gilt Goblet, sitting in my Dolphin-chamber at the round table, by a sea-cole fire, on Wednesday in Whitson week, when the Prince broke thy head for lik'ning him to a singing-man of Windsor; Thou didst sweare to me then (as I was washing thy wound) to marry me, and make mee my Lady thy wife. Canst thou deny it? Did not goodwife *Keech* the butchers wife come in then, and cal me gossip *Quickly*? comming in to borrow a messe of Vinegar: telling vs, she had a good dish of Prawnes: whereby thou didst desire to eat some: whereby I told thee they were ill for a greene wound? And didst thou not (when she was gone downe staires) desire me to be no more familiar with such poore people, saying, that ere long they should call me Madam? And didst thou not kisse me, and bid mee fetch thee 30.s? I put thee now to thy Book-oath, deny it, if thou canst.

> (II.i.82–99)[5]

The striking thing here is not simply the number of words Quickly speaks, an aspect which the analytical framework of the previous section would cover, as would the Maxim of Manner, but the apparently excessive level of detail she includes. Successive prepositional phrases and subordinated clauses elaborate information. Quickly breaks the conversational norm represented by the Maxim of Quantity, thus inviting an implicature to be drawn. What is this implicature? As I pointed out in section 3.8.1, referring to Short (1989: 149), the embedded nature of drama may lead us to believe that this is a message about Quickly's character — she enjoys hammering her point home. However, it is possible that contextual factors in the fictional world may partially discount this inference. Note that the Lord Chief Justice is listening to Quickly's speech. This is her opportunity to convince him that Falstaff really did make the promise, and her strategy might be to anchor her claims in as much detail as possible. Thus, the truth about Quickly's character cannot be resolved on the basis of this evidence alone. We need low distinctiveness information to reinforce a character inference (that is, Quickly talking in similar ways in other contexts). This can indeed be found in the play. Quickly breaks the maxim of quantity, as well as the maxim of manner, when talking in other contexts (for example II.i.22–36, II.iv.68–74, II.iv.53–8, II.iv.78–91). Within the same play, Justice Shallow is a good example of another character whose conversational behaviour can be captured by the maxims of quantity and manner. He provides unnecessary detail, unnecessary repetition, and presents information in a disorderly manner (see his contributions to *Henry IV, Pt. II*, Act III, Scene ii). For example, whilst recruiting some law officers, he examines the roll call:

> Where's the Role? Where's the Role? Where's the Role?
> Let me see, let me see, let me see: so, so, so, so: yea marry
> sir. Raphe Mouldie: let them appeare as I call: let them do
> so, let them do so: Let mee see, Where is Mouldie?
>
> *Henry IV, Pt. II* (II.ii.96–100)

The implicature here is likely to be that he is somewhat senile.

4.4.3 Lexis

Intuitively, it is reasonable to suggest that lexis plays a significant role in shaping people's impressions of others. For example, the tendency to use formal lexis may give the impression that someone is rather aloof or pompous, informal lexis that someone is 'down to earth'. However, research undertaken to examine the relationship between lexis and personality or character is patchy. This is no surprise when one considers the problems involved in establishing and isolating what the salient dimensions of lexical variation are, and in applying those dimensions to data. For example, consider the dimension of abstractness versus concreteness. How would you order the following: 'atom', 'human', 'love', 'martian', 'pen'? 'Love' is clearly at the abstract end of the scale, whereas 'pen' is more concrete. But what about physical concepts like 'atom' that can't be sensed by humans, or generic concepts like 'human', or fictional concepts like 'martian'? And what would you make of the abstractness of the word 'love' in a sentence like 'They're making love.'? In context, 'love' may have a rather concrete sense. In spite of these difficulties, in the following sections I identify some dimensions which are important in characterisation and can be quantified. In the final section, I change tack and introduce an empirical methodology to help reveal what the salient lexical features of a particular character are.

4.4.3.1 Germanic versus latinate lexis

One way of pinning down the relationship between lexis and character is to look at the predominant etymological origin of the words that a character uses.[6] This is useful insofar as different stylistic dimensions correlate with lexical source. The more common words of English, particularly the words of speech, tend to be Germanic in origin, whereas Latin words tend to be rare and appear more often in written language. Germanic words are more likely to be used in informal, private contexts, whereas Latin words are the words of formal, public occasions. Germanic words tend to be simple, often words of one syllable, whereas Latin words are usually polysyllabic. Concrete things are often referred to by words of Germanic origin (for example wood, earth, house, pan, knife, fork), whilst Latin words tend to refer to more abstract concepts. Germanic words often express some kind of attitude, whether negative or positive, whereas Latin words tend to be more neutral (for example, compare the pairs 'whore—prostitute' and 'cheap—inexpensive'). These stylistic differences are summarised in Table 4.1. In terms of these scales, French words lie between Germanic and Latin vocabulary. Adamson (1989) has produced some evidence for the correlation of different degrees of formality with Germanic, French and Latinate lexis. Subjects rated 30 words (each word in isolation) according to formality. Results

Table 4.1   Stylistic dimensions associated with German and Latinate lexis

GERMANIC		LATIN
Frequent	⟵——————⟶	Rare
Spoken	⟵——————⟶	Written
Informal	⟵——————⟶	Formal
Private	⟵——————⟶	Public
Simple	⟵——————⟶	Complex
Concrete	⟵——————⟶	Abstract
Affective	⟵——————⟶	Neutral

of the experiment revealed a 'marked polarization' between highly formal Latinate lexis and informal Germanic lexis (1989: 212). French seemed to occupy the middle ground.

The issue of *why* these areas of vocabulary have acquired particular characteristics can be explained by looking at the historical development of English loanwords. In fact, the contrasting stylistic flavour of Germanic and Latinate lexis was even more marked in Shakespeare's time. The bulk of Latin vocabulary entered the language during the Renaissance, which was a period of lexical upheaval. The important point is that unlike the earlier borrowing of French vocabulary into speech, Latin vocabulary was the language of the written medium, the language of books or the 'inkhorn'. Much of it was difficult to understand (and still is!), and was perceived as 'alien' by some. Not surprisingly it is in the very early seventeenth century that the first dictionaries appeared, in order to help people cope with these 'hard words'. This state of affairs gave rise to the so-called 'inkhorn controversy', a debate about the merits or otherwise of the acquisition of 'artificial' 'bookish' Latin vocabulary in place of 'natural' 'common' Germanic vocabulary (see Baugh and Cable 1993: 212–18).

In Shakespeare's plays, differences in lexical source can be linked to differences in character. The Nurse's speech in *Romeo and Juliet*, for example, is dominated by Germanic lexis. Consider the speech below, spoken in the presence of Lady Capulet and Juliet:

> Euen or odde, of all daies in the yeare come *Lammas* Eue
> at night shall she be fourteene. *Susan* & she, God rest all

Christian soules, were of an age. Well *Susan* is with God, she was too good for me. But as I said, on *Lammas* Eue at night shall she be fourteene, that shall she[,] marrie, I remember it well. 'Tis since the Earth-quake now eleuen yeares, and she was wean'd I neuer shall forget it, of all the daies of the yeare, vpon that day: for I had then laid Worme-wood to my Dug [= breast] sitting in the Sunne vnder the Douehouse wall, my lord and you were then at *Mantua*, nay, I doe beare a braine. But, as I said, when it did tast the Worme-wood on the nipple of my Dugge, and felt it bitter, pretty fool, to see it teachie, and fall out with the Dugge, Shake quoth the Doue-house, 'twas no neede I trow to bid mee trudge: and since that time it is a eleuen yeares, for then she could stand alone, nay, bi' th' roode she could haue runne, & waddled all about: for euen the day before she broke her brow, & then my Husband God be with his soule, a was a merry man, tooke vp the Child, yea quoth hee, doest thou fall vpon thy face? thou wilt fall backeward when thou hast more wit, wilt thou not *Iule*? And by my holy-dam, the pretty wretch lefte crying, & said I: to see now how a jest shall come about. I warrant, & I shall liue a thousand yeares, I neuer should forget it: wilt thou not, *Julet* quoth he? and pretty fool it stinted, and said I.

(I.iii.17–49)[7]

In the whole 32 lines of this speech there is not one Latinate word.[8] And there are only a handful of French loanwords: *warrant, face, age* and *fool,* which are all well-established loanwords. Compare this with nine lines from Lady Capulet a few speeches later:

This night you shall behold him at our Feast,
Read ore the volume of young *Paris* face,
And find delight, writ there with Beauties pen,
Examine euery seuerall liniament,
And see how one another lends content:
And what obscur'd in this faire volume lies,
Find written in the Margent of his eyes.
This precious Book of Love, this vnbound Louer,
To Beautifie him, onely lacks a Couer.

(I.iii.81–9)

The lexical mix is clearly different here. Latinate lexis includes *volume* (x 2), *liniament*, *obscur'd*, and *Margent*.[9] French lexis includes *Examine*, *delight*, *Beauties* (*Beautifie*), *precious*, *content*, and *Couer*. Approximately one word in five is non-Germanic.

The Germanic lexis of the Nurse's speech creates or reinforces a number of stylistic effects. The words she uses tend to be simple, mono-syllabic, and informal. This, coupled with relatively short sentence length, makes her speech — in contrast with that of Lady Capulet — sound like naturally occurring conversation (and, indeed, she actually reports speech). This is reinforced by the fact that she uses a number of typically colloquial expressions (note her weakness for mild oaths — *I warrant*, *I trow*, *bi' th' roode*, *by my holy-dam*), and the odd dialectal form such as *a* for the singular third person pronoun, a form that is common in southern and western dialects (see *OED*). In addition, her Germanic lexis reflects her concern for the physical: in the extract above, for example, she makes several references to parts of the body (*dug* x 2, *braine*, *nipple*, *brow*, *face*). Overall, the Nurse's lexis is likely to give the impression to people reading or watching the play that she is straight-forward, spontane-ous, natural, down to earth, and intimate. The absence of French and Latinate loan words also reflects her low social status and, presumably, her low level of education. Additional evidence for this is suggested in her occasional attempts to use Latinate words in other parts of the play which often misfire: for example, her odd usage of the adjective 'senten-tious' as a noun in 'she hath the prettiest sententious of it' (II.iv.204–5).

The Latinate and French lexis of Lady Capulet fosters a contrasting style of speech. Her vocabulary is more complex, formal and rare. It is less physical, more befitting the idealistic language of romantic love. This aspect is reinforced by an extended metaphor (the tenor being Paris's face and the vehicle a *volume*) which conspires to make Paris's face non-physical. Furthermore, her speech is couched in tight rhyming couplets. In sum, Lady Capulet's lexis is likely to give an audience the impression that she is a rather detached and artificial person. The fact that she uses such French and Latinate lexis also suggests that she is of high status and well educated.

In drawing attention to the Germanic lexis of the Nurse and the more Latinate and French lexis of Lady Capulet, one can begin to account for how we might gain particular impressions of these characters. These lexical differences provide evidence for McLeish's claim that the Nurse provides 'earthiness' and 'the warmth, affection and plain human dign-ity which all the upper-class characters lack' (1985: 176), and that Lady Capulet is 'cool' and 'worldly-wise' (1985: 47). Of course, it should not be thought, however, that these lexical issues only apply to historical texts. The extract below is from the BBC comedy series *Yes Prime Minister*, whose principal characters are the government minister James Hacker and the civil servant Sir Humphrey. In his diary, Hacker recalls the time when Humphrey told him that he was going to move to another department:

> Humphrey had said that 'the relationship, which I might tentatively venture to aver has not been without a degree of reciprocal utility and even perhaps occasional gratification, is approaching the point of irreversible bifurcation and, to put it briefly, is in the propinquity of its ultimate regrettable termination'.
>
> I asked him if he would be so kind as to summarise what he's just said in words of one syllable. He nodded in sad acquiescence. 'I'm on my way out', he explained.

(Lynn and Jay 1989: 16)

Sir Humphrey uses a mysterious bureaucratic language to disguise the indiscretions of government and defuse any moments of potential embarrassment. Hacker is a relatively straightforward person who needs things to be put in simple language. It is almost as if they speak two different languages. There is a contrast between the loftiness of Sir Humphrey's first utterance and the mundane tone conveyed by the vocabulary of his final speech. This can be explained by noticing that the two sets of words differ in their origin: the majority of the first set comes from Latin or French; the second set is Germanic.

Before we leave the topic of Germanic and Latinate lexis, two further characterisation issues should be raised. Firstly, characters that are able to switch from one type of lexis to another are liable to be perceived as rounder characters. Adamson (1989: 222) illustrates this well with the speech of Othello:

> But that I love the gentle Desdemona
> I would not my unhoused free condition
> Put into circumscription and confine
> For the seas' worth.

(I.ii.25–8)

The final line not only deviates from the Latinate lexis of the previous two lines (*condition, circumscription, confine*), but also disrupts the metre of those lines. It is more like naturally occurring speech. This is the line in which Othello assesses the extent of his love for Desdemona. In Adamson's words, 'The effect is curiously moving, as though we have been given a glimpse of a private man behind the public hero, of a sincere feeling behind the rhetorical splendour' (1989: 222).

Secondly, the fact that much of the new Latinate vocabulary was relatively obscure also provided Shakespeare with the opportunity of creating a particular sort of comic character. In *Much Ado About Nothing*, Dogberry's scatter-brained nature is reflected in his lexical confusion. For example, he uses *comprehend* when he means *apprehend*, *auspicious* when he means *suspicious* ('our watch sir haue indeede comprehended two aspiitious persons', III.v.42–4). Such characters have become part of a traditional comic type, the most famous exemplar being Sheridan's eponymous Mrs Malaprop.

4.4.3.2 Lexical richness

The richness or diversity of lexis within a person's or character's speech can suggest certain characteristics. Some research has been undertaken in this area. The conclusion seems to be that 'Generally, lower diversity results in receiver judgements of lower communicator competence, lower socio-economic status, and higher anxiety' (Bradac 1982: 107; see also Bradac 1990: 396–7). One can calculate the lexical richness of a particular character by working out a type/token ratio. In other words, by dividing the number of *different* words by the *total* number of words spoken one can end up with a figure that reflects the diversity of lexis relative to the size of the total sample of speech. Thus somebody who speaks 1000 different words out of a total of 2000 words would achieve a type/token ratio of 0.5. The closer the ratio is to 1, the richer the lexis.

One needs to be wary of contrasting the type/token ratio of characters who speak different volumes of speech, particularly if the total volume is small. A character who speaks just ten words could end up with a ratio of 1. To avoid this problem, I compared relatively large and similar volumes of speech. The Nurse, Capulet and Mercutio in *Romeo and Juliet* are good subjects for comparison. Their type/token ratios are given in Table 4.2.

In order to investigate whether the difference between the ratios for the Nurse and Capulet was statistically significant, I calculated a z-score. The critical value for significance at the 1% level is 2.58: the value obtained was 3.4. This shows the statistical difference to be highly

Table 4.2   Lexical richness: type/token ratios for three characters[10]

Character	Type	Token	Ratio
Nurse	647	2205	0.293
Capulet	723	2121	0.341
Mercutio	816	2093	0.390

significant. This being so, one can readily assume that there are also significant differences between Mercutio and Capulet, and Mercutio and the Nurse.

The fact that the Nurse, Capulet and Mercutio differ in lexical richness reflects differences of character. Firstly, let us consider the Nurse and Capulet. One might suspect that differences in education and social status might account for Capulet's richer lexis, but there is more to it than this. The Nurse at any tense moment in the play gives vent to her emotions with remarkably persistent repetitions. For example, upon discovering Juliet's apparently dead body she says:

> O wo, O wofull, wofull, wofull day,
> Most lamentable day, most wofull day,
> That euer, euer, I did yet behold.
> O day, O day, O day, O hatefull day,
> Neuer was seene so blacke a day as this:
> O wofull day, O wofull day.

(IV.v.49–54)

Compare this with Capulet's reaction to the same event five lines later:

> Despis'd, distressed, hated, martir'd, kill'd,
> Vncomfortable time, why cam'st thou now
> To murther, murther our solemnitie?
> O Child, O Child; my soule, and not my Child,
> Dead art thou, alacke, my Child is dead,
> And with my Child, my ioyes are buried.

(IV.v.59–64)

Admittedly, Capulet does use repetition too, but he never matches the Nurse. The Nurse, for example, repeats *day* ten times; Capulet repeats *child* five times. In his first line, Capulet produces a carefully-constructed

189

list of past participles, related in meaning and creating a crescendo from *Despis'd* to *kill'd*. His reaction to Juliet's death is altogether more controlled, more measured. We may conclude that he lacks the emotional spontaneity of the Nurse.

The fact that Mercutio's lexis is so rich can be attributed to his education, his social status and also his character. He spends most of his time playing with words, so much so that at one point Romeo pleads for peace (I.iv.95). He is highly creative in devising additional vocabulary, for example, *how art thou fishified* (II.iv.38) and *she had a better Loue to berime her* (II.iv.41). Even when fatally wounded he contrives a pun: *aske for me tomorrow, and you shall find me a graue man* (III.i.95–6). His diverse lexis suggests a character that cannot be contained, a dazzling volatile character. These are the characteristics that lead to his quarrel with Tybalt, and ultimately to his death.

4.4.3.3 Surge features

Some linguistic features are associated with personal affect, a term which in linguistics has been used to encompass people's feelings, emotions, moods and attitudes, as well as personality (Caffi and Janney 1994: 328). Although the link between language and affective *impressions* does not appear to have been subjected to empirical investigation, numerous linguists have claimed that affect is expressed by a wide range of different linguistic features, including, for example, evaluative lexis, hedges, modal verbs, lexical repetition and pronouns. In this section, I will follow the work of Taavitsainen (1999), who examines the role of features of personal affect in characterisation, specifically in *The Canterbury Tales*.

Taavitsainen defines the useful term 'surge features' thus:[11]

> Personal affect is a component of participant relations and finds outlets in various forms; thus it gives us a picture of the person's behavioral patterns and mental characteristics. It may exhibit more permanent qualities of emotion, with a long term realisation, e.g. love, fondness, sadness or dislike, or more transient and volatile states of mind like anger, or dislike erupting into telling someone off. These outbursts of emotion can be called surge features. [. . .] According to my earlier studies, outbursts of emotion in surge features of personal affect include exclamation, swearing, and pragmatic particles.
>
> (1999: 219–20)

The status of exclamation as a surge feature can clearly be seen in the speech of the Nurse (IV.v.49–54) quoted above: modern editions supply numerous exclamation marks (such as 'O day! O day! O day! O hateful day!' (Alexander 1951)). Note also here that lexical repetition is a marker of emotional anxiety. Exclamations are often marked by a particular lexical item, and that item itself may be associated with a particular attitude. For instance, as the examples below illustrate, 'alas' often expresses regret (Taavitsainen 1995: 447), and 'fie' often expresses disdain (Taavitsainen 1995: 449):

Pro.	Not so: I thinke she liues.
Jul.	Alas.
Pro.	Why do'st thou cry alas?
Jul.	I cannot choose but pitty her.

(*The Two Gentlemen of Verona* IV.iv.71–4)

La.	What? quite vnmann'd in folly.
Macb.	If I stand heere, I saw him.
La.	Fie for shame.

(*Macbeth* III.iv.73–4)

Swearing, oaths, profanities, or taboo words in general, may signal emotions such as anger or surprise (a typical reaction, if, say, you drop something on your foot). What gives such words power and what may make them foregrounded is that they are, to varying degrees, linguistic taboos. Of course, swearing is very sensitive to context. For example, having dropped something on your foot, you would probably not swear, if you were standing in the middle of a nursery school. Furthermore, swearing need not be the result of anger or surprise. It could, for example, be a means of cementing in-group cohesion, as Labov (1972) revealed in his study of banter amongst black adolescents. With regard to drama, taboo words have already been noted as important. In the informant study I discussed in section 3.8.3, I pointed out that three of the segments of text which were considered as important in the characterisation of Billy contained mildly taboo words: 'bloody' (x 2) and 'hell'. I argued that these words contributed to an explanation of some of the character descriptors informants supplied, such as 'grumpy' and 'irritable', and, particularly, 'prone to swearing mildly' (x 2), 'offensive', 'aggressive', and 'gruff'. I also claimed that these taboo words explained, at least in part, the emotional state descriptors 'feels oppressed', 'frustrated', 'miserable', 'unsatisfied'.

Pragmatic particles have also been referred to as 'discourse markers', 'pragmatic markers' (the term I shall adopt here) or 'implicit modifiers'. They include items such as 'well', 'why', 'what', 'I mean' and 'you know'. These items are not integrated into the grammar of accompanying linguistic segments; in speech they normally constitute a tone group, whilst in writing they are often separated by punctuation marks (see Brinton 1996 for a summary of characteristics). Compare, for example, the sentences 'Well, he did it in the end' and 'He did it well'. In the first, 'well' acts as a pragmatic marker; in the second, it is an adverb in the grammatical structure of the sentence. Blake (1992–3) argues that pragmatic markers play an important role in the construction of Shakespeare's characters by signalling attitudes to what has been said or done. For example, 'what' can express surprise or indignation, whilst 'why' can express mild condescension. These usages are illustrated by the speech of the Nurse from *Romeo and Juliet* given below, when the Nurse discovers Juliet still in bed late in the day. In fact, this particular speech also illustrates all of the other features discussed in this section.

> Mistris, what Mistris? *Iuliet*? Fast I warrant her she.
> Why Lambe, why Lady, fie you sluggabed,
> Why Loue I say? Madam, sweet heart: why Bride?
> What not a word? You take your peniworths now.
> Sleepe for a weeke, for the next night I warrant
> The Countie *Paris* hath set vp his rest,
> That you shall rest but little, God forgiue me:
> Marrie and Amen: how sound is she a sleepe?
> I must needs wake her: Madam, Madam, Madam,
> I, let the Countie take you in your bed,
> Heele fright you vp yfaith. Will it not be?
> What drest, and in your clothes, and downe again?
> I must needs wake you: Lady, Lady, Lady?
> Alas, alas, helpe, helpe, my Ladyes dead,
> O weladay, that euer I was borne,
> Some Aqua-vitae ho, my Lord, my Lady?

(IV.v.1–16)[12]

Of course, none of the features in this section, or indeed in this chapter, necessarily reflects a character's personality. Such features can be used for strategic purposes (to elicit sympathy, for example). However, it is clear that they are frequently used by authors, such as Shakespeare, as a conventional way of signalling that a character has a particular emotion or attitude. As Taavitsainen (1999) argues, they are 'style markers'. In addition, we should remember that the features discussed in this section are generally more frequent in speech (see, for example, Taavitsainen 1999; Culpeper and Kytö 1999, 2000). In Shakespeare, speech-like language is usually reserved for the middle and lower classes (see Salmon [1967] 1987). Hence, it is no surprise that such features cluster in the speech of the Nurse.

4.4.3.4 Social markers: Terms of address and second person pronouns

Terms of address, including vocatives and pronouns, can be an important means of signalling social information. Characters can be rapidly placed within particular social groups, and their social relations with other characters can be indicated. In this section, my aim is to establish the richness of terms of address as a tool for characterisation. I shall start by briefly considering present-day terms of address. I then turn to Elizabethan terms of address, and supply some Shakespearian examples. Finally, I briefly touch on the issue of the second person pronouns 'you' and 'thou'.

The classic description of present-day English terms of address must be Ervin-Tripp's (1972) study. However, this is now somewhat dated, and so I will refer to Leech's (1999) study, which, being corpus-based, also has the advantage of solid empirical support. The main semantic categories identified in Leech (1999: 109–13) are ordered approximately from those indicating a familiar or intimate relationship to those indicating a more distant or respectful one, and include:

Endearments (e.g. (my) darling, love, sweetie) Typical address between close female family members, sexual partners and 'favourite' people.

Family terms (e.g. (mum)my, (dad)dy, ma, pa, grandma, granny, grandpa, granddad) Typical address to family members of an elder generation.

Familiarisers (e.g. guys, mate, folks, bro) Typical address between males signalling solidarity.

First names Typical address between friends and family members, as well as other (even casual) acquaintances. A sub-group of first names is familiarised first names, shortened first names, and names with the pet suffix -y/-ie (e.g. Marj, Tom, Jackie).

Title and surname (e.g. Mrs Johns, Mr Graham, Ms Morrisey) Typical means of marking a more distant and respectful relationship.

Honorifics (e.g. sir, madam, ma'am) Relatively rare in English, they may occur in situations, such as formal service encounters, where there is a markedly asymmetrical relation between speakers.

(Summarised from Leech 1999: 109–13)

Of course, this summary does not capture all nuances of terms of address, and, in particular, does not do justice to the *usages* of terms of address, but at least it conveys a sense of the richness of terms of address as a means of marking social groups and relations in present-day English.[13]

Unlike today, honorifics were generally important in Elizabethan England (see Replogle [1973] 1987; Salmon 1987). The Elizabethans had a relatively precise system for using names and terms of address to indicate social status. In the terminology of Brown and Gilman (1960), whereas today the emphasis is generally on the horizontal plane (encompassing notions such as solidarity, familiarity, and intimacy, as well as their opposites), in Elizabethan England there was also an emphasis on the vertical plane (encompassing notions such as power and social status, and the opposite notion of equality). Unfortunately, the exact nature of the Elizabethan address system is still a matter for future research, though Nevalainen and Raumolin-Brunberg (1995) have made a significant start. Similarly, there is work to be done on address terms in Shakespeare's plays, though some descriptions can be found in Replogle (1987), Salmon (1987), and Busse (1998). Here, I shall simply outline some broad categories of terms of address that have relevance in Shakespeare's plays, and include examples from those plays.

In Shakespeare, typical terms of address used by subordinates for royalty include: 'your highness', 'your majesty', 'my Lord', 'madam' and 'sir'. The nobility often receive the placenames of their titles, for example, Buckingham, York, Dorset, Kent, and Exeter, and more generally terms of address such as 'your grace', my lord', 'your lordship/ ladyship', 'sir', and 'madam'. Knights tend to receive the title 'Sir' plus a first name (such as Sir John, Sir James) or first name and surname (for instance Sir John Falstaff), and sometimes just a surname (Falstaff, Catesby). Untitled characters, who are also property holders, may receive the title 'Master' or 'Mistress' plus surname (Master Ford, Mistress Ford). Servants may receive first names, though men often use surname or both names to their male servants. In addition to the above terms of address, the names of particular social groups could be used as terms of address (e.g. Nurse, Huntsman, Friar, Shepherd, Woman, Man, Son, Wife). This is still possible today (e.g. Nurse Smith, or simply Nurse, as a term of address), but it is much less common. In Shakespeare's plays, names of social groups are also used to identify or refer to particular characters. These social groups vary according to such factors as social status (e.g. Citizen, Gentleman), occupation (e.g. Boatswain, Fisherman, Host, Hostess, Gardner, Captain, Officer, Guard, Gravedigger, Doctor, Porter, Servant), and age (e.g. Child, Young Boy, Old Man). All these are, of course, generalisations.

It must be emphasised that the usage of terms of address will depend on a variety of factors, including the nature of the relationship between addresser and addressee, the affective state of the speaker, and the situation. Moreover, it should not be assumed that terms of address are in any sense fixed or given. Often it is the dynamic usage of terms of address in Shakespeare that is the source of character interest. For example, in *Henry IV, Parts 1 and 2*, Falstaff, a disreputable knight, addresses Prince Hal, the heir apparent, as 'Hal' (in Leech's (1999) terms a familiarized first name) and 'lad', 'boy' and 'wag' (in Leech's (1999) terms familiarizers). Replogle (1987: 110) points out that though a superior may use familiar terms to an inferior (Prince Hal addresses Falstaff as 'Jack'), this gives the inferior no right to return such address terms. Falstaff's choice of terms of address reveal his shocking audacity. Moreover, they reveal Prince Hal's character:

> The acceptance of this incredible degree of familiarity from anyone, particularly from an inferior of so low a degree and questionable background, would have shown that the prince was weak, dissolute, and a fool — a potential disaster for the country.
>
> (Replogle 1987: 111)

At the end of the play (V.v), when Hal is made king, Falstaff's terms of address are his usual ones of familiarity: 'King *Hall*, my Royall *Hall*', and 'my sweet Boy'. But Hal has now, from the Elizabethan point of view, come to his senses. He says to his Lord Chief Justice 'speak to that vain man' (V.v.45) — Falstaff's over-familiarity is characterised as vanity. When Falstaff persists, Hal says, 'I know thee not, old man', a total rejection of any familiarity.

Apart from the address terms outlined above, Elizabethan second person pronouns could have significant social or pragmatic implications. Elizabethan English offered a choice between two forms for the second person pronouns: the plural forms *ye, you, your/yours* and the singular forms *thou, thee, thy/thine* (hereafter referred to collectively as You-forms and Thou-forms respectively). After the late thirteenth century, however, usage ceased to be a relatively straightforward grammatical matter, as the plural You-forms began to be used for the singular in particular contexts (Pyles and Algeo 1993: 188). A great deal of research has investigated the usage of the second person pronouns in Early Modern English, although much of this research has floundered on simplification, insufficient quantity of textual data, and sheer confusion. The theoretical underpinning for much of the research in this area is Brown and Gilman's (1960), referred to above. Table 4.3 summarises their arguments with regard to Elizabethan second person pronoun usage.

Table 4.3 Elizabethan second person pronoun usage according to power and solidarity

	You	Thou
Power	To social superiors	To social inferiors
Solidarity	Between social equals of high status	Between social equals of low status

According to the theory, in Shakespeare one would expect the following pattern of social use: You-forms would be used reciprocally at court amongst the upper ranks who would also receive You-forms from social inferiors such as messengers and murderers; Thou-forms would be used reciprocally amongst the low ranks — the two grave diggers in *Hamlet*, for example. The low ranks would also receive Thou-forms as an address from social superiors. Richard III, for instance, uses Thou-forms frequently when addressing characters of lower rank.

However, even a cursory glance at Shakespeare's plays will show that the pattern of usage is not so simple. Characters fluctuate between the pronouns, not only in the same interaction, but often in the same utterance. To account for these fluctuations, McIntosh (1963) and Mulholland ([1967] 1987) add an expressive or emotional dimension to the usage of second person pronouns. The idea that pronominal shifts reflect emotional or attitudinal change had in fact already been argued by Abbott [1871] (1881) and Byrne [1936] (1970). You-forms are considered dispassionate and emotionally unmarked, while Thou-forms can be used to express negative emotions (such as anger and contempt), or positive emotions (like affection and love). Thus Sir Toby Belch can offer Sir Andrew Aguecheek the following advice on how to write a provocative challenge: 'taunt him with the license of Inke, if thou thou'st him some thrice, it shall not be amisse' (*Twelfth Night* III.ii.41–3).

Whilst it is true that the social relationship between participants and emotional factors explain a number of cases, it is clear that many problems remain. Why, for example, do Bottom and his men (near the bottom of the social hierarchy) in *A Midsummer Night's Dream* (I.ii) use You-forms to each other? Moreover, shifts to Thou-forms cannot always be accounted for simply in terms of an expression of emotion. Richard of Gloucester, for example, appears to switch from 'you' to 'thou' in order to mark a social difference, when dealing with the insolence of Sir Robert Brakenbury (*Richard III* I.i.88–102).

> Rich.   Euen so, and please your Worship Brakenbury,
> You may partake of any thing we say:
> We speake no Treason man; We say the King
> Is wise and vertuous, and his Noble Queene
> Well strooke in yeares, faire, and not iealious
> We say, that Shores Wife hath a pretty Foot,
> A cherry Lip, a bonny Eye, a passing pleasing tongue:
> And that the Queenes Kindred are made of gentle
> Folkes.
> How say you sir? can you deny all this?
> Bra.   With this (my Lord) my selfe haue nought to doo.
> Rich.   Naught to do with Mistris Shore?
> I tell thee Fellow, he that doth naught with her
> (Excepting one) were best to do it secretly alone.

Note that 'your' in the first line collocates with the flattering title 'Worship' (Brakenbury is a mere knight) and the politeness formula 'and please' (= 'and if it please'). But also note the sarcasm: Richard is going overboard with politeness to a man he considers (and who is) well beneath him. In the penultimate line, he has switched to 'thee', which collocates with 'Fellow', a term that could express contempt in this period. Pragmatic factors are involved in the switch in pronoun forms here; it cannot be accounted for simply in terms of relatively fixed social properties, such as power and solidarity. Clearly, a more flexible approach to You- and Thou-forms is necessary.

A number of researchers (such as Barber [1981] 1987; Brown and Gilman 1989; Quirk [1971] 1987; Wales 1983) have employed the concept of markedness to explain some aspects of second person pronoun usage. In Shakespeare's time, You-forms were in general the unmarked forms (Wales 1983; Hope 1993). The fact that in Shakespeare the number of You-forms roughly equals the number of Thou-forms, as Barber

(1987: 177) points out, does not disprove that You-forms are unmarked in general. In drama, fluctuation between You-forms and Thou-forms may be, for example, an important means of indicating character relations, shifts in those relations, or attempts to shift those relations. Drama thrives on dynamic interaction. An important consequence, however, of this more even distribution of You-forms and Thou-forms is that there is no clearly marked form for Shakespeare. And there are other problems with the markedness approach: (1) it still fails to explain rapid fluctuation between You-forms and Thou-forms, (2) once a 'norm' is established, the tendency is to focus on only one form — the marked form — and ignore the function of the unmarked form, and (3) shifts to the marked form are usually explained in terms of social and emotional factors so that other interpersonal and discoursal factors are overlooked.

Calvo (1992: 16) offers a different approach to the usage of the second person pronouns. She suggests that sometimes they act as social markers:

> [. . .] not because their usage correlates with membership of a particular social group or class — as in Brown and Gilman (1960, 1989) — but because they can suggest what type of relationship exists between addresser and addressee.

Regarded thus, their usage can be described within a politeness framework. They are 'indicators of in-group or out-group social relations and as such they are often manipulated intentionally by speakers' (Calvo 1992: 17). Margaret's linguistic behaviour in *Richard III* can be used to illustrate this point. Margaret almost always uses Thou-forms. In doing so, Margaret disassociates herself from the other characters: Thou-forms here indicate out-group relations. But when speaking to Dorset she shifts to singular You-forms:

Dor.   Dispute not with her, she is lunaticke.
Q. Mar.   Peace Master Marquesse, you are malapert,
    Your fire-new stampe of Honour is scarce currant.
    O that your yong Nobility could iudge
    What 'twere to lose it, and be miserable!

(I.iii.255–8)

Here, the shift to You-forms *appears* to be an in-group marker. But in the pragmatic context, she employs this as mock politeness or sarcasm to put the upstart Dorset in his place.

Calvo's (1992) approach is flexible and dynamic, and can account for many occurrences of the second person pronoun. Moreover, it can readily be incorporated within a more general politeness (and impoliteness) framework — an area which, as I will demonstrate in Chapter 5, has important implications for characterisation.

4.4.3.5 Keywords

So far the above sub-sections have focussed on particular dimensions of lexis that capture dimensions of characterisation. In this section, I want to focus on an empirical methodology for identifying what might be the 'key' words of a character's speech. One way of getting at a character's keywords might be to look at the frequencies with which particular features occur. Whilst this can yield some points of interest, it also produces many meaningless results. The high frequency words of characters tend to be words that characters have in common (for example 'the'): they tell us nothing about the individual character. The high frequency words of a particular character have little stylistic significance, unless they are compared with an appropriate norm. Enkvist (1964, 1973) emphasises that the stylistic significance of what he called 'style-markers' comes about when there is a significant differential between the densities of linguistic features in a text and the densities of corresponding linguistic features in a *contextually* related norm (that is, we are more likely to compare a sonnet with other sonnets than the telephone book).

A computer program that does the kind of analysis required of Enkvist's definition is the *Keywords* facility in Mike Scott's *WordSmith Tools* (1999). *Keywords* conducts a statistical comparison between the words of a corpus (or wordlist) and a bigger reference corpus. According to Scott:

> To compute the 'key-ness' of an item, the program therefore computes
>
> - its frequency in the small wordlist
> - the number of running words in the small wordlist
> - its frequency in the reference corpus
> - the number of running words in the reference corpus
>
> and cross-tabulates these.
> Statistical tests include:
>
> - the classic chi-square test of significance with Yates correction for a 2 x 2 table

- Ted Dunning's Log Likelihood test, which gives a better estimate of keyness, especially when contrasting long texts or a whole genre against your reference corpus.

A word will get into the listing here if it is unusually frequent (or unusually infrequent) in comparison with what one would expect on the basis of the larger wordlist.

(Scott 1999: Help Menu)

I prepared some files from an electronic version of *Romeo and Juliet* (the First Folio), downloaded from the Oxford Text Archive. I put the speech (minus speaker identification, stage directions, etc.) of the following characters into separate files: Romeo (4,803 words), Juliet (4,291 words), Capulet (1,643 words), the Nurse (2,233 words), and Mercutio (2,056 words).[14] I then standardised the spelling, so that the computer would not treat spelling variants of the same word as different words. I then used *Keywords* to compare each file against a reference corpus made up of the sum total of all the other files (for example Juliet was compared against Romeo, Capulet, the Nurse and Mercutio). I set the minimum frequency for a word to be considered for keyness at four, selected the chi-square test for significance, and the probability value at smaller than or equal to 0.05 (that is, there is a 5% chance or less of the result being a fluke).[15] Having generated a list of a keywords for each character, I examined the function and context of each instance of a keyword, in order to validate and account for the results. This step is not required by Enkvist's definition, but was necessary, since not all keywords reflected character (some keywords, for example, arose as a result of a particular context). A particular issue relates to the *dispersion* of the keyword instances.[16] For example, if all the instances of a particular keyword are clustered within a particular speech, they are more likely to reflect something about that speech and its particular context, and not the character of the speaker. In terms of covariation theory (see 3.3.4), in order to draw conclusions for character, we need, in theory, the instances of a keyword to occur in reaction to different stimuli, at different times and in different situations.

To do justice to the results generated by the program would require much more space than I have here. Instead, I shall confine myself to a limited number of observations, rather than a more systematic presentation and explanation of results. I will only report keywords which are key because they are unusually frequent in a particular character's speech.

For Romeo, the two most key keywords are 'beauty' and 'death'.[17] Given that he extols Juliet's beauty and laments her death, these results are not surprising. More surprising perhaps is that the most key keyword for Juliet is 'if'. What this seems to reflect is that she spends much of the play in a state of anxiety. This includes worries about whether Romeo is already married ('If he be married, /My grave is like to be my wedding-bed (I.v.134–5)), worries about Romeo's safety ('If they do see thee, they will murther thee' (II.ii.70)), and worries about Romeo's intentions ('But if thou meanest not well' (II.ii.150)). Capulet's most key keyword is 'go'. In most instances of 'go' he is issuing commands, and this points to the role he assumes for himself as head of the household, organising those around him, including Tybalt (I.v.82), Paris (III.iv.31), the Nurse (III.v.171), his servants (IV.ii.2), and Juliet (IV.ii.9). Amongst the most key keywords for the Nurse are 'woeful', 'God', Lord', and 'warrant'. All of these are surge features. Clearly, the repetitions of 'woeful' discussed in 4.4.3.2 account for its identification as a keyword. The keywords 'God' and 'Lord' are used in oaths and exclamations (see 4.4.3.3 for an example). Salmon (1987: 62) suggests that '(O) Lord is a favourite expletive of the lower classes'. 'Warrant' appears in expressions such as 'I warrant thee' (roughly equivalent to present-day 'I bet you') that assert the truth of a claim and imply the speaker's emotional involvement. Such expressions can be seen as pragmatic markers. Also, 'warrant' was considered to be colloquial (cf. *OED*). All these keywords characterise the Nurse as someone who expresses her emotions (she is the emotional mirror for the events of the play), and, to a lesser extent, someone who is lower class. With Mercutio, the results are surprising because they include items that have high frequencies in general. The articles predominate: the most key keyword is 'a' and the eighth, 'the'. The fourth most key keyword is 'of'. I suspect these words reflect Mercutio's enthusiastic elaboration of information by means of successive noun phrases, when he tells stories or provides commentaries. By way of illustration, I have underlined Mercutio's noun phrases in the following extract:

Ben. Why what is *Tibalt*?
Mer. More then <u>Prince</u> of <u>Cats</u>. O <u>hee</u>'s <u>the Couragious Captaine</u> of <u>Complements</u>: <u>he</u> fights as <u>you</u> sing <u>pricksong</u>, keeps <u>time</u>, <u>distance</u>, and <u>proportion</u>, <u>he</u> rests <u>his minum</u>, one, two, and <u>the third</u> in <u>your bosom</u>: <u>the very butcher</u> of <u>a silk button</u>, <u>a Dualist</u>, <u>a Dualist</u>: <u>a Gentleman</u> of <u>the very first house</u> of <u>the</u>

first and the second cause: ah the immortal Passado
the Punto reuerso, The hay.

(II.iii.18–26)[18]

Clearly, the *Keywords* program offers unique opportunities for revealing the style markers of characters' speech.

4.4.4 Syntactic features

There is some evidence that syntactic features are perceived to be less
salient than other linguistic features in distinguishing speech styles. In
a number of studies involving Quebec French, syntactic features were
consistently perceived to be less salient than pronunciation or vocabulary (Giles and Powesland 1975: 5–6). However, research is thin on
the ground. Scherer, in his review of personality markers in speech,
is surprised that 'there is no systematic research on personality differences in cognitive processing and the complexity of syntactic structure'
(1979: 170). What the precise relationship between cognitive organisation and syntactic complexity is remains to be discovered. A particular
issue for the data addressed in this book is the fact that it is dialogue.
Scherer (1979: 172) notes the possibility that personality differences flow-
ing from cognitive organisation may only be apparent in monologue,
since dialogue requires the allocation of cognitive resources to matters
such as turn-taking, which may lead to simpler syntax in order to reduce
the overall cognitive burden.

These comments on real-life research tally with work on fictional
texts in general, and Shakespeare's plays in particular. Page (1988: 57),
examining speech in the English novel, states: 'Grammar and syntax are,
apart from the most obvious differences, less readily absorbed by the
casual listener, and are used relatively little by writers.' Blake (1983),
considering Shakespeare, concludes that syntactic differences between
characters' speech are less important than other aspects because they are
less likely to be noticed: they are 'more subtle than marked features of
vocabulary or dialect and can readily be overlooked, particularly in the
theatre' (1983: 28). However, no systematic research has investigated
whether grammar really is less important in creating an impression of a
character. It might be the case that the cumulative effect of grammatical
features is an issue. Although it is beyond the scope of this book, the
way forward may be in the computational analysis of characters' speech,
for example, by adopting the methodology laid out in Biber (1988).

Here, I shall simply illustrate some of the ways in which playwrights have used grammatical features in characterisation.

Whilst research on real-life talk has not established a clear relationship between syntactic complexity and cognitive organisation, fictional texts, whether in dialogue or monologue, have exploited what appears to be a schematic relationship between syntax and cognitive organisation, such that the more simple the syntax the more simple-minded the character, and vice versa. Brook (1976: 183) points out that the old men in Shakespeare tend to speak in 'short, jerky sentences, as though out of breath'. This is exemplified by the shepherd's speech in *The Winter's Tale*:

> Good lucke (an't be thy will) what haue we heere? Mercy on's, a Barne? A very pretty barne; A boy, or a Childe I wonder? (A pretty one, a verie prettie one) sure some Scape; Though I am not bookish, yet I can read Waiting-Gentle-woman in the scape [. . .]
>
> (III.iii.65–71)[19]

Of course, a discussion of sentences in Shakespearean texts needs caution. The sentence is a feature of writing, not speech. Since the sentence is partly defined by punctuation, we need to be wary of editorial practices. Also, the prototype of the sentence was not the same four hundred years ago as it is today. Generally speaking, sentences (broadly defined as a unit of text beginning with a capital and ending with a full-stop, exclamation mark or question mark) were longer in Early Modern English texts.[20]

Perhaps one of the clearest uses of syntax to suggest a simple-minded character is Steinbeck's ([1937] 1992) characterisation of Lennie, a gentle giant, in *Of Mice and Men*. For example:

> 'We gonna have a little place,' Lennie explained patiently. 'We gonna have a house an' a garden and a place for alfalfa, an' that alfalfa is for the rabbits, an' I take a sack and get it fulla alfalfa and then I take it to the rabbits.'
>
> (1992: 94)

The very simple coordinated structures are reminiscent of child-talk. Note, also, that the simple structures cannot be attributed to excitement, since Lennie is explaining *patiently*. A good example of a character at the other end of the simple/complex grammatical scale is Oscar Wilde's ([1894] 1973) Lady Bracknell in *The Importance of Being Earnest*. Consider this last sentence in one of her turns:

> It is my last reception, and one wants something that will encourage conversation, particularly at the end of the season when everyone has practically said whatever they had to say, which, in most cases, was probably not much.

(1973: 352)

The second main clause of this sentence is remarkably complex, as this bracketing of clauses makes clear:

> [It is my last reception], and [one wants something [that will encourage conversation], particularly at the end of the season [when everyone has practically said whatever [they had to say, [which, in most cases, was probably not much]]]].

Clearly, Lady Bracknell's speech here, as elsewhere, is at odds with the norms of spoken language — and even perhaps the norms of written language. She exhibits an abnormally high level of control over her syntactic production. This, of course, contributes to her characterisation: she exudes massive psychological presence, controlling all who surround her. We might also note that this sentence was part of a turn lasting 171 words. Not only does this indicate her power, but it is also relevant to an earlier observation above regarding real–life speech, namely that complex syntax is more achievable in the context of monologue than the ebb and flow of dialogue.

My examples thus have been of relatively flat characters. Shakespeare's Lear is an example of a character who shifts from flatness to roundness, and this shift is partly suggested by a shift in syntactic style. Compare these two speeches, the first being Lear's second speech of the play, and the second occurring after his madness on the heath, when he awakes to discover his daughter Cordelia.

> Tell me my daughters
> (Since now we will diuest vs both of Rule,
> Interest of Territory, Cares of State)
> Which of you shall we say doth loue vs most,
> That we, our largest bountie may extend
> Where Nature doth with merit challenge. *Gonerill,*
> Our eldest borne, speake first.

(I.i.47–53)

Lear.   Where haue I bin?
Where am I? Faire day light?
I am mightily abus'd; I should eu'n dye with pitty
To see another thus. I know not what to say:
I will not sweare these are my hands: let's see,
I feele this pin pricke, would I were assur'd
Of my condition
[. . .]
Pray do not mocke me:
I am a very foolish fond old man,
Fourescore and vpward,
Not an houre more, nor lesse:
And to deale plainely,
I feare I am not in my perfect mind.
Me thinkes I should know you, and know this man,
Yet I am doubtfull: For I am mainely ignorant
What place this is: and all the skill I haue
Remembers not these garments [. . .]

(IV.vii.52–67)

The syntax of the first speech is complex. Note that the object (*Which of you shall we say doth love us most*) is delayed by the subordinated adverbial clause in parentheses, and that the object itself contains an embedded clause. Also, the sentence finishes with another subordinated adverbial clause, which itself contains an embedded adverbial clause.[21] In contrast, Lear's second speech contains relatively short clauses, often held together with simple coordination. This shift in syntactic style does not mean that Lear has become simple minded; rather, this syntactic simplicity reflects the fact that he has switched from a mind fogged by pompous notions of his own kingliness, to a clear vision of his daughters' true worth. He moves toward the straight-talking style of his daughter Cordelia.

Hussey (1992: 169–70), discussing Lear's speeches quoted above, points out that there is a style shift involving not just syntax, but also vocabulary (note, for example, the decrease in polysyllabic vocabulary). This is a useful reminder that syntactic features usually operate in conjunction with features at other linguistic levels to create a more salient impression. For example, complex syntax and complex lexis (such as polysyllabic, formal, rare) may give rise to a 'high style', and in turn that 'high style' may be salient and revealing about a character. Conversely, simple syntax and simple lexis (monosyllabic, informal, common) may give rise to a 'low style', which may be revealing about a character.[22]

4.4.5 Accent and dialect

As far as social and personality evaluation is concerned, the most salient dimension of accent variation in Britain is the degree to which it varies from the standard. As I noted in section 1.4.1, the overall research conclusion seems to be that 'standard accents usually connote high status and competence; regional accents may be seen to reflect greater integrity and attractiveness' (Edwards 1982: 25). Non-standard and standard accents are stereotypically associated with different personality traits:

> [. . .] speakers of RP may attract stereotyped personality impressions of greater *competence* from listeners than speakers of nonstandard regional accents [. . .] However, both regional accented judges and to a lesser extent RP judges seem to consider nonstandard speakers as possessing greater personal integrity and social attractiveness than RP speakers.
>
> (Giles and Powesland 1975: 67–8)

By 'competence' Giles and Powesland meant that speakers are considered more ambitious, intelligent, self-confident, determined and industrious; by 'personal integrity and social attractiveness' they meant that speakers are considered less serious and more talkative, good-natured and humorous.

A brief example from Arthur Miller's *The Crucible* (1986) demonstrates how dramatists can capitalise upon the attitudes stereotypically associated with particular accents and dialects. The following turns are part of a much longer interaction in which Hale (the official witchfinder) interrogates Tituba (a slave servant), in order to establish that she is guilty of being a witch (see 3.3.3 for further analysis of this interrogation):

Hale:	Woman, have you enlisted these children for the devil?
Tituba:	No, no, sir, I don't truck with no Devil!
Hale:	Why can she not wake? Are you silencing this child?
Tituba:	I love me Betty!

(*The Crucible* 1986: 45)

The spelling, grammar and lexis of Hale's words are all standard. This, and our knowledge of his social standing, would presumably lead us to infer that he would speak, if the play were performed, with a non-regional standard accent.[23] In contrast, Tituba's speech contains two features of non-standard grammar: the much stigmatised double negative, and the use of the objective pronoun *me* instead of the possessive *my*. Although it is not signalled in the spelling, our knowledge about the speaker and the fact that she speaks a non-standard dialect would presumably lead us to infer that she would speak with a non-standard regional accent. These dialects and the interaction between them is likely to reinforce the impression of an intelligent, confident, and determined Hale running linguistic rings round a good-natured but vulnerable Tituba.

A general problem, however, with research in the area of accents is the issue of what constitutes 'the standard'. In Giles and Powesland (1975), and indeed many other studies, the standard is assumed to be Received Pronunciation (RP), a particularly high-prestige accent spoken by a small elite (only a few percent of the total population of Britain) and not marked for region (that is, theoretically, an RP speaker from the north should sound more or less the same as an RP speaker from the south). The standard, then, is defined primarily in social and evaluative terms. One specific problem that flows from this is that, outside the language laboratory, contextual factors determine what constitutes that prestige dialect. In my local Lancashire pub, for example, the regional accent carries more prestige than RP, which in that context may attract negative attributions of snootiness. In the context of the family dinner table, a different dialect yet again may be the prestige accent. Moreover, in some fictional contexts RP has developed negative associations. In Hollywood films over the last few decades, RP has become associated with the dramatic role of villain. Let's consider a few examples of RP speaking villains. Shere Khan, the tiger in Walt Disney's *The Jungle Book*, has a very conservative RP accent (supplied by George Sanders), contrasting with the friendly jovial Baloo, who has a marked regional accent. In the last Robin Hood production, *Robin Hood: Prince of Thieves*, the Sheriff of Nottingham sports a RP accent, delivered with great aplomb by Alan Rickman, contrasting with Robin, played by the American actor Kevin Costner. There are also many action or thriller films that include an RP speaking villain. In *Rush Hour*, for example, Tom Wilkinson (better known as a British northern accent speaker in the films *Brassed Off* and *The Full Monty*) is the RP speaking villain, masterminding an international art smuggling operation, and contrasts with the 'good guys', a wise-cracking black American police officer from

Los Angeles and a police officer (played by Jackie Chan) from Hong Kong. As is clear from these examples, RP speaking villains are actually part of a specific subset of villains: they are sophisticated villains, usually in some position of power.

Another general problem, and one that is particularly pertinent to this study, is that the research mentioned above pertains to speech. As I have already indicated in 4.2.2, the possibilities and assumptions relating to accent and dialect in speech cannot be straightforwardly transferred to writing. Although standard written English is developed from the Middle English dialects of the Midlands, it is now no longer regionally marked. In fact, the spelling and grammar of standard written English is used with remarkably little variation throughout the world. The notion of standard here can mean a relatively uniform and fixed variety. An important consequence of this is that deviations from the writen standerd aa straiking very. Such deviations are also stigmatised. Let us crystallise the discussion thus far with some examples. I will begin with some present-day fictional examples, since historical texts have additional complications which will need consideration.

Sue Townsend's (1992) novel *The Queen and I* depicts a world in which a Republican government is elected in Britain, and the royal family, stripped of its trappings, is sent to live on a council estate — the significantly named *Hell Close* — in the Midlands. In this social satire, much of the humour comes about through characterisation, in particular, prototypicality distortions (see 2.5.2). I noted in 2.4.3 that person prototypicality judgements depend on the *interaction* between behaviours and situations (Cantor and Mischel 1979: 36–42), and that people are perceived as highly prototypical if they exhibit the same behaviours consistently across situations, and particularly in situations where those behaviours are not expected, or, indeed, if they simply appear in situations where they are not expected. Townsend takes a group from the top of the social scale and places them in the context of those groups at the bottom. This is the reverse of what happens to Sly in the prologue to *The Taming of the Shrew* and Bottom in *A Midsummer Night's Dream*, where commoners find themselves in an aristocratic, or even royal, context.

One of the techniques Townsend utilises to highlight the distinct social group memberships of the characters is to signal that they have different dialects. For example the Queen, talking to Beverley, her new next-door neighbour, says:

> 'Harris found a rat,' said the Queen.
> 'A *ret*?'

'A *rat* look!' Beverley looked down at the dead rodent at the Queen's feet.

(p. 54)

The unusual spelling *ret* signals that the Queen's pronunciation of the vowel in *rat* is typical of conservative RP, where it rhymes with 'net'. Note that for us to easily understand the language here, the word is first spelt conventionally as *rat*, even though it is in the mouth of the Queen. *Ret*, we must infer, is a representation of Beverley's representation of the Queen's accent.

In another example, Mr Christmas, a resident of Hell Close, talks with the Queen:

'Yeah, turkey! Din't cure 'im though. Says 'e don't care if 'e dies young. 'E says 'e 'ates the world and there's nowt for 'im to live for.'

'How very sad', said the Queen.

(p. 238)

The most striking feature of the spelling is the apostrophes marking the absence of 'h'. Clearly, the spelling signals 'h-dropping', a characteristic of working-class and lower middle-class speech in much of Britain. In addition, apart from the reduced form 'din't', Mr Christmas uses the word 'nowt' (meaning 'nothing'), a well-known regional term associated with the northern dialects. Interestingly, the Queen does not drop the 'h' in her speech here, even though 'h-dropping' is also a characteristic of some upper-class speakers.[24] The point to note here is that Townsend, like other writers, is not aiming at the systematic and accurate representation of real-life sociolinguistic facts, but at supplying some markers of particular varieties, leaving readers to fill in the gaps with background knowledge. If Townsend's Queen had also dropped her aitches, a considerable risk is taken that the reader will be able to apply the relevant real-life knowledge. In fact, the reader is much more likely to be aware of the stigmatised phenomenon of 'h-dropping', which is stereotypically associated with lack of education, regional accents (particularly Cockney) and the lower classes. Thus, the reader might have been misled into thinking that the Queen was accommodating the speech characteristics of another group (those of the working-class community she finds herself in). Moreover, if the Queen had also dropped her aitches, that would have disrupted the convention established for her in this novel that standard spelling signals her RP accent. Remember that, as with *ret* above, we learn about the precise nature of the Queen's conservative RP accent through the non-standard spelling of *other* characters.

My final example from *The Queen and I* is spoken by another resident of Hell Close:

'Well, I wun't exactly say jus' like you an' me', said Wilf.

(p. 195)

The spelling of Wilf's speech apparently conveys no information about the distinctive nature of his accent. The use of 'u' in *wun't* conveys nothing distinctive about the pronunciation of that word. Similarly, the absence of 't' in *jus'* and 'd' in *wun't* and *an'* is uninformative. One should remember that the alveolar consonants 't' and 'd' in word-final position are particularly susceptible to assimilation or elision in English: assuming informal, fairly rapid speech, most speakers would not pronounce a word-final 't' or 'd'. The point is that the writer is creating an illusion of regional accent in writing and against the norms of writing. This is what has been referred to as 'eye-dialect', a graphologically-based dialect.

If we turn to the historical situation, a further set of problems arises. In earlier periods — including the early seventeenth century, the period within which Shakespeare was writing — although there was an emerging written standard, there was certainly nothing comparable to the generally-accepted written standard of today. Regarding accent, there was great variability, and this is borne out by clues in surviving written records. As for a spoken 'standard', the evidence is slight. George Puttenham, the assumed author of *The Arte of English Poesie* (1589), attached great social value to London-based speech. He famously advised the poet: 'ye shall therefore take the usuall speach of the court, and that of London and the shires lying about London within lx. myles and not much above'. But note that he is advising the poet: we do not know whether this advice holds good for all kinds of writing. There is evidence in Shakespeare's plays which is consistent with Puttenham's advice. For example, in the following exchange from *As You Like It*, how 'fine' an accent is seems to depend on regional and social factors:

Orl.   Your accent is something finer, then you could purchase in so remoued a dwelling.

Ros.   I haue bin told so of many: but indeed, an olde religious Vnckle of mine taught me to speake, who was in his youth an inland man [. . .]

(III.ii.318–23)

Remote regions (presumably those removed from the centres of population, government, trade, and culture, such as London and the other
major cities) are associated with 'rougher' accents, but education can
cut across this dimension. For the purposes of this book, when I use the
term 'non-standard' in reference to historical forms, I refer to forms that
are regionally or socially marked. The more restricted a feature is to a
particular regional or social context, the more marked it is.

Shakespeare's graphological presentation of English accents is sketchy,
usually not more than a few hints to the actor. Similarly, his presentation of English dialects is confined to the odd lexical item or grammatical form. As Blake comments, 'there is a marked absence of cant, slang
and dialect in all Shakespearean plays' (1983: 30). For example, it is
clear from the above exchange between Orlando and Rosalind in as *As
You Like It* that the locals of the Forest of Arden (the shepherds Corin,
Silvius, and Phebe, and the country folk William and Audrey) should
speak a regional dialect. There is, however, no indication at all of dialect
in lexis, grammar or spelling. One can only guess at why this might be
so. Perhaps he left it to his actors to supply relevant dialectal features. In
fact, the actor's job here was relatively easy, since there was no need for
an actor to attempt the realistic representation of a dialect, for the reason
that a conventional stage dialect was frequently used in the Elizabethan
period, usually for poking fun at rustic characters such as those in *As You
Like It*. This dialect was based on the southern dialect, including Kent. (To
the present-day ear, the nearest equivalent would be a south-western
British dialect.) It still has some currency today in plays and films, and
is often referred to as 'Mummerset'. The best example in Shakespeare
occurs in the exchanges between Edgar and Oswald in *King Lear*:

Edgar	Chill not let go Zir,
	Without vurther 'casion.
Oswald	Let go Slaue, or thou dy'st.
Edgar	Good Gentleman goe your gate, and let poore volke
	passe: and 'chud ha' bin zwaggerd out of my life,
	'twould not ha' bin zo long as 'tis, by a vortnight.
	Nay, come not neere th' old man: keepe out, che
	vor' ye, or ice try whither your Costard, or my
	Ballow be the harder; chill be plaine with you.
Oswald	Out Dunghill.
Edgar	Chill picke your teeth Zir: come, no matter vor
	your foynes.

(IV.vi.237–47)

These exchanges supposedly take place in Kent. The non-standard nature of Edgar's speech is indicated by the spelling. The initial consonants /f/ and /s/ are voiced to /v/ and /z/ (e.g. *vurther, volke, vortnight, vor; zir, zwaggerd, zo*). These consonantal features would have been relatively distinctive, since there was (and still is) generally less variation among consonants compared with vowels. He also uses a non-standard form of the first person singular. The initial *ch* in the words *chill* and *chud* is the consonant of the Middle English first person singular *ich* (from Old English *ic*). The vowel has been dropped, and the word attached to the following verb to give *chill* (I will) and *chud* (I would or should). *Che* seems to be the dialectal form of the pronoun preceding a consonant-initial word. The features mentioned so far may well have been consistent with the real Kentish dialect of the period. However, the word *gate* is a Northern word for 'way'. Shakespeare's concern is to produce some recognisably regional forms in order to create a rustic persona for Edgar, not to reproduce accurate Kentish. Finally, with regard to this particular example, one might note that Edgar is a nobleman, he is not a rustic character. He uses dialectal forms for pragmatic reasons — he is attempting to disguise himself from Oswald — not sociolinguistic reasons.

Shakespeare's clearest use of dialect for sociolinguistic reasons (the speech reflects the speech communities to which the fictional speaker supposedly belongs) is in the characterisation of non-English characters: the Welshmen Sir Hugh Evans (*The Merry Wives of Windsor*) and Captain Fluellen (*Henry V*), the Scotsman Captain Jamy (*Henry V*), and the Irishman Captain Macmorris (*Henry V*). Clearly, their dialects would be more distinctly non-standard, since they are spoken in areas geographically remote from London, the centre of the evolving standard English. Features of the Welshmen's speech include the unvoicing of initial /b/ and /v/ ('pig' for 'big', 'falorous' for 'valorous'), the use of non-standard grammar (such as lack of subject–verb concord — 'if there is not better directions' (Fluellen, *Henry V*, III.ii.60)), and the use of words or phrases associated with Welsh speakers (like *look you*). Macmorris's features include the use of /ʃ/ for /s/ or /z/ ('Chrish' for 'Christ', 'ish' for 'is'), the use of non-standard grammar (such as unusual past participles — 'I would have blowed up the town' (*Henry V*, III.ii.85–60)), and the frequent occurrence of the word *la* ('law'). Jamy's Scottish accent is best suggested in the words 'gud' (see Kökeritz 1953: 42) and 'tway'. He also uses non-standard grammar (for instance the omission of the auxiliary 'have' in 'I wad full fain heard some question' (*Henry V*, III.ii.112–13)). As with the Kentish spoken by Edgar, the evidence suggests that Shakespeare was not overly concerned with accurately producing a Welsh,

Scottish or Irish dialect. Of the examples given above, the grammatical examples in particular are not peculiar to those dialects, but serve in creating the impression of a number of non-standard dialects. This suits Shakespeare's nationalistic purpose in *Henry V*: an Englishman, a Welshman, a Scotsman, and an Irishman, all officers in the King's army, are brought together in the same scene (*Henry V*, III.ii) — they unite for the national good. Simultaneously, Shakespeare achieves some comedy for the London audience, who could laugh at their differing dialects. This, of course, echoes the long tradition in jokes of bringing together the regional stereotypes of the British Isles (see the discussion on jokes in Further Directions and Exercises on page 156).

By way of conclusion, it is worth noting that writers primarily use graphological devices, and to a lesser extent grammatical, to convey a sense of dialect. If dialectal words are used, they tend to be well-known items stereotypically associated with a particular dialect. This strategy ensures comprehensibility for readers, who would rapidly be flummoxed by the general use of dialectal vocabulary.

4.4.6 Verse and prose

Shakespeare is well known for supplying his lower class characters with prose, and higher class characters with verse (see for example Morgan 1987: 155). Whilst there is a broad basis of truth to this, the distribution of verse and prose is in fact more complex. Consider the distribution in *Romeo and Juliet*. The total percentage of speech spoken in verse for each character is listed in Table 4.4.

Looking at this table, one can see that social status plays a part in whether a character speaks verse or prose. Juliet, Capulet, Lady Capulet, Prince Escalus, Paris, Montague, Lady Montague, Romeo, Benvolio, and Tybalt are all predominantly verse-speaking characters who have high social status. The servants Peter, Sampson, Abraham, Anthony, Gregory, Potpan, the Page, eight nameless servants, and the three musicians are all predominantly prose-speaking characters who have low social status. There are, however, a number of complications. The two Friars, the Page, the three Watchmen, Balthasar (Romeo's servant), the Apothecary, and the Nurse are all predominantly verse-speaking characters of low social status. Mercutio is of 'gentle' status, but speaks prose and verse in roughly equal measure. Clearly, other variables are involved in the distribution of verse and prose.

Topic influences the choice between verse and prose. Serious and emotionally charged topics are broached in verse. Balthasar, the page,

Table 4.4 Percentages of verse spoken by each character in *Romeo and Juliet*[25]

Characters who speak <u>more</u> than 50% verse	Actual percentage of verse	Characters who speak <u>less</u> than 50% verse	Actual percentage of verse
Juliet	100%	Mercutio	47.6%
Friar Lawrence	100%	Peter	12.7%
Capulet	100%	Sampson	0.0%
Lady Capulet	100%	Abraham	0.0%
Prince Escalus	100%	Anthony	0.0%
Paris	100%	Gregory	0.0%
Friar John	100%	Potpan	0.0%
Balthasar	100%	Musicians (x 3)	0.0%
Apothecary	100%	Servants (x 8)	0.0%
Watchmen (x 3)	100%		
Montague	100%		
Page	100%		
Lady Montague	100%		
Romeo	93.4%		
Benvolio	92.4%		
Tybalt	88.6%		
Nurse	76.6%		

Friar John, the Apothecary, and the three watchmen only appear in the final act. This act revolves around the aftermath of Juliet's supposed suicide — Romeo's discovery of her apparent death, his suicide, her suicide, and the finding of their bodies. Thus, they speak in verse. The effect of this variable can be seen if one compares the percentage of verse in five tragedies (*Hamlet, Lear, Macbeth, Othello,* and *Romeo and Juliet*) with the percentage of verse in five comedies (*Love's Labour's Lost, As You Like It, Twelfth Night, A Midsummer Night's Dream, The Merry Wives of Windsor*). These tragedies consist of 81.8% verse, and the comedies 48.2% verse. Even allowing for some variation in play length and possible bias in the particular choice of plays, the difference — 33.6% —

is significant, but not surprising. The tragedies are racked with the torments of guilt, bereavement, misplaced trust, passionate love, and so on. In Shakespeare, verse is the vehicle for such topics.

The Nurse and Mercutio in *Romeo and Juliet* require some explanation. The Nurse speaks a reasonably high percentage of verse, 76.6%. It is true that her social status is 'non-gentle', but she is a senior servant and much respected. Furthermore, she is full of her own self-importance. Whilst Mercutio is of 'gentle' status, the fact that he speaks so much prose reflects his character: he takes nothing seriously. He serves as a contrast to the passion of Romeo's love.

It should be remembered that verse and prose usually operate in tandem with lexical and grammatical features to create a particular style — high, middle or low (see 4.4.4). Also, verse and prose are not discrete categories. For example, Pistol's speech (*The Merry Wives of Windsor*, *Henry IV Pt 2*, and *Henry V*) tends to be in the border between prose and verse. As Brook points out, Pistol speaks 'a kind of metrical prose which in the early editions is printed as verse' (1976: 200). This, coupled with his fondness for literary allusion and rich vocabulary, makes him stand out from his prose-speaking companions, and reinforces his tendency to show off his linguistic dexterity.

4.4.7 Paralinguistic features

A number of studies have suggested that non-content cues (phonological and paralinguistic features), can be more significant with respect to social evaluation than the content of speech (see Giles and Powesland 1975: 1–4 for a review). I have already considered the importance of accent, specifically the correlation of certain phonemic features with certain social groups, especially those based on region and social status. In addition, the way one speaks can trigger information about other group memberships, such as age and sex, and also information about personality. There is a strong relationship between certain voices and certain personality types. The notion of *vocal stereotypes*, the idea that particular vocal characteristics are conventionally associated with particular personality traits, is a well-established finding (see for example Addington 1968: 493; Scherer and Scherer 1981: 131). The precise nature of this association is, however, still little understood.

Brown's (1990) discussion of paralinguistic features is exceptional in that it draws examples from literary fiction. At its onset, she defines paralinguistic features thus:

> Paralinguistic features are those which contribute to the expression of an attitude by the speaker. They are phonetic features of speech which do not form an intrinsic part of the phonological contrasts which make up the verbal message: they can be discussed independently of the sequences of vowels and consonants, of the stress patterns of words, of the stressing of lexical rather than grammatical words, and of intonation structure which determines where the tonic syllable falls. [. . .] [they are] aspects of speech that contribute to the meaning over and above what the verbal element of the message means.
>
> (1990: 112)

As Brown points out (1990: 112), paralinguistic features are not the only way in which a speaker can express an attitude. For example, a smile in a suitable context may suggest happiness. Such non-verbal cues will be considered in the following section (4.4.8.), whilst here I shall confine myself to paralinguistic features, and examine their stereotypical relationships with aspects of personality and character. It should be remembered, however, that paralinguistic cues and non-verbal cues often work together in suggesting a particular attitude.

This section clearly involves discussion of aspects of performance. As I have already suggested (see 1.7.2), such aspects of performance can be inferred from the play text. Stage directions are an obvious mechanism whereby performance aspects are directly indicated, but we can also infer appropriate performance aspects from the speech of characters (see Short 1998). For example, in *Romeo and Juliet* the surge features of the Nurse's speech, when she discovers the apparently dead Juliet, indicate that she is in a state of considerable anxiety, and from here it is easy to infer appropriate performance aspects (such as wide fluctuations in pitch). A comprehensive treatment of how the text triggers paralinguistic performance features, directly or indirectly, and how those paralinguistic features correlate with certain language attitudes, is well beyond the scope of this book. In this section, I have the more limited aim of giving the flavour of some areas that could benefit from further study. For expository convenience, I discuss these areas separately. There is, of course, the issue of interaction amongst these areas, but space precludes me from discussing this.

1. Speech tempo and non-fluency features
Scherer (1979), reviewing empirical work on speech markers of personality (the bulk of which took place in an Anglo-American context), pointed out that

> Experimental research on observers' reactions to manipulated hesitancy and speech rate show quite conclusively that absence of hesitation pauses and generally faster speech rate yield more speaker evaluations in terms of extroversion, competence and likeability.
>
> (Scherer 1979: 166)

At the other end of the tempo scale, I suspect that slow speech is more likely to suggest seriousness, ponderousness, or pretentiousness. In *Twelfth Night*, Malvolio thinks he has received advice from Olivia about how to increase his status and act like a man of importance (though it is in fact a trick). He should adopt 'a sad face, a reuerend carriage, a slow tongue, in the habite of some Sir of note' (III.iv.64–5). Some caution, however, is needed in the interpretation of *slow tongue*, since it is possible that it could mean 'speaking little' (that is, being reluctant to speak), rather than speaking slowly.

Hesitation is one of a number of non-fluency features such as needless repetitions, re-starts, and syntactic anomalies. These features are so much a normal part of impromptu, informal speech that we barely notice their occurrence, unless they are particularly frequent. In plays the discoursal context is different (see 1.7.1). Short comments:

> '[. . .] if features normally associated with normal non-fluency do occur [in drama dialogue], they are perceived by readers and audience as having a *meaningful* function precisely because we know that the dramatist must have included them *on purpose*.'
>
> (1996: 177)

The non-fluency features of a character's speech may suggest lack of control and lead to impressions of nervousness, lack of confidence, shyness and so on. Such features play a part in characterisation in Shakespeare's texts. For example, in *Richard III*, the second Murderer's tender conscience is suggested in his needless repetition:

> | Clarence | Who sent you hither? Wherefore do you come? |
> |----------|---|
> | 2nd Murd | To, to, to —— |
> | Clarence | To murther me? |
>
> (I.iv.167–9)

2. Pitch range

Physique and height correlate well with a person's vocal apparatus. As Laver and Trudgill (1979: 7–9) point out, '[a] tall, well-built man will tend to have a long vocal tract and large vocal folds', and such a vocal set-up will tend to produce a lower pitch range. As a consequence of these physical correlations, pitch range is a good indicator of sex, the typical female range being higher (see references cited in Laver and Trudgill 1979: 11–12). Age is marked by a lowering of the mean pitch for a particular sex as age increases, but then a rise with extreme age (see references cited in Laver and Trudgill 1979: 9–10).

According to Scherer (1979: 186), for a male speaker whose pitch remains within the normal male pitch range, higher pitch may suggest extroversion, assertiveness, confidence or competence. These are states that may cause muscular tension, and thus a rise in pitch. If the pitch of a male speaker nears the normal female pitch range, then that high pitch may suggest weakness, effeminacy, lack of competence, nervousness, or emotional instability. There is no clear evidence as to what happens if the pitch of a male speaker is placed lower than the normal pitch range. I suspect that lowered pitch may be associated with impressions of responsibility, sadness, or even sexiness. The situation for women is under-researched.

In Shakespeare's plays, there is evidence that high pitch range is associated with argumentative, bad-tempered or emotional women, and low pitch range with submissive and attractive women. Much of Octavia's character in *Antony and Cleopatra* is revealed in a scene (III.iii) in which Cleopatra quizzes a messenger about how Octavia speaks, looks and acts. The truth of the messenger's information with regard to Octavia's character is somewhat open to question. This is particularly so as the scene progresses and it becomes clear that Cleopatra, in her jealousy, wants to hear that Octavia has a foul character in all respects. Nevertheless, this scene provides us with some evidence about what characteristics might be schematically associated with various paralinguistic and non-verbal features. In the exchange below, it is plain that positive characteristics are associated with women who have a low pitch range.

> Cleo. Didst heare her speake?
>   Is she shrill-tongu'd or low?
> Mess. Madam, I heard her speake, she is low voic'd.
> Cleo. That's not so good [. . .]

(III.iii.12–14)

3. Variation in pitch

According to research, 'High variability is seen as indicative of a dynamic, extroverted and outgoing and benevolent person, and seems to connote potency in terms of the semantic differential' (Scherer 1979: 187). Conversely, a flat voice with restricted pitch movement tends to suggest that the speaker is 'more masculine, more sluggish, colder, and generally more withdrawn' (Addington 1968: 502). No significant differences have been revealed between men and women.

Very restricted pitch movement would be consistent with the characterisation of Nym in *The Merry Wives of Windsor* and *Henry V*. Nym is very much a phlegmatic clod, and provides a good contrast with the dynamic blustering of Pistol in the same plays. High variability in pitch would be consistent with Pistol's character.

4. Loudness

Rather like pitch range, a larger physique is likely to correspond with larger respiratory volume, and thus greater loudness (Laver and Trudgill 1979: 7–9). Consequently, greater loudness could be an marker of a male speaker. However, loudness has been subject to little empirical research.

In Shakespeare's plays loudness is often associated with strong emotion, whereas softness is associated with calmness or humility. In the Induction to *The Taming of the Shrew*, the Lord's advice to his page is that in order to play the humble wife he should speak 'With soft low tongue' (Induction. i.112). We might also note Lear's famous line upon the death of Cordelia: 'Her voice was euer soft, / Gentle, and low, an excellent thing in woman' (*King Lear* V.iii.273–4). These suggest the positive evaluation of quietness (and perhaps low pitch range) in relation to women. In contrast, Katherina is renowned for her 'scolding tongue' (*The Taming of the Shrew* I.ii.98). This aspect of her character is not enough to put off Petruchio, who claims that he will take her on 'though she chide as loud / As thunder when the clouds in Autumne cracke' (I.ii.93–4).

5. Voice quality

In this sub-section I shall consider a rag-bag of voice qualities. Voice quality can mark one's age, most notably the 'breaking' voice of male puberty, as well as the hoarse, thin voice of old age, brought about by physiological changes (see references cited in Laver and Trudgill 1979: 10). Regarding personality features, Addington (1968) carried out a study using American subjects, in order to discover the aspects of personality that are stereotypically associated with a number of descriptive labels for voice qualities such as 'breathy', 'throaty', and so on. His study is often cited as evidence of particular speech and personality correlations (e.g. Scherer 1979; Zebrowitz 1990). Unfortunately, whilst some of the labels he uses are relatively transparent, others are less so, and none are explained. 'Breathiness' results when the vibration efficiency of the vocal folds is affected. For example, sexual arousal results in changes to the mucus covering the vocal folds, and hence causes a 'breathy' voice. Marilyn Monroe, of course, was famous for her breathy voice. A 'nasal' voice results from 'a tendency to keep the soft palate lowered throughout speech' (Laver and Trudgill 1979: 14). A nasal quality is characteristic of RP speakers. A 'tense' voice quality is 'frequently marked, but not always, especially by the hardening of the musculature in the pharyngeal cavity — the part that is affected when one suffers from a sore throat' (Brown 1990: 129). Such a tense quality is a characteristic of old age. Addington's label 'throaty' or 'guttural' is probably what other researchers call a 'velarised voice', resulting from 'the tendency to keep the tongue raised towards the soft palate' (Laver and Trudgill 1979: 14). Such a voice is characteristic of speakers from Liverpool and Birmingham. Finally, Addington's 'orotund' is probably what other researchers call a 'labialised voice', resulting from 'the tendency to maintain the lips in a rounded posture throughout speech' (Laver and Trudgill 1979: 14). By way of example, this feature is more characteristic of Italian speakers than English. Addington's results are summarised in Table 4.5.

Table 4.5   Voice quality and personality impressions (adapted from Addington 1968)

Voice quality	Tendency for male speakers to be perceived as	Tendency for female speakers to be perceived as
Breathy	Youthful, artistic	Feminine, pretty, effervescent, highly strung, shallow
Nasal	Wide array of socially undesirable characteristics	Wide array of socially undesirable characteristics
Tense	Old, unyielding	Youthful, emotional, feminine, high-strung, less intelligent
Throaty	Older, realistic, mature, sophisticated, well-adjusted	Oafish or cloddish
Orotund	Vigorous, artistic, sophisticated	Lively, gregarious, aesthetically sensitive, proud, humourless

In Shakespeare's plays, Suffolk (*Henry VI, Pts 1 and 2*) comments on his own voice quality: 'Suffolkes Imperial tongue is sterne and rough: /

Vs'd to command, vntaught to plead for fauour' (IV.i.121–2). 'Stern-ness' suggests, according to Brown (1990: 129), a tense voice. Addington's results indicate that tenseness is associated with an unyielding person-ality. This is in accord with Suffolk's character, which revolves around imperiousness, inflexibility and unbridled passion. In *Twelfth Night*, Sir Toby Belch instructs Sir Andrew Aguecheek how to make an effective challenge to a rival lover:

> [. . .] so soon as euer thou seest him, draw, and as thou draw'st, swear horrible: for it comes to pass oft, that a terrible oath, with a swaggering accent sharpely twang'd off, giues manhoode more approbation than euer proof it selfe would haue earn'd him. Away.
>
> (III.iv.167–73)[26]

It is not easy to determine precisely what a 'a swaggering accent sharpely twang'd off' is. Clearly, it is one that leads to a supercilious, boastful impression of the speaker. Perhaps 'swaggering' suggests orotundity. Addington's (1968) present-day research would support the idea that this would help lend Sir Andrew an air of superiority. Perhaps 'sharpely twang'd off' suggests a nasal quality, which, according to Addington (1968), would be likely to result in a negative impression. In fact, these voice qualities suggest a persona that is very much at odds with Sir Andrew's real character: he is at heart a complete coward. Presumably, Sir Toby is trying to equip him with voice qualities which could foster such a forbidding impression that he may not have to prove himself in actually fighting his rival.

4.4.8 Visual features

Visual or appearance cues such as stature, clothing, facial expression, and posture play a key role in person perception and characterisation. As Jones puts it, 'the importance of *appearance cues* is almost impossible to overestimate in a first-impression situation' (1990: 7). As I pointed out in section 2.4.4, some researchers (such as Brewer 1988, Fiske and Neuberg 1990) have argued that a small number of 'primitive' social cognitive categories (notably sex, race and approximate age) are used relatively automatically and universally in perception. These categories are linked to salient visual cues (it is difficult not to notice somebody's sex, race and age). With regard to fictional plays, the importance of visual cues is reflected in my empirical investigation (see 2.6.2). Appearance features are amongst the descriptors elicited for both Jean and Billy, but particularly Jean. In fact, they are the only descriptors given which are concerned with concrete and perceptible aspects of character; all other descriptors are concerned with social, psychological, demographic, physiological or emotional characteristics.

This section is divided into two sub-sections, according to whether the visual cue is dynamic or static. Firstly, I will consider kinesic features (features that relate to body motion), and then appearance features (relatively static features of one's person such as physique). Within kinesic features, I also discuss the relative positioning of characters in terms of spatial distance. This aspect is often treated independently of kinesic factors under the heading 'proxemics'. As with the previous section on paralinguistic features, this section clearly concerns complex performance issues, and so my aim here is just to outline some crucial areas.

4.4.8.1 Kinesic features

How one positions oneself in relation to other people broadly correlates with the degree of social distance that pertains. This has been a well-established research finding since Edward Hall (1966) first comprehensively investigated spatial distance between people. We would expect intimates to be relatively close together, and strangers to be relatively far apart. Another important dimension is the relative power between people: one can maintain the respectful distance of a subordinate or the nearness of an equal. In the performance of plays, the arrangement of characters on stage should give the audience some idea of the social relations amongst them. *Richard II* is interesting with respect to spatial distance between characters, because the positioning of characters on stage can be a means of signalling that the 'normal' social order has been disrupted. Bushy, Green and Bagot have the love of the King, and thus might position themselves close to him. The rebels, notably Bolingbroke and Northumberland, who are of considerably higher social standing, construe Bushy, Green and Bagot as upstarts who have perverted the normal order, whereby social status and power is paramount in determining who is near the King, not social distance. As Green puts it, 'our neereness to the King in loue, / Is neere the hate of those loue not the King' (II.ii.127–8).

Facial expressions may be described with reference to the state of specific facial components: the forehead, eyebrows, eyes (including eyelids), nose, cheeks, mouth (including lips), and chin. When the face is neutral, and thus relatively uninformative, the facial muscles are relaxed.

The bulk of empirical research on facial expressions has investigated their correlation with particular emotions, notably surprise, fear, anger, disgust, sadness, and happiness (see Ekman *et al.* 1971). In Shakespeare's plays, the descriptions of facial expressions associated with particular emotions are accurate, when compared with present-day research. For example, Pericles (in *Pericles, Prince of Tyre*) describes sadness as 'dull-ey'd melancholy' (I.ii.2), and Olivia (in *Twelfth Night*) refers to an angry expression as 'the contempt and anger of his lip' (III.i.143). Both descriptions are in accord with Ekman *et al.* (1971). It is worth noting here that, although emotions are often transitory, they can be habitual. Some people or characters are dispositionally sad, happy, angry, and so on. For example, the lovers of Shakespeare's comedies (such as Lysander, Demetrius, Hermia and Helena in *A Midsummer Night's Dream*) are characteristically happy, the melancholic characters (like Jacques in *As You Like It*) are characteristically sad, and Queen Margaret in *Richard III* is characteristically angry and bitter.

A person's or character's gait can influence how they are perceived. Zebrowitz, reviewing various studies, concludes that:

> [. . .] impressions of adult walkers are influenced by the extent to which their gait resembles that of a young person. Youthful walking adults are perceived as happier and more powerful than their older walking peers.

> (1990: 78)

Broadly speaking, this is also reflected in Shakespeare's plays. In particular, gait reflects social as well as physical power. In *The Winter's Tale*, Autolycus declares that the old shepherd should have recognised that he was a courtier from his gait: 'Hath not my gate in it, the measure of the Court?' (IV.iv.729). In *Antony and Cleopatra*, Cleopatra is concerned about the gait of Octavia, her rival in love. The messenger dutifully condemns Octavia with a gait that characterises her as timorous and powerless.

> Cleo. What Maiestie is in her gate, remember
>   If ere thou look'st on Maiestie.
> Mess. She creepes: her motion, & her station are as one.
>   She shewes a body, rather than a life,
>   A Statue, than a Breather.

> (III.iii.17–21)

In addition to the aspects mentioned so far, there is a vast array of body movements and postures that have the potential to suggest or reinforce a characterisation. For example, solidarity between two people or characters could be conveyed by increased touching, eye contact, and the orientation of the torso towards each other (Mehrabian 1972). A bowed posture may suggest old age, depression or, especially in the historical context of Shakespeare's plays, social inferiority. This sense is clear in Queen Margaret's comment that her interlocutors 'bow like subjects' (*Richard III*, I.iii.161).

4.4.8.2 Appearance features

There is a strong body of evidence to support the idea that people attribute positive qualities to physically attractive people and negative qualities to unattractive people (see Zebrowitz 1990: 70–3, for a review). This correlation is evident in the characterisation of some Shakespearean characters. For example, Richard of *Richard III*, in his opening of the play, makes it clear that he is both ugly and evil. In *Othello*, Desdemona is both beautiful and good.

Stature can also convey characterising information. Indeed, the word stature can be used of both physical height and social standing. This hints at the fact that a tall person may give the impression of social power, as well as of physical power. In a play, one would not normally expect a short character to occupy a position of power, such as the throne.[27] There is some evidence indicating that taller men are viewed more positively than shorter men (Zebrowitz 1990: 76). In Shakespeare, this may also apply to women. Cleopatra, upon hearing that Octavia is not as tall as she is, concludes that she is *dwarfish* (III.iii.16), a word that obviously carries negative associations in this context. (See, also, Hermia and Helena's quarrel in *A Midsummer Night's Dream* III.ii, where Hermia's relative shortness is at issue.)

Other salient physical dimensions include the body's fatness or thinness. In Shakespeare's plays, fatness typically has positive associations and thinness negative associations. Falstaff (*Henry IV, Pts 1 and 2*, and *The Merry Wives of Windsor*) jokes about the girth of his belly. His fatness suggests his ebullience and self-indulgence. Physiognomy and even hair colour can furnish character information. For example, in Shakespeare's plays (and indeed more generally in fictional texts) white hair may suggest old age. A face that is very round or long, or a forehead that is very low, is viewed negatively. All this is clear in Cleopatra's conversation with the messenger, who does his best to paint an unpleasant picture of Octavia:

Cleo.   Bear'st thou her face in mind? is't long or round?
Mess.   Round, euen to faultinesse.
Cleo.   For the most part too, they are foolish that are so.
        Her haire what colour?
Mess.   Browne Madam: and her forehead
        As low as she would wish it.
Cleo.   There's Gold for thee.

(III.iii.28–33)

Clothing is obviously less static than the other features examined in this sub-section. It is an aspect a character can change. Dress codes play an important role in indicating social group membership. Dress varies according to such factors as social status, age, occupation, and income. In Sue Townsend's novel *The Queen and I* (1992), dress, as well as hair-cut, is a sign that Prince Charles has embraced the life of the lower classes. In this extract, PC Ludlow identifies Charles, who is in court on a charge of assault:

'Yes,' Ludlow said, also turning towards the dock. 'He's the one in the shell suit and pony tail.'
    The Queen was furious with Charles, she had told, no *ordered* him, to have a short back and sides and wear his blazer and flannels, but he had stubbornly refused. He looked like, well, a *poor*, uneducated person.

(p. 215)

In Shakespeare's plays, nobles may be instantly recognisable from their finery, the youth from their fashionable garb, clergymen from their habits, soldiers from their uniforms, and paupers from their rags. In addition, individuals may adopt specific items that have strong associations. For example, a walking stick suggests an old person, a crown suggests royalty. It should be noted that such associations are culture-specific. For example, Elam (1980: 11) notes that a twentieth-century audience is unlikely to associate the crown in *Richard II* with 'divine providence', as would have been the case with an Elizabethan audience.[28]

4.4.9 Context: A character's company and setting

Henry James was aware that a person's surroundings can tell us much about that person. Madame Merle spells this out to Isabel in *A Portrait of a Lady*:

> When you've lived as long as I you'll see that every human being has his shell and that you must take the shell into account. By the shell I mean the whole envelope of circumstances. There's no such thing as an isolated man or woman; we're each of us made up of a cluster of appurtenances. What shall we call our 'self'? Where does it begin? where does it end? It overflows into everything that belongs to us — and then it flows back again. I know a large part of myself is in the clothes I choose to wear. I've a great respect for *things*! One's self — for other people — is one's expression of one's self; and one's house, one's furniture, one's garments, the books one reads, the company one keeps — these things are all expressive.
>
> ([1881] 1947: 216)

Just as it is possible for a person or character to choose what to do or say and how to do it or say it, so it is also possible, assuming an absence of constraint, for a person or character to choose their surroundings, both physical and human. We associate certain choices with certain types of people. For example, one might generate schematic expectations about a present-day British accountant (a social role) such as: they live in a fashionable part of town, drive a BMW, have a mobile phone to hand, and mix with other grey-suited, conservative, townie types (whether they actually do or not is, of course, another matter).

In a Shakespearean play, one might expect a king to be at court or on the battlefield, surrounded by regal paraphernalia and consorting with the nobility or courtiers. The fact that Falstaff is frequently seen in taverns and mixes with disreputable characters reflects his nefarious character. That we also see Hal (*Henry IV, Pts 1 and 2*), the heir to the throne, in taverns and mixing with characters like Falstaff is highly foregrounded, since we would expect him to be at court. One might be tempted to infer that Hal has rather dramatically 'come off the rails'. Hal, however, soon announces to the audience in a soliloquy (*Henry IV, Pt 2*, I.ii.188–210) that his carousing with Falstaff does not reflect his true self, and thus we can discount such an inference. Occasionally, the setting chosen by a character suggests their emotional state. For example, Lear's breakdown is reflected in his choice of the wild heath.

The characters within a play can form patterns of similarity or contrast along particular dimensions. Here, I am touching on a structuralist approach to characterisation, that of 'semic' analysis (see 2.2.1). In *King Lear*, there are not only two similar plots centring around Lear and

Table 4.6   Character appearances on stage for each scene of *King Lear*

Act	I					II				III							IV							V		
Scene	1	2	3	4	5	1	2	3	4	1	2	3	4	5	6	7	1	2	3	4	5	6	7	1	2	3
Lear	1			1	1				1		1		1		1							1	1			1
Edgar		1				1		1					1		1		1					1		1	1	1
Kent	1			1	1		1		1	1	1		1		1				1				1			1
Gloucester	1	1				1	1		1			1	1		1	1	1					1				
Edmund	1	1				1	1					1		1		1		1						1		1
Fool				1	1				1		1		1		1											
Goneril	1		1	1					1									1						1		1
Regan	1					1	1		1							1					1			1		1
Albany	1			1														1						1		1
Cordelia	1																			1			1		1	1
Cornwall	1					1	1		1					1		1										
Oswald			1	1			1		1									1			1	1				
France	1																									
Doctor																				1			1			
Knight				1																						
Curan						1																				
Burgundy	1																									
Herald																										1
Old Man																	1									
Captain																										1
Gentlemen										1										1		1	1			1
Messengers																		1		1						
Servants																1										

Gloucester, but also two similar sets of characters. Both Lear and Gloucester are old and parents. Their offspring consist of good characters and bad. Gloucester's Edmund is rotten and disloyal like Lear's Regan and Cordelia, and Gloucester's Edgar is virtuous and faithful like Lear's Cordelia. These are very general semantic character patterns. In order to take a closer look at how the reader's *perception* of similarities or oppositions may be enhanced or suppressed, one can consider who actually appears with whom. For *King Lear*, I have followed Pfister (1988: 171–6) and constructed a matrix for the whole play, to display which character, or characters, appear with another character (see Table 4.6). If a character appears within a particular scene, I have inserted a '1' in the relevant box. One cannot assume from the resulting display that if, say, two characters both receive a '1' for a particular scene, they spoke to each other or even that they were on stage at the same time, since within a scene there may be many entrances or exits. One can assume, however, that characters receiving a '1' for a certain scene are at least in close temporal proximity to each other. The matrix also gives some idea of the relationship between the timing of a character's appearance and the play as a whole. I have included an additional layer of information in the list of characters by ordering them according to how much they speak (starting from Lear, who speaks the most). (This ordering does not apply to 'Gentlemen' or 'Messengers', since it is not clear how many different Gentlemen or Messengers there are.)

There is close correspondence in scene appearance between Kent and Lear. In fact, in only one scene (IV.vi) does Lear appear without Kent. This pattern reinforces an impression of Kent's dogged loyalty to Lear. A stronger pattern of correspondence is that between Lear and the Fool. The Fool only appears when Lear does and he only appears in the first half of the play during the period of Lear's 'madness'. This pattern not only reinforces an impression of the Fool's loyalty to Lear, but also the sense of Lear's foolishness. Cordelia has the longest gap between appearances of any character. Lear's failure to perceive Cordelia's reticence as a positive feature of her character sets off a chain of events that leads to his own downfall. Towards the end of the play she enters at the head of the French forces to 'save' Lear. Although Lear recovers his mind and discovers the truth of Cordelia's love, her death at the end of the play causes Lear to die of grief. It is worth noting at this point that, in terms of how much she speaks, Cordelia is positioned tenth, even lower than such characters as Albany. Cordelia's part *appears* to be a relatively minor one: she speaks in only four scenes and is on stage at the close of the play as a corpse. However, Cordelia's importance is in her relationship with Lear and in her dramatic role — she is the 'victim' of the play — rather than in the weight of her conversational participation.

The flat characters, broadly speaking those below Oswald in the list, do not appear frequently enough to form a pattern, but seem to function chiefly in relation to matters of the plot. For example, France's presence in the first scene facilitates our knowledge of his marriage to Cordelia, and this explains how she can return with French forces at the end of the play. The Old Man guides the blinded Gloucester and facilitates the meeting with Gloucester's son Edgar. Both of Kent's meetings with a Gentleman (III.i and IV.iii) are used to motivate events (for instance Kent commissions the Gentleman to link up with Cordelia), and to inform the audience of the current state of characters (especially Lear and Cordelia) and of the political events (such as France's plans to invade England). The servants enhance the tension and pathos in the scene in which Gloucester's eyes are put out (III.vii). One servant loyally tries to prevent Cornwall from blinding Gloucester's other eye, but is killed in the process, though he does succeed in administering a wound to Cornwall that proves fatal. The other servants comment on the wickedness of the act and determine to help Gloucester. Curan appears in II.i solely to inform Edmund (and, of course, the audience) of the fact that Albany and Cornwall are at loggerheads.

4.5 Authorial cues

In this section, I turn to cues that do not arise directly from the character concerned. These are cues over which the character notionally has no power of choice. As a consequence, I shall treat them as more closely associated with the author. The areas I shall consider here are names and stage directions.

4.5.1 Proper names

Proper names not only *refer* to particular individuals, but may also have *sense*. The vast majority of English first names communicate the referent's gender (exceptions include such names as 'Terry'). Moreover, Joseph Kasof, having reviewed a vast quantity of research (most of it North American) and conducted studies of his own, concludes that both first names and surnames 'differ in attractiveness and connote impressions of the name bearer's age, intellectual competence, race, ethnicity, social class, and other attributes' (1993: 140). It is not difficult to understand how these different associations have developed: at different times different names have been fashionable, and different social groups have preferred particular names. For example, according to Dunkling (1995), in England and Wales 'Florence' was the most popular name for girls in 1900 (presumably, the effect of Florence Nightingale), but now it sounds dated. Thus, the name Florence may lead to the expectation that the name-bearer is relatively old. The names 'Kevin' and 'Tracey', though popular in the mid-eighties, have experienced rapid decline (see figures in Dunkling 1995), presumably because they became strongly associated with the young, moneyed, working-class people of late Thatcherite Britain. Clearly, a writer can exploit the meaning potential of names in constructing a character.

Although the nuances of Elizabethan names may be lost, in the overlapping groups below I have tried to capture some of the characterising functions performed by character names in Shakespeare.

1. Reference to historical figures
A considerable number of Shakespeare's characters, particularly his rounder characters, are modelled on writings about real-life historical figures. This applies most obviously to the history plays which draw upon figures of English history. Other plays, such as *Antony and Cleopatra*, *Macbeth*, and *Hamlet*, also allude to real-life figures, namely those of Ancient Rome, Scotland, and Denmark. For plays such as these, it is worth noting that Shakespeare was drawing from medieval quasi-legendary history (such as Saxo Grammaticus), and thus the representation (or even existence) of some of the figures is even more unreliable. But the accuracy or otherwise of those historical figures is not the issue. The important factor is that the audience may already have a relatively well-formed impression of a character before even seeing the play. For instance, Richard III's supposed wickedness had made him a well-known figure well before Shakespeare put pen — or rather quill — to paper.

2. Nationality markers
Shakespeare's character names often suggest nationality, for example, the Italian names of *The Two Gentlemen of Verona* (such as Silvia, Lucetta, Antonio) or the Scottish names of *Macbeth* (Macbeth, Donalbain, Caithness). Shakespeare, however, was not overly concerned with consistency in indicating nationality or using the names of the country in which a play was set. *Hamlet*, for example, has many Italian or Latin names for Danish characters (for example Polonius, Bernardo, Marcellus). But there

are occasions when a name marked for nationality suited Shakespeare's purposes. In *Love's Labour's Lost*, Armado's name marks him as Spanish and this helps enhance his eccentricity, especially in contrast with the Englishness of his Page, Moth. The Spanish were favourite comic targets at the time the play was written, because England was at war with Spain and feeling a sense of superiority, having defeated the Spanish Armada three or four years previously. Other examples include Fluellen (the spelling presumably reflecting a typical English pronunciation of Llewellyn), Macmorris and Jamy whose names signal that they are respectively Welsh, Irish and Scottish.

3. Meaningful names

A number of Shakespearean names are meaningful in themselves, not just through their associations: they have conceptual meaning. For example, in *Love's Labour's Lost*, Anthony Dull is very much a clod; in *The Two Gentlemen of Verona*, Proteus is whimsical, fickle, and changeable; in *Henry IV, Pt 2* and *The Merry Wives of Windsor*, Shallow is shallow in nature; in *Henry IV, Pt 2* Silence is silent most of the time. Sometimes a character's name contrasts with their actual character. In *Henry IV, Pt 2*, Feeble, a woman's tailor, is the only one of Falstaff's recruits with the stomach for a fight. Falstaff takes the opportunity to point up the contrast: 'courageous Feeble' (III.ii.157), 'forcible Feeble' (III.ii.164). In *Love's Labour's Lost*, Moth's name achieves its meaning through its phonetic similarity with the French 'mot', meaning 'word'. Moth frequently uses his linguistic skills to upstage Armado, something that is made all the more humorous by the fact that Moth is a child.

4.5.2 Stage directions

Plays vary enormously with respect to how stage directions are employed. In Shakespeare's plays, stage directions are minimal (usually indicating entrances and exits, and possibly the setting), and almost certainly come from the hand of editors. The extreme opposite end of the scale is probably best represented by Bernard Shaw's plays, which contain such lengthy opening stage directions that they begin to look distinctly novel-like. Stage directions offer one way in which playwrights can characterise their characters. The key place where this happens is at the beginning of plays, for it is often here that characters are set up.

As an illustration of the richness of characterisation possible in an opening stage direction, I will consider the first part of the opening stage direction in Edward Albee's *The Zoo Story* ([1958] 1962: 113):

> PETER: A man in his early forties, neither fat nor gaunt, nei-
> ther handsome nor homely. He wears tweeds, smokes a pipe,
> carries horn-rimmed glasses. Although he is moving into
> middle age, his dress and his manner would suggest a man
> younger.
> JERRY: A man in his late thirties, not poorly dressed, but
> carelessly. What was once a trim and lightly muscled body
> has begun to go to fat; and while he is no longer handsome,
> it is evident that he once was. His fall from physical grace
> should not suggest debauchery; he has, to come closer to it,
> a great weariness.

First, we are supplied with group membership information. We learn
the sex of the characters from their names and *a man*, and their age
groups, *early forties* and *late thirties*. The characters are similar in age, but
in most other respects dissimilar. The next information we receive for
both characters concerns appearance. Peter's physique is *neither fat nor
gaunt, neither handsome nor homely*: he seems to be rather average. This is
reinforced by his clothes — *tweeds, pipe,* and *horn-rimmed glasses* — suggesting that his life has settled into a comfortable middle-class groove.
Jerry, on the other hand, is *not poorly dressed, but carelessly* and he has
experienced a *fall from physical grace*. Here, we learn something of Jerry's
history: there is a suggestion that there has been some change in his life,
a change for the worse. This impression of misfortune is reinforced by
the fact that he has a *great weariness*. This contrasts with Peter's manner
which should *suggest a man younger*. In terms of personal characteristics,
Peter has vitality and is in good spirits; Jerry is exhausted and has some
kind of latent depression. In sum, even though the stage direction is
fairly short, we are given group membership information, appearance
information, personal information, and character history. In addition,
each character's stage direction is clearly set up for us to infer aspects of
similarity and contrast between the two characters.

4.6 Conclusion

This chapter has revealed the numerous ways in which the text can be
manipulated in order to create a particular impression of a character. Two
areas, however, are in particular need of further research. Firstly, more
informant testing is needed in order to discover the relative importance

of different textual cues in fictional texts and to discover their schematic associations. Secondly, computer analysis of fictional texts would help identify linguistic dimensions of variation according to character. As far as automated analysis in the areas of grammar and semantics is concerned, there is at present no grammatically tagged version of Shakespeare and content analysis is very much in its infancy (see Wilson and Leech 1993 for first steps in this area).

Apart from the discussion of conversational structure in 4.4.1 and conversational implicature in 4.4.2, this chapter has not attempted to explore the interaction between different linguistic variables, and between language and contextual factors. The following chapter addresses some of these issues through the framework of linguistic politeness.

Notes

1 Of course, it is not the case that one's idiolect or dialect remains static. For example, although originally a Londoner, I sometimes find myself 'accommodating' to certain features of my local, Lancashire dialect in my own speech (see the example introducing section 1.4.2). Clearly, context can influence one's speech style.

2 An analysis of this passage can be found in Short (1996: 207–10).

3 The text of *Richard III* has a particularly troubled history. Davison (1996: 1) suggests that there are some 2,000 differences — roughly 10% of the play — between the First Quarto (1597) and the First Folio (1623). This particular part of the play varies considerably in different editions. Most significantly, the First Folio does not include turns 9 to 20. The text I use is that of *The Arden Shakespeare* (Hammond 1981). This text, like all the modern editions I consulted, is biased towards the First Quarto. Needless to say, punctuation is supplied by the editor, and thus is not necessarily a reliable basis for interpretation.

4 Admittedly, he gives Lady Anne a ring, but that is so he can possess her as his wife.

5 Lineation is not as in the original.

6 The main traditional etymological groupings in English are Germanic (including Old English, Old Norse, and Old Danish), French (including French and Old French), and Latinate (including Latin which had itself acquired many Greek words). These groups are not unproblematic. Many Latinate words have passed relatively unchanged into English via French, and sometimes there is doubt about whether a particular word was borrowed directly from Latin or indirectly via French (particularly if the Latin word appeared in English and French at a similar time) (see, for example, Baugh and Cable 1993: 221–2).

7 Lineation is not as in the original.

8 I exclude *Christian*, since it is a very early Latin loanword borrowed into Old English.

9 Some of these words may have been borrowed from Latin via French.

10 The type and the token statistics are taken from Spevack (1968).

11 Taavitsainen (personal com.) took some inspiration for the term 'surge feature' from Martin (1992: 533).

12 In Alexander's (1985) edition, all the First Folio's question marks in this passage, except those in lines 4, 11 and 12, are replaced by exclamation marks, as are a number of the commas.

13 In fact, Leech (1999) also considers terms of address in American English, but I have not presented those observations here.

14 I also generated a file for Lady Capulet, but it contained too few words (only 795) for useful and reliable analysis.

15 I repeated the analysis with the Log Likelihood test, but this made no difference to the results reported here.

16 *WordSmith Tools* has a facility for plotting keyword dispersion.

17 My meaning of 'the two most key keywords' is the two keywords that have the lowest probability value, i.e. the two words that are — relatively speaking — most unusual. I am not using the term 'key keyword' in Mike Scott's more technical sense.

18 Lineation is not as in the original.

19 Lineation is not as in the original.

20 Some possible reasons for this are: (a) other punctuation marks, such as the colon, did some of the duties which we would expect of the full-stop today, and (b) conjunctions and adverbs may have played a more important role in segmenting text.

21 The complexities of this sentence are famous (see, for example, Downes 1988). Some editors (e.g. Alexander 1985) split the sentence by placing a question mark after *most*.

22 See Gilbert (1979: ch. 2) for a discussion of 'high-style', 'middle-style' and 'low-style' in Shakespeare.

23 Although Miller's play is based on an actual event — the Salem Witchcraft Trials — that took place in the seventeenth century, and although the existing records of the event contain dialectal features in Tituba's talk (see Rissanen 1997), there is no evidence that Miller is trying to accurately represent the historical linguistic facts, including the little we know about dialects at that time. As a consequence, my interpretation here assumes a present-day reader applying knowledge about present-day dialects.

24 'H-dropping' does not characterise the middle classes, a fact which some commentators explain by noting the higher levels of literacy amongst the middle classes — they are more aware of the 'h' in the written form.

25 All statistics are taken from Spevak (1968).

26 Lineation is not as in the original.

27 Interestingly, in the real-life presidential campaigns in the USA there is a strong tendency for the tallest candidate to be elected.

28 For a semiotic account of dress, and theatre in general, see Elam (1980).

CHAPTER 5

(IM)POLITENESS AND CHARACTERISATION

5.1 Introduction

Any analysis of dialogue needs to be sensitive to the social dynamics of interaction. Broadly speaking, politeness is about the strategic manipulation of language, about expediting conversational goals by saying what is socially appropriate. In this chapter, I open with some examples designed to act as a preliminary justification as to why we need to think about politeness phenomena, if we are to study characterisation. I continue this justification in more detail in 5.5, where I argue that politeness theory encompasses linguistic areas that are key in person perception, and I make a case for the importance of politeness in fictional characterisation. I shall first describe the politeness theory of Brown and Levinson (1987). In addition, I shall note a possible extension to politeness theory, namely, 'impoliteness', which, I argue, is of special importance in explaining characterisation in drama.

5.2 Speech acts, politeness and characterisation: Opening examples

As I pointed out in 3.3.3, for a speech act to achieve success certain 'felicity conditions' (Austin 1962) need to be in place. For example, for a command to receive compliance it presumably requires a 'preparatory condition' (Searle 1969) such that the balance of power lies with the speaker. The types of speech act that people tend to produce may be related to the amount of power they have in relation to other people, as well as to their objectives, personality, and so on. As with other aspects of conversational behaviour, one's speech acts may be determined by social role, as much as personality. The fact that somebody issues many commands may be a reflection of their role as, for example, an instructor or a parent, or of their tendency to be bossy and aggressive, or a combination of the two. Clearly, analysing a character's speech acts is likely to reveal much about their character, and this has been demonstrated in a number of studies (for example Hurst 1987; Short 1989) (see also 3.3.3). By way of example, in 4.4.3.5 my *KeyWords* analysis revealed that the word 'go' is a highly salient aspect of Capulet's speech in *Romeo and Juliet*. Further analysis established that in almost all cases 'go' was used with the force of a command. It is this speech act that sets him up as a controlling figure in the play. In most cases his commands are successful, something which is not surprising given his power as head of the household. However, an exception is his spectacular failure to control his daughter's love. That he thought he could control Juliet in the same way that he controlled other people is, of course, part of the tragedy of the play.

In addition to analysing *what* speech acts characters use, we also need to consider *how* they perform their speech acts. Searle (1975b), for example, drew attention to the fact that grammatical sentence types did not always match the illocutionary force traditionally associated with them. For example, 'Pass the salt' contains a match between imperative form and requestive force. However, 'Can you pass the salt' uses an interrogative form to achieve the request. This is, in Searle's (1975b) terms, an indirect speech act. To crystallise the discussion, let us return to the passage from *Richard III* discussed in 4.4.1.1, and examine the two speech acts lying at the heart of this interaction: the request and the promise. Buckingham introduces his request for the title and wealth very indirectly. Literally, he makes a statement to the effect that he has considered the fact that Richard had requested his help in killing Hastings. Given the fact that he has now fulfilled this request, it is not difficult to infer, via the maxim of relation (Grice 1975), that he now wants Richard to fulfil his promise. Clearly, Richard is the more powerful participant and so Buckingham must soften the imposition of his request with indirectness. However, it is important to note that Buckingham has managed to make it clear that it was Richard who sought his help and it is Richard who now is indebted to him. Buckingham is more direct in turn 5 — *I claim the gift*. This is more than a straightforward request. A claim assumes that the speaker has some specific right to have the request complied with. His claim is based on the fact that Richard had earlier promised him the wealth and title. The fact that the promise has been made is reinforced by lexical repetition: the gift is his *due by promise*, and it is Richard who has made the promise — *you have promised*. Buckingham appeals to feudal values in pointing out that

Richard's *honour* and *faith* are in jeopardy, if he reneges on his promise. The impact of this is increased in light of the fact that other people can hear Buckingham speak. Buckingham has the moral balance of power. Buckingham's next utterance (turn 7) is an indirect request couched as a question. Here, as I noted earlier, Buckingham is also concerned to control the topic. Interestingly, Buckingham describes the speech act he has been trying to perform as a *demand*, suggesting that he sees it as stronger than a request, and made from a position of moral power.[1] As Buckingham's next three turns (9, 11, 13) are incomplete, one cannot be certain about the speech act involved, although one can note that in turn 11 he is able to reinforce the fact that Richard has made a promise. In turn 15 Buckingham makes an indirect request similar to that of turn 1, only this time reminding Richard that he has made him a promise. However, Richard's perspective is rather different. Buckingham's conversational behaviour is characterised as the speech act of *begging*, implying that the 'request' is made from a position of complete powerlessness — it is more of an appeal to Richard's largesse.

Analysing how characters, or indeed people, perform their speech acts tells us much about their goals, how they perceive interpersonal relationships, and how they manage the social context. All this is very much the business of politeness.

5.3 Linguistic politeness

Over the last 20 years politeness theories have concentrated on how we employ communicative strategies to maintain or promote social harmony:

> [The role of the Politeness Principle is] to maintain the social equilibrium and the friendly relations which enable us to assume that our interlocutors are being cooperative in the first place.

> (Leech 1983: 82)

> . . . politeness, like formal diplomatic protocol (for which it must surely be the model), presupposes that potential for aggression as it seeks to disarm it, and makes possible communication between potentially aggressive parties.

> (Brown and Levinson 1987: 1)

> Politeness can be defined as a means of minimizing confrontation in discourse — both the possibility of confrontation occurring at all, and the possibility that a confrontation will be perceived as threatening.
>
> (Lakoff 1989: 102)

It is particularly important to note Craig *et al.*'s distinction between 'politeness as a system of *message strategies* and politeness as a *social judgement*' (1986: 456). In this chapter I shall concentrate on politeness as the strategic manipulation of verbal and non-verbal behaviour in the pursuit of social harmony, not as a judgement of social 'niceness' (the lay person's notion of 'politeness'). This is not to say that a politeness analysis does not involve social judgements of any sort. In order to decide, for example, whether somebody is being over-polite or polite enough in a particular context, a complex social judgement is required.

In the field of politeness Brown and Levinson's work (1978, 1987) is the best known and the most researched, though by no means without weaknesses and faults.[2] In their work they attempt to relate the following aspects: (1) face, (2) acts that threaten face, (3) sociological variables influencing face threat, and (4) five general ways (or 'superstrategies'), with their associated linguistic strategies, of counterbalancing face threat. I shall provide a critical introduction to (1), (2) and (3) in 5.3.1, and then (4) in 5.3.2.

5.3.1 Face, face-threatening acts, and degree of face threat

What is face? Notions such as reputation, prestige, and self-esteem all involve an element of face. The term is perhaps most commonly used in the idiom *losing face*, meaning that one's public image suffers some damage, often resulting in humiliation or embarrassment. Such reactions are suggestive of the emotional investment in face. Much modern writing on face draws upon the work of Goffman (for example 1967, 1971), though the concept can be traced back to the fourth century BC in China (Tracy 1990). Brown and Levinson's conception of face consists of two related components, which they assume are universal: '*every* member wants to claim for himself' (1987: 61) [my italics]. Their conception of *positive* face, characterised in terms of wants, is as follows:

the want of every member that his wants be desirable to at least some others . . . in particular, it includes the desire to be ratified, understood, approved of, liked or admired.

(1987: 62)

I may assume, for example, that you want me to acknowledge your existence (for instance say 'Hello'), approve of your opinions ('You're right about that student'), or express admiration ('I thought you did a good job'). *Negative* face wants are defined as 'the want of every *competent adult member* that his actions be unimpeded by others' (1987: 62). I may assume, for example, that you want me to let you attend to what you want, do what you want, and say what you want.

It is worth noting that the way face is manifested outside the theorist's vacuum seems to be less clear-cut than Brown and Levinson imply. In particular, they underestimate the impact of context: positive and negative face cannot be assumed to apply in quite the same way across cultures, individuals, situations, acts, time, and so on. Furthermore, it should be stressed that face is not confined to the self, but includes all that the self identifies with. Thus an insult directed at the colour of my shoes will hurt less than one levelled at this chapter: I have invested much more of myself in the latter and see it as a reflection upon my abilities as an academic, a key face component given my career goals. Of course, it is not difficult to think of someone for whom shoe colour is a primary face concern, reflecting a fashion-conscious self. Face varies from person to person.

Any action that impinges in some degree upon a person's face (typically, orders, insults, criticisms) is a 'face-threatening act' (hereafter, FTA). Facework can be designed to maintain or support face by counteracting threats, or potential threats, to face. This kind of facework is often referred to as redressive facework, since it involves the redress of an FTA. Brown and Levinson's discussion of politeness is confined to this kind of redressive facework. For example, compare the following two utterances, 'I wondered if I could trouble you to do this for me', and, 'Do this'. Both threaten the negative face of the hearer in exacting some sort of cost or effort from them. The first utterance, however, is considerably 'softened' through politeness strategies. The fact that the speaker takes the trouble to avoid a direct and concise means of pursuing a particular goal implicates (1) the speaker's acknowledgement of the face-threatening potential of the act, and (2) concern to maintain the hearer's face. A point to note about FTAs is that they are not restricted to threatening the hearer's face. Brown and Levinson make a distinction (1987: 65–8) between those that primarily threaten the hearer's face (such as orders, requests, threats, criticism, contradictions, and the mention of taboo topics), and those that primarily threaten the speaker's face (like expressing thanks, unwilling promises and offers, apologies, the breakdown of physical control over one's body, and confessions).

An issue that Brown and Levinson's model fails to tackle is the fact that acts can, and often do, contain multiple face threats. The sort of decontextualised speech acts they use do not reflect the indeterminacies of utterances and the face-threatening ramifications they may have for any of the participants in a particular speech event. Moreover, a face-threatening act can take place over a sequence of utterances. Requests, for example, are often played out over a series of turns. An utterance such as 'Could you do me a favour?' could function as a pre-request and have important politeness implications for the main request. Brown and Levinson's work includes no extended examples. The root of these problems is that Brown and Levinson's work is based on the theory of speech acts which has been criticised for tending to focus on single acts with a single force (see Levinson 1981; Thomas 1985b; Leech 1983). Brown and Levinson's work is also weakened by the fact that it is confined to facework designed to *maintain* face. Facework can also be designed to *enhance* face. For example, giving a compliment out of the blue or wishing somebody 'Happy Birthday' can enhance positive face; lending a helping hand or offering directions to somebody who is lost can enhance negative face. Such facework is not linked to a FTA. Facework can also be designed to *attack* face. An FTA is deliberately performed with the aim of damaging face. For example, sarcasm, calling names, and snubs are strategies typically used to attack face. It is this kind of facework that I shall pay special attention to when I consider 'impoliteness' in 5.4.

Brown and Levinson argue that an assessment of the amount of face threat of a particular act involves three sociological variables: (1) the social distance between participants, (2) the relative power of the hearer over the speaker, and (3) the absolute ranking of the imposition involved in the act. For example, asking a new colleague for a cup of tea is more face-threatening than asking a long-standing colleague (the distance variable); asking one's employer for a cup of tea is more face-threatening than asking a colleague (the power variable); and asking for a glass of vintage port is more face-threatening than asking for a glass of water (the ranking variable). Brown and Levinson defined these variables thus:

1) *Distance (D)* is a symmetric social dimension of similarity/difference between the speaker and the hearer. It is often based on the frequency of interaction. The reciprocal giving and receiving of positive face is symptomatic of social closeness.

2) *Relative Power (P)* of the hearer over the speaker is an asymmetric social dimension. It is the degree to which a participant can impose his own plans and self-evaluation (face). Deference is symptomatic of a great power differential.

3) *Absolute Ranking (R)* refers to the ordering of impositions according to the degree to which they impinge upon an interactant's face wants in a particular culture and situation. Negative face impositions can be ranked according to the expenditure (a) of *services* (including the provision of time) and (b) of *goods* (including non-material goods like information, as well as the expression of regard and other face payments). Positive face impositions can be ranked according to the amount of 'pain' suffered by the other, based on the discrepancy between the other's self-image and that presented in the FTA.

(summarised from 1987: 74–8)

Brown and Levinson claim that these three variables subsume all other factors that can influence an assessment of face threat. They suggest (1987: 76) that numerical values could be attached to each variable, and that the variables can be summed according to the following formula to provide an act's weightiness or expected amount of face threat: $W_\chi = D(S,H) + P(H,S) + R_\chi$. W_χ refers to the weightiness of an act, $D(S,H)$ refers to the distance between speaker and hearer, $P(H,S)$ refers to the hearer's power in relation to the hearer, and R_χ refers to the degree of imposition of the act. The point of calculating face threat, according to Brown and Levinson, is that it will lead to 'a determination of the level of politeness with which, other things being equal, an FTA will be communicated' (1987: 76). They do not, however, attempt to apply this formula in a quantitative analysis of face threat.

Research has supported Brown and Levinson's claims for the power variable: the more powerful speaker being associated with less politeness (see for example Falbo and Peplau 1980; Baxter 1984; Holtgraves 1986;

Brown and Gilman 1989). Similarly, research has generally supported claims about the rank variable: the greater imposition being associated with more politeness (Cody *et al.* 1981; Lustig and King 1980; Brown and Gilman 1989; Holtgraves and Yang 1990). However, evidence for claims about the distance variable, that politeness increases with distance, has been inconsistent. Evidence for or against the distance variable is very difficult to assess. This is mainly due to the lack of agreement as to what constitutes 'distance' ('solidarity' in Brown and Gilman's (1960) terminology, or 'social distance' in Leech's (1983)). Brown and Gilman base their 'solidarity' dimension on 'similarities' that 'make for like-mindedness or similar behaviour dispositions' (1960: 258). Baxter (1984) assumes that it is to do with affect (liking) in a relationship. Craig *et al.* (1986) base distance on familiarity (that is, frequency of interaction). Brown and Levinson arrive at a definition of distance (1987: 76–7) that can encompass all three aspects: similarity, affect, and familiarity. However, some research (Slugoski and Turnbull 1988; Brown and Gilman 1989) indicates that affect should be treated as a separate variable. For affect, their data suggest the opposite of Brown and Levinson's predictions; in other words, they found that more politeness was associated with greater liking.

Brown and Levinson concede (1987: 12) that they 'underplay the influence of other factors' in determining the seriousness of face threat. The rights and obligations involved in a social role relationship receive inadequate attention. For example, a salesperson is obliged to serve a customer, and a customer has the right to be served. A result of such a relationship is that certain acts are legitimised, but not others. A customer could not ask the salesperson to tie his or her shoelace without radically increasing the face threat (assuming no exceptional mitigating circumstance such as the customer having no arms!). Other factors such as the presence of a third party, formality or mood may be important. One might, for instance, tone down a criticism of somebody because the face damage that person might suffer would be increased by the presence of a third party (for example a student's peers in a seminar).

Brown and Levinson assume that the effects of power, distance and rank on the perceived degree of face threat are independent of each other and additive; that is to say, each variable would have the same effect regardless of the other variables. This understanding is implicit in their formula $W_\chi = D(S,H) + P(H,S) + R_\chi$. However, there is some empirical evidence which suggests that the combination of these variables is not that simple. For example, Blum-Kulka *et al.* (1985) and Holtgraves and Yang (1990) both found a relationship between power and distance such that when the speaker and hearer differed in power, distance had little effect. Moreover, Myers (1991: 44–5) notes a more general difficulty with the combination of variables: values for these variables are not given, but are constructed in interaction. For each variable 'there is not one value, but a tension between at least two interpretations of the situation' (Myers 1991: 44). An interesting example of this occurred during the meeting of the Vice-Chancellor and Student Union President at my university. The Student Union President perceived the relationship as more equal than did the Vice-Chancellor. He consistently used the Vice-Chancellor's first name in spite of the fact that this was not reciprocated: the Vice-Chancellor used title plus surname to address the Student Union President. In other words, they both used discourse strategies — terms of address — in an attempt to shape the nature of the social relationship between them.[3]

5.3.2 Superstrategies

Brown and Levinson proposed five superstrategies (general orientations to face) that are systematically related to the degree of face threat. A rational actor will select an appropriate superstrategy to counterbalance the expected face threat. Thus, the less the imposition of the act, the less powerful and distant the other is, the less polite one will need to be. The individual superstrategies are briefly outlined below. The first superstrategy is associated with lowest face threat, and the last with the most.

1) *Bald on record*
The FTA is performed 'in the most direct, clear, unambiguous and concise way possible' (Brown and Levinson 1987: 69); in other words, in accordance with Grice's Maxims (1975). No attempt is made to acknowledge the hearer's face wants. This strategy is typically used in emergency situations (such as shouting 'Get out' when a house is on fire), when the face threat is very small (such as 'Come in', said in response to a knock at the door), and when the speaker has great power over the hearer (like 'Stop complaining', said by a parent to a child).

2) *Positive politeness*
The use of strategies designed to redress the addressee's positive face wants. The speaker indicates that in general they want some of the hearer's positive face wants, by, for example, paying attention to the hearer ('Hello'), expressing interest, approval or sympathy ('That was

so awful, my heart bled for you'), using in-group identity markers ('Liz, darling'), seeking agreement ('Nice weather today'), avoiding disagreement ('Yes, it's kind of nice'), assuming common ground ('I know how you feel'), and so on. The sphere of relevant redress is not restricted to the imposition incurred in the FTA itself. The idea is that the general appreciation of the hearer's wants will serve to counter-balance the specific imposition. The expression of positive politeness as a motivated strategy of face threat redress is marked by exaggeration (Brown and Levinson 1987: 101). It is this that serves to distinguish it from normal familiar behaviour. A general spin-off of positive politeness techniques is that they act as 'a kind of social accelerator' (1987: 103), since in using them one indicates a wish to be closer to the addressee.

3) *Negative politeness*
The use of strategies designed to redress the addressee's negative face wants. The speaker indicates respect for the hearer's face wants and the wish not to interfere with the hearer's freedom of action. It includes such strategies as mollifying the force of an utterance with questions and hedges ('Actually, I wondered if you could help?'), being pessimistic ('I don't suppose there would be any chance of a cup of tea?'), giving deference, that is, treating the addressee as a superior and thereby emphasising rights to immunity ('I've been a real fool, could you help me out?'), apologising ('I'm sorry, I don't want to trouble you but . . .'), impersonalising the speaker and the hearer ('It would be appreciated if this were done'), and so on. In contrast with positive politeness, negative politeness focusses on the redress of the particular face threat caused by an act. One might say that positive politeness attempts to provide the pill with a sugar coating, but that negative politeness attempts to soften the blow. A further contrast is that a spin-off of negative politeness techniques increases social distance, it acts as a 'social brake'.

4) *Off-record*
The FTA is performed in such a way that 'there is more than one unambiguously attributable intention so that the actor cannot be held to have committed himself to one particular intent' (Brown and Levinson 1987: 69). In other words, it is performed by means of an implicature (Grice 1975). The speaker's face-threatening intention can be worked out by means of an inference triggered by the flouting of a maxim. Such implicatures may be denied. For example, 'I'm thirsty', said with the goal of getting a cup of tea, flouts the maxim of relation (Grice 1975). In a suitable context the hearer may be able to infer that the speaker is

asking for a cup of tea, but, if challenged, the speaker could always deny this.

5) *Withhold the FTA*
The speaker actively refrains from performing the FTA. As Craig *et al.* point out, 'an option every communicator has is not to talk' (1986: 442).

Brown and Levinson admit that they 'may have been in error to set up the three super-strategies, positive politeness, negative politeness, and off record, as ranked unidimensionally to achieve mutual exclusivity' (1987: 18), but they argue that there is an 'absence of definitive evidence' that they 'got the ranking wrong' (1987: 20), and resist the idea that strategies can be mixed (for example, positive politeness markers occurring in negative politeness strategies such as indirect requests) (1987: 17–20). However, a number of researchers have challenged the ranking. Blum-Kulka *et al.* (1985) suggests that off–record strategies could be less polite than negative politeness strategies, since it is impolite to require a superior to calculate the force of an off-record request. Baxter (1984) suggests that positive politeness may presuppose negative politeness and should therefore occupy a higher position in the hierarchy. Several researchers (for example Scollon and Scollon 1981; Craig *et al.* 1986; Tracy 1990; Lim and Bowers 1991) argue that, because positive and negative politeness are different in type, they cannot be ranked unidimensionally. Like the superstrategies, the output strategies for positive and negative politeness are not linked to any single underlying dimension of politeness. As Shimanoff (1977) notes, sometimes they are defined functionally ('Be pessimistic') and sometimes linguistically ('Question, hedge') (see also Craig *et al.* 1986). In general, an important point to note is that politeness is not just determined by a particular strategy: it is determined by a particular strategy in a particular context.

5.4 A note on impoliteness

So far I have considered issues to do with politeness: how we use linguistic strategies to maintain or promote harmonious social relations. However, as I pointed out in 5.3.1, there are times when people use linguistic strategies to attack face — to *strengthen* the face threat of an act. I will used the label 'impoliteness' to describe this kind of linguistic strategy. A full description of impoliteness can be found in Culpeper (1996a).[4] Here, I will confine myself to an illustrative example.

Imagine the different ways in which the face-threatening act of criticism might be conveyed — say, criticism of a paper you have written:

Perhaps it could have been improved   POLITENESS

It wasn't good

It was bad

It was crap

You must have shit for brains   IMPOLITENESS

Here we have a scale varying from very polite to very impolite. At one end of the scale, the utterance 'Perhaps it could have been improved' could be interpreted as polite, given a suitable context, for two reasons: (1) the hedge 'perhaps' reduces the force of the speaker's criticism, and (2) 'it could have been improved' is an oblique way of expressing the criticism. The speaker flouts Grice's maxim of manner (Grice 1975), and conveys the criticism in an implicature. This is an example of what Brown and Levinson (1987) would call an off-record strategy. At the other end of the scale, the utterance 'You must have shit for brains' could be interpreted as extreme positive impoliteness, given a suitable context, for several reasons: (1) 'shit' is a taboo word (more so than 'crap'), (2) the criticism is personalised through the use of 'you', and (3) the speaker flouts Grice's maxim of quality, in order to implicate the impolite belief that the writer has absolutely no intelligence. What about the utterance 'It was bad' in the middle of the scale? Whether one interprets this as polite or impolite would depend very much on the context, as well as prosodic and paralinguistic features. For example, if it were not part of someone's role (as a tutor, say) to make the criticism, and if it were known that the addressee was particularly sensitive to criticism, then 'It was bad' would seem to be impolite. It should be noted that the key difference between politeness and impoliteness is a matter of *intention*: whether it is the speaker's intention to support face (politeness) or to attack it (impoliteness). Of course, there are a number of other types of rudeness. For example, a speaker might unintentionally cause offence or might use *mock* impoliteness (banter), perhaps to reinforce social solidarity. These would not constitute cases of 'genuine' impoliteness, as I have defined it here.

Leech claims that conflictive communication tends to be 'rather marginal to human linguistic behaviour in normal circumstances' (1983: 105).

In general this is true, but of course there are some contexts where such behaviour is not so marginal. Researchers (such as Lakoff 1989, Penman 1990) have found that the language of the courtroom, for example, is characterised by its aggression. I would suggest that drama, particularly in recent decades, is also a context where verbal conflict is not so marginal. Aggression has for thousands of years been a source of entertainment. Consider the fact that the courtroom has been the basis for numerous films and television dramas. The courtroom provides a socially respectable and legitimate form of verbal aggression. Moreover, I would argue that there are good reasons why drama in general thrives on verbal conflict. Impolite behaviour, either as a result of social disharmony or as the cause of it, does much to further the development of character, as well as plot, as I will demonstrate in 5.6.

5.5 The case for the importance of (im)politeness in characterisation

In spite of criticisms, Brown and Levinson's work is formidable in its range and descriptive power, and remains the most significant contribution to the study of politeness. But why is the study of politeness (or impoliteness) important for characterisation? In this section I make a case for its importance, first concentrating on (im)politeness and real-life person perception, and then (im)politeness and fictional characterisation.

5.5.1 (Im)politeness, power and person perception

Holtgraves, considering the ramifications of politeness theory for person perception, sees politeness theory as a way of accounting for impressions: '[politeness theory] provides a means for assessing how raw sensory input (i.e. language structure) is converted into specific impressions' (1992: 153). From the study of (im)politeness choices we can infer much about the dimensions that are important in the mediation of face in interaction, and as a result increase our understanding of personality. Brown and Levinson put it thus: 'an understanding of the significant dimensions on which interaction varies should provide insights into the dimensions on which personality is built, as well as social relationships' (1987: 232). Lachenicht (1980), discussing what he calls 'aggravating language', argues for individual variation in (im)politeness use:

> There seems to be good grounds for suspecting that particular individuals may favour particular [aggravation] strategies. Certainly this seems to be the case for politeness strategies: we are all acquainted with people who prefer to be informal, and others who prefer distance and formality. This does not mean that individuals may lack sensitivity to contextual changes, only that their flexibility is constrained to some degree by a preferred style of interaction. I think we can assume this to be the case for aggravation as well. Some 'hotheads' make abundant use of positive aggravation; some dangerous individuals habitually employ negative aggravation, particularly those in authority in total institutions [. . .] The acquisition of these strategies, then, must be at least partly linked to general social and personality development.

(1980: 682–3)

I have argued above that politeness is sensitive to context. There is evidence to suggest that person impressions are influenced by mismatches between politeness features and context. Holtgraves et al. (1989) showed that subjects are more sensitive to the assertiveness of conversational remarks made by same-status speakers than those made by a higher-status individual. Presumably, such assertiveness to an equal clashes with the predictions of the power variable (see 5.3.2 above). Holtgraves and Srull (1989) discovered that self-aggrandising statements decreased liking when not justified by the context (for example as responses to an enquiry or equivalent self-disclosure). Such statements would conflict with Leech's 'modesty maxim' (1983). Furthermore, there is evidence that, other things being equal, impolite remarks attract more attention than polite remarks (Wyer et al. 1994). Presumably, this is because they conflict with a conversational norm to be polite (see, for example, Grice 1975). This would support my argument above (5.4) for the particular importance of impoliteness in characterisation.

It should be noted that one of the sociological variables underpinning the usage of politeness is power. Erickson et al. (1978) investigated the effects of speech style on impression formation in a courtroom setting. They note that hedges (such as 'I think', 'I guess') are amongst the linguistic features typically associated with individuals who have low social power and status. Similarly, O'Barr's work (for example 1982) on courtroom discourse reveals a cluster of features associated with people with low power, including hesitations, tag questions, deictic phrases, polite forms, intensifiers and hedges. Such features are also reminiscent of the features Lakoff (1975) attributes to a 'women's language' (see 1.4.2). They may also, depending on context, be described within a politeness framework. Of course, the argument here is primarily that there is a schema that links such features to attributes like weakness, uncertainty, passiveness and ineffectiveness, not that there is an empirically true correspondence or that the schema is applicable in all contexts.

Let us briefly illustrate the discussion with a couple of examples from Sue Townsend's *The Queen and I* (1992). Here, Charles attempts to admonish his mother for being patronising:

> 'Mummy, I really think that you er — shouldn't . . . isn't it frightfully patronising . . . I mean, in our present circumstances . . . to call anyone "a little man"?'
>
> (p. 45)

Charles exhibits a string of negative politeness features. Charles's opening strategy is to be indirect: rather than saying something like 'You should/ought not . . .', he embeds the criticism in a personal statement *I really think that you*. But he even shies away from this, and re-starts the admonition as a negative question (*shouldn't . . .*), thereby removing his personal involvement and making the admonition yet more indirect. However, the obligation signalled in the modal *shouldn't* is also clearly too forceful for Charles, who re-phrases this with *isn't*. This search for indirectness, coupled with hedges and pauses, suggests Charles's relative weakness when compared to his mother. This second example illustrates how linguistic features conventionally associated with polite behaviour are also schematically associated with 'women's language':

> Tony Threadgold lit a cigarette and passed it to his wife. Then he lit one for himself. His good manners were often mocked at the Flowers Estate Working Men's Club. He had once said, 'Excuse me', as he struggled through the scrum at the bar with a tray of drinks, only to have his sexuality challenged.
>
> '"Excuse me?"' mocked a fat man with psychotic eyes. 'What are you, a poofter?'
>
> Tony had brought the tray of drinks crashing down on the man's head: but then had immediately gone to Bev and apologised for the delay in obtaining more drinks. Lovely manners.
>
> (pp. 34–5)

Features of speech that are schematically linked to powerfulness have not been well researched. One might reasonably expect devices that attenuate the force of a speech act to be associated with relatively powerless people, and devices that boost illocutionary force to be associated with relatively powerful people. Thomas (1984, 1985a, 1986) has examined 'unequal encounters' (interactions in which one participant is in a position of relative authority) and described the pragmatic and discoursal devices used by the powerful participant to maintain control. These include illocutionary force-indicating devices (such as 'I order you to go'), metapragmatic comments ('That was an order'), and reformulations ('I mean, get out of my sight now'). What these devices have in common is that they remove pragmatic ambivalence, they deny the subordinate participant the possibility of 'leaving the precise illocutionary intent of his or her utterance diplomatically unclear' (Thomas 1984: 227). Thomas (1995: 48) notes that people often avoid using an explicit performative, because 'in many circumstances it seems to imply an unequal power relationship or a particular set of rights on the part of the speaker'. As an example of power talk, consider Richard of Gloucester's attempts to stop the funeral procession of Henry VI led by Lady Anne (widow of Henry VI's son):

Glo.	Stay you that beare the Coarse [=corpse], & set it down.
Anne	What blacke Magitian coniures vp this Fiend, To stop deuoted charitable deeds?
Glo.	Villaines set down the Coarse, or by S. Paul, Ile make a Coarse of him that disobeyes.
1 Gent.	My Lord stand backe, and let the Coffin passe.
Glo.	Vnmanner'd Dogge, Stand'st thou, when I commaund: Aduance thy Halberd higher than my breast, Or by S. Paul Ile strike thee to my Foote And spurne vpon thee Begger for thy boldnesse.

(I.ii.33–42)

Initially, Richard uses imperatives (*stay, set*) to perform the command, but this strategy fails to achieve the required effect. Later he uses a metapragmatic comment, *when I commaund*, to make the force of his speech act clear. In addition, he uses impoliteness strategies. He employs abusive terms of address (*Villaines, Vnmanner'd Dogge, Begger*), all of which imply the social inferiority of the addressee. He also uses threats *(set down the Coarse, or by S. Paul, / Ile make a Coarse of him that disobeyes,* and *Aduance thy Halberd higher than my breast, / Or by S. Paul Ile strike thee to my Foote / And spurne vpon thee Begger for thy boldnesse).* That these threats are reinforced by reference to Saint Paul would, in the strongly Christian world of Shakespeare's England, have given them considerable clout. Such language implies Richard's relative power. In fact, whether Richard actually has the authority to support his command is debatable, considering that he is not yet king. The point is that he uses language to give such an impression of power that he achieves his goal. This, of course, fits Richard's characterisation in the play: he uses language to create for himself whatever persona suits his purposes. Immediately after the above exchanges he switches into love talk, in order to play the ardent lover and thereby seduce Anne.

5.5.2 (Im)politeness and characterisation: The study of *The Entertainer* revisited

A number of studies have shown that frameworks of linguistic politeness can be used to shed light on literary critical issues, and, in particular, characterisation (see for example Leech 1992; Simpson 1989; Bennison 1993). Why is politeness so useful in the study of drama? A framework that brings together face (an emotionally-sensitised concept about the self) and sociological variables (such as power and social distance) and relates them to motivated linguistic strategies is going to be particularly useful in helping us understand how characters position themselves relative to other characters, and how they manipulate others in pursuit of their goals. Such a framework will allow us to describe systematically, for example, how characters might ingratiate themselves with others, or how one character might offend another.

In the empirical investigation I undertook (see 2.6 and 3.8.3), respondents seemed to react in particular to (im)politeness factors. A number of the descriptors given characterise Billy and particularly Jean at the beginning of *The Entertainer* in '(im)politeness' terms. Thus, for example, Billy is *rude* (x 4), and *offensive*, whilst Jean is *polite* (x 10), and *deferential* (x 3). Of course, what my respondents understood by these terms may not coincide with my description above of linguistic (im)politeness. Let us briefly re-examine the data elicited in the second task where I asked respondents to indicate and comment on aspects of the text which they thought were important in Billy's or Jean's characterisation. Half or more of my twenty respondents marked the following segments of text as relating to their impression of Billy. (The number of markings are indicated in brackets, as are the text line numbers. The segments are presented in the order in which they occur.

1. Can't get any peace in this damned house (x 15) (line 5)
2. Can't even read the paper in peace (x 15) (lines 11–12)
3. I wondered who the hell it was. (x 10) (line 24)
4. I'd just sat down to read the evening paper (x 10) (line 30)
5. bloody farm-yard (x 14) (line 31)
6. Bloody farm-yard (x 11) (line 33)
7. Some black fellow (x 12) (lines 35–6)
8. I'd only just sat down to read the evening paper (x 12) (line 46)
9. give your Grandad a kiss (x 14) (line 52)
10. it's nice to see you, my darling (x13) (line 55)

As I pointed out earlier (3.8.3), segments 1, 2, 4 and 8 are complaints. Complaints are acts which threaten both positive and negative face (Brown and Levinson 1987: 67). Consider again Wierzbicka's suggestion that the meaning of the speech act verb of complaining is

I say: something bad is happening (to me)

I feel something bad because of that

I say this because I want to cause someone to know about it and to do
   something because of that that would cause me to feel better

(1987: 241–3)

To make someone aware of bad news is a threat to positive face; to want them to do something about it is a threat to negative face. Billy's complaints are bald on record: the FTA is performed in a direct, clear, unambiguous and concise way in circumstances where face is not irrelevant or minimal.[5] Bald on record is something of a grey zone lying between politeness and impoliteness. Whether one considers Billy's utterances as bald on record politeness or bald on record impoliteness depends crucially on intention: does Billy want to damage Jean's face, or does he just use the least polite strategy in an appropriate context? Jean has indeed disturbed him, and so this must justify the complaint to some degree. Note that Billy does not attempt to exacerbate the complaints, as one might expect with impoliteness. He does not, for example, explicitly attribute responsibility to Jean for being disturbed. So, bald on record politeness may be the more likely interpretation.

Respondents indicated, either through written comment in the questionnaire or in the group discussions, that the racist language of segment 7, *Some black fellow*, and the mild swearword *bloody* in segments 5 and 6 all break some kind of taboo. Taboo words can be used as a positive impoliteness strategy (Culpeper 1996a). However, it does not seem to be the case that Billy is pursuing an impoliteness strategy here. It is not clear that this language is designed to have face-damaging implications for Jean. The use of taboo language here has an expressive function: it has more to do with the fact that he is angry.

The change in Billy's behaviour is reflected in a shift from lack of politeness to considerable politeness. I have already commented on the fact that segment 9, *give your Grandad a kiss*, functions as an act of forgiveness (see 3.8.3). Billy cancels the debt or FTA for which Jean is apologising. Moreover, it affirms social relations between them, a characteristic of positive politeness. Kissing, in this context, is an act of reconciliation. If somebody asks for a kiss, one can assume that the speaker wants the kiss and feels close to whomever is being asked for the kiss. Such an act implies a polite belief, and thus being direct in expressing the act — in this case using the imperative *give* — increases the politeness. Billy also uses positive politeness in segment 10, *it's nice to see you, my darling*. The want to be liked lies at the heart of positive face concerns. In asserting that it is *nice* to see Jean, Billy satisfies this face want of hers. The term of endearment *my darling* claims in-group solidarity with and affection for Jean.

I observed in 3.8.3 that Jean's apologies attracted more comment than her other linguistic features. Brown and Levinson list apologising as a separate negative politeness strategy (1987: 187–90). However, their discussion concerns facework that precedes the performance of an FTA. Jean's apologies follow the performance of the FTA (disturbing Billy). She engages in what Goffman (1971) called 'remedial work', which functions

> [. . .] to change the meaning that otherwise might be given to an act, transforming what could be seen as offensive into what can be seen as acceptable. This change seems to be accomplished, in our Western society at least, by striking in some way at the moral responsibility otherwise imputed to the offender.
>
> (1971: 109)

suggests that three devices are used to accomplish remedial accounts, requests, and apologies. The kind of apologising discussed by Brown and Levinson (1987) is similar to Goffman's notion of priming. Requests take place prior to the FTA and (according to Goffman 1971: 114) involve 'asking license of a potentially offended person to engage in what could be considered a violation of his rights' (for example, 'Excuse me, could I . . . ', 'I'm sorry to bother you, but . . .'). Accounts and apologies are similar in that they both take place after the FTA. In brief, accounts consist of transferring responsibility for the offence ('The train was late', 'I had no idea you were so sensitive about this'), and apologies involve expressing regret for the offence ('I'm sorry about . . .'). However, the distinction between accounts and apologies is blurred. Fraser (1981) includes them both in his discussion of apologies, and in the literature on accounts, apologies are usually included (see for example Holtgraves 1992: 146–70).

Jean's remedial work consists of the apology *I'm sorry*, which she utters four times. She expresses personal regret for the offence. The penultimate time she apologises she says, *I am sorry*. Presumably, this is a cue for the actor to put additional stress on *am* and not to elide the vowel. By being unnecessarily long-winded in pronunciation, Jean flouts the maxim of manner (Grice 1975). She implicates that she is truly sorry. The final time she apologises she also says, *I disturbed you.* This might be described as a 'concession', which is a particular type of account. A concession involves admitting offensiveness and responsibility, and is distinctive in a number of respects (Holtgraves 1989). Firstly, Holtgraves provides evidence to support the claim that concessions are perceived as more supportive of the hearer's face than other types of account, such as excuses or justifications. In other words, Jean uses the type of account that is perceived as most polite to the hearer. Secondly, concessions are also least supportive of the speaker's face. In admitting fault, the speaker simultaneously supports the hearer's and threatens her own. Jean opts for a strategy that means personal sacrifice.

Politeness theory is effective in accounting for the conversational behaviour in the passage from *The Entertainer*, and also seems to correspond with the kind of impressions that my respondents had of the characters. Billy's shift from distinct lack of politeness to politeness corresponds with a shift in impression from negative characteristics like grumpiness to positive, affection. Similarly, Jean's politeness behaviour corresponds with her positive characteristics (affectionate, generous).

5.6 Characterisation in the film *Scent of a Woman*

In this section, I demonstrate how (im)politeness phenomena can be used in characterisation. I shall focus on the character of the Colonel in the film *Scent of a Woman* (1992), directed by Martin Brest. This is a re-make of the Italian film *Profumo di Donna* (1974). Of course films are not plays, but the differences relate primarily to the nature of the medium, not the dynamics of the dialogue. Short (1998) points out that a film embodies one particular performance; it lacks the variation of different stage performances. Also, film allows greater possibilities for the creation of realism or special effects, and it allows the exploitation of camera techniques for the manipulation of point of view, for instance.

Scent of a Woman revolves around two characters, Charlie and the Colonel, and is set in North America. Charlie is a student at a prestigious private school, but he is not rich and is supported by student aid. In order to make ends meet, rather than go home for Thanksgiving he responds to an advertisement asking for somebody to act as a carer for a blind relative — the Colonel. The dialogue below is the first encounter between Charlie and the Colonel. (Charlie = CH, Colonel = COL)[6]

    (1) CH: Sir?

    (2) COL: Don't call me sir.

    (3) CH: I'm sorry, I mean mister, sir.

    (4) COL: Uh–ooh, we've got a moron here, is that it?

    (5) CH: No mister . . . I . . . er . . . that is . . . er . . . lieu-
tenant, yes sir, lieu —

    (6) COL: Lieutenant-Colonel. 26 years on the line, no-
body ever busted me four grades before. Get in here, you idiot. [Pause] Come a little closer, I want to get a better look at you. How's your skin, son?

    (7) CH: My skin, sir?

    (8) COL: Ah, for Christ's sake!

    (9) CH: I'm sorry, I don't —

  (10) COL: Just call me Frank. Call me Mr. Slade. Call me Colonel, if you must. Just don't call me sir.

  (11) CH: Alright, Colonel.

  (12) COL: Simms, Charles, a senior. You on student aid, Simms?

  (13) CH: Ah, yes I am.

> (14) COL: For student aid read crook. Your father peddles card telephones at a 300 per cent mark-up; your mother works on heavy commission in a camera store, graduated to it from expresso machines. Ha, ha! What are you . . . dying of some wasting disease?
>
> (15) CH: No . . . I'm right here.
>
> (16) COL: I know exactly where your body is. What I'm looking for is some indication of a brain.

The Colonel's conversational behaviour comes as something of a surprise. We might have expected much politer behaviour, given that he and Charlie are complete strangers. Furthermore, it is likely that our prior knowledge of the role relationship between Charlie and the Colonel — that of 'carer' and 'cared for' — would have given rise to other expectations about their relationship and thus their behaviour. For example, we might have expected that the balance of power, at least in some respects, lay with Charlie. From the outset, the Colonel's conversational behaviour is contrary to expectations, and thus a possible trigger for a correspondent inference. His first utterance is oddly brusque. We might have expected reciprocal greetings, phatic activity of some kind; instead, in turn 2 the Colonel uses an imperative to command Charlie not to use *Sir*.[7] Thus, the deference encoded in Charlie's first utterance receives something of a slap in the face — negative face, in this case. The Colonel proceeds in his next turn (4) to refer to Charlie as a *moron*. Clearly, this is threatening to Charlie's positive face, as is the Colonel's term of address *you idiot* in turn 6. In the same turn, the Colonel's imperative command *Get in here* is particularly face-threatening. The Colonel's question *You on student aid, Simms?* (turn 12) transgresses social rules. It is taboo in western cultures for strangers to ask someone about their income. Moreover, earlier in the film we have been made aware that being on student aid is stigmatised. Charlie's response, the filled pause *Ah*, suggests that he is taken aback. In the following turn, the Colonel presents an offensive account of Charlie's parents' professions. Moreover, the Colonel has no evidence for this account: he flouts Grice's maxim of quality, in order to implicate an impolite belief about Charlie's parents. One should remember here that face is not confined to the self, but is invested in other things related to the self, including other people. Thus, an attack on Charlie's parents is an attack on Charlie's extended positive face. In the same turn (14), the Colonel asks *What are you . . . dying of some wasting disease?* Obviously, Charlie is not dying of a wasting disease. The Colonel flouts the maxim of quality and implicates the impolite belief that Charlie acts as if he were moribund. Similarly, the Colonel's utterance *What I'm looking for is some indication of a brain* (turn 16) flouts the maxim of quality, since there is no evidence that Charlie lacks intelligence, and implicates the impolite belief that Charlie exhibits no intelligence.

Charlie's contribution to this dialogue is restricted. He speaks much less than the Colonel — 32 words compared with 133 words — and, moreover, is interrupted twice (turns 5 and 9). The Colonel controls the dialogue, impeding Charlie's contributions and thus damaging his negative face. What Charlie does say is always polite. His use of *sir* as a deferential term of address back-fires, since the Colonel has some peculiar objection to it. This leads to two apologies from Charlie (turns 3 and 9) — a politeness strategy addressed to the Colonel's negative face. In addition, Charlie always attempts to comply with the Colonel's requests to do something (for instance, turn 3) or his requests for information (turn 13). Charlie's responses are 'preferred', that is to say, they are structurally unmarked (see 3.7.1). The key point to note about Charlie's politeness and the Colonel's impoliteness is the interaction — or rather the lack of interaction — between them: Charlie is polite in spite of the Colonel's impoliteness, and the Colonel is impolite in spite of Charlie's politeness. Each type of behaviour is made more significant in the context of the other. This significance can be explained by reference to the augmenting principle — greater significance will be attached to a behaviour if it is done in spite of reasons for not doing it.

The fact that the Colonel's behaviour is unexpected, consistently breaking social norms, invites explanation. A strong possibility is to attribute his behaviour to his character and draw a correspondent inference: the Colonel is an embittered man, a man with a warped personality, a misanthropist. But we should also note that the Colonel is no mindless antisocial being. His impoliteness is achieved through a range of strategies, some of them quite sophisticated, even a touch humorous. Charlie also exhibits a pattern of consistent and unexpected behaviour, given his unpleasant reception from the Colonel. Again, we can attribute this to his character and draw a correspondent inference: Charlie is the prototypical 'nice guy'. Perhaps he might also be thought rather shy, even passive or spineless, since he does nothing to counter the abuse. Clearly, Charlie and the Colonel are contrasting characters. As is often the case in drama, a system of contrasts helps in defining character. We shall see that these early impressions of the Colonel and Charlie develop as the film proceeds.

The Colonel takes Charlie to New York for, as he puts it, 'a final tour of the field'. He plans to enjoy himself and then kill himself. In what is probably the most famous scene in the film, the Colonel and Charlie are ensconced in a high-class restaurant, when the Colonel smells the scent of a woman. Charlie describes the woman to the Colonel, and seems to find her attractive himself. The Colonel determines that they should introduce themselves to the woman, Donna, and initiates the conversation below. (Colonel = COL, Donna = DON)

(1) COL: Excuse me, señorita, do you mind if we join you? I'm feeling you're being neglected.
(2) DON: Well, I'm expecting somebody.
(3) COL: Instantly?
(4) DON: No, but any minute now.
(5) COL: Some people live a lifetime in a minute. What are you doing right now?
(6) DON: I'm waiting for him.
(7) COL: Well, would you mind if we waited with you? Just to keep the womanisers from bothering you.
(8) DON: No, I don't mind.
(9) COL: Thank you.

As in the previous extract, this is the Colonel's first conversation with a particular stranger, but here his conversational behaviour is dramatically different. He opens the conversation with the apology *Excuse me*, a negative politeness strategy. His request for permission to join her, *do you mind if we join you?*, is indirect: it is couched as a question about whether she minds, not whether they can do it. He supports her positive face in expressing apparent concern for her: *I'm feeling you're being neglected.* When Donna fails to invite them to join her, the Colonel in turn 7 reiterates the request and increases the politeness: *would you mind if we waited with you?* The possibility that they might wait with her is further distanced — and thus made more indirect — by the fact that it is set in a hypothetical context indicated by the modal *would* and the use of the past tense. The Colonel also provides a reason why they should wait with her: *Just to keep the womanisers from bothering you.* Ostensibly, the Colonel is offering to do her a favour, a negative politeness strategy. Of course, there is also a touch of humour here in that the Colonel and Charlie themselves appear to be the womanisers. Donna agrees to their request, and the Colonel expresses gratitude, *Thank you*, a negative politeness strategy.

Thus, impoliteness is not the sole behaviour of the Colonel; he is capable of a far wider range. Moreover, we see that the Colonel can produce context-sensitive language: if he wants to produce face-supporting behaviour, in order to pursue particular goals in a particular context, he can. Category-based, flat characters tend to exhibit the same behaviour regardless of context. Our impression of the Colonel's character is likely to develop, but to what? Earlier we had an apparently embittered man taking gratuitous verbal pot-shots at Charlie; now we have someone laying on the linguistic honey, partly, so it seems, to help Charlie meet Donna. This contradiction forces us to pay more attention to the Colonel's character. The combination of the fact that he cannot easily be categorised within a social schema and the presence of motivational factors encouraging the audience to attend to him (for example he is the protagonist, he is intriguing, his linguistic dexterity and humour are attractive) may encourage the audience to move towards piecemeal processing, the basis for a round character.

Charlie's character remains fairly flat for the bulk of the film. He is the predictably polite Charlie in all contexts. However, in a tense scene three-quarters of the way through the film, Charlie develops suddenly and dramatically beyond a simple category-based character. The Colonel, in his hotel bedroom, is preparing to kill himself with a pistol. Charlie has been trying to persuade the Colonel to give him the gun, and has, characteristically, relied on politeness strategies. For example, in *Colonel, why don't you just give me the gun . . . alright?* he (1) uses a deferential term of address (and one approved by the Colonel!), (2) performs the request indirectly by asking a question about why the Colonel should not give him the gun, (3) uses the hedge *just* to minimise the imposition of the request, and (4) adds the tag question *alright?* which softens the presumptuousness involved in making the request. But Charlie fails to get the gun. At the point when the Colonel looks as if he is going to pull the trigger, Charlie grapples for the gun, and the Colonel threatens him with it, in order to get him out of the room. The following dialogue ensues:

    (1) COL: Get out of here.
    (2) CH: I'm staying right here.
    (3) COL: Get out of here.
    (4) CH: I'm staying right here.
    (5) COL: I'll blow your fucking head off.
    (6) CH: Do it. You want to do it, do it. Let's go. [*Pause*]
    (7) COL: Get out of here.

(8) CH: Look, you fucked up, alright, so what? So every-body does it. Get on with your life would you.

(9) COL: What life? I got no life. I'm in the dark here, you understand? I'm in the dark.

(10) CH: So give up. You want to give up, give up. Because I'm giving up too. You say I'm through, you're right, I'm through. We're both through. It's all over. So let's get on with it, let's fucking do it. Let's fucking . . . pull the trigger . . . you miserable blind motherfucker. [*Pause*] Pull the trigger.

Charlie's conversational behaviour is suddenly very different from what we have seen. This is the first time he directly defies the Colonel's commands (turns 2 and 4). This is also the first time he uses taboo words (turns 8 and 10). Clearly, in this kind of extreme situation, such verbal behaviour is not inappropriate. However, more strikingly, this is the first time he is impolite — 'you miserable blind motherfucker' (turn 10). This 'name-calling' strategy seems calculated to cause maximum positive face damage to the Colonel.

Charlie deviates dramatically from his usual pattern of behaviour. Deviation from a target-based expectancy (what we expect Charlie to do) can trigger a correspondent inference. Of course, how we interpret Charlie's behaviour depends on the context. There is no necessary equation that impolite behaviour results from a nasty personality. Charlie's goal seems to be to call the Colonel's bluff (note how Charlie handles the Colonel's violent threat in turn 5) and to shock him out of his present course of action. Charlie's attack on the Colonel's face is a short-term goal designed to bring long-term benefit to the Colonel. Thus we might infer that Charlie is not simply a 'nice guy', but somebody who has determination and bravery, somebody who is prepared to employ whatever means are necessary to achieve what he believes in, somebody who — as the Colonel puts it — has 'integrity'. The audience's impression of Charlie, then, moves away from being category-based towards piecemeal processing.

In *Scent of a Woman* (im)politeness is crucial to the construction of character. Thus, at the beginning of the film the extreme impoliteness of the Colonel and the extreme politeness of Charlie are likely to result in strong interpretative assumptions about their respective characters. The polarisation in their (im)politeness behaviour works in tandem with the polarisation or contrast of character. Later in the film, in episodes like that of the second extract above, the relationship between Charlie and the Colonel becomes more complex, as a result of changes in the Colonel's behaviour and, as a consequence, a shift in our impression of his character. In the third extract above, this contrast between the characters begins finally to be resolved. Charlie changes from exclusively polite behaviour and from this we understand a shift in his character. Moreover, the change in Charlie is also a catalyst for change in the Colonel. Charlie's impoliteness is more than an attempt to get the Colonel's gun. He tackles the causes of the Colonel's embitterment and his consequent drive towards suicide: his self-blame for his blindness (caused by playing with a grenade) and his self-pity for his blindness (see turn 8 in the third extract above). Moreover, Charlie is successful: he gets the gun and brings about a change in the Colonel. Needless to say, the Colonel uses no more impoliteness towards Charlie for the rest of the film.

5.7 Conclusion

The main objective of this chapter has been to argue that politeness and impoliteness features can be a central textual technique in characterisation. Moreover, (im)politeness goes some way towards capturing some of the more dynamic and functional aspects of language used in characterisation. Of course, one would not want to overstate the role of (im)politeness in characterisation. (Im)politeness theory has only an indirect contribution to make towards characterisation, since it focusses on the dynamics of social relations between participants, and not on *whether* a particular strategy might reveal the character of a participant or *what* a particular strategy might reveal about a participant. The issues of 'whether' and 'what' have already been addressed in Chapters 2 and 3, where I discussed schema theory and attribution theory.

Notes

1   In fact, the First Folio has the word 'request', not 'demand'.
2   See Fraser (1990) for a good review of other approaches to politeness.
3   I owe this example to Mick Short.
4   See also Lachenicht (1980).
5   Brown and Levinson's politeness model (1987: 64–5) assumes a rational actor, as indeed does my impoliteness framework. However, Billy's rationality may be an issue here. Respondent 6 suggests that Billy is possibly 'senile'. However, I think there is insufficient evidence to dismiss all of Billy's conversation as the product of an irrational speaker.

6   My transcriptions in this section do not attempt to capture performance-related aspects in any detail.

7   In fact, the same utterance could in other contexts be polite, if it were interpreted as a move in the direction of informality and equality. However, in the film prosodic and paralinguistic aspects of the utterance (e.g. the heavy stress on *Don't*) preclude a polite interpretation, and Charlie's following utterance, an apology, is evidence that he did not interpret it as polite.

CHAPTER 6

CONCLUSION: THE CHARACTERISATION OF KATHERINA IN SHAKESPEARE'S *THE TAMING OF THE SHREW*

6.1 Introduction

In this chapter, I bring together the various strands of this book and demonstrate that literary characterisation can be fruitfully approached by drawing upon theories from psychology, particularly social cognition. My analysis focusses on Katherina, the protagonist in Shakespeare's *The Taming of the Shrew*, who has been the subject of fierce literary critical debate. I will engage in this debate by showing how the psychological theories I have introduced can be used to shed light on the characterisation of Katherina and to support or refute particular literary interpretations. My analysis of Katherina encompasses her characterisation throughout the play. I first outline the kind of schema the Elizabethans probably had for a 'shrew'. I then argue that in the first part of the play the evidence is largely consistent with this schema, and thus our impression of Katherina is largely category-based. However, I show that as the play progresses a number of changes create the conditions for a more complex and personalised character. As a consequence of this analysis, I claim that Katherina is not, as some critics have argued, simply a shrew, or an inconsistent character, or a typical character of a farce.

6.2 Literary criticism and Katherina

The Taming of the Shrew has received less critical attention than most of Shakespeare's plays. In some critical works, even those on Shakespeare's comedies (such as Bradbury and Palmer 1972; Evans 1985), it is almost ignored. Similarly, several studies of Shakespeare's characters barely mention it (such as Kirschbaum 1962; Palmer 1962; Newman 1985). Admittedly, it is not one of Shakespeare's more complex plays. In terms of characterisation, there are relatively few characters, little psychological trauma in any character, and, as I shall demonstrate, relatively clear delineation of character. However, literary critics and producers of the play seem to have been troubled by the characterisation of the protagonist, Katherina. In particular, there has been controversy over the extent to which Katherina is a 'shrew': an evil, ill-tempered woman. Charlton is adamant that she is a shrew: 'curst and shrewd and froward' (1938: 97). Tillyard suggests that there is evidence for and against, but rather oddly concludes that, because of this, Shakespeare's play 'remains in its chief outlines not quite consistent, not completely realised or worked out' (1965: 80). Dash argues that she is not a shrew, but 'an alert, creative intelligence, rational and able to develop an idea with skill' (1981: 58–9).

Other issues which critics have addressed have also concerned Katherina's characterisation. A particular controversy revolves around whether *The Taming of the Shrew* is a farce or a comedy. Heilman argues that it is a farce, because the characters, including Katherina, lack 'the physical, emotional, intellectual, and moral sensitivity that we think of as "normal"' (1972: 324). Abrams (1988) and Tillyard (1965) suggest that the play is farce in parts. Coghill (1950) and Bean (1980) see it as a comedy, and view Katherina as more complex than a character of farce. Another issue that has attracted attention is whether, or to what extent, Katherina is transformed during the course of the play. Is she 'tamed', and if so, in what way? Critics have focussed on Katherina's final so-called 'obedience' speech, where she declares to the other women that 'Thy husband is thy lord, thy life, thy keeper' (V.ii.147). Hazlitt ([1817] 1906: 239) argues that Katherina's self-will is subdued by Petruchio's, which is greater: at the end of the play we are left with a pitiable, broken woman. In contrast, Kahn (1977) and Dash (1981), taking feminist lines, argue that Katherina remains unbroken. In order to sustain this interpretation, they take the 'obedience' speech to be ironic. Other commentators (such as Tillyard 1965; Morris 1981) have opted for what might be seen as the compromise interpretation: Katherina finally recognises the game Petruchio has been playing and joins him in it. The irony of the 'obedience' speech lies in the context: the audience knows that Katherina and Petruchio have made their peace, but the other characters do not. As Janet Suzman put it, 'That hyperbolic speech at the end of the play, reviled by feminists, can now become Kate playing, in public, the exact game she has been taught in private' (quoted in J. Cook 1990: 29).

No critic has comprehensively and systematically examined the construction of Katherina's character in order to support their interpretations, and many have focussed on the 'obedience' speech almost to the exclusion of other parts of the play. My analysis is designed to fill this gap. A key event in the play is the first meeting between Katherina and Petruchio which occurs in Act II, Scene i. This event represents an important structural turning point in Katherina's characterisation and is the fulcrum of my analysis. Before this event, I will show how Katherina appears to be a prototypical shrew. After this event, I shall argue that a number of changes create the conditions for a richer, more personalised impression of Katherina, which is not at all consistent with the argument that she is simply a shrew or a typical character of farce.

6.3 Analysis of Katherina in *The Taming of the Shrew*

6.3.1 The SHREW schema

For an Elizabethan audience, would the title of the play have activated a schema for a particular type of person — a SHREW schema? In my view, it is highly likely that most people would have had, or at the very least known of, a SHREW schema and what constituted some of its central features.

What might have been the features of the SHREW schema? According to the *Oxford English Dictionary (OED)*, the word *shrew* originally referred to any animal of the genus *sorex* (resembling mice but having a long sharp snout). Superstitions about the shrew developed, so that it came to be seen as wicked and evil. By the thirteenth century, these associations were transferred to men so that it was also used to mean 'a wicked, evil-disposed, or malignant man' (*OED*: Sb.1.a). By the end of the fourteenth century, it was often used to refer to the devil (*OED*: Sb.1.b). During the medieval period the word was also applied to women. One of the earliest such usages is in Chaucer's Epilogue to *The Merchant's Tale* (c. 1386): 'But of hir tonge a lobbyng shrewe is she'. In this context it meant 'a woman given to railing or scolding' (*OED*: Sb.3.a). This was apparently the dominant meaning in Shakespeare's time. Of course, one cannot rely purely on what a historical, literary-based dictionary has to say about one word, in order to describe the SHREW schema. At the end of the sixteenth century, the notion of a 'shrew' overlapped considerably with the notion of a 'scold', and to a lesser extent with a 'wanton' and a 'witch'.[1] In Table 6.1, I have reconstructed what might have been the Elizabethan SHREW schema, drawing upon evidence in the *OED*, Shepherd (1985), Mills (1991), and, more particularly, de Bruyn (1979).[2]

Table 6.1   Schematic elements in an Elizabethan shrew schema

Personal	*Habit*	Talkative
	Goal	To cause evil or harm
	Trait	Ill-tempered, assertive, disobedient, jealous, cruel, aggressive
Social Role	*Supernatural*	The devil's mistress (i.e. controller)
	Marital	Wife
Group membership	*Gender*	Female

De Bruyn (1979), which is in fact a much-used source for Mills (1991), examines stereotypes of women in the sixteenth century, drawing upon an array of evidence from poems, plays, treatises, legends, sermons, diaries, jests, tales and ballads. Needless to say, there can be no claim that statements about women in such evidence reflected what was happening in the actual lives of women; indeed, many historians agree that there was a gap between theory and practice (see Krontiris 1992: 7–8).

The connection with the devil, the shrew's presumed source of power, needs some comment. According to de Bruyn (1979), ancient legends and sagas had related the shrew to Lilith, who, in rabbinical mythology, was Adam's first wife and the person who led him astray. In these legends, Lilith was made the mother of the demons. In the literature of the Early Modern English period, the Devil himself is frequently shown to be unable to cope with the shrew, and is even compared quite favourably with her (for many examples, see de Bruyn 1979: 139–47). De Bruyn (1979: 138) suggests a reason for this characterisation:

> [For man] To be ruled by a woman showed up his own weakness, it meant loss of freedom, and this may well have been the reason why a shrew [. . .] was depicted as a devil-ish creature, the worst evil on earth.

The situation of man being ruled by a woman was exploited in sixteenth century literature, so that 'the shrew grew to be a stock figure for laughter and amusement' (de Bruyn 1979: 138). This is the dramatic role of the fictional shrew: a character who functions to subdue a male character (normally a husband), and thereby to amuse the audience (see 2.2.3 and 2.5.1, for dramatic roles).[3]

In essence then, the SHREW schema consists of a specific constellation of social categories: someone who was female, a wife, talkative, and so on. Central to the SHREW schema was the belief in the shrew's evil. In the Early Modern English period, the SHREW schema described here was very much part of the dominant, patriarchal ideology. This ideology would have influenced the way the schema was employed in the interpretation and production of social discourse, which in turn would influence the development of the schema (see 2.4.2 and 2.4.5.1 for the link between social schemata and ideology). This is not to say that there were no resistant voices to conceptions of women — or, in other words, schemata — produced and sustained by this ideology (see, for example, the pamphlets by women writers in Shepherd 1985), though there was 'no very definite sense of a female alternative' (Shepherd 1985: 23) (see also Krontiris 1992: 18–19).

For a twentieth-century audience, two issues need to be addressed. Firstly, does the word *shrew* in the title of the play function as a trigger for a schema relating to a particular kind of woman? In the *Collins COBUILD English Language Dictionary* (1987), the second sense, after that concerning the animal, is stated thus: 'If you refer to a woman as a shrew, you mean that she is very bad-tempered or mean; an offensive use', and illustrated with an example, 'He found himself married to a vulgar shrew'.[4] In the British National Corpus (approximately 100 million words of British English from the late 1980s and early 1990s), of the 73 instances of the word *shrew*, 45 refer to the animal, 16 to women, 11 to Shakespeare's play, and one is a proper name. Collocations, where the word refers to women, include: 'shrill shallow shrew', 'shrilled the shrew' and 'nagging shrew'. All 21 instances of *shrewish* refer to a woman, and collocations include: 'shrewish and ill-tempered' and 'shrewish tongue'. So, although the word is clearly rare, one might suppose that there is at least some knowledge of the word *shrew* used to refer to a particular kind of woman.

Secondly, is a contemporary audience likely to possess a schema for the particular type of woman that corresponds to my description of the patriarchal Elizabethan SHREW schema (see Table 6.1)? Given the cultural and social changes that have occurred over the last 400 years, it is improbable that the audience today will have knowledge of this exact schema, and thus may arrive at different interpretative conclusions. As I pointed out in 2.3.3.2, Bartlett's ([1932] 1995) experiment on the North American Indian folk tale *The War of the Ghosts* revealed that British informants tended to reconstruct the story in terms of their own cultural schemata. In particular, the secularisation of society means that a relationship with the devil is now unlikely to constitute part of a conception of any person. This is not to say, however, that today nobody has a schema which is similar. Some of the collocations mentioned above ('shrill', 'nagging', 'ill-tempered') suggest features that were likely to have been part of the patriarchal Elizabethan SHREW schema. Stereotypes of the nagging woman have proved durable, in spite of the fact that competing ideologies have evolved and such stereotypes are now abhorred by many and acknowledged as highly offensive. It is quite possible that some features, which may have constituted part of the patriarchal Elizabethan SHREW schema, now constitute part of other conceptions of women. For example, it is likely that for many Elizabethans Katherina's challenge to her father's authority would have been perceived as disorderly and disrespectful behaviour (thus prototypically shrewish behaviour), and would probably have triggered the SHREW schema. For some members of a modern audience, such behaviour may seem to be a spirited rebellion against an unfair and repressive patriarchal system, and trigger quite different social schemata. Some of these differences can be seen in the latest film version of the play, *10 Things I Hate About You* (directed by Gil Junger 1999). Katherina is characterised as a nonconformist: she drives an old banger, reads feminist literature, plays football aggressively, and despises boys and the dating game. Compared with her air-headed, boy-besotted sister Bianca, her individuality and lively intelligence seem refreshing.

My analysis below will concentrate on the dominant Elizabethan SHREW schema, and address the issue of whether or not Katherina possesses the kind of personality that fits this schema. This is, after all, the central issue in the play. It is important to note that my analysis concentrates on what I have described as the dominant Elizabethan perspective. Thus references to the SHREW schema are references to the Elizabethan schema as it appears in Table 6.1. My use of the term 'shrewish' to describe particular behaviour should be understood as meaning 'consistent with the Elizabethan SHREW schema'. References to an audience are references to an Elizabethan audience which had knowledge of that schema.

6.3.2 First impressions: Instantiating the SHREW schema

The first woman encountered in the play is Katherina interacting with her father, Baptista. A cohesive interpretative pattern emerges in the following passage to the effect that Katherina is shrewish.

Baptista   Gentlemen, importune me no farther,
For how I firmly am resolv'd you know;
That is, not to bestow my youngest daughter
Before I have a husband for the elder.
If either of you both love Katherina,
Because I know you well and love you well,
Leave shall you have to court her at your
pleasure.

Gremio   To cart her rather. She's too rough for me.
There, there, Hortensio, will you any wife?

Katherina   I pray you, sir, is it your will
To make a stale of me amongst these mates?

Hortensio   Mates, maid! how mean you that? No mates for you
Unless you were of gentler, milder mould.

Katherina   I' faith, sir, you shall never need to fear;
Iwis it is not half way to her heart;
But if it were, doubt not her care should be
To comb your noddle with a three-legg'd stool,
And paint your face, and use you like a fool.

(I.i.48–65)[5]

Gremio's reaction to Baptista's permission to court Katherina is foregrounded. An assumption made in granting permission is that the hearer wants to do what you permit (see 'The Permit Group' of speech act verbs in Wierzbicka 1987: 109–25). Gremio, however, clearly wants nothing to do with Katherina. This is highlighted by his pun on *court/ cart*. The phonological parallelism reinforces the semantic contrast — from romantic courtship to the punishment of bawds or whores by carting them through the streets. Gremio's low opinion of Katherina is made more explicit in his following sentence, *She's too rough for me.* Hortensio's attitude towards Katherina is the same. The evidence so far of Katherina's shrewish behaviour is indirect in that it comes from other characters, but there is some consensus amongst them, which lends support to a stimulus attribution (that is, their actions and attitudes are caused by some aspect of Katherina). Furthermore, Katherina herself provides us with evidence. Her first utterance, though apparently deferential (*I pray you, sir*), questions her father's will. In her second, she asserts that if she were married, she would beat her husband's head with a stool, scratch his face, and use him as if he were a fool. Clearly, her behaviour and purported intentions are unusual. These utterances, if taken at face value, might lead to a correspondent inference that she is disrespectful, violent and malicious.

So far, the configuration of information about Katherina neatly fits the SHREW schema, though there are some discounting factors: Baptista has granted permission to two fools to court her, and so it may not seem entirely unreasonable that she should question his will.

6.3.3 Character context: The role of Bianca

The categorisation of people may be strongly influenced by context (see 2.3.3.2). The characterisation of Bianca plays an important role in how Katherina is perceived. Lucentio is the first to comment on Bianca, and in doing so points up the contrast with Katherina:

> But in the other's silence do I see
> Maid's mild behaviour and sobriety.

> (I.i.70–1)

Lucentio's inference about Bianca here seems to be based on an assumption about the correlation between volume of speech and personality. In other words, he uses a particular causal schema to make the inference. For women in the period of the play, little or no speech was often stereotypically associated with the characteristics of being demure and submissive, whereas a lot of speech was often stereotypically associated with being headstrong, rebellious and quarrelsome, or, in other words, shrewish.[6]

Bianca has a single turn in Act I, the effect of which is likely to reinforce the impression of Katherina's shrewishness. Her response to her father's instruction to go indoors contrasts with Katherina's earlier refusal to do so:

> Bianca   Sister, content you in my discontent.
>   Sir, to your pleasure humbly I subscribe;
>   My books and instruments shall be my company,
>   On them to look, and practise by myself.

> (I.i.80–3)

Not only does she comply, but she also emphasises her deference to her father. This is achieved through the adverb *humbly*, which is syntactically foregrounded through its unusual positioning before the subject of the sentence.[7] Furthermore, Bianca highlights the unpleasant nature of her father's wishes: *My books and instruments shall be my company, / On them to look and practise by myself* (I.i.82–3). She will be in solitary confinement. One might argue here that Bianca provides Katherina with a discounting factor, justifying why Katherina refuses to obey her father. However, what is perhaps the more salient issue here is the contrast: the fact that Bianca, unlike Katherina, complies despite the discomfort. Bianca's ploy seems to be to utilise the augmenting effect: she invites the correspondent inference that she is a 'good' daughter, respectful and obedient even in the face of hardship. As perhaps her name suggests, she is the Elizabethan establishment's social ideal of the obedient and submissive woman, a patient Griselda.[8]

The general effect of Bianca on the Elizabethan audience's perception of Katherina is likely to be one of foregrounding Katherina's behaviour by contrast and enhancing a category-based impression of her as a shrew.

6.3.4 Inferring shrewish characteristics

In Act I Katherina's behaviour has already begun to form a pattern suggesting her shrewishness. This pattern is strengthened by two events that occur in Act II before Katherina meets Petruchio (II.i.182).

At the beginning of Act II, we learn that Katherina has tied Bianca up and is interrogating her in order to find out which suitor she loves best.

Bianca	Good sister, wrong me not, nor wrong yourself,
	To make a bondmaid and a slave of me —
	That I disdain; but for these other gawds,
	Unbind my hands, I'll pull them off myself,
	Yea, all my raiment, to my petticoat;
	Or what you will command me will I do,
	So well I know my duty to my elders.
Katherina	Of all thy suitors here I charge thee tell
	Whom thou lov'st best. See thou dissemble not.
Bianca	Believe me, sister, of all the men alive
	I never yet beheld that special face
	Which I could fancy more than any other.
Katherina	Minion, thou liest. Is't not Hortensio?

(II.i.1–13)

The politeness and impoliteness strategies used by the two characters contrast and have implications for the way they might be perceived. Bianca pays at least lip service to politeness. In addressing Katherina as *Good sister*, she is positively polite in expressing approval and in using an in-group marker. She is also deferential: *what you will command me will I do*. On the other hand, Katherina uses an explicit performative command (that is, the force of the utterance is named), *I charge thee tell / Whom thou lov'st best*. Thomas (1995: 48) notes that people often avoid using an explicit performative, because 'in many circumstances it seems to imply an unequal power relationship or a particular set of rights on the part of the speaker'. However, Bianca did license Katherina to command her, and so one cannot assume that Katherina is simply exerting power, though one may wonder whether Bianca's license would extend to the revelation of personal information. In her next turn, Katherina is positively impolite: she attacks Bianca's positive face with an abusive, condescending term of address (*Minion*) and through her assertion that Bianca is lying. One might also note that Bianca uses the *you* form of the second person pronoun, whereas Katherina uses the *thou* form. The usage of these variants in this period is very complex (see 4.4.3.4), but Katherina's use of *thou* in this context probably carries a hint of condescension, whereas Bianca's use of *you* is consistent with her appearance of respectfulness to her elder sister. Finally and importantly, this interaction ends with Katherina striking Bianca.

The second event is not actually witnessed by the audience, though the physical results are revealed. According to the stage direction, Hortensio enters *with his head broke* (II.i.141). Katherina had apparently broken a lute over his head and called him names.

Clearly, Katherina's behaviour in these two events is very unusual. She breaks normative expectations at a variety of behavioural levels, both linguistic and non-linguistic. Whilst there are some discounting factors, tying up somebody and breaking a musical instrument on somebody's head are strikingly unreasonable behaviours. Moreover, her behaviours are low in distinctiveness — key information for a person attribution — in that she acts in a similar way to different stimuli: she treats Baptista, Bianca and Hortensio in the same way. The importance of this behavioural pattern is that it allows us to infer that the cause of her behaviour lies not in external phenomena, but in her personality; in other words, it allows us to infer that she is dispositionally aggressive, an element of the SHREW schema.

6.3.5 Characterisation through other-presentation

In 4.3.3, I emphasised that an important aspect of characterisation is what other characters say about a particular character. In the first third of the play (before II.i.182), the audience gains little information about Katherina on the basis of her own conversation or behaviour. She is on stage for only 93 lines and speaks only 219 words — 4% of the total number of words spoken. The bulk of the evidence comes from what other characters say about her. Almost all the descriptive terms used for Katherina by Hortensio, Gremio, Tranio, Grumio and Baptista are negative evaluations:

> **Hortensio**: shrewd ill-favour'd (I.ii.57); [. . .] intolerable curst, / And shrewd, and froward, so beyond all measure (I.ii.87–8); curst Katherine (I.ii.181). **Gremio**: She's too rough for me (I.i.55); fiend of hell (I.i.88); hell (I.i.125); with a most impatient devilish spirit (I.i.151); wildcat (I.ii.193). **Tranio**: stark mad or wonderful froward (I.i.69); so curst and shrewd (I.i.180). **Grumio**: Katherine the curst (I.ii.127); **Baptista**: hilding of a devilish spirit (II.i.26).

Clearly, there is very high consensus, the key to a covariation pattern for a stimulus attribution (that is, it is something about Katherina that causes these utterances) (see Table 3.1). This is particularly evident in the lexical repetition. Crucially, all of these evaluations fit the prototypical features of the SHREW schema (note, for example, the lexical items referring in some way to hell).

Contrary to this negative pattern, Petruchio uses positive descriptive terms for Katherina throughout the play (for example, addressing Baptista, 'Pray, have you not a daughter / Call'd Katherina, fair and virtuous?' (II.i.42–3)). However, in the first third of the play, there are clear discounting factors to be taken into consideration. Petruchio appears to be a fortune hunter: 'Haply to wive and thrive as best I may' (I.ii.55); 'wealth is the burden of my wooing dance' (I.ii.67). Saying positive things about Katherina, and thereby demonstrating his love for her, would support his goal of obtaining Baptista's permission to marry Katherina. These are reasons why he might violate the maxim of quality (Grice 1975). Also, he claims that his positive description of Katherina is based on 'that report which I so oft have heard' (II.i.53). The audience knows that this flies in the face of the facts which they have been given so far. That Petruchio wishes to marry Katherina in spite of the bad press she is given in his hearing, makes it likely that the audience will make an attribution to the effect that he is hell-bent on gaining wealth, or that there is another strong reason not yet revealed. The reasoning here is captured by the augmenting principle: if somebody does something in spite of reasons for not doing it, a perceiver would be likely to infer that that person had a particularly strong reason for doing it.

I have earlier demonstrated that the behaviour of Katherina and Bianca constitutes a clear contrast between them. This contrast is reinforced by evidence inferred from what other characters say about them. As with Katherina, in constructing Bianca's character we rely largely upon what the other characters say. All the descriptive terms used for her by Lucentio, Baptista, Hortensio, Gremio and Tranio are positive evaluations:

> **Lucentio**: But in the other's silence do I see / Maid's mild behaviour and sobriety (I.i.70–1); Minerva (I.i.84); young modest girl (I.i.156); O yes, I saw sweet beauty in her face, / Such as the daughter of Agenor had. (I.i.167–8); Sacred and sweet was all I saw in her (I.i.176). **Baptista**: good Bianca (I.i.76). **Hortensio**: Sweet Bianca! (I.i.139); beautiful Bianca (I.ii.117); fair Bianca (I.ii.172). **Gremio**: Sweet Bianca (I.i.110); Fair Bianca (I.i.165). **Tranio**: fair Bianca (I.ii.241); The one as famous for her scolding tongue / As is the other for beauteous modesty (I.ii.250–1); Bianca, fair and virtuous (II.i.91).

As is the case with Katherina, consensus is very high, suggesting a stimulus attribution (it is something about Bianca that causes these utterances). Moreover, all these evaluations refer to aspects of the Elizabethan establishment's ideal of the 'good woman', the diametric opposite of the SHREW schema. In particular, note that the evaluations mix or even fuse visible, concrete aspects with abstract (consider *beauteous modesty*). This was part of the establishment's conception of a 'good woman', whereby '[w]oman's sobriety and reticence in dress and behaviour, her surrender to her husband's wishes, her perfect self-control in difficult situations, all these were only the visible counterparts of her inward state of mind' (de Bruyn 1979: 23).[9]

What the other characters say is likely to have the effect of hardening the structural opposition between Katherina and Bianca. The two sisters contrast in terms of patriarchal Elizabethan social schemata: Katherina exhibits disruptive behaviour and is said to have an ill-tempered personality (she fits the SHREW schema); Bianca exhibits compliant behaviour and is said to have a pleasant personality and be physically attractive (she fits the patriarchal conception of the 'good woman').

6.3.6 A close-up on Katherina

As I mentioned earlier, Petruchio's meeting with Katherina, II.i.182–317, is a key point in the play. For the first and only time in the play, the audience has prolonged exposure to her. It is also a key event in terms of the play's plot; here Petruchio must win Katherina's love, if he is going to marry her. One should remember Baptista's precondition to allowing the marriage to proceed, namely, that Katherina's love should be gained (II.i.128–9).

For reasons of space, I cannot present a comprehensive analysis of the interaction between Katherina and Petruchio.[10] Instead I shall focus on one important aspect: how Petruchio dominates Katherina. In the final quarter of the interaction, Petruchio's strategy is to falsely claim to Baptista that he has won Katherina's love. Presumably, we are to understand that he hopes either he will be believed or that Baptista, being desperate to marry Katherina, will pretend to believe him. In order to pull off the trick, Petruchio needs to control what Katherina says to Baptista: it is important that she does not contradict him. Katherina is apparently in a powerless position — as Petruchio points out: *will you, nill you, I will marry you* (II.i.264). With the entrance of Baptista, Gremio and Tranio, Petruchio constructs a direct discourse act specifically designed to determine what Katherina says: *Never make denial* (II.i.272). By hogging the conversational floor, he forces Katherina into a subordinate position. Figure 6.1 displays word-counts for Katherina and Petruchio at quarterly intervals.

Katherina seems to have no power in determining her marriage, but her conversational powerlessness is not predicted by the SHREW schema.[11] According to this schema, one might expect her character to consist of

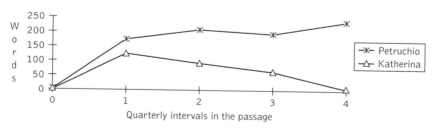

Figure 6.1   Distribution of words: Katherina and Petruchio (II.i.182–317)

a talkative headstrong woman hell-bent on causing trouble. Note also that the dramatic role associated with the SHREW schema (see 6.3.1) predicts that the shrew subdues the male character, the opposite of what happens here. As a result, it is difficult to maintain a purely category-based impression of Katherina. There may be a shift towards a personalised impression, and thus towards the piecemeal integration of characteristics. There are also motivational factors supporting this shift. Not only has Katherina been established as an important and interesting character, but also she may evoke some sympathy, because she is cheated and forced into marrying an 'oddball', unscrupulous character, Petruchio. This character shift is given increasing impetus during the rest of the play.

6.3.7 Character context: Petruchio replaces Bianca

In the remainder of the play (after Petruchio's meeting with Katherina, II.i.182–317), Katherina and Bianca do not appear on the stage together until the fifth act, and even here they do not address each other individually. Bianca is detached from Katherina: she no longer plays an important role in influencing the perception of Katherina. More importantly, Bianca undergoes a radical change of character, giving rise to a cohesive pattern of information that clashes with a 'good woman' conception.

The very next time we hear Bianca speaking to Lucentio and Hortensio she is being assertive:

> Why, gentlemen, you do me double wrong
> To strive for that which resteth in my choice.
> I am no breeching scholar in the schools,
> I'll not be tied to hours nor 'pointed times,
> But learn my lessons as I please myself.
> And to cut off all strife: here sit we down.
> Take you your instrument, play you the whiles;
> His lecture will be done ere you have tun'd.

> (III.i.16–23)

Bianca's challenge to Lucentio's and Hortensio's authority in organising her time is reminiscent of Katherina's earlier challenge to Baptista's authority. Furthermore, her exercise of power is apparent in her use of direct commands, each formulated with an imperative (*sit*, *take*, and *play*), to organise Lucentio and Hortensio.

Later in the play, Petruchio reveals that Bianca has married Lucentio. This is foregrounded behaviour: Bianca has married Lucentio behind her father's back, going against the expectations associated with the obedient daughter. This is further evidence of her lack of respect for authority and her secretiveness. In the final scene of the play, Bianca fails the obedience test in refusing to appear when she is summoned by her husband.

Clearly, an Elizabethan impression of Bianca based on conformity to the establishment's ideal of a daughter and a 'good woman' becomes untenable. This, however, does not necessarily result in a more complex characterisation of Bianca. In the first third of the play, all the evidence supports her categorisation as the social ideal; in the remainder of the play, all the evidence supports her categorisation as a SHREW. This contradiction can be resolved by simply *recategorising* her as a SHREW. Her earlier goodliness can be construed as further evidence of her duplicity. An important consequence of Bianca's character change is that it may help to further destabilise a SHREW-based impression of Katherina.

Petruchio becomes the most important part of Katherina's human context. After their first meeting, he appears whenever Katherina does and also interacts with her. His behaviour after the first encounter with Katherina *appears* to reinforce his hot-headedness and craziness, and, in addition, to suggest that he is disorderly and rebellious. He is late for his wedding and produces no excuse. Moreover, he turns up in inappropriate dress for a wedding. During the wedding service, he swears loudly at the Priest, *by gogs-wouns* (III.ii.156), and cuffs him, causing him to fall down. After the ceremony,

> He calls for wine: 'A health!' quoth he, as if
> He had been aboard, carousing to his mates
> After a storm; quaff'd off the muscadel,
> And threw the sops all in the sexton's face

(III.ii.166–9)

Then he kisses Katherina, leaving the church echoing with a *clamorous smack* (III.ii.174). The fact that Petruchio's behaviour is utterly inappropriate for the event, and as a consequence unexpected, is made clear in Gremio's description of the celebratory drink: it is more suited to a sailor's *carousing*. When Petruchio and Katherina next appear (IV.i.104), having arrived at Petruchio's house, the audience is again exposed to Petruchio's wild behaviour. He calls his servants names, and he is physically violent: he strikes two servants and throws dishes and food at

277

them. This behaviour is unwarranted, since there is no discounting factor: there is nothing the servants do that could justify such behaviour. The cause of it seems, at this point, to lie in Petruchio's personality. However, Petruchio later informs the audience in a soliloquy (IV.i.175–98) that all his behaviour was in fact a ploy to 'tame' Katherina.

The particular issue I want to address with regard to Petruchio's behaviour is its likely effect on the Elizabethan audience's perception of Katherina. Petruchio produces a series of behaviours that are prototypically shrewish. He has no respect for order, he is domineering, he is aggressive, both verbally and physically, and he is loud. Curtis's comment on Petruchio's behaviour reflects this: 'By this reckoning he is more shrew than she' (IV.i.74). No longer is Katherina contrasted in the heavenly light of Bianca, but in the hellfire of Petruchio. As a result, in the remainder of the play there is likely to be a strong bias toward perceiving Katherina as less shrewish.

6.3.8 Characterisation through other-presentation: A reversal

An important ramification of Bianca's character change is that it casts doubt on the credibility of characterisation by other characters. The way Lucentio, Baptista, Hortensio, Gremio and Tranio described Bianca was clearly wrong. This may lead the audience to doubt their accuracy about Katherina. The actual contribution made to the characterisation of Katherina by other characters in the final two-thirds of the play is much reduced in importance compared with the first third. There are fewer cues (clustering in certain scenes), and they do not exhibit the same kind of strong consensus. Nevertheless, they are evidence that the other characters' conceptions of Katherina have changed. There is now more of a mixture of positive and negative descriptions (the ratio of positive to negative being 3 to 4), and this may encourage the audience to change from a SHREW-based impression of Katherina.

> **Tranio:** good Katherine (III.ii.21); she's a devil, a devil, the devil's dam (III.ii.151). **Gremio:** she's a lamb, a dove, a fool to him (III.ii.152).[12] **Bianca:** mad (III.ii.240). **Curtis:** Poor soul (IV.i.168). **Baptista:** a shrew of thy impatient humour (III.ii.29); the veriest shrew of all (V.ii.64).

Regarding Petruchio's positive descriptions in the final two-thirds of the play (*lovely* (III.ii.88); *sweet* (III.ii.231); *bonny* (III.ii.223); *sweet*

(IV.i.143); *sweeting* (IV.iii.36)), although some of the former discounting factors no longer apply, since Katherina is now his wife, other discounting factors are present. These positive descriptions could be seen as part of his shrewish act: a sarcastic impoliteness strategy designed to provoke Katherina. However, his reference to Katherina as a *gentlewoman* (IV.v.61) is particularly significant. Two scenes earlier (IV.iii.70–2), he denies Katherina the right to have the cap of a *gentlewoman* on the basis that she is not *gentle* ('When you are gentle, you shall have one too' (IV.iii.71)). Several meanings could be suggested in the use of this word: that she does not have the character appropriate to one of noble birth (*OED*: adj.3.a.); that she is not courteous or polite (*OED*: adj.3.c.); and that she does not have a mild disposition (*OED*: adj.8.). Clearly, he now thinks Katherina has some of these qualities, and, clearly, if she has these qualities, she cannot be thought a SHREW.

6.3.9 Katherina's behaviour

After Katherina's and Petruchio's first meeting, Katherina next appears waiting for Petruchio to turn up for the wedding. Baptista's sympathy for her predicament is evident from his reaction to Katherina's departure from the stage in tears:

> Go, girl, I cannot blame thee now to weep,
> For such an injury would vex a saint;
> Much more a shrew of thy impatient humour.

(III.ii.27–9)

These are not the tears of anger and frustration which we saw earlier (II.i.35–6), but the legitimate tears of suffering. This is another facet that is inconsistent with the SHREW schema. Shrews, as far as the ideology of the establishment is concerned, are prototypically despised and disliked: they do not attract sympathy.

In Gremio's report of the wedding ceremony he comments on Katherina's physical behaviour: she *Trembled and shook* (III.ii.163). Such body movements are strongly associated with fear, and induce sympathy. This is further information that seems inconsistent with the SHREW schema. When Katherina and Petruchio reappear, Katherina's first words, addressed to Petruchio, are polite — *Let me entreat you* (III.ii.196). She uses the negative politeness strategy of giving deference. This strategy assumes the superior power of the addressee. This is the first time in the play that Katherina appears to acknowledge a social order and place herself in an inferior position. It is unusual behaviour for Katherina — a deviation from her own norm — and, on the face of it, it is inconsistent with the relative power predicted by the SHREW schema. This pattern of behaviour is reinforced later in the play when Katherina goes out of her way to help Petruchio's servants. Such a pattern of behaviour supports a person attribution, since Katherina reacts in the same way to different stimuli (that is, low distinctiveness). However, Katherina exhibits different behaviour when Petruchio insists that they must forgo the wedding feast. She refuses to comply and asserts her own authority: 'I will be angry; what hast thou to do? / Father, be quiet; he shall stay my leisure' (III.ii.212–13). She uses the modal *will* to express her own desire.[13] Her rhetorical question *what hast thou to do?* strongly asserts that Baptista has no right to interfere. This attacks his negative face. Her command *be quiet* is a clear example of bald on record impoliteness. It is obviously too direct in this context, bearing in mind Baptista's status. Katherina's behaviour here (defiance of authority, verbal aggression, and anger) is prototypically shrewish, although one should note that the fact that Petruchio's behaviour is unreasonable is likely to exert some influence as a discounting factor.

The audience thus receives contrasting information about Katherina at this point in the play. There is no simple change from one schema to another, as with Bianca, but a move down the continuum towards *piecemeal processing*. This move is supported by the presence of motivational factors. Katherina is a central and interesting figure: it is worth the audience investing cognitive effort in attending to her character. In addition, as I have already suggested, she may have elicited some sympathy from the audience, and this affective factor may increase the amount of attention she gains. In the following parts of the play, this contrasting mixture of information is continued.

6.3.10 Katherina and the run-up to the 'obedience' speech (V.ii.137–80)

On the journey to Baptista's house, Petruchio presents Katherina with stark alternatives: she either agrees with him that the sun is the moon and they continue to her father's house in order to join in festivities, or she disagrees with him and they turn back to Petruchio's house. As she is in a less powerful position, Katherina has little choice but to give in, if she wants to go to her father's house. As Hortensio points out, 'Say as

he says, or we shall never go' (IV.v.11). The form of her capitulation is
significant:

> Forward, I pray, since we have come so far,
> And be it moon, or sun, or what you please;
> And if you please to call it a rush-candle,
> Henceforth I vow it shall be so for me.

> (IV.v.12–15)

The speech act of promising is couched as an explicit performative.
Furthermore, six lines later she reiterates the promise:

> What you will have it nam'd, even that it is,
> And so it shall be so for Katherine.

> (IV.v.21–2)

It should be noted that in each promise Katherina uses the modal *shall*.
In Early Modern English *shall* was more widely used to express obligation than it is today (Barber 1976: 159–60; Görlach 1991: 114), and it is
perhaps this which made it particularly forceful when used to promise
or predict a future act.[14]

Because Katherina makes a promise to do whatever Petruchio commands, does this mean that she has undergone some dramatic change
of character from shrew to obedient woman? The fact that Petruchio
extracted the promise from her by virtue of his superior power is a clear
discounting factor in attributing obedience to her. However, it is significant that she makes the promise so forcefully: more forcefully than is
strictly necessary. It is also significant that she keeps the promise over
time — in fact, for the rest of the play. Furthermore, in the first scene
of Act V she kisses Petruchio, in spite of the fact that he presents her
with a way of avoiding a kiss, and also addresses him with a term of
endearment: *love* (V.i.33). This may be evidence that her attitude towards
Petruchio has changed.[15] Is Katherina then a case for recategorisation
like Bianca, only from shrew to obedient woman rather than the other
way round? This is what some critics (such as Hazlitt [1817] 1906) have
argued for. However, there are two objections to this. Firstly, there is
no obvious means of explaining away her earlier shrewish behaviours.
This is unlike the case with Bianca where, it may be remembered, one
can simply reassess her earlier behaviour as further evidence of duplicity.

Secondly, as I stated above and as I will briefly show in relation to the 'obedience' speech scene, Katherina never relinquishes completely her shrew-like behaviour. Again this is unlike Bianca who relinquishes all obedient behaviour. Can one then argue, as some critics have done (such as Charlton 1938; Tillyard 1965), that the characterisation of Katherina is simply inconsistent? There are two objections to this. Firstly, there are reasons why an audience might attempt piecemeal integration. Not only does the audience have a configuration of information that is likely to be inconsistent with any schema, but there are also motivational factors present which justify the expenditure of cognitive effort. Apart from emotive factors such as sympathy, Katherina presents an intriguing puzzle that will not go away. Bianca, in contrast, after the point where one might recategorise her as a shrew, recedes into the background of the play. Katherina remains centrally involved. For example, in the final act of the play, Bianca has ten lines of dialogue, whereas Katherina has 55. Secondly, it is during the final scene of the play that the audience may see how the apparently inconsistent facets of Katherina's character can be integrated.

As I pointed out in 6.2, my aim in this chapter is to focus on the parts of the play which have generally been neglected by the critics, who typically have focussed on the 'obedience' speech (V.ii.137–80). However, I will offer some brief remarks on the 'obedience' speech here. A particularly important aspect of the final scene of the play, where we hear the famous 'obedience' speech, is the fact that Petruchio licenses Katherina to engage in behaviours that appear to be consistent with the SHREW schema. When Bianca and the Widow disobey the summonses of their husbands, Katherina is sent to get them and licensed, if they refuse to come, to 'Swinge [. . .] them soundly forth unto their husbands' (V.ii.104). Petruchio licenses Katherina to 'tell' (V.ii.130) Bianca and the Widow about the duty they owe their husbands. Significantly, the Widow objects specifically to this speech act: 'We will have no telling' (V.ii.132). Katherina is also given the opportunity to speak at length. She has the longest turn in the play overall, extending to 364 words. These behaviours — using physical violence, strongly asserting a particular state of affairs, and hogging conversational space — are, on the face of it, prototypically shrewish behaviours. However, they are licensed and used, from the Elizabethan establishment's perspective, for socially-approved purposes. It is also worth noting that Petruchio enables Katherina to gain the revenge on Bianca which she had sought earlier in the play (II.i.36). Bianca has to submit to a 'telling off' from Katherina. Not surprisingly, Katherina emphasises the obedience owed to a husband, because this highlights Bianca's faults.

My general argument then is not that Katherina has had to suppress aspects of her behaviour, but to adapt them to new contexts. Petruchio provides her with opportunities where she can legitimately, from the Elizabethan establishment's point of view, unleash the more spirited side of her personality. In effect, Katherina's 'shrewish' behaviour is now context-sensitive and not merely general, the mode of behaviour of a category-based character. For example, whereas a character based on the SHREW schema will exercise power over all, Katherina now accepts the superior power of some, but wields power over others. She is a 'personalised' or round character, based on piecemeal integration.

6.4 Conclusion

In this book I have outlined an interdisciplinary approach to characterisation, which draws in particular upon theories from social and cognitive psychology. This approach attempts to explain how characters are constructed in the interaction between readers and play texts. It goes beyond pragmatic analyses of plays, which hitherto have been used within stylistics to account for characterisation in drama (see, for example, Herman 1995; Short 1996; Culpeper *et al.* 1998). Such pragmatic analyses do not, nor do they intend to, postulate theories of characterisation, but rather explore the dynamics of dialogue, noting implications for characterisation. For example, these analyses do not explain what a coherent impression of character might be, the ways in which a character impression might change, or why a particular conversational inference might be considered a character inference. I have demonstrated how my approach works in relation to Katherina in *The Taming of the Shrew*. Here, my method was to focus on the text and, within the constraints of the theories I introduced, to generate hypotheses about the construction of character, hypotheses which account for the available textual evidence in a systematic and parsimonious way. In addition, I have shown how my cognitive approach to characterisation accommodates and accounts for various characterisation concepts postulated in literary theory, in particular the notion of flat and round characters.

My analysis in this chapter, focussing on an Elizabethan perspective, has demonstrated that Katherina is not a character of farce. She is not a flat character, a caricature, or lacking in 'the physical, emotional, intellectual, and moral sensitivity that we think of as "normal"' (Heilman 1972: 324). At the end of the play, she ends up neither a broken woman nor simply a shrew. In fact, in order to sustain one of these interpretations, literary critics have had to turn a blind eye to some of her characteristics, or weakly dismiss them as 'out of character':

> [Katherina] is intolerably curst and shrewd and froward so beyond all measure, that although her extravagant bullying of her sister and of her teacher is within her physical compass, her complaint that her father is committing her to an old maid's life, and her lament that she will sit and weep until she finds some occasion of revenge, seem widely out of character. Even more disconcerting are the tears she sheds because she anticipates that Petruchio will fail her at the church, or will surely overlook some item or other of the arrangements ordained by fashionable propriety for a bourgeois wedding.
>
> (Charlton 1938: 97)

Contrary to Tillyard (1965: 80), I would argue that Shakespeare has not simply created an inconsistent character, but created the potential for the piecemeal integration of these inconsistencies. In the final act, the audience is shown how elements of two diverse Elizabethan social schemata — the SHREW schema and the contrasting concept of the socially ideal woman — may be brought together in Katherina. Shakespeare creates the conditions for a degree of 'schema refreshment' (Cook 1994) (see 2.5.4). Following Semino's (1997) partial redefinition of schema refreshment, schema refreshment may involve not only changing our schemata, as Cook (1994) argues, but also stretching or challenging them, or 'connecting normally separate schemata in unusual ways' (Semino 1997: 251). Shakespeare created the conditions in which normally separate schemata might be connected. Indeed, this is Shakespeare's contribution to the vibrant debate at the time about the role of women in society. It might be noted that Shakespeare does not challenge the social order, but appears strongly conservative in showing the reconciliation of disparate personality elements *within* the established order. My portrayal of Katherina's characterisation is entirely consistent with Belsey's (1985) discussion of the contest in art and literature over new and old meanings of the family, and hence of women, in the sixteenth and seventeenth centuries. On the one hand, there was the old view of the dynastic family, where the model woman was like the character Griselda, obedient, patient, uncomplaining and silent. This is reminiscent of the Bianca of the first third of *The Taming of the Shrew*. The opposite of this model woman is the SHREW schema. On the other hand, there was marriage viewed as an affective relationship, where the woman was in partnership with her husband. This is reminiscent of Katherina at the end of the play. However, this newer model is not necessarily less patriarchal: 'Patriarchy reasserts itself within the affective family. Perhaps the marriage of true minds had never implied equality for women, but only [. . .] a new kind of pliability' (1985: 177).[16] Importantly, Belsey argues that the contest between the old and the new

> [. . .] momentarily unfixed the existing system of [sexual] differences, and in the gap thus produced we are able to glimpse a possible meaning, an image of a mode of being, which is not asexual, nor bisexual, but which disrupts the system of differences on which sexual stereotyping depends.

> (1985: 190)

This disruption of sexual stereotyping is part of the piecemeal integration or schema refreshment which I have attributed to Katherina's characterisation.

And what about the 'obedience' speech? My analysis precludes both the interpretation that it is 'genuine' and that it is ironic, since the former implies that Katherina has been broken and the latter implies that she remains unbroken. Both these views are overly simplistic and do not account for all the evidence in the play. However, the third interpretation, that the irony is in the context, is still viable. What I referred to as the compromise interpretation, the idea that Katherina recognises the game Petruchio has been playing and joins him in it, is a plausible interpretation. She agrees to let him take the lead, and in return he channels the more spirited aspects of her personality into, from the Elizabethan establishment's perspective, legitimate areas, and together they play tricks on the other characters.

I make no claim that my reading of Katherina's characterisation is the only one possible. I have stressed at a number of points the relativity of schemata. My claim is rather that, given a certain set of schemata, my characterisation theory explains how certain interpretative conclusions come about in the interaction between the text and the reader.

Notes

1   See, for example, the entries in the dictionary of 'Womanwords' (Mills 1991).

2   The frequency of 'shrew' in existing historical corpora (e.g. the Helsinki Corpus) is too slight to allow conclusions to be drawn. Hence, I was forced to rely on other sources.

3   De Bruyn (1979: 138) points out that the shrew-tamers 'were few and their taming had little effect upon future literature'.

4   This dictionary is primarily based on the *COBUILD* corpus of English, compiled mainly from texts of the 1970s and 1980s, and thus in theory should reflect contemporary usage. However, some dictionary examples were made up, if no corpus example could be found, and this could be one of those rare examples.

5   All quotations in this chapter from *The Taming of the Shrew* are taken from *The Arden Shakespeare*, edited by Morris (1981).

6   Evidence for these associations can be found in Shepherd (1985) and de Bruyn (1979) (see also the references given in Newman 1991: 53). However, it should be noted that the ideal of silence did not apply equally to the women of all social groups. In particular, it did not apply to a small courtly elite, for whom measured conversation was the ideal, rather than silence (Krontiris 1992: 14–15).

7   *Humbly* occurs 61 times in Shakespeare. In 51 instances (representing 84% of the total) it occurs after the subject.

8   See, for example, Shepherd (1985: 26, 195), Belsey (1985: 172–3), Krontiris (1992: 7), and de Bruyn (1979: Chapter 2) for discussions of the concept of the 'good woman'.

9   De Bruyn (1979) does not consider sub-types of the ideal of the 'good woman', although they clearly existed. For example, Krontiris (1992) points out that a small elite group of courtly women had 'a slightly different version of feminine conduct' (1992: 14).

10 For an illuminating Gricean analysis of this interaction, see Cooper (1981).

11 Also, it might be noted that in Early Modern England it was not normally the case that a daughter had no input into the marriage arrangements. Within the upper classes, marriages were normally arranged, since such marriages had a solidly financial basis. However, for the mass of the population, 'the idea of marriage as a voluntary mutually supportive relationship seems to have been widely accepted' (Briggs 1983: 44). Both of these notions of marriage are relevant to *The Taming of the Shrew*.

12 *Fool* could have a favourable sense in Shakespeare's period.

13 The volitional use of *will*, as opposed to predictive, was much more common in the Early Modern English period (cf. Traugott 1972: 116).

14 Coriolanus's comments (III.i.86–112) on Sicinius's use of *shall* make clear the power attributed to that word.

15 Bean's (1980) interpretation of the play as a romantic comedy relies upon the idea that Katherina falls in love with Petruchio, and that this brings about her change of character.

16 See also Bean (1980) for marriage seen as both a partnership and a hierarchy.

FURTHER DIRECTIONS AND EXERCISES

1. Narrative

Generally speaking, the major difference between dialogue texts (such as theatrical plays, screenplays, and transcriptions of conversation) and narrative texts (such as prose fiction, biographies and newspapers) is the presence of the narrator in the latter. I have already pointed out (see 3.8.2) how the manipulation of key aspects of narrative may influence how characters are perceived. In narrative, the more frequent the use of first-person narration, internal narration (i.e. the expression of a character's thoughts and feelings), and direct speech/thought presentation, the more the reader may be predisposed to attribute behaviours to contextual causes rather than the character; and vice versa, the less frequent these aspects are, the more the reader may be predisposed towards a character attribution. Of course, these narrative aspects are just some of the features which relate to point of view — the angle or perspective from which the fictional world is presented, whether spatial, temporal, ideological or cognitive. Narrative characterisation includes constructing a character's viewpoint, and this can be conveyed through a variety of linguistic features, such as verbs of cognition, deictic expressions and ideologically loaded lexis (see Short 1996: Chapter 9, for an overview). Manipulating point of view, bearing in mind the attribution bias, may have an important effect on how readers perceive characters: for example, it may affect whether or not a character is perceived to be a victim of circumstances, and thus whether or not they are likely to evoke sympathy. However, the relationship between point of view and reader sympathy is currently rather more a matter of hypothesis than empirical fact (but see van Peer and Pander Maat 1996, for some progress in this area).

You could set up a small-scale study to probe this area further. Taking a couple of prose extracts such as the Diana and Charles passages in 3.8.2, you could devise a questionnaire or conduct a structured interview to probe readers' perceptions. Or, you could take a single extract (for example the Diana passage in 3.8.2) and re-write it to encourage an opposite attribution, and then investigate each extract.

Another important feature of narrative, and one that is closely related to point of view, deserves a mention: 'mind style'. Mind style is the way in which the world is conceptualised by the mind whose point of view is being presented. According to Fowler (1977), mind style comes about when '[c]umulatively, consistent structural options, agreeing in cutting the presented world to one pattern or another, give rise to an impression of a world-view' (1977: 76); it refers 'to any distinctive linguistic representation of an individual mental self' (1977: 103). In other words, mind style is a particular aspect of characterisation: one's impression of the mental properties and habits of an individual. Note that Fowler's definition talks about a 'consistent' set of choices 'agreeing' in some way. In covariation attribution theory, this corresponds to the low distinctiveness pattern (the target person does not react in a distinctive way to different stimuli) that is so crucial to a person attribution. Bockting (1995) is a book-length study that explores the relationship between mind style and characterisation in the novels of William Faulkner. Here and generally, analyses of mind style have focussed on grammatical features (especially, transitivity patterns) and lexical features (especially, under/overlexicalisation and value-laden vocabulary) (see also Halliday 1971; and Leech and Short 1981). The focus on grammatical features tallies with my comments in 4.4.4, where I hypothesised a schematic relationship between syntax and cognitive organisation. All the examples I gave in that section, whether from prose or drama, could be considered instances of mind style. More recently, Semino and Swindlehurst (1996) and Black (1993) have explored the role of metaphor in the creation of mind style. Semino and Swindlehurst (1996) explore the theoretical merits of combining the notion of mind style with the cognitive theory of metaphor, and demonstrate how patterns of metaphor lie at the heart of the narrator's mind style in Ken Kesey's *One Flew Over the Cuckoo's Nest* (1973). For example, the narrator Bromden, an inmate of a mental institution, tends to perceive the world in terms of machines. Thus, he describes the nurse:

> She works the hinges in her elbows and fingers. I hear a small squeak. She starts moving, and I get back against the wall, and when she rumbles past she's already big as a truck, trailing that wicker bag behind her exhaust like a semi behind a Jimmy Diesel. Her lips are parted, and her smile's going out before her like a radiator grill. I can smell the hot oil and

magneto spark when she goes past, and every step hits the
floor she blows up a size bigger, blowing and puffing, roll
down anything in her path!

(1973: 79)

Bromden, who used to be an electrical engineer, uses the source domain
of machinery to conceptualise the world around him.

There is no reason why the notions discussed here — point of view
and mind style — cannot also be of relevance to drama. Verbs of
cognition, deictic expressions and ideologically-loaded lexis may also
(supposing no discounting factors) reflect a character's point of view.
However, given the conversational format of drama, it is likely that
other linguistic features need to be taken into account. For example, the
sincerity condition of speech acts is the speaker's psychological state
(Searle 1969). Clearly, more work needs to be done in this area (see
McIntyre 1999, for some valuable first steps). Regarding mind style, its
most obvious relevance to drama is in soliloquies and asides, which
frequently give an impression of the mental view of the speaker. You
could, for example, explore Macbeth's soliloquies and asides for the
techniques used to convey his mental world view.[1]

2. Verse

Characterisation should not be overlooked in verse (including mainstream poetry, limericks, song lyrics, nursery rhymes). Minimally, in
verse we construct a 'speaking voice', which we can treat as a deictic
anchorage point. Consider these opening words from some of Philip
Larkins's poems:

'This was Mr Bleaney's room. [. . .]'

Mr Bleaney

Now night perfumes lie upon the air [. . .]

Summer Nocturne

If my darling were once to decide [. . .]

If, My Darling

In the first example, 'this' signals the spatial proximity between the
speaking voice and Mr Bleaney's room; in the second example, 'Now'

signals the temporal proximity between the speaking voice and the state of the night air; in the third example, 'darling' signals a close social relationship between the speaking voice and the referent of 'my darling'.

Perhaps the view that characterisation in verse is less important results from the naïve assumption that the speaking voice in the text world is that of (or at least closely related to) the writer. The truth of the matter is that the relationship between the speaking voice and the writer is complex, as is the nature of that speaking voice, and both may vary from text to text and even within a text (see Semino 1997: 38–49). For example, our knowledge of Sylvia Plath's life, relationships and experiences may lead us to infer a close identity between her and the speaking voices in her poems, whereas the speaking voices of Chaucer's *Troilus and Criseyde*, with their Homeric background, can hardly be thought to have much to do with Chaucer. Moreover, Chaucer creates relatively independent characters through specific and detailed third-person narratorial characterisation, including character description, action, and participation in reported dialogue. Thus, the discourse structure of much of Chaucer's verse resembles the three-level structure of the prototypical novel, with the narrator–narratee level intervening between the author–reader and character–character levels. In contrast, Sylvia Plath's poems, which frequently adopt first-person narration, allow greater potential for collapsing the discourse levels and assuming that the 'I' is not only the main character of the poem, but also the author.

Investigate characterisation in song lyrics. In order to whet your appetite, consider the rich diversity found in Beatles's song titles alone, for example: 'Paperback Writer' (triggers a social role schema), 'The fool on the hill' (triggers a personal schema), 'Here comes the sun' (the point of view of the speaking voice is indicated through deictic 'here' and 'come': the sun moves toward the speaker), 'Hey Jude' ('hey' is an attention-getter, and 'Jude' suggests first-name familiarity), 'Don't let me down' (implicates, via the maxim of quantity, that the speaker has reason to believe that he or she might be let down), and 'I am the walrus' (implicates, via the maxim of quality, that the speaker has qualities in common with 'the walrus').

Note

1   It is worth noting that Macbeth's mental expression sometimes spills out of soliloquies and asides and is overheard by characters on stage, as, for example, in the famous banquet scene (III.iv.1–121).

REFERENCES

Abbott, E.A. [1871] (1881) *A Shakespearean Grammar*, 3rd edn, London: Macmillan.

Abrams, D. and Hogg, M.A. (eds) (1990a) *Social Identity Theory: Constructive and Critical Advances*, Hemel Hempstead: Harvester Wheatsheaf.

Abrams, D. and Hogg, M.A. (1990b) 'The context of discourse: Let's not throw out the baby with the bathwater', *Philosophical Psychology*, 3, 2, 219–225.

Abrams, M.H. (1988) *A Glossary of Literary Terms*, 5th edn, New York: Holt, Rinehart and Winston.

Adamson, S. (1989) 'With double tongue: Diglossia, stylistics and the teaching of English', in Short, M. (ed.) *Reading, Analysing and Teaching Literature*, London: Longman, 204–240.

Addington, D.W. (1968) 'The relationship of selected vocal characteristics to personality perception', *Speech Monographs*, 35, 492–503.

Albee, E. [1958] (1962) 'The Zoo Story', in Albee, E., *The Zoo Story and Other Plays*, London: Jonathan Cape, 111–142.

Alexander, P. (1951) *William Shakespeare: The Complete Works*, London: Collins.

Amussen, S.D. (1988) *An Ordered Society: Gender and Class in Early Modern England*, Oxford: Basil Blackwell.

Andersen, S.M., Klatsky, R.L. and Murray, J. (1990) 'Traits and social stereotypes: Efficiency differences in social information processing', *Journal of Personality and Social Psychology*, 59, 2, 192–201.

Anderson, N.H. (1981) *Foundations of Information Integration Theory*, New York: Academic Press.

Anderson, R.C. and Pichert, J.W. (1978) 'Recall of previously unrecallable information following a shift in perspective', *Journal of Verbal Learning and Verbal Behaviour*, 17, 1–12.

Antaki, C. (1994) *Explaining and Arguing: The Social Organisation of Accounts*, London: Sage.

Antaki, C. and Widdicombe, S. (1998a) 'Identity as an achievement and as a toll', in Antaki, C. and Widdicombe, S. (eds) *Identities in Talk*, London: Sage, 1–14.

Antaki, C. and Widdicombe, S. (eds) (1998b) *Identities in Talk*, London: Sage.

Aristotle (1940) *Aristotle's Art of Poetry*, trans. by I. Bywater, Oxford: Oxford University Press.

Asch, S.E. (1946) 'Forming impressions of personality', *Journal of Abnormal and Social Psychology*, 41, 258–290.

Ashmore, R.D. (1981) 'Sex stereotypes and implicit personality theory', in Hamilton, D.L. (ed.), *Cognitive Processes in Stereotyping and Intergroup Behaviour*, Hillsdale, NJ: Lawrence Erlbaum, 37–81.

Ashmore, R.D. and Del Boca, F.K. (1981) 'Conceptual approaches to stereotypes and stereotyping', in Hamilton, D.L. (ed.), *Cognitive Processes in Stereotyping and Intergroup Behaviour*, Hillsdale, NJ: Lawrence Erlbaum, 1–35.

Augoustinos, M. and Walker, I. (1995) *Social Cognition: An Integrated Perspective*, London: Sage.

Austin (1962) *How to Do Things with Words*, Oxford: Oxford University Press.

Ayckbourn, A. [1969] (1998) 'Ernie's Incredible Illucinations', in Ayckbourn, A., *Alan Ayckbourn: Plays 2*, London and Boston: Faber & Faber, 1–29.

Baddeley, A.D. (1986) *Working Memory*, New York: Oxford University Press.

Barber, C. (1976) *Early Modern English*, London: Andre Deutsch.

Barber, C. [1981] (1987) ' "You" and "thou" in Shakespeare's *Richard III* ', reprinted in Salmon, V. and Burness, E. (eds), *A Reader in the Language of Shakespearian Drama*, Amsterdam and Philadelphia: John Benjamins, 163–179.

Baron, R.A. and Byrne, D. (1991) *Social Psychology: Understanding Human Interaction*, Boston: Allyn and Bacon.

Barsalou, L.W. (1982) 'Context-independent and context-dependent information in concepts', *Memory and Cognition*, 10, 82–93.

Barsalou, L.W. (1989) 'Intra-concept similarity and its implications for inter-concept similarity', in Vosniadou, S. and Ortony, A. (eds) *Similarity and Analogy*, Cambridge: Cambridge University Press, 76–121.

Barthes, R. [1970] (1975) *S–Z*, trans. by Richard Miller, London: Cape.

Bartlett, F.C. [1932] (1995) *Remembering: A Study in Experimental and Social Psychology*, Cambridge: Cambridge University Press.

Baskervill, C.R. [1911] (1967) *English Elements in Jonson's Early Comedy*, New York: Gordian Press.

Baugh, A.C. and Cable, T. (1993) *A History of the English Language*, 4th edn, London: Routledge.

Bavelas, J.B., Black, A., Chovil, N. and Mullet, J. (1990) 'Truths, lies, and equivocations. The effects of conflicting goals on discourse', *Journal of Language and Social Psychology*, 9, 135–161.

Baxter, L.A. (1984) 'An investigation of compliance-gaining as politeness', *Human Communication Research*, 10, 3, 427–456.

Bean, J. (1980) 'Comic structure and the humanizing of Kate in *The Taming of the Shrew*', in Lenz, G.R.S., Greene, G. and Neely, C.T. (eds) *The Woman's Part*, Urbana: University of Illinois Press, 65–78.

Belsey, C. (1985) 'Disrupting sexual difference: Meaning and gender in the comedies', in Drakakis, J. (ed.), *Alternative Shakespeares*, London: Routledge, 166–190.

Bem, S.L. (1983) 'Gender schema theory and its implications for child development: Raising gender-aschematic children in a gender-schematic society', *Signs: Journal of Women in Culture and Society*, 8, 4, 598–616.

Bennison, N. (1993) 'Discourse analysis, pragmatics and the dramatic character: Tom Stoppard's *Professional Foul*', *Language and Literature*, 2, 2, 79–99.

Bennison, N. (1997) *Unfolding the Process: Character, Narratology, and the Fiction of George Eliot*, unpublished PhD thesis, Lancaster University.

Biber, D. (1988) *Variation across Speech and Writing*, Cambridge: Cambridge University Press.

Black, E. (1993) 'Metaphor, simile and cognition in Golding's *The Inheritors*', *Language and Literature*, 2, 37–48.

Blake, N.F. (1983) *Shakespeare's Language: An Introduction*, London: Macmillan.

Blake, N.F. (1992–3) 'Shakespeare and discourse', *Stylistica*, 2, 3, 81–90.

Blum-Kulka, S. (1987) 'Indirectness and politeness in requests: Same or different?', *Journal of Pragmatics*, 11, 131–146.

Blum-Kulka, S., Danet, B. and Gherson, R. (1985) 'The Language of requesting in Israeli Society', in Forgas, J. (ed.) *Language and Social Situations*, New York: Springer-Verlag, 113–139.

Bockting, I. (1995) *Character and Personality in the Novels of William Faulkner: A Study in Psychostylistics*, Lanham, Maryland: University Press of America.

Bohner, G., Bless, H., Schwarz, N. and Strack, H. (1988) 'What triggers causal attributions? The impact of valence and subjective probability', *European Journal of Social Psychology*, 18, 335–348.

Bradac, J.J. (1982) 'A rose by another name: Attitudinal consequences of lexical variation', in Ryan, E.B. and Giles, H. (eds), *Attitudes toward Language Variation: Social and Applied Contexts*, London: Arnold, 99–115.

Bradac, J.J. (1990) 'Language attitudes and impression formation', in Giles, H. and Robinson, W.P. (eds), *Handbook of Language and Social Psychology*, Chichester: Wiley, 387–412.

Bradbury, M. and Palmer, D. (1972) *Stratford-Upon-Avon Studies 14: Shakespearian Comedy*, London: Edward Arnold.

Bradley, A.C. [1905] (1960) *Shakespearean Tragedy: Lectures on Hamlet, Othello, King Lear, Macbeth*, 2nd edn, London: Macmillan.

Bransford, J.D. and Johnson, M.K. (1972) 'Contextual prerequisites for understanding: Some investigations of comprehension and recall', *Journal of Verbal Learning and Verbal Behaviour*, 11, 717–726.

Brecht, B. (1964) *Brecht on Theatre*, trans. by J. Willett, London: Methuen.

Brewer, M.B. (1988) 'A Dual Process Model of Impression Formation', in Srull, T.K. and Wyer, R.S. (eds) *Advances in Social Cognition, Vol. 1*, Hillsdale, NJ: Lawrence Erlbaum.

Brewer, M.B., Dull, V. and Layton, L. (1981) 'Perceptions of the elderly: Stereotypes as prototypes', *Journal of Personality and Social Psychology*, 41, 4, 656–670.

Brewer, W.F. and Nakamura, G.V. (1984) 'The Nature and Function of Schemas', in Wyer, R.S. and Srull, T.K. (eds) *Handbook of Social Cognition, Vol. 1*, Hillsdale, NJ: Lawrence Erlbaum.

Briggs, J. (1983) *This Stage-Play World: English Literature and its Background 1580–1625*, Oxford: Oxford University Press.

Brinton, L. (1996) *Pragmatic Markers in English* (Topics in English, 19), Berlin and New York: Mouton de Gruyter.

Britton, B.K. and Graesser, A.C. (eds) (1996) *Models of Understanding Text*, Mahwah, NJ: Lawrence Erlbaum.

Brook, G.L. (1976) *The Language of Shakespeare*, London: Andre Deutsch.

Brooke, M.E. (1988) *Topic change and social influence: A pilot study*, Unpublished report, University of Otago, New Zealand: Department of Psychology.

Brown, B.R. (1970) 'Face-saving following experimentally induced embarrassment', *Journal of Experimental Social Psychology*, 6, 255–271.

Brown, G. (1990) *Listening to Spoken English*, 2nd edn, London: Longman.

Brown, G. and Yule, G. (1983) *Discourse Analysis*, Cambridge: Cambridge University Press.

Brown, P. and Levinson, S.C. (1978) 'Universals in language usage: Politeness phenomena', in Goody, E.N. (ed.) *Questions and Politeness: Strategies in Social Interaction*, Cambridge: Cambridge University Press, 56–289.

Brown, P. and Levinson, S.C. (1987) *Politeness: Some Universals in Language Usage*, Cambridge: Cambridge University Press.

Brown, R. and Gilman, A. (1960) 'The pronouns of power and solidarity', in Sebeok, T.A. (ed.) *Style in Language*, Cambridge, MA: MIT Press, 253–276.

Brown, R. and Gilman, A. (1989) 'Politeness theory and Shakespeare's four major tragedies', *Language in Society*, 18, 159–212.

Burton, D. (1980) *Dialogue and Discourse: A Sociolinguistic Approach to Modern Drama Dialogue and Naturally Occurring Conversation*, London: Routledge & Kegan Paul.

Burton, D.M. (1973) *Shakespeare's Grammatical Style: A Computer-Assisted Analysis of 'Richard II' and 'Antony and Cleopatra'*, Austin and London: University of Texas Press.

Busemann, A. (1925) *Die Sprache der Jugend als Ausdruck der Entwicklungsrhythmik*, Jena.

Busemann, A. (1948) *Stil und Charakter: Untersuchungen zur Psychologie der individuellen Redeform*, Meisenheim, Glan.: A. Hain.

Busse, U. (1998) 'Forms of address in Shakespeare's plays: Problems and findings', in R. Schulze (ed.) *Making Meaningful Choices in English: On Dimensions, Perspectives, Methodology and Evidence*, Tübingen: Gunter Narr, 33–60.

Byrne, Sister St. G. [1936] (1970) *Shakespeare's Use of the Pronouns of Address; its Significance in Characterization and Motivation*, New York: Haskell House.

Caffi, C. and Janney, R.W. (1994) 'Toward a pragmatics of emotive communication', *Journal of Pragmatics*, 22, 325–373.

Calvo, C. (1992) 'Pronouns of address and social negotiation in "As You Like It"', *Language and Literature*, 1, 1, 5–27.

Cameron, D. (1992) *Feminism and Linguistic Theory*, 2nd edn, London: Macmillan.

Cameron, D., McAlinden, F. and O'Leary, K. (1989) 'Lakoff in context: the social and linguistic functions of tag questions', in Coates, J. and Cameron, D. (eds) *Women in Their Speech Communities*, Harlow: Longman, 74–93.

Cantor, N. and Mischel, W. (1977) 'Traits as prototypes: Effects on recognition memory', *Journal of Personality and Social Psychology*, 35, 38–48.

Cantor, N. and Mischel, W. (1979) 'Prototypes in person perception', in Berkowitz, L. (ed.) *Advances in Experimental Social Psychology, Vol. 12*, New York: Academic Press, 3–52.

Charlton, H.B. (1938) *Shakespearian Comedy*, London: Methuen.

Chatman, S. (1972) 'On the formalist–structuralist theory of character', *Journal of Literary Semantics*, 1, 57–79.

Chatman, S. (1978) *Story and Discourse: Narrative Structure in Fiction and Film*, Ithaca and London: Cornell University Press.

Cheyne, W. (1970) 'Stereotyped reactions to speakers with Scottish and English regional accents', *British Journal of Social and Clinical Psychology*, 9, 77–79.

Coates, J. (1989) 'Introduction', in Coates, J. and Cameron, D. (eds), *Women in Their Speech Communities*, Harlow: Longman, 63–73.

Coates, J. and Cameron, D. (eds) (1989) *Women in Their Speech Communities*, Harlow: Longman.

Cody, M., McLaughlin, M. and Schneider, J. (1981) 'The impact of relational consequences and intimacy on the selection of interpersonal persuasion tactics: A reanalysis', *Communication Quarterly*, 29, 91–106.

Coghill, N. (1950) 'The basis of Shakespearean comedy: A study in medieval affinities', *Essays and Studies of the English Association*, 3, 1–28.

Coleman, L. and Kay, P. (1981) 'Prototype semantics: The English word "Lie"', *Language*, 57, 1, 26–44.

Collins Cobuild English Language Dictionary (1987), ed. in chief Sinclair, J., London: Collins.

Collins, A.M. and Quillian, M.R. (1969) 'Retrieval time from semantic memory', *Journal of Verbal Learning and Verbal Behaviour*, 8, 240–247.

Condor, S. and Antaki, C. (1997) 'Social cognition and discourse', in van Dijk, T.A. (ed.), *Discourse as Structure and Process*, London: Sage, 320–347.

Conway, M.A. and Bekerian, D.A. (1987) 'Situational knowledge and emotions', *Cognition and Emotions*, 1, 2, 145–191.

Cook, G. (1990) *A Theory of Discourse Deviation: The Application of Schema Theory to the Analysis of Literary Discourse*, Ph.D. dissertation, University of Leeds.

Cook, G. (1994) *Discourse and Literature*, Oxford: Oxford University Press.

Cook, J. (1990) *Women in Shakespeare*, London: Virgin.

Cooper, M. (1981) 'Implicature, convention and "The Taming of the Shrew" ', *Poetics*, 10, 1–14.

Coulmas, F. (ed.) (1981) *Conversational Routine: Explorations in Standardised Communication Situations and Prepatterned Speech*, The Hague: Mouton.

Coulthard, M. (1985) *An Introduction to Discourse Analysis*, London: Longman.

Coupland, N., Grainger, K. and Coupland, J. (1988) 'Politeness in context: Intergenerational issues (Review article)', *Language in Society*, 17, 253–262.

Craig, R.T., Tracy, K. and Spisak, F. (1986) 'The discourse of requests: Assessment of a politeness approach', *Human Communication Research*, 12, 4, 437–468.

Crawford, M. (1995) *Talking Difference: On Gender and Language*, London and New Delhi: Sage.

Crosby, F. and Nyquist, L. (1977) 'The female register: An empirical study of Lakoff's hypotheses', *Language in Society*, 6, 313–322.

Culler, J. (1975) *Structuralist Poetics: Structuralism, Linguistics and the Study of Literature*, London: Routledge & Kegan Paul.

Culpeper, J. (1994) 'Why relevance theory does not explain "The relevance of reformulations" ', *Language and Literature*, 3, 1, 43–48.

Culpeper, J. (1996a) 'Towards an anatomy of impoliteness', *Journal of Pragmatics*, 25, 349–367.

Culpeper, J. (1996b) 'Inferring character from text: Attribution theory and foregrounding theory', *Poetics*, 23, 335–361.

Culpeper, J. (1998) '(Im)politeness in dramatic dialogue', in Culpeper, J. *et al.* (eds), *Studying Drama: From Text to Context*, London: Routledge, 83–95.

Culpeper, J. (2000) 'An approach to characterisation: The case of Katherina in Shakespeare's *The Taming of the Shrew*', *Language and Literature*, 9, 4, 291–316.

Culpeper, J. and Kytö, M. (1999) 'Modifying pragmatic force: Hedges in a corpus of Early Modern English dialogues', in Jucker, A.H., Fritz, G. and Lebsanft, F. (eds), *Historical Dialogue Analysis*, Amsterdam: John Berjamins, 293–312.

Culpeper, J. and Kytö, M. (2000) 'Data in historical pragmatics: Spoken interaction (re)cast as writing', *Journal of Historical Pragmatics*, 1, 2, 175–199.

Culpeper, J., Short, M. and Verdonk, P. (1998) (eds) *Studying Drama: From Text to Context*, London: Routledge.

Cunico, S. (2000) An Anatomy of Madness: (Dis)ordered speech in drama, unpublished Ph.D. dissertation, Lancaster University.

Dash, I.G. (1981) *Wooing, Wedding, and Power: Women in Shakespeare's Plays*, New York: Columbia University Press.

Davison, P. (ed.) (1996) *The First Quarto of King Richard III* (The New Cambridge Shakespeare), Cambridge: Cambridge University Press.

de Bruyn, L. (1979) *Woman and the Devil in Sixteenth-century Literature*, Tisbury, Wiltshire: Compton Press.

Della Casa, G. [1558] (1958) *Il Galateo*, trans. by R.S. Pine-Coffin, Harmondsworth: Penguin.

Dessen, A.C. (1977) *Elizabethan Drama and the Viewer's Eye*, Chapel Hill: University of North Carolina Press.

Diderot, D. (1875) *Œuvres Complètes de Diderot*, ed. by Assézat, J. and Huitième, T., Paris: Garnier Frères.

Doran, M. (1976) *Shakespeare's Dramatic Language*, Wisconsin: University of Wisconsin Press.

Dore, J. (1985) 'Children's conversations', in van Dijk, T.A. (ed.) *Handbook of Discourse Analysis, Vol. 3, Discourse and Dialogue*, London: Academic Press, 47–65.

Downes, W. (1988) 'King Lear's question to his daughters', in van Peer, W. (ed.), *The Taming of the Text*: Explorations in Language, Literature and Culture, London: Routledge, 225–257.

Drakakis, J. (ed.) (1985) *Alternative Shakespeares*, London: Routledge.

Dubois, B.L. and Crouch, I. (1975) 'The question of tag questions in women's speech: They don't really use more of them, do they?', *Language in Society*, 4, 289–294.

Dunkling, L. (1995) *The Guinness Book of Names*, 7th edn, London: Guinness Publishing.

Edmondson, W.J. (1981) 'On saying you're sorry', in Coulmas, F. (ed.), *Conversational Routine: Explorations in Standardised Communication Situations and Prepatterned Speech*, The Hague: Mouton, 273–287.

Edwards, D. and Potter, J. (1992) *Discursive Psychology*, London: Sage.

Edwards, J.R. (1982) 'Language attitudes and their implications among English speakers', in Ryan, E.B. and Giles, H. (eds), *Attitudes Toward Language Variation: Social and Applied Contexts*, London: Arnold, 20–33.

Edwards (1998) 'The relevant thing about her: Social identity categories in use', in Antaki, C. and Widdicombe, S. (eds), *Identities in Talk*, London: Sage.

Ekman, P., Fiesen, W.V. and Tomkins, S.S. (1971) 'Facial affect scoring technique (FAST): A first validity study', *Semiotica*, 3, 37–58.

Elam, K. (1980) *The Semiotics of Theatre and Drama*, London and New York: Methuen.

Ellegård, A. (1978) *The Syntactic Structure of English Texts: A Computer-based Study of Four Kinds of Text in the Brown University Corpus* (Gothenburg Studies in English, 43), Gothenburg: Gothenburg University Press.

Emmott, C. (1997) *Narrative Comprehension: A Discourse Perspective*, Oxford: Oxford University Press.

Enkvist, N.E. (1964) 'On defining style', in Enkvist, N.E., Spencer, J. and Gregory, M. (eds) *Linguistics and Style*, Oxford: Oxford University Press, 1–56.

Enkvist, N.E. (1973) *Linguistic Stylistics*, Berlin: Mouton.

Erickson, B., Lind, E.A., Johnson, B.C. and O'Barr, W.M. (1978) 'Speech style and impression formation in a court setting: The effects of "powerful" and "powerless" speech', *Journal of Experimental Social Psychology*, 14, 266–279.

Ervin-Tripp, S. (1972) 'On sociolinguistic rules: Alternation and co-occurrence', in Gumperz, J.J. and Hymes, D. (eds) *Directions in Sociolinguistics: The Ethnography of Communication*, New York: Holt Rinehart & Winston, 213–250.

Evans, M. (1985) 'Deconstructing Shakespeare's comedies', in Drakakis, J. (ed.), *Alternative Shakespeares*, London: Routledge, 67–94.

Ewen, J. (1980) *Character in Narrative*, Tel Aviv: Sifri'at Po'alim.

Eysenck, M.W. and Keane, M.T. (1990) *Cognitive Psychology: A Student's Handbook*, Hillsdale, NJ: Lawrence Erlbaum.

Fairclough, N. and Wodak, R. (1997) 'Critical discourse analysis', in van Dijk, T.A. (ed.) *Discourse as Social Interaction*, London: Sage, 258–284.

Falbo, T. and Peplau, L.A. (1980) 'Power strategies in intimate relationships', *Journal of Personality and Social Psychology*, 38, 4, 618–628.

Fishelov, D. (1990) 'Types of character, characteristics of types', *Style*, 24, 3, 422–439.

Fiske, S.T. (1988) 'Compare and contrast: Brewer's dual process model and Fiske *et al.*'s continuum model', in Srull, T.K. and Wyer, R.S. (eds), *Advances in Social Cognition, Vol. I: a Dual Process Model of Impression Formation*, Hillsdale, NJ: Lawrence Erlbaum, 65–76.

Fiske, S.T. and Neuberg, S.L. (1990) 'A continuum of impression formation, from category-based to individuating processes: Influences of information and motivation on attention and interpretation', in Zanna, M.P. (ed.) *Advances in Experimental Social Psychology*, Vol. 23, New York: Academic Press, 1–74.

Fiske, S.T. and Taylor, S.E. (1984) *Social Cognition*, Reading, MA: McGraw-Hill.

Fiske, S.T. and Taylor, S.E. (1991) *Social Cognition*, 2nd edn, New York: Addison-Wesley.

Forster, E.M. [1927] (1987) *Aspects of the Novel*, Harmondsworth: Penguin.

Fowler, R. (1977) *Linguistics and the Novel*, London: Methuen.

Fowler, R. (1986) *Linguistic Criticism*, Oxford and New York: Oxford University Press.

Fowler, R. (1991) *Language in the News: Discourse and Ideology in the Press*, London and New York: Routledge.

Fraser, B. (1981) 'On apologizing', in Coulmas, F. (ed.), *Conversational Routine: Explorations in Standardised Communication Situations and Prepatterned Speech*, The Hague: Mouton, 259–271.

Fraser, B. (1990) 'Perspectives on politeness', *Journal of Pragmatics*, 14, 219–236.

Fraser, B. and Nolan, W. (1981) 'The association of deference with linguistic form', *International Journal of the Sociology of Language*, 27, 93–109.

Freeman, D.C. (1995) ' "Catch[ing] the nearest way": Macbeth and cognitive metaphor', *Journal of Pragmatics*, 24, 689–708.

Frege, G. (1952) 'On sense and reference', in Geach, P. and Black, M. (eds) *Translations from the Philosophical Writings of Gottlob Frege*, Oxford: Blackwell, 56–78.

Frye, N. (1957) *Anatomy of Criticism: Four Essays*, Princeton, NJ: Princeton University Press.

Garber, M. (1996) *Vice Versa: Bisexuality and the Eroticism of Everyday Life*, London: Hamish Hamilton.

Garfinkel, H. (1967) *Studies in Ethnomethodology*, Englewood Cliffs, NJ: Prentice Hall.

Garnham, A. and Oakhill, J. (1996) 'The mental models theory of language comprehension', in Britton, B.K. and Graesser, A.C. (eds), *Models of Understanding Text*, Mahwah, NJ: Lawrence Erlbaum, 313–339.

Gernsbacher, M.A., Goldsmith, H.H. and Robertson, R. (1992) 'Do readers represent characters' emotional states?', *Cognition and Emotion*, 6, 89–111.

Gerrig, R.J. and Allbritton, D.W. (1990) 'The construction of literary character: A view from cognitive psychology', *Style*, 24, 3, 380–391.

Gilbert, A.J. (1979) *Literary Language from Chaucer to Johnson*, London: Macmillan.

Gilbert, D.T. (1989) 'Thinking lightly about others: Automatic components of the social inference process', in Uleman, J.S. and Bargh, J.A. (eds) *Unintended Thought: Limits of Awareness, Intention, and Control*, New York: Guilford, 189–211.

Gilbert, D.T. and Hixon, J.G. (1991) 'The trouble of thinking: Activation and application of stereotypic beliefs', *Journal of Personality and Social Psychology*, 60, 509–517.

Gilbert, D.T. and Jones, E.E. (1986) 'Perceiver-induced constraint: Interpretation of self-generated reality', *Journal of Personality and Social Psychology*, 50, 269–280.

Giles, H. (1970) 'Evaluative reactions to accents', *Educational Review*, 22, 211–227.

Giles, H. and Powesland, P.F. (1975) *Speech Style and Social Evaluation*, London: Academic Press.

Giles, H. and Robinson, W.P. (eds) (1990) *Handbook of Language and Social Psychology*, Chichester: Wiley.

Giles, J. (1997) *The Crying Game*, London: British Film Institute.

Goffman, E. (1959) *The Presentation of Self in Everyday Life*. New York: Doubleday.

Goffman, E. (1967) *Interaction Ritual: Essays on Face-to-face Behavior*, New York: Anchor Books.

Goffman, E. (1971) *Relations in Public*, New York: Harper & Row.

Goodwin, C. (1996) 'Transparent vision', in Ochs, E, Schegloff, E.A. and Thompson, S.A. (eds) *Interaction and Grammar* (Studies in Interactional Sociolinguistics, 13), Cambridge: Cambridge University Press, 370–404.

Görlach, M. (1991) *Introduction to Early Modern English*, Cambridge: Cambridge University Press.

Graesser, A.C., Gernsbacher, M.A. and Goldman, S.R. (1997) 'Cognition', in van Dijk, T.A. (ed.), *Discourse as Social Interaction*, London: Sage, 292–319.

Graesser, A.C., Singer, M. and Trabasso, T. (1994) 'Constructing inferences during narrative text comprehension', *Psychological Review*, 101, 3, 371–395.

Graumann, C.F. (1992) 'Speaking and understanding from viewpoints: Studies in perspectivity', in Semin, G.R. and Fiedler, K. (eds), *Language, Interaction and Social Cognition*, London, Sage: 237–255.

Greene, J. (1987) *Memory, Thinking and Language: Topics in Cognitive Psychology*, London and New York: Methuen.

Greimas, A.J. (1966) *Sémantique Structurale*, Paris: Larousse.

Grice, H.P. (1975) 'Logic and conversation', in Cole, P. and Morgan, J.L. (eds) *Syntax and Semantics 3: Speech Acts*, New York: Academic Press, 41–58.

Grice, H.P. (1981) 'Presupposition and conversational implicature', in Cole, P. (ed.) *Radical Pragmatics*, New York: Academic Press, 183–198.

Hall, E. (1966) *The Hidden Dimension*, New York: Doubleday.

Hall, K. and Bucholtz, M. (1995) *Gender Articulated. Language and the Socially Constructed Self*, New York and London: Routledge.

Halliday, M.A.K. (1971) 'Linguistic function and literary style: An inquiry into the language of William Golding's "The Inheritors" ', in Chatman, S. (ed.) *Literary Style: A Symposium*, Oxford: Oxford University Press: 330–365.

Hamilton, D.L. (ed.) (1981) *Cognitive Processes in Stereotyping and Intergroup Behaviour*, Hillsdale, NJ: Lawrence Erlbaum.

Hamilton, D.L. (1988) 'Causal attribution viewed from an information processing perspective', in Bar-Tal, D. and Kruglanski, A.W. (eds) *The Social Psychology of Knowledge*, New York: Cambridge University Press, 359–385.

Hamilton, D.L. and J.W. Sherman (1994) 'Stereotypes', in Wyer, R.S. and Srull, T.K. (eds.) *Handbook of Social Cognition, Volume 2: Applications*, 2nd edn, New Jersey: Lawrence Erlbaum, 1–68.

Hammond, A. (ed.) (1981) *King Richard III* (The Arden Shakespeare), London and New York: Routledge.

Hanks, P. and Hodges, F. (1990) *A Dictionary of First Names*, Oxford: Oxford University Press.

Harris, L., Gergen, K. and Lannaman, J. (1986) 'Aggression rituals', *Communication Monographs*, 53, 252–265.

Harris, M.A. (1949) 'The origin of the seventeenth century idea of humours', *Modern Language Notes*, 10, 44–46.

Harvey, W.J. (1965) *Character and The Novel*, London: Chatto & Windus.

Hastie, R. (1984) 'Causes and effects of causal attribution', *Journal of Personality and Social Psychology*, 46, 44–56.

Hayes, N. (1994) *Foundations of Psychology*, London: Routledge.

Hazlitt, W. [1817] (1906) *Characters of Shakespear's Plays*, London: Dent and Sons Everyman's Library.

Heider, F. (1944) 'Social perception and phenomenal causality', *Psychological Review*, 51, 358–374.

Heider, F. (1958) *The Psychology of Interpersonal Relations*, New York: Wiley.

Heilman, R.B. (1972) 'Introduction to *The Taming of the Shrew*', in Barnet, S. (ed.) *The Complete Signet Classic Shakespeare*, New York: Harcourt Brace Jovanovich, 321–329.

Herman, V. (1991) 'Dramatic dialogue and the systematics of turn-taking', *Semiotica*, 83, 97–121.

Herman, V. (1995) *Dramatic Discourse: Dialogue as Interaction in Plays*, London: Routledge.

Hewstone, M. (1983) 'The role of language in attribution processes', in Jaspars, J. *et al.* (eds), *Attribution Theory and Research: Conceptual, Developmental and Social Dimensions*, London: Academic Press, 241–259.

Higgins, E.T. (1981) 'The "communication game": Implications for social cognition and persuasion', in Higgins, E.T., Zanna, M.P. and Herman, C.P. (eds), *Social Cognition: The Ontario Symposium, Vol. 1*, Hillsdale, NJ: Lawrence Erlbaum, 343–392.

Hochman, B. (1985) *Character in Literature*, Ithaca and London: Cornell University Press.

Holmes, J. (1984) 'Modifying illocutionary force', *Journal of Pragmatics*, 8, 345–365.

Holmes, J. (1992) 'Women's talk in public contexts', *Discourse and Society*, 3, 2, 131–150.

Holmes, J. (1995) *Women, Men and Politeness*, London and New York: Longman.

Holtgraves, T. (1986) 'Language structure in social interaction: Perceptions of direct and indirect speech acts and interactants who use them', *Journal of Personality and Social Psychology*, 51, 2, 305–314.

Holtgraves, T. (1989) 'The form and function of remedial moves: Reported use, psychological reality, and perceived effectiveness', *Journal of Language and Social Psychology*, 8, 1–16.

Holtgraves, T. (1992) 'The linguistic realization of face management: Implications for language production and comprehension, person perception, and cross-cultural communication', *Social Psychology Quarterly*, 55, 2, 141–159.

Holtgraves, T. and Srull, T.K. (1989) 'The effects of positive self-descriptions on impressions: General principles and individual differences', *Personality and Social Psychology Bulletin*, 15, 425–462.

Holtgraves, T. and Yang, J-N. (1990) 'Politeness as universal: Cross-cultural perceptions of request strategies and inferences based on their use', *Journal of Personality and Social Psychology*, 59, 4, 719–729.

Holtgraves, T., Srull, T.K. and Socall, D. (1989) 'Conversation memory: The effects of speaker status on memory for the assertiveness of conversation remarks', *Journal of Personality and Social Psychology*, 56, 149–160.

Holyoak, K.J. and Gordon, P.C. (1984) 'Information processing and social cognition', in Wyer, R.S. and Srull, T.K. (eds), *Handbook of Social Cognition, Vol. I*, Hillsdale, NJ: Lawrence Erlbaum, 39–70.

Hope, J. (1993) 'Second-person singular pronouns in records of Early Modern "spoken" English', *Neuphilologische Mitteilungen*, XCIV, 83–100.

Hughes, R. (1996) *English in Speech and Writing: Investigating Language and Literature*, London and New York: Routledge.

Hurst, M.J. (1987) 'Speech acts in Ivy Compton-Burnett's *A Family and a Fortune*', *Language and Style*, 20, 4, 342–358.

Hussey, S.S. (1982) *The Literary Language of Shakespeare*, London: Longman.

Hussey, S.S. (1992) *The Literary Language of Shakespeare*, 2nd edn, London: Longman.

Ionesco, E. (1962) *Notes et Contre-Notes*, Paris: Gallimard.

Ionesco, E. (1964) *Eugene Ionesco: Notes and Counter-Notes*, trans. by D. Watson, London: John Calder.

Jakobson, R. (1960) 'Closing statement: Linguistics and poetics', in Sebeok, T.A. (ed.) *Style and Language*, Cambridge, MA: MIT Press, 350–377.

James, H. [1881] (1947) *The Portrait of a Lady*, Oxford: Oxford University Press.

Jardine, L. (1983) *Still Harping on Daughters: Women and Drama in the Age of Shakespeare*, Sussex: Harvester Press.

Jaspars, J., Fincham, F.D. and Hewstone, M. (eds) (1983) *Attribution Theory and Research: Conceptual, Developmental and Social Dimensions*, London: Academic Press.

Jespersen, O. (1958) *A Modern English Grammar on Historical Principles*, Part IV, London: Allen & Unwin.

Johnson, S. [1765] (1908) *Johnson on Shakespeare*, Oxford: Oxford University Press.

Johnson, S.A. and Meinhof, U. (eds) (1997) *Language and Masculinity*, Oxford: Blackwell.

Johnson-Laird, P.N. (1983) *Mental Models*, Cambridge: Cambridge University Press.

Jones, D. (1980) 'Gossip: Notes on women's oral culture', in Kramarae, C. (ed.), *The Voices and Words of Women and Men*, Oxford: Pergamon Press, 193–198.

Jones, E.E. (1979) 'The rocky road from acts to dispositions', *American Psychologist*, 34, 107–117.

Jones, E.E. (1990) *Interpersonal Perception*, New York: W.H. Freeman.

Jones, E.E. and Davis, K.E. (1965) 'From acts to dispositions: The attribution process in person perception', in Berkowitz, L. (ed.) *Advances in Experimental Social Psychology, Vol. 2*, New York: Academic Press, 219–266.

Jones, E.E. and Harris, V.A. (1967) 'The attribution of attitudes', *Journal of Experimental Social Psychology*, 3, 1–24.

Jones, E.E. and McGillis, D. (1976) 'Correspondent inferences and the attribution cube: A comparative reappraisal', in Harvey, J.H., Ickes, W.J. and

Kidd, R.F. (eds), *New Directions in Attribution Research, Vol. 1*, Hillsdale, NJ: Lawrence Erlbaum.

Jones, E.E. and Nisbett, R.E. (1972) 'The actor and the observer: Divergent perceptions of the causes of behavior', in Jones, E.E. *et al.* (eds), *Attribution: Perceiving the Causes of Behavior*, Morristown, NJ: General Learning Press, 79–94.

Jones, E.E., Kanouse, D.E., Kelley, H.H., Nisbett, R.E., Valins, S. and Weiner, B. (eds) (1972) *Attribution: Perceiving the Causes of Behavior*, Morristown, NJ: General Learning Press.

Josephs, H. (1969) *Diderot's Dialogue of Language and Gesture*, Ohio: Ohio State University Press.

Jucker, A.H. (ed.) (1995) *Historical Pragmatics: Pragmatic Developments in the History of English* (Pragmatics and Beyond, New Series, 35), Amsterdam and Philadelphia: John Benjamins.

Jucker, A.H., Fritz, G. and Lebsanft, F. (eds) (1999) *Historical Dialogue Analysis*, Amsterdam: John Benjamins.

Kahn, C. (1977) '*The Taming of the Shrew*: Shakespeare's mirror of marriage', in Diamond, A. and Edwards, L.R. (eds) *The Authority of Experience: Essays in Feminist Criticism*, Amherst, MA: University of Massachusetts Press, 84–100.

Kanouse, D.E. (1972) 'Language, labeling and attribution', in Jones, E.E. *et al.* (eds), *Attribution: Perceiving the Causes of Behavior*, Morristown, NJ: General Learning Press, 121–135.

Kasof, J. (1993) 'Sex bias in the naming of stimulus persons', *Psychological Bulletin*, 113, 1, 140–163.

Kelley, H.H. (1967) 'Attribution theory in social psychology', in Levine, D. (ed.) *Nebraska Symposium on Motivation*, Lincoln, Nebraska: University of Nebraska Press, 192–238.

Kelley, H.H. (1972) 'Attribution in social interaction', in Jones, E.E. *et al.* (eds), *Attribution: Perceiving the Causes of Behavior*, Morristown, NJ: General Learning Press, 1–26.

Kelley, H.H. (1973) 'The processes of causal attribution', *American Psychologist*, 28, 107–128.

Kesey, K. (1973) *One Flew Over the Cuckoo's Nest*, London: Pan Books.

Kintsch, W. (1988) 'The role of knowledge in discourse comprehension: A construction–integration model', *Psychological Review*, 95, 163–182.

Kintsch, W., Schmalhofer, F., Welsch, D. and Zimny, S. (1990) 'Sentence memory: A theoretical analysis', *Journal of Memory and Language*, 29, 133–159.

Kirschbaum, L. (1962) *Character and Characterization in Shakespeare*, Detroit: Wayne State University Press.

Knapp, J.V. (1990) 'Introduction: Self-preservation and self-transformation: Interdisciplinary approaches to literary character', *Style*, 23, 3, 349–364.

Knights, L.C. [1933] (1963) *Explorations: Essays in Criticism Mainly on the Literature of the Seventeenth Century*, London: Chatto & Windus.

Kökeritz, H. (1953) *Shakespeare's Pronunciation*, New Haven: Yale University Press.

Kökeritz, H. [1954] (1963) *Mr. William Shakespeares Comedies, Histories, & Tragedies*. (Facsimile edition of the First Folio, 1623.) New Haven and London: Yale University Press.

Kramarae, C. (1974) 'Stereotypes of women's speech: The word from cartoons', *Journal of Popular Culture*, 8, 622–638.

Kramarae, C. (1977) 'Perceptions of male and female speech', *Language and Speech*, 20, 151–161.

Kramarae, C. (ed.) (1980) *The Voices and Words of Women and Men*, Oxford: Pergamon Press.

Krontiris, T. (1992) *Oppositional Voices: Women as Writers and Translators of Literature in the English Renaissance*, London and New York: Routledge.

Labov, W. (1972) *Language in the Inner City: Studies in the Black English Vernacular*, Oxford: Blackwell.

Labov, W. (1973) 'The boundaries of words and their meanings', in Bailey, C.-J.N. and Shuy, R.W. (eds) *New ways of Analyzing Variation in English*, Washington DC: Georgetown University Press, 340–373.

Labov, W. (1990) 'The intersection of sex and social class in the course of linguistic change', *Language Variation and Change*, 2, 205–254.

Labov, W. (1994) *Principles of Linguistic Change. Vol 1: Internal Factors* (Language in Society, 20), Oxford: Blackwell.

Lachenicht, L.G. (1980) 'Aggravating language: A study of abusive and insulting language', *International Journal of Human Communication*, 13, 4, 607–687.

Lakoff, G. (1977) 'Linguistic gestalts', *Papers from the Thirteenth Regional Meeting of the Chicago Linguistic Society*, Chicago: Chicago University Press, 236–287.

Lakoff, G. (1987) *Women, Fire, and Dangerous Things*, Chicago: Chicago University Press.

Lakoff, R. [1973] (1975) 'The logic of politeness; or, minding your P's and Q's', *Papers from the Ninth Regional Meeting of the Chicago Linguistic Society*, Chicago: University of Chicago Press, 292–305.

Lakoff, R. (1989) 'The limits of politeness: Therapeutic and courtroom discourse', *Multilingua*, 8, 101–129.

Lakoff, R. (1990) *Talking Power: The Politics of Language*, New York: Basic Books.

Lambert, W.E., Hodgson, R., Gardner, R.C. and Fillenbaum, S. (1960) 'Evaluational reactions to spoken languages', *Journal of Personality and Social Psychology*, 60, 44–51.

Laver, J. (1981) 'Linguistic routines and politeness in greeting and parting', in Coulmas, F. (ed.), *Conversational Routine: Explorations in Standardised Communication Situations and Prepatterned Speech*, The Hague: Mouton, 289–304.

Laver, J. and Trudgill, P. (1979) 'Phonetic and linguistic markers in speech', in Scherer, K.R. and Giles, H. (eds), *Social Markers in Speech*, Cambridge: Cambridge University Press, 1–32.

Leech, G.N. (1969) *A Linguistic Guide to English Poetry*, London: Longman.

Leech, G.N. (1970) ' "This bread I break" — Language and interpretation', in Freeman, D.C. (ed.) *Linguistics and Literary Style*, New York: Holt, Rinehart & Winston, 119–128.

Leech, G.N. (1981) *Semantics*, Harmondsworth: Penguin.

Leech, G.N. (1983) *Principles of Pragmatics*, London: Longman.

Leech, G.N. (1985) 'Stylistics', in van Dijk, T.A. (ed.) *Discourse and Literature*, Amsterdam: John Benjamins, 39–57.

Leech, G.N. (1992) 'Pragmatic principles in Shaw's *You Never Can Tell*', in Toolan, M. (ed.) *Language, Text and Context*, London: Routledge, 259–278.

Leech, G.N. (1999) 'The distribution and function of vocatives in American and British English conversation', in Hasselgård, H. and Oksefjell, S. (eds) *Out of Corpora: Studies in Honour of Stig Johansson*, Amsterdam and Atlanta, GA: Rodopi, 107–118.

Leech, G.N. and Short, M. (1981) *Style in Fiction*, London: Longman.

Leith, D. (1983) *A Social History of English*, London: Routledge.

Leith, D. (1989) 'A pragmatic approach to ballad dialogue', in van Peer, W. (ed.), *The Taming of the Text: Explorations in Language, Literature and Culture*, London: Routledge, 35–60.

LePage, R.B. and Tabouret-Keller, A. (1985) *Acts of Identity: Creole-based Approaches to Language and Ethnicity*, Cambridge: Cambridge University Press.

Lester, G. (ed.) (1999) *Chaucer in Perspective: Middle English Essays in Honour of Norman Blake*, Sheffield: Sheffield Academic Press.

Levin, S.R. (1965) 'Internal and external deviation in poetry', *Word*, 21, 225–237.

Levinson, S. ([1979] 1992) 'Activity types and language', in Drew, P. and Heritage, J. (eds) *Talk at Work*, Cambridge: Cambridge University Press, 66–100.

Levinson, S. (1981) 'The essential inadequacies of speech act models of dialogue', in Parret, H., Sbisa, M. and Verschueren, J. (eds) *Possibilities and Limitations of Pragmatics*, Amsterdam: John Benjamins, 473–489.

Levinson, S. (1983) *Pragmatics*, Cambridge: Cambridge University Press.

Lewicki, P. (1985) 'Nonconscious biasing effects of single instances on subsequent judgments', *Journal of Personality and Social Psychology*, 48, 563–574.

Lim, T-S. and Bowers, J.W. (1991) 'Face-work: Solidarity, approbation, and tact', *Human Communication Research*, 17, 415–450.

Lingle, J.H., Altom, M.W. and Medin, D.L. (1984) 'Of cabbages and kings: Assessing the extendibility of natural object concept models to social things', in Wyer, R.S. and Srull, T.K. (eds), *Handbook of Social Cognition, Vol. I*, Hillsdale, NJ: Lawrence Erlbaum, 72–117.

Liu, R. (1986) *The Politeness Principle and 'A Dream of Red Mansions'*, unpublished M.Phil. dissertation, Lancaster University.

Livingstone, S. (1998) *Making Sense of Television: The Psychology of Audience Interpretation*, 2nd edn, London and New York: Routledge.

Long, D.L. (1994) 'The effects of pragmatics and discourse style on recognition memory for sentences', *Discourse Processes* 17, 213–234.

Lowe, V. (1998) ' "Unhappy" confessions in *The Crucible*', in Culpeper, J. *et al.* (eds), *Studying Drama: From Text to Context*, London: Routledge, 128–141.

Lustig, M.W. and King, S. (1980) 'The effect of communication apprehension and situation on communication strategy choices', *Human Communication Research*, 7, 74–82.

Lynn, J. and Jay, A. (1989) *The Complete Yes Prime Minister*, London: BBC Books.

Mandler, J.M. and Johnson, N.S. (1977) 'Remembrance of things parsed: Story structure and recall', *Cognitive Psychology*, 9, 111–151.

Mani, K. and Johnson-Laird, P.N. (1982) 'The mental representation of spatial descriptions', *Memory and Cognition*, 10, 181–187.

Margolin, U. (1983) 'Characterization in narrative: Some theoretical prolegomena', *Neophilologus*, 67, 1–14.

Margolin, U. (1986) 'The doer and the deed: Action as a basis for characterization in narrative', *Poetics Today*, 7, 2, 205–225.

Margolin, U. (1989) 'Structuralist approaches to character in narrative: The state of the art', *Semiotica*, 75, 1/2, 1–24.

Margolin, U. (1990) 'The what, the when, and the how of being a character in literary narrative', *Style*, 24, 3, 453–468.

Martin, J.R. (1992) *English Text: System and Structure*, Philadelphia and Amsterdam: John Benjamins.

Martin, W. (1986) *Recent Theories of Narrative*, Ithaca and London: Cornell University Press.

McArthur, L.Z. and Baron, R.M. (1983) 'Toward an ecological theory of social perception', *Psychological Review*, 90, 215–247.

McCann, C.D. and Higgins, E.T. (1990) 'Social cognition and communication', in Giles, H. and Robinson, W.P. (eds), *Handbook of Language and Social Psychology*, Chichester: Wiley, 13–32.

McCann, C.D. and Higgins, E.T. (1992) 'Personal and contextual factors in communication: A review of the "Communication Game" ', in Semin, G.R. and Fiedler, K. (eds), *Language, Interaction and Social Cognition*, London: Sage, 144–172.

McClelland, J.L. (1987) 'The case for interactionism in language processing', in Coltheart, M. (ed.) *Attention and Performance, XII*, London: Lawrence Erlbaum Associates, 3–36.

McClelland, J.L., Rumelhart, D.E. and the PDP Research Group (1986) *Parallel Distributed Processing: Explorations in the Microstructure of Cognition*,

(Vol. 2: Psychological and Biological Models), Cambridge, MA: MIT Press.

McConnell-Ginet, S., Borker, R. and Furman, N. (eds) (1980) *Women and Language in Literature and Society*, New York: Praeger.

McGill, A.L. (1989) 'Context effects in judgements of causation', *Journal of Personality and Social Psychology*, 57, 189–200.

McIntosh, A. (1963) ' "As You Like It": A grammatical clue to character', *A Review of English Literature*, 4, 2, 68–81.

McIntyre, D. (1999) *Towards a Systematic Description and Explanation of Point of View Dramatic Texts, with Special Reference to Dennis Potter's 'Brimstone and Treacle'*, unpublished MA dissertation, Lancaster University.

McLeish, K. (1985) *Longman Guide to Shakespeare's Characters: A Who's Who of Shakespeare*, London: Longman.

McMillan, J.R., Clifton, K.A., McGrath, D. and Gale, W. (1977) 'Woman's language: Uncertainty or interpersonal sensitivity and emotionality?', *Sex Roles*, 3, 6, 545–559.

Mead, G. (1990) 'The representation of fictional character', *Style*, 24, 3, 440–452.

Medin, D.L. and Schaffer, M.M. (1978) 'Context theory of classification learning', *Psychological Review*, 85, 207–238.

Mehrabian, A. (1972) *Nonverbal Communication*, Chicago: Aldine-Atherton.

Meutsch, D. (1986) 'Mental models in literary discourse: Towards the integration of linguistic and psychological levels of description', *Poetics*, 15, 307–331.

Miller, A. [1953] (1986) *The Crucible*, Harmondsworth: Penguin.

Mills, J. (1991) *Womanwords: A Vocabulary of Culture and Patriarchal Society*, London: Virago.

Milroy, L. (1980) *Language and Social Networks*, Baltimore: University Park Press.

Minsky, M. (1975) 'A framework for representing knowledge', in Winston, P.H. (ed.) *The Psychology of Computer Vision*, New York: McGraw-Hill, 211–277.

Montagu, A. (1973) *The Anatomy of Swearing*, London and New York: Macmillan and Collier.

Morgan, M. (1987) *Drama Plays, Theatre and Performance*, London: Longman.

Morris, B. (ed.) (1981) *The Arden Shakespeare: 'The Taming of the Shrew'*, London: Routledge.

Morton, A. (1995) *Diana: Her New Life*, London: O'Mara.

Muhlhausler, P. and Harre, R. (1990) *Pronouns and People: The Linguistic Construction of Social and Personal Identity*, Oxford: Blackwell.

Muir, K. (1984) *The Arden Shakespeare: Macbeth*, London and New York: Methuen.

Mukařovský, J. (1970) 'Standard language and poetic language', ed. and trans. by Garvin, P.L., in Freeman, D.C. (ed.) *Linguistics and Literary Style*, New York: Holt, Rinehart & Winston, 40–56.

Mulholland, J. [1967] (1987) ' "Thou" and "you" in Shakespeare: A study in the second person pronoun', reprinted in Salmon, V. and Burness, E. (eds), *A Reader in the Language of Shakespearian Drama*, Amsterdam and Philadelphia: John Benjamins, 153–161.

Myers, G.A. (1991) 'Politeness and certainty: The language of collaboration in an AI project', *Social Studies of Science*, 21, 1, 37–73.

Neisser, U. (1976) *Cognition and Reality: Principles and Implications of Cognitive Psychology*, San Francisco: W.H. Freeman.

Nevalainen, T. and Raumolin-Brunberg, H. (1995) 'Constraints on politeness: The pragmatics of address formulae in Early English correspondence', in Jucker, A.H. (ed.) *Historical Pragmatics: Pragmatic Developments in the History of English* (Pragmatics and Beyond, New Series, 35), Amsterdam and Philadelphia: John Benjamins, 541–601.

Nevalainen, T. and Raumolin-Brunberg, H. (eds) (1996) *Sociolinguistics and Language History: Studies Based on the Corpus of Early English Correspondence*, Amsterdam: Rodopi.

Newman, K. (1985) *Shakespeare's Rhetoric of Comic Character: Dramatic Convention in Classical and Renaissance Comedy*. New York and London: Methuen.

Newman, K. (1991) *Fashioning Femininity and English Renaissance Drama*, Chicago: University of Chicago Press.

Ng, S.H. (1990) 'Language and control', in Giles, H. and Robinson, W.P. (eds), *Handbook of Language and Social Psychology*, Chichester: Wiley, 271–285.

Nisbett, R.E., Caputo, C., Legant, P. and Maracek, J. (1973) 'Behavior as seen by the actor and as seen by the observer', *Journal of Personality and Social Psychology*, 27, 154–164.

O'Barr, W.M. (1982) *Linguistic Evidence: Language, Power, and Strategy in the Courtroom*, New York: Academic Press.

O'Barr, W.M. and Atkins, B.K. (1980) ' "Women's language" or "powerless language"?', in McConnell-Ginet, S. *et al.* (eds), *Women and Language in Literature and Society*, New York: Praeger, 93–110.

One Foot in the Grave, Series One (originally transmitted 1990), *The Big Sleep*, produced and directed by Susan Belbin, London: BBC Worldwide.

Onions, C.T. (1986) *A Shakespeare Glossary*, ed. by Eagleson, R., Oxford: Clarendon Press.

Ortony, A., Clore, G.L. and Collins, A. (1988) *The Cognitive Structure of Emotions*, Cambridge: Cambridge University Press.

Orvis, B.R., Cunningham, J.D. and Kelley, H.H. (1975) 'A closer examination of causal inference: The roles of consensus, distinctiveness, and consistency information', *Journal of Personality and Social Psychology*, 32, 605–616.

Osborne, J. (1957) *The Entertainer*, London: Faber & Faber.

(The) Oxford English Dictionary (1989) (2nd edn.) prepared by Simpson, J.A. and Weiner, E.S.C., Oxford: Clarendon Press.

Page, N. (1988) *Speech in the English Novel*, 2nd edn, Houndmills, Hampshire: Macmillan.

Palmer, J. (1962) *Political and Comic Characters of Shakespeare*, London: Macmillan.

Penman, R. (1990) 'Facework and politeness: Multiple goals in courtroom discourse', *Journal of Language and Social Psychology*, 9, 15–38.

Pfister, M. (1988) *The Theory and Analysis of Drama*, Cambridge: Cambridge University Press.

Phelan, J. (1990) 'Character and judgment in narrative and in lyric: Toward an understanding of the audience's engagement in "The Waves" ', *Style*, 24, 3, 408–421.

Poetics Today (1986) *Theory of Character*, 7, 2, Jerusalem: Israel Science Publishers.

Pollard-Gott, L. (1993) 'Attribution theory and the novel', *Poetics*, 21, 499–524.

Potter, J. and Wetherell, M. (1987) *Discourse and Social Psychology: Beyond Attitudes and Behaviour*, London: Sage.

Potter, R.G. (1981) 'Character definition through syntax: Significant within-play variability in 21 modern English-language plays', *Style*, 15, 4, 415–434.

Potter, R.G. (1992) 'Reader responses to dialogue', in Nardocchio, E.F. (ed.) *Reader Response to Literature: The Empirical Dimension*, Berlin: Mouton de Gruyter, 15–33.

Propp, V. [1928] (1968) *The Morphology of the Folktale*, 2nd edn, trans. by Scott, L., Austin: University of Texas Press.

Pyles, T. and Algeo, J. (1993) *The Origins and Development of the English Language*, 4th edn, Fort Worth, TX: Harcourt Brace Jovanovich.

Quirk, R. [1971] (1987) 'Shakespeare and the English language', reprinted in Salmon, V. and Burness, E. (eds), *A Reader in the Language of Shakespearian Drama*, Amsterdam and Philadelphia: John Benjamins, 3–21.

Quirk, R., Greenbaum, S., Leech, G. and Svartvik, J. (1985) *A Comprehensive Grammar of the English Language*, London: Longman.

Ramisch, H. and Wynne, K. (eds) (1997) *Language in Time and Space. Studies in Honour of Wolfgang Viereck on the Occasion of His 60th Birthday* (Zeitschrift für Dialektologie und Linguistik — Beihefte 97), Stuttgart: Franz Steiner Verlag.

Raskin, V. (1985) *Semantic Mechanisms of Humor* (Synthese Language Library), Dordrecht: Reidel.

Replogle, C. [1973] (1987) 'Shakespeare's salutations: A study in stylistic etiquette', reprinted in Salmon, V. and Burness, E. (eds), *A Reader in the Language of Shakespearian Drama*, Amsterdam and Philadelphia: John Benjamins, 101–115.

Rhys, E. (1925) *The Complete Plays of Ben Jonson, Vol. 1*, Everyman's Library, No. 489, London: Dent.

Rimmon-Kenan (1983) *Narrative Fiction: Contemporary Poetics*, London: Methuen.

Rissanen, M. (1997) ' "Candy no witch, Barbados" ': Salem witchcraft trials as evidence of Early American English', in Ramisch, H. and Wynne, K. (eds), *Language in Time and Space. Studies in Honour of Wolfgang Viereck on the Occasion of his 60th Birthday.* Stuttgart: Franz Steiner Verlag, 183–193.

Robinson, L.F. and Reis, H.T. (1989) 'The effects of interruption, gender, and status on Interpersonal Perceptions', *Journal of NonVerbal Behaviour*, 13, 3, 141–153.

Robinson, W.P. and Giles, H. (1990) Prologue, in H. Giles and W.P. Robinson (eds) *Handbook of Language and Social Psychology*, Chichester: Wiley, 1–8.

Rosch, E. (1973) 'Natural categories', *Cognitive Psychology*, 4, 328–350.

Rosch, E. (1975) 'Cognitive reference points', *Cognitive Psychology*, 7, 532–547.

Rosch, E. (1977) 'Human categorization', in Warren, N. (ed.) *Studies in Cross-Cultural Psychology, Vol. 1*, London: Academic Press, 1–49.

Rosch, E. (1978) 'Principles of categorization', in Rosch, E. and Lloyd, B.B. (eds.) *Cognition and Categorization*, Hillsdale, NJ: Lawrence Erlbaum, 27–48.

Rosch, E. and Mervis, C.B. (1975) 'Family resemblances: Studies in the internal structure of categories', *Cognitive Psychology*, 7, 573–605.

Rosch, E., Mervis, C.B., Gray, W.D., Johnson, D.M. and Boyes-Braem, P. (1976) 'Basic objects in natural categories', *Cognitive Psychology*, 8, 382–439.

Ross, L. (1977) 'The intuitive psychologist and his shortcomings: Distortions in the attribution process', in Berkowitz, L. (ed.) *Advances in Experimental Social Psychology, Vol. 10*, New York: Academic Press, 173–220.

Rumelhart, D.E. (1975) 'Notes on a schema for stories', in Bobrow, D.G. and Collins, A. (eds) *Representation and Understanding*, New York: Academic Press, 211–236.

Rumelhart, D.E. (1980) 'Schemata: The building blocks of cognition', in Spiro, R., Bruce, B. and Brewer, W. (eds) *Theoretical Issues in Reading Comprehension*, Hillsdale, NJ: Lawrence Erlbaum, 35–58.

Rumelhart, D.E. (1984) 'Schemata and the cognitive system', in Wyer, R.S. and Srull, T.K. (eds), *Handbook of Social Cognition, Vol. 1*, Hillsdale, NJ: Lawrence Erlbaum, 161–188.

Rumelhart, D.E. and Norman, D.A. (1981) 'Analogical processes in learning', in Anderson, J.R. (ed.), *Cognitive Skills and their Acquisition*, Hillsdale, NJ: Lawrence Erlbaum, 335–359.

Rumelhart, D.E. and Ortony, A. (1977) 'The representation of knowledge in memory', in Anderson, R.C., Spiro, R.J. and Montague, W.E. (eds) *Schooling and the Acquisition of Knowledge*, Hillsdale, NJ: Lawrence Erlbaum, 99–135.

Rumelhart, D.E., Smolensky, P., McClelland, J.L. and Hinton, G.E. (1986) 'Schemata and sequential thought processes in PDP models', in McClelland, J.L. *et al.* (eds), *Parallel Distributed Processing: Explorations in the Microstructure of Cognition* (Vol. 2: Psychological and Biological Model(s), Cambridge, MA: MIT Press, 7–57.

Ryan, E.B. and Giles, H. (eds) (1982) *Attitudes toward Language Variation: Social and Applied Contexts*, London: Arnold.

Sacks, H. (1992) *Lectures on Conversation (Volumes I and II)* (edited by Gail Jefferson, with an introduction by Emanuel A. Schlegloff), Oxford: Blackwell.

Sacks, H., Schegloff, E.A. and Jefferson, G. (1974) 'A simplest systematics for the organisation of turn-taking for conversation', *Language*, 50, 4, 383–396.

Salmon, V. [1967] (1987) 'Elizabethan colloquial English in the Falstaff plays', reprinted in Salmon, V. and Burness, E. (eds), *A Reader in the Language of Shakespearean Drama*, Amsterdam and Philadelphia: John Benjamins, 39–70.

Salmon, V. and Burness, E. (eds) (1987) *A Reader in the Language of Shakespearean Drama*, Amsterdam and Philadelphia: John Benjamins.

Sanford, F.H. (1942) 'Speech and personality', *Psychological Bulletin*, 39, 811–845.

Schank, R.C. and Abelson, R.P. (1977) *Scripts, Plans, Goals, and Understanding: An Inquiry into Human Knowledge Structures*, Hillsdale, NJ: Lawrence Erlbaum.

Scherer, K.R. (1979) 'Personality markers in speech', in Scherer, K.R. and Giles, H. (eds), *Social Markers in Speech*, Cambridge: Cambridge University Press. 147–209.

Scherer, K.R. and Giles, H. (eds) (1979) *Social Markers in Speech*, Cambridge: Cambridge University Press.

Scherer, K.R. and Scherer, U. (1981) 'Speech behaviour and personality', in Darby, J.K., Jr. (ed.) *Speech Evaluation in Psychiatry*, New York: Grune & Stratton, 115–135.

Scollon, R. and Scollon, S. (1981) *Narrative, Literacy and Face in Inter-ethnic Communication*, New Jersey: Ablex.

Scollon, R. and Scollon, S. (1995) *Intercultural Communication: A Discourse Approach* (Language in Society, 21), Oxford: Blackwell.

Scott, M. (1999) *WordSmith Tools*, Oxford: Oxford University Press.

Searle, J.R. (1969) *Speech Acts: An Essay in the Philosophy of Language*, Cambridge: Cambridge University Press.

Searle, J.R. (1975a) 'The logical status of fictional discourse', *New Literary History*, 6, 319–332.

Searle, J.R. (1975b) 'Indirect speech acts', in Cole, P. and Morgan, J.L. (eds) *Syntax and Semantics 3*, New York: Academic Press.

Searle, J.R. (1979) *Expression and Meaning*, Cambridge: Cambridge University Press.

Semin, G.R. and Fiedler, K. (eds) (1992) *Language, Interaction and Social Cognition*, London: Sage.

Semino, E. (1997) *Language and World Creation in Poems and Other Texts*, London: Longman.

Semino, E. and Swindlehurst, K. (1996) 'Metaphor and mind style in Ken Kesey's *One Flew over the Cuckoo's Nest*', *Style*, 30, 1, 143–166.

Shepherd, S. (ed.) (1985) *The Women's Sharp Revenge: Five Women's Pamphlets from the Renaissance*, London: Fourth Estate.

Sherman, R.C. (1988) 'Are two modes better than one? A critique of Brewer's Dual Process model', in Srull, T.K. and Wyer, R.S. (eds), *Advances in Social Cognition, Vol. I: A Dual Process Model of Impression Formation*, Hillsdale, NJ: Lawrence Erlbaum, 155–164.

Shimanoff, S. (1977) 'Investigating politeness', in Keenan, E.O. and Bennett, T.L. (eds) *Discourse across Time and Space*, Southern California Occasional Papers in Linguistics, 5, 213–41.

Short, M. (1989) 'Discourse analysis and the analysis of drama', in Carter, R. and Simpson, P. (eds) *Language, Discourse and Literature: An Introductory Reader in Discourse Stylistics*, London: Unwin Hyman, 139–168.

Short, M. (1996) *Exploring the Language of Poems, Plays and Prose*, London: Longman.

Short, M. (1998) 'From dramatic text to dramatic performance', in Culpeper, J. *et al.*, *Studying Drama: From Text to Context*, London: Routledge, 6–18.

Short, M. and Semino, E. (forthcoming) 'Stylistic analysis and evaluation'.

Simpson, P. (1989) 'Politeness phenomena in Ionesco's *The Lesson*', in Carter, R. and Simpson, P. (eds) *Language, Discourse and Literature: An Introductory Reader in Discourse Stylistics*, London: Unwin Hyman, 171–193.

Simpson, P. (1993) *Language, Ideology and Point of View*, London: Routledge.

Simpson, P. (1996) *Language through Literature: An Introduction*, London: Routledge.

Simpson, P. (1998) 'Odd talk: Studying discourses of incongruity', in Culpeper, J. *et al.* (eds), *Studying Drama: From Text to Context*, London: Routledge, 34–53.

Sinclair, J. and Coulthard, R. (1975) *Towards an Analysis of Discourse*, Oxford: Oxford University Press.

Slugoski, B.R. and Turnbull, W. (1988) 'Cruel to be kind and kind to be cruel: Sarcasm, banter, and social relations', *Journal of Language and Social Psychology*, 7, 101–121.

Smith, E.R. (1988) 'Impression formation in a general framework of social and nonsocial cognition', in Srull, T.K. and Wyer, R.S. (eds), *Advances in Social Cognition, Volume I: A Dual Process Model of Impression Formation*, Hillsdale, NJ: Lawrence Erlbaum, 165–176.

Smith, E.R. and Zarate, M.A. (1990) 'Exemplar and prototype use in social categorisation', *Social Cognition*, 8, 243–262.

Smyth, M.M., Collins, A.F., Morris, P.E. and Levy, P. (1994) *Cognition in Action*, 2nd edn, Hove, East Sussex: Psychology Press.

Souriau, E. (1950) *Les Deux Mille Situations Dramatiques*, Paris: Flammarion.

Spencer-Oatey, H. (1992) *Cross-Cultural Politeness: British and Chinese Conceptions of the Tutor–Student Relationship*, Ph.D. dissertation, University of Lancaster.

Sperber, D. and Wilson, D. (1986) *Relevance: Communication and Cognition*, Oxford: Blackwell.

Sperber, D. and Wilson, D. (1995) *Relevance: Communication and Cognition*, 2nd edn, Oxford: Blackwell.

Spevack, M. (1968) *A Complete and Systematic Concordance to the Works of Shakespeare*, Hildesheim: Georg Olms Verlagsbuchhandlung.

Srull, T.K. and Wyer, R.S. (eds) (1988) *Advances in Social Cognition, Volume I: A Dual Process Model of Impression Formation*, Hillsdale, NJ: Lawrence Erlbaum.

Stanislavski, C. (1968) *Building a Character*, trans. by E.R. Hapgood, London: Methuen.

Steckler, N.A. and Cooper, W.E. (1980) 'Sex differences in color naming of unisex apparel', *Anthropological Linguistics*, 22, 373–381.

Steinbeck, J. [1937] (1992) *Of Mice and Men*, London: Heinemann.

Stewart, J.I.M. (1949) *Character and Motive in Shakespeare*, London: Longman.

Storms, M.D. (1973) 'Videotape and the attribution process: Reversing actors' and observers' points of view', *Journal of Personality and Social Psychology*, 27, 165–175.

Strongman, K. and Woolsey, J. (1967) 'Stereotyped reactions to British accents, *British Journal of Social and Clinical Psychology*, 6, 164–167.

Stubbs, M. (1983) *Discourse Analysis: The Sociolinguistic Analysis of Natural Language*, Oxford: Blackwell..

Styan, J.L. (1969) *The Elements of Drama*, Cambridge: Cambridge University Press.

Style (1990) *Literary Character*, 24, 3, Illinois: Northern Illinois University.

Sunderland, J. (2000) 'Baby entertainer, bumbling assistant and line manager: discourses of fatherhood in parentcraft texts', *Discourse and Society*, 11(2), 249–274.

Synder, M.L. and Frankel, A. (1976) 'Observer bias: A stringent test of behavior engulfing the field', *Journal of Personality and Social Psychology*, 34, 857–864.

Taavitsainen, I. (1995) 'Interjections in Early Modern English: From imitation of spoken to conventions of written language', in Jucker, A.H. (ed.), *Historical Pragmatics: Pragmatic Developments in the History of English* (Pragmatics and Beyond, New Series, 35), Amsterdam and Philadelphia, John Benjamins, 439–465.

Taavitsainen, I. (1999) 'Personality and styles of affect in *The Canterbury Tales*', in Lester, G. (ed.), *Chaucer in Perspective: Middle English Essays in honour of Norman Blake*, Sheffield: Sheffield Academic Press, 218–234.

Taylor, S.E. (1981) 'A categorisation approach to stereotyping', in Hamilton, D.L. (ed.) *Cognitive Processes in Stereotyping and Intergroup Behaviour*, Hillsdale, NJ: Lawrence Erlbaum, 83–114.

Taylor, S.E. and Fiske, S.J. (1975) 'Point-of-view and perceptions of causality', *Journal of Personality and Social Psychology*, 32, 439–445.

Taylor, S.E., Fiske, S.J., Etcoff, N.L. and Ruderman, A. (1978) 'Categorical bases of person memory and stereotyping', *Journal of Personality and Social Psychology* 36, 778–793.

Thomas, J.A. (1984) 'Cross-cultural discourse as 'unequal encounter': Towards a pragmatic analysis', *Applied Linguistics*, 5, 3, 226–235.

Thomas, J.A. (1985a) 'The language of power: Towards a dynamic pragmatics', *Journal of Pragmatics*, 9, 765–783.

Thomas, J.A. (1985b) 'Complex illocutionary acts and the analysis of interaction', *Lancaster Papers in Linguistics*, No. 11.

Thomas, J.A. (1986) *The Dynamics of Discourse: a Pragmatic Analysis of Confrontational Interaction*, Ph.D. dissertation, University of Lancaster.

Thomas, J.A. (1994) 'The conversational maxims of H.P. Grice', in Asher, R.E. (ed.) *The Encyclopedia of Language and Linguistics*, Vol. 2: 754, Oxford: Pergamon Press.

Thomas, J.A. (1995) *Meaning in Interaction*, London: Longman.

Thorndyke, P.W. (1977) 'Cognitive structures in comprehension and memory of narrative discourse', *Cognitive Psychology*, 9, 77–110.

Thorndyke, P.W. and Yekovich, F.R. (1980) 'A critique of schema-based theories of human story memory', *Poetics*, 9, 23–49.

Thorne, B., Kramarae, C. and Henley, N. (eds) (1983) *Language, Gender and Society*, Rowley, Massachusetts: Newbury House.

Tillyard, E.M.W. (1965) *Shakespeare's Early Comedies*, London: Chatto & Windus.

Tillyard, E.M.W. (1967) *The Elizabethan World Picture*, London: Chatto & Windus.

Toolan, M.J. (1985) 'Syntactical styles as a means of characterisation in narrative, *Style*, 19, 1, 78–93.

Toolan, M.J. (1988) *Narrative: A Critical Linguistic Introduction*, London: Routledge.

Townsend, S. (1992) *The Queen and I*, London: Mandarin Paperbacks.

Tracy, K. (1990) 'The many faces of facework', in Giles, H. and Robinson, W.P. (eds), *Handbook of Language and Social Psychology*, Chichester: Wiley, 209–226.

Traugott, E.C. (1972) *A History of English Syntax: A Transformational Approach to the History of English Sentence Structure*, New York: Holt, Rinehart & Winston.

Trudgill, P. (1978) 'Introduction: Sociolinguistics and sociolinguistics', in Trudgill, P. (ed.) *Sociolinguistic Patterns in British English*, London: Edward Arnold, 1–18.

Trudgill, P. (1983) *On dialect: Social and Geographical Perspectives*, Oxford: Basil Blackwell.

Tulving, E. (1972) 'Episodic and semantic memory', in Tulving, E. and Donaldson, W. (eds), *Organisation of Memory*, New York: Academic Press, 382–403.

Tversky, A. and Kahneman, D. (1974) 'Judgment under uncertainty: Heuristics and biases', *Science*, 185, 1124–1131.

van Dijk, T.A. (1987) *Communicating Racism: Ethnic Prejudice in Thought and Talk*, Newbury Park: Sage.

van Dijk, T.A. (1988) 'Social cognition, social power and social discourse', *Text* 8 (1–2): 129–157.

van Dijk, T.A. (1990) 'Social cognition and discourse', in Giles, H. and Robinson, W.P. (eds) *Handbook of Language and Social Psychology*, Chichester: Wiley, 163–183.

van Dijk, T.A. (1991) *Racism and the Press*, London: Routledge.

van Dijk, T.A. (ed.) (1997a) *Discourse as Structure and Process* (Discourse Studies: A Multidisciplinary Introduction, Volume 1), London: Sage.

van Dijk, T.A. (ed.) (1997b) *Discourse as Social Interaction* (Discourse Studies: A Multidisciplinary Introduction, Volume 2), London: Sage.

van Dijk, T.A. and Kintsch, W. (1983) *Strategies of Discourse Comprehension*, London: Academic Press.

van Leeuwen, T. (1995) Representing social action, *Discourse and Society* 6, 1, 81–106.

van Leeuwen, T. (1996) 'The representation of social actors', in Caldas-Coulthard, C.R. and Coulthard, M. (eds), *Texts and Practices: Readings in Critical Discourse Analysis*, London and New York: Routledge, 32–70.

van Peer, W. (1986) *Stylistics and Psychology: Investigations of Foregrounding*, London: Croom Helm.

van Peer, W. (ed.) (1989) *The Taming of the Text: Explorations in Language, Literature and Culture*, London: Routledge.

van Peer, W. and Pander Maat, H. (1996) 'Perspectivation and sympathy: Effects of narrative point of view', in Kreuz, R.J. and MacNealy, M.S. (eds), *Empirical Approaches to Literature and Aesthetics*, Norwood, NJ: Ablex, 3–22.

Wales, K. (1983) '*Thou* and *you* in Early Modern English: Brown and Gilman re-appraised', *Studia Linguistica*, 37, 2, 107–125.

Weber, J.J. (1992) *Critical Analysis of Fiction*, Amsterdam and Atlanta: Rodopi.

Weiner, B. (1985) ' "Spontaneous" causal thinking', *Psychological Bulletin*, 97, 74–84.

Weinsheimer, J. (1979) 'Theory of character: Emma', *Poetics Today*, 1, 185–211.

Werth, P.W. (1976) 'Roman Jakobson's verbal analysis of poetry', *Journal of Linguistics*, 12, 21–73.

Wierzbicka, A. (1987) *English Speech Act Verbs: A Semantic Dictionary*, London: Academic Press.

Wilde, O. [1894] (1973) 'The importance of being Earnest', in Trilling, L. and Bloom, H. (eds), *Victorian Prose and Poetry* (The Oxford Anthology of English Literature), New York: Oxford University Press, 345–390.

Wilson, A. and Leech, G.N. (1993) 'Automatic content analysis and the stylistic analysis of prose literature', *Revue Informatique et Statistique dans les Sciences Humaines*, 29, 219–234.

Wittgenstein, L. (1958) *Philosophical Investigations*, 2nd edn, Oxford: Blackwell.

Wyer, R.S. and Carlston, D.E. (1994) 'The cognitive representation of persons and events', in Wyer, R.S. and Srull, T.K. (eds) *Handbook of Social Cognition*, 2nd edn, *Vol. 1 Basic Processes*, Hillsdale, NJ: Lawrence Erlbaum, 41–98.

REFERENCES

Wyer, R.S. and Srull, T.K. (eds) (1984) *Handbook of Social Cognition, Vol. 1*, Hillsdale, NJ: Lawrence Erlbaum.

Wyer, R.S., Budesheim, T.L., Lambert, A.J. and Swan, S. (1994) 'Person memory and judgment: Pragmatic influences on impressions formed in a social context', *Journal of Personality and Social Psychology*, 66(2), 254–267.

Zebrowitz, L.A. (1990) *Social Perception*, Milton Keynes: Open University Press.

Zimmerman, D.H. (1998) 'Identity, context and interaction', in Antaki, C. and Widdicombe, S. (eds.) *Identities in Talk*, London: Sage, 87–106.

Zwaan, R.A. (1991) 'Some parameters of literary and news comprehension: Effects of discourse-type perspective on reading rate and surface-structure representation', *Poetics*, 20, 13–156.

Zwaan, R.A. (1993) *Aspects of literary comprehension*, Amsterdam and Philadelphia: John Benjamins.

Zwaan, R.A. (1994) 'Effect of genre expectations on text comprehension', *Journal of Experimental Psychology: Learning, Memory, and Cognition*, 20, 920–933.

Zwaan, R.A. (1996) 'Toward a model of literary comprehension', in Britton, B.K. and Graesser, A.C. (eds), *Models of Understanding Text*, Mahwah, NJ: Lawrence Erlbaum, 241–255.

INDEX